The USS *Puffer*
in World War II

The USS *Puffer* in World War II

A History of the Submarine and Its Wartime Crew

CRAIG R. MCDONALD

Foreword by John D. Alden
Foreword by Maurice Rindskopf

McFarland & Company, Inc., Publishers
Jefferson, North Carolina, and London

LIBRARY OF CONGRESS CATALOGUING-IN-PUBLICATION DATA

McDonald, Craig R., 1951–
The USS Puffer in World War II : a history of the submarine and its wartime crew / Craig R. McDonald ; foreword by John D. Alden ; foreword by Maurice Rindskopf.
    p.   cm.
Includes bibliographical references and index.

ISBN 978-0-7864-3209-7
softcover : 50# alkaline paper

1. Puffer (Submarine)   2. World War,
1939–1945 — Naval operations — Submarine.
3. World War, 1939–1945 — Naval operations, American.
4. World War, 1939–1945 — Campaigns — Pacific Ocean.
5. World War, 1939–1945 — Regimental histories — United States.
I. Title.
D783.5.P85M34   2008   940.54'510973 — dc22   2007047176

British Library cataloguing data are available

©2008 Craig R. McDonald. All rights reserved

No part of this book may be reproduced or transmitted in any form or by any means, electronic or mechanical, including photocopying or recording, or by any information storage and retrieval system, without permission in writing from the publisher.

On the cover: Both photographs from November 1944: crew of the USS *Puffer* (courtesy Craig McDonald); the USS *Puffer* at sea (U.S. Navy)

Manufactured in the United States of America

McFarland & Company, Inc., Publishers
Box 611, Jefferson, North Carolina 28640
www.mcfarlandpub.com

*To the memory of my father, Donald B. McDonald, Jr.
(February 25, 1924–January 29, 2007), and
the other thousands of men who quietly
served in submarines during World War II*

*and to the memory of my mother, Bernice McDonald
(May 29, 1922–November 16, 2006).*

Acknowledgments

When I began doing research for this book, one of the first sources of information I found was a Web site dedicated to the more recent nuclear submarine, USS *Puffer* (SSN 652). Don Cook was the webmaster of www.usspuffer.org, and he had included information on "Our Combat Heritage," which was a reference to the World War II *Puffer* (SS 268)—the *Puffer* I was looking for. Much to my amazement there were pictures of the original *Puffer* on the Web site. Cook's *Puffer* Web site contained a guest registry where the names and e-mail addresses of a few World War II *Puffer* veterans or their family members were listed. Like me, many of these people were looking for details of their fathers' submarine service or were attempting to contact old shipmates. I wanted to help; I enjoyed detective work. As a result I was hooked on finding more of the *Puffer*'s history. I enhanced Cook's Web site with additional crew pictures and more details of the *Puffer*'s wartime actions. Over the last six years via the Web site I have found *Puffer* people, and they have found me. We have shared information. I thank Cook for creating the Web site.

The next step in the search for the history of the *Puffer* took me to the National Archives Web site. There I found two key items that detailed the history of the *Puffer* and the men who served in the boat. At the end of each patrol into enemy waters the submarine commander wrote a detailed report of his actions against the enemy. This report was known as a War Patrol Report (WPR). I transcribed some of the highlights from a few of the patrols, and Cook posted the texts on his Web site.

The other documents obtained from the National Archives were the key to finding the names of the over 200 men who served on the *Puffer*—the personnel reports or muster roll lists. These reports were made every three months, and detailed changes in rate (rank) and the transfer or arrival of new crew members. After a detailed analysis of the reports, I was able to create a complete list of every enlisted man who had served on the *Puffer* and during which war patrols. I organized this information, and it was also posted on the *Puffer* Web site.

I had cold data, but I had no human details from people that had served on the *Puffer*. How and why did these young men come to serve on submarines? What was daily life like on a submarine? I needed to talk with real people. As a member of the Washington State Chapter of the World War II Submarine Veterans, my father had been invited to the National World War II Submarine Veterans conventions. At these conventions a *Puffer* reunion breakfast was first organized in 1990 by John Gutensohn, and later by Bob Polk, Tony Sasso, Ken

Martinson, and John Sanders. In early 2001 my father put me in contact with Bob Polk and John Sanders, who were the chairmen of the 2001 *Puffer* reunion. Polk and Sanders gave me videos of the reunions from the early 1990s and a list of names, addresses, and phone numbers of the living *Puffer* veterans.

I was motivated to collect the personal recollections and perspectives from the *Puffer* crew. I wanted to collect the words of the men who were there. I used Tom Brokaw's book *The Greatest Generation — In Their Own Words* as a guide to create a questionnaire. I mailed a biographical questionnaire to about 50 *Puffer* veterans. On the biographical sheets, they provided their accounts of boot camp, submarine school, best times and worst times during the war, crew member friends, what they wanted most during the war, and other stories. I have woven these experiences into the text. Also as a result of this mailing I received an enthusiastic telephone offer from Tom Metz. He supplied me with typed versions of the hundreds of pages of the nine war patrol reports. This was a great improvement over the microfilm copies I possessed. In 1976 Metz had written a personal account of his wartime service; he supplied me with a copy. He also copied the biographical sketches of numerous *Puffer* veterans.

Another *Puffer* veteran to offer aid to my project was Andrew Jackson Thoman. Thoman was a retired librarian and schoolteacher. After retirement he continued to share with grade school children his Submarine Service experiences, and as part of his presentations the children chimed a bell once for each of the 52 boats lost during the war. Much to my excitement, about the same time, I found 16 minutes of 16 mm color film at the National Archives Web site that was shot on the *Puffer* during July of 1945. I had the film converted to VHS video format. I gave Thoman a copy of the video, which he added to his presentation. He noted the children were interested in what he said, but the images on the video heightened their interest. They saw the *Puffer* crew shooting the 5-inch deck gun and exploding a Japanese fuel dump on Bali. We had planned to meet in August at the 2001 World War II Submarine Veterans Convention in St. Louis. He was going to help me identify faces in the crew pictures and share more *Puffer* stories. My phone conversations with Thoman inspired me to continue the hunt for the *Puffer*'s history. For health reasons Thoman was unable to attend and tragically died shortly thereafter. I lost a friend.

Using an Internet telephone directory, in 2002 I located another *Puffer* veteran, Glenn Stoy. Until I contacted him, he had no knowledge of the World War II Submarine Veterans organization. He meticulously made an exact reproduction of his *Puffer* diary. His contemporary personal comments gave an enlisted man's viewpoint.

I found another treasure in early 2004. Again using the Internet directory, I located Jon Golay, son of the *Puffer* officer Frank Golay. Golay served on the *Puffer* for seven war patrols. From Jon I learned his mother, Clara Golay-Bradford, had preserved over 100 pages of letters Frank had written to her during the war. She kindly allowed me to use the texts in the *Puffer* history. Frank Golay had also taken many photos which recorded images of the officers and crew. The Golay letters and photos captured the details of daily life on the *Puffer*—exactly what I had been looking for.

Other persons who have contributed to the *Puffer* history include: Avis Nelson, who searched Australian newspapers and archives for events related to the *Puffer* sailors during the war in Perth and Fremantle; Edward Dauplaise, who wrote how he became chief of the boat; Timothy T. Petitt at the Operational Archives of the Naval Historical Center at the Washington Navy Yard, DC, who supplied naval biographies and commendations for the USNA officers; Jon Bernard, who offered pictures of his father, Lawrence Bernard; Charles Brown, Charles Brockhausen, Jay Deem, Russell Tidd, Ladislaus Topor, Ray Roberts, John Solak, Norman Trudeau, Walter Mazzone, and Ken Dobson, who provided details of the First War Patrol; Corwin Maupin, who provided the names of the 20th Torpedo Class of 1943; Dan Hess, who gave me information about his father, Franklin Hess, and photos of the *Puffer* cribbage board; Debbie Selk, who located the letters of Ralph W. Christie at the Library of Congress; John Crouse, manager of the St. Mary's Submarine Museum, who searched his files for *Puffer* related materials; Cristin Waterbury at the Wisconsin Maritime Museum, who found archive photos and local newspaper articles about the *Puffer*; Nancy Webber, who created the map template; Ethan Bernhardt and Phil Namy, who offered suggestions after reading the text from a non-submariner's perspective; William Somerville, who located Japanese information about the First War Patrol and the sinking of the *Teiko Maru*; and Commander John Alden, USN (Retired) and Rear Admiral Maurice Rindskopf, USN (Retired), who supplied technical corrections and suggestions. And most of all thanks to my friends, the *Puffer* veterans, who shared their experiences and recollections and helped identify their shipmates in numerous photos. My apologies to any person misidentified; faces and memories fade with time.

During the writing of the book a number of my friends have gone on eternal patrol: John Allen, who candidly talked with me in St. Louis over dinner about the First War Patrol; Charles Brockhausen, whom I also met in St. Louis and interviewed by phone about the First War Patrol; Tony Sasso, who helped organize numerous *Puffer* reunions; and Carl Dwyer, the last commander of the *Puffer*, who also shared details and answered questions about the First War Patrol.

Table of Contents

Acknowledgments vii
Foreword by Commander John D. Alden, USN (Retired) 1
Foreword by Rear Admiral Maurice H. Rindskopf, USN (Retired) 3
Preface 5

1. QUALIFYING FOR THE SUBMARINE SERVICE
   Boot Camp 7
   Specialty School 11
   Submarine School 13

2. BUILDING THE *PUFFER* AND THE BONDING OF THE CREW
   Submarines in Wisconsin 16
   Building the *Puffer* 18
   Plank Owners 22
   The Bonding of the Crew 29
   Down the Mississippi River 30
   Final Training and on to Brisbane 32

3. THE INITIAL OFFICERS OF THE *PUFFER*
   Commander Marvin J. Jensen 34
   Franklin G. Hess 36
   Lawrence G. Bernard 38
   Carl R. Dwyer 40
   William M. Pugh II 41
   Walter Mazzone 41
   Kenneth Dobson 42

4. The Political, Physiological and Psychological

- Torpedo Politics 43
- The Physical Environment 45
- Lack of Light 47
- Sleep Deprivation and Irregular Sleep 47
- Perception of Time 48
- Heat and Humidity 48
- Hypoxia and Carbon Dioxide Poisoning 50
- Adrenaline 51
- Summary 52

5. The First War Patrol Beginnings

- Repairs and Rest at Brisbane 54
- The First Attack 56
- Bad Weather and Disaster 58

6. The Depth Charging of the *Puffer*

- The Dangerous Escorts 61
- Caught at Periscope Depth 64
- Heat and Humidity Rise 68
- Sinking Deeper 70
- Waiting It Out 72
- Decision Time 73
- Surface! Surface! 76
- The *Puffer*'s Return 78
- Awards 80

7. The Second War Patrol

- Distorted History 81
- Corrected History 82
- New Crew and Boat Repairs 84
- The New Commander 86
- Departure for Subic Bay 87
- The First Attack 88
- Frustration Again 89
- Waiting for Action 90
- No Christmas Presents 92
- Happy New Year 93
- Deck Gun Action 95

8. THE THIRD WAR PATROL
- New Crew Members and Training 98
- Lombok and Makassar Straits 101
- Invasion Scare 102
- A Second Chance 103
- A Dangerous Destroyer 110
- No Contacts and Return to Fremantle 112

9. R & R AT PERTH AND FREMANTLE
- Companionship and Craziness 114
- The Extreme 116
- The Tragic 117

10. THE FOURTH WAR PATROL
- New Crew Members 120
- Repairs and More Repairs 121
- Lifeguard Duty 124
- Tawi Tawi — Carrier Carrier 130
- Tanker Tanker 134
- Mechanical Troubles 138
- Resistance in the Sibutu Passage 139
- Friendly Natives 140
- Awards 140

11. THE FIFTH WAR PATROL
- New Men and New Equipment 142
- Return to the Makassar Strait 144
- Shallow Water 147
- Sibutu Passage 149
- Basilan Strait Attack 153
- Torpedo Transfer 154
- Cape Calavite Attack 156
- Another Assignment? 161
- Awards 162
- 30 Days Leave 162

12. THE SIXTH WAR PATROL
- A New Commander and a Larger Crew 166
- New Weapons and Technology 170

    Waikiki Bound 171
    Okinawa 177
    Dive! Dive! 180
    Heavy Seas and Heavy Action 181
    A Trap 186
    R & R at Guam 187

13. THE SEVENTH WAR PATROL
    A Full Boat and Refit 189
    Lifeguard Duty 192
    A Near Miss 193
    Man Overboard! 196
    Thirsty Lookouts 197
    Air Support 200
    Junks 201
    Artillery Action 203
    Return to Saipan 203
    Midway via Wake 206

14. R & R AT MIDWAY
    Arrival 211
    Fun and Games 213
    Navy Cross 216
    Victory in Europe Day 220
    Training 220
    Good-Bye 224

15. THE EIGHTH WAR PATROL
    More Personnel Changes 226
    Back to Saipan 229
    Back to War 231
    Tragedy 233
    The South China Sea 235
    Java Sea and Bali 237
    Fremantle 240
    R & R in Perth 241

16. THE NINTH WAR PATROL
    The Last Departure 248
    The Numbers Game 251

       Peace 254
       The Last Loss 256

17. BACK TO THE STATES
       54 or Bust 258
       Subic Bay Wait 260
       Off to Pearl Harbor 267
       San Francisco 275
       Navy Day Celebration 277
       Home Again 279
       What Next? 282

18. POSTWAR SERVICE
       Hawaii 284
       Seattle 289
       The End of the *Puffer* 292
       Reunions 293

Glossary of Terms and Abbreviations   295
Appendix 1. List of Awards   301
Appendix 2. Summary of Claimed Successful Attacks   303
Appendix 3. Postwar Puffer Service Roster   306
Bibliography   309
Index   315

Foreword
by John D. Alden

Among World War II submarines, neither the USS *Puffer* nor any of her three skippers are listed with the famous few top scorers. On the other hand, her record was respectable enough to rate her as one of 37 recipients of the coveted Navy Unit Commendation. In short, the *Puffer* was a typical representative of the hard-working but uncelebrated majority of U.S. submarines that decimated the Japanese naval and merchant fleets during the war in the Pacific.

Similarly, among the men who served on the *Puffer*, Donald B. McDonald, Jr., was just one of many volunteers who signed up for "the duration plus six months" and performed their duties faithfully and quietly. After basic training he came on board as a lowly seaman second class, joined the torpedo gang, pulled his weight without special reward or complaint, and advanced to the rank of torpedoman second class by the war's end. Like so many other veterans of the Silent Service, he never told his family much about his wartime experiences. Consequently, his son had to seek out other voices in compiling this history of the *Puffer* and his father's role in it.

In telling this story, author Craig McDonald has chosen to rely heavily on the words, both written and spoken, of men who actually experienced the moments of terror and long stretches of boredom, the isolation as well as the comradeship of overly close quarters, the homesickness of long weeks at sea punctuated by brief sojourns in foreign ports, that were the lot of most submariners. The men of the *Puffer* were no strangers to all of these conflicting sensations.

The author traces the 18-year career of the submarine from the laying of her keel until her departure for the scrapyard, and his father's naval career from boot camp to postwar service in a reserve unit. The *Puffer* was a Manitowoc boat, that is, she was built in Wisconsin by the Manitowoc Shipbuilding Company, and like most of her sisters spent much of her wartime service in the Southwest Pacific. Manitowoc sailors are unanimous in praising the warm hospitality of their Wisconsin hosts and the high quality of the shipyard's work. They are similarly united in their appreciation of their welcoming acceptance by the Australians at Brisbane and Fremantle, whenever the boats were lucky enough to find respite there between war patrols.

The *Puffer* and Donald McDonald didn't meet until after the First War Patrol, when the submarine limped into Fremantle after probably the longest period of submergence under constant depth charging and harassment by Japanese anti-submarine forces experienced by any U.S. submarine during the war — 37 hours and 45 minutes. In researching this episode and its physiological and psychological implications, the author convincingly debunks certain legends that were based on the *Puffer*'s ordeal: that such experiences necessitated wholesale transfers of crews because of psychic complications, and that new men could never penetrate the supposed "mystic bond" shared only by the survivors.

Although Seaman McDonald missed that patrol, he bonded readily with his shipmates and encountered enough excitement of his own during the *Puffer*'s next eight patrols. In addition to torpedo attacks, both successful and unsuccessful, these included the transfer of torpedoes from aft to forward while surfaced in enemy waters, the loss of the chief of the boat overboard, a wild bombardment of Japanese shore installations with the 5-inch deck gun, and equally wild shenanigans during refits at Fremantle, Midway, Guam, and Saipan, as well as stops at Pearl Harbor, Darwin, Onslow, and Subic Bay. In recording these and other adventures, the author has accurately captured the feeling of submarine service during World War II in the Pacific.

John D. Alden
Commander, USN (Retired)

Foreword
by Maurice H. Rindskopf

I can say, "I was there and done that!"

I served in *Drum* (SS 228) from 11 November 1941 until 11 November 1944. That *Drum* preceded *Puffer*'s entry into the war by some 15 months gives me a different perspective because every officer and man who deployed on our first patrol did so in the same boat — inexperienced.

The USS Puffer *in World War II* tells the story of the life of a U.S. Navy submarine. The leading character is *Puffer* (SS 268) which came alive when her crew commissioned her at the Manitowoc Shipbuilding Company, her builder, in Manitowoc, Wisconsin, on April 27, 1943. She fought with honor, and was decommissioned on June 27, 1946, at Mare Island Naval Shipyard, Vallejo, California.

Craig McDonald sets the stage by explaining in adequate detail the process by which submariners are selected, screened, and educated as they ply the road from officer and enlisted recruit to qualified submariner, a proud dolphin pin wearer, a true member of an elite band. It is not totally surprising to learn that Craig's father, Donald B. McDonald, Jr., followed that path. He reported prior to the second patrol as a reserve seaman second class and remained in *Puffer* until he was released from active duty as a torpedoman second class after the war was over.

There are also brief biographies of the seven commissioning officers emphasizing that four had prior war patrol experience before reporting to *Puffer*. The commanding officer graduated from the Naval Academy in 1933, with others following in 1935, 1937, 1938, and 1942. Other submarines joining the fray at the same time had like talent in their wardrooms.

I was *Drum*'s fourth officer, and the original torpedo data computer operator, just like my *Puffer* classmate, Carl Dwyer. I made 11 war patrols, the last two as commanding officer from June until November 1944. Carl Dwyer's experience in *Puffer* was eerily similar.

McDonald has spent some seven years researching other published material, including Navy archives, and conducting lengthy interviews with officers and men who served in *Puffer*. He makes effective use of these deck-plate tales, and utilizes the thorough recall of the officers to let the reader make virtual patrols.

He has chosen to tell the *Puffer* story patrol by patrol, recognizing that submarine warfare in World War II was hours of patient searching, sometimes under boring conditions, mixed with minutes of high stress accompanied by exhilarating triumph. To *Puffer*, the latter came early on October 9, 1943, some two weeks after arrival on station in the South China Sea, on her First War Patrol. *Puffer* was the victim of a horrendous depth charging by a highly skilled Japanese patrol craft. Over a period of 32 hours, *Puffer* was subject to persistent, accurate attacks which caused considerable damage and flooding. She was driven to depths far in excess of her 300-foot test depth and forced to operate with a large up angle to maintain depth, finally approaching the point of battery exhaustion.

Captain Marvin Jensen, in consultation with his officers, considered several options, finally choosing to surface after about 38 hours (perhaps the longest submergence of any submarine in the war) where he found room to escape from his pursuers under cover of darkness. He brought the ship into Fremantle, Australia, for refit. She was ready in a month for a second patrol under a new skipper, Commander Gordon Selby.

Drum experienced a depth charging on her first patrol which lasted 22 hours. The men of the enemy patrol craft, aroused by the sinking of the large seaplane tender *Mizuho* under their watch, were inexperienced and not persistent enough to gain a kill or even damage *Drum*. But, similarly, *Drum*'s inexperienced crew may well have prolonged the evasion long after the enemy had departed the scene. And like Captain Marvin Jensen, *Drum*'s Captain Bob Rice consulted his officers before electing to surface after dark into an empty Sea of Japan. In November 1943, *Drum* suffered her only depth charge damage when dogged patrol craft dropped large deep charges close above the engine room, causing a crack in the conning tower after bulkhead — and sending *Drum* to Mare Island via Pearl Harbor for a new conning tower.

According to McDonald previous histories alleged that the *Puffer* crew was dispersed after the severe depth charging because morale was forever damaged, and that those who joined the ship subsequently would never be integrated into a truly dedicated crew. McDonald firmly refutes this historical inaccuracy. He has included enlisted personnel sailing lists for each patrol, showing those transferred and those reporting. He shows that the transfer of 20 of the original complement of 71, leaving 51 to make the second patrol, was not out of the ordinary. By happenstance, my personal records show that *Drum* sailed on her second patrol with 51 of the 67 men who made the initial patrol.

Puffer enjoyed considerable success over four more war patrols under Selby, during which he was awarded two Navy Crosses, and the boat a Navy Unit Citation. Had *Puffer* not been the victim of several Mk XIV torpedo failures including premature explosions and duds, she might well have sunk several more ships. I can vouch for the frustration these erratic torpedoes caused, for *Drum* was on the line very early in the war and suffered through the entire sad history of premature torpedo detonations, deep running, magnetic exploder failures, and duds from firing pin deformation. Commander Selby was succeeded in *Puffer* by my 1938 classmate Lt. Commander Carl R. Dwyer, who likewise won a Navy Cross.

The USS Puffer *in World War II* is an easy read because anecdotes from officers and enlisted personnel add to the detailed blow by blow reporting of *Puffer*'s many contacts, approaches, attacks, sinkings, and evasions. It is a reward for McDonald's diligent research and a valuable addition to World War II submarine lore for the submarine veterans of World War II who are still with us as well as mature history buffs and the next generation who will man our submarines well into the 21st century.

Rear Admiral Maurice H. Rindskopf, USN (Retired)
USS Drum *(SS 228), November 1941–November 1944*
Commanding Officer, June–November 1944
Annapolis, Maryland

Preface

As a child I was aware that my father, Donald B. McDonald, Jr., had been in the Submarine Service during World War II, and the experience made him special. Many kids growing up in the 1950s had fathers who had been in World War II, but none of my friends had fathers who had been in the Submarine Service. In 1999 my interest in my father's submarine service was rekindled. As a longtime stamp collector I was aware the United States Postal Service was planning a set of stamps for the 100th anniversary of the Submarine Service. I wanted to commemorate my father's service by giving him a framed photo of the boat he served on, the USS *Puffer*, and a commemorative envelope with one of the new stamps. I also found a commemorative envelope postmarked on the day the *Puffer* was commissioned in 1943 at Manitowoc, Wisconsin. How were submarines built in Wisconsin?

About the same time, I began reading the first definitive history of the Submarine Service. In *Silent Victory* by Clay Blair I discovered that my father and others who served in submarines truly were very special: only 1 in 10 men who volunteered for submarine duty passed the tough mental and physical testing. All were volunteers. The Submarine Service was small, only about 16,500 men or 1.6 percent of the wartime Navy, but it had the highest casualty rate of any branch of the military services, roughly 22 percent. When a submarine sank, there were rarely survivors. All told, 3,617 men were lost on 52 boats from the 272 submarines which saw action during the war. However, during World War II the Submarine Service accounted for about 55 percent of the tonnage sunk of the Imperial Japanese Navy and the merchant fleets.

I wanted to determine the *Puffer*'s contribution to the war effort. I read in Blair that after the First War Patrol of the *Puffer* the commanding officer had been relieved of his command. The boat was submerged an incredible 38 hours and nearly lost. In 1946 naval historians wrote that the crew had been broken up after the first patrol for psychological reasons—a mystic bond existed among the crew. Such a mass exodus of the crew also cast aspersions upon their performance. Blair confirmed these events.

My father was not present for the First War Patrol of the *Puffer*, so I could not ask him about the events. I did ask him what he had heard. Even though my father served with crew members from the first patrol for over a year, he knew virtually nothing about the first patrol. He had heard horror stories of men taken off the boat in straitjackets, but no one wanted to talk much about the events. The Submarine Service was the Silent Service. As a result, the first aspect of the *Puffer*'s history I wanted to research was the First War Patrol. What really happened? I was skeptical about the mystic bond.

For all men in submarines the harsh physiological and psychological strains were very real — usually hidden by the day-to-day routine, but accentuated during attacks and counterattacks by the enemy. From my graduate studies in biomechanics and human performance I knew the conditions were extreme. An understanding of human physiology is necessary to appreciate the taxing conditions of submarine duty. No other submarine history has dealt with the connection between the physiology and psychology in as much detail, of which the *Puffer*'s First War Patrol was the extreme example.

The most accurate approach to telling the history of the *Puffer* was by using primary sources—the contemporary documents and the recollections and writings of the men who were there. The extent to which I used original documents is unique in a submarine history. I corresponded with many *Puffer* veterans by mail, phone, and e-mail, digging into the details of the First War Patrol. As a result of these interviews and the data from the personnel records at the National Archives, I was able to correct the distorted history of the First War Patrol. I shared my findings with the *Puffer* sailors at the 2002 World War II Submarine Veterans reunion. I was encouraged by their positive responses to continue my research and turned my attention to the accomplishments of the *Puffer* during the remainder of the war.

There was more to the *Puffer*'s history and service than the difficulties of the First War Patrol. The early chapters contain the veterans' recollections of boot camp, specialty schooling, submarine school, and the building of the *Puffer* in Wisconsin. Also included are the previous naval experiences of the officers, which influenced their actions while on the *Puffer*. Some officers had much submarine experience; some had none. The same was true for the enlisted men — the crew was typically a mix of old salts and new recruits. Political factors within the Navy also affected the effectiveness of a submarine crew. Officers and crew alike had little control over the internal naval politics of faulty torpedo manufacture. The torpedo politics were remote and unknown to most enlisted men, but they knew the weapon didn't always work properly.

Attacks made by the *Puffer* are detailed in the words of the commanding officers. The antics of the men during rest and recuperation are retold. The Japanese records, the commanding officers' patrol reports, and the letters, diaries, and recollections of the men who served on the *Puffer* are woven together with my own insights. Also included are Internet resources that will allow the reader to explore maps and aspects of submarines and the Submarine Service in greater detail. Those readers unfamiliar with the terminology of submarines should first check out the *Glossary* section at the end of the text.

Although the events detailed were those that surrounded my father and the *Puffer*, I hope the reader will feel, understand, and appreciate the experiences of all the men who served in the Silent Service.

1

Qualifying for the Submarine Service

Boot Camp

After enlistment or being drafted into the Navy, the first stop was 6 to 8 weeks in boot camp. There were eight boot camps in various locations around the United States. The largest two camps were in San Diego, California, and Great Lakes Naval Station, Illinois. Experiences varied from place to place, and from season to season. Donald McDonald, a native of Tacoma, Washington, went to Farragut, Idaho, a smaller boot camp serving the northwestern states of Colorado, North and South Dakota, Wyoming, Oregon, Idaho and Washington.

McDonald, along with other drafted men, left from the Seattle train station among hugs and tears on a relatively warm day in early January 1943. Having lived all his life in the moderate climate of western Washington, McDonald expected the same in Idaho. When he arrived at Farragut, Idaho, the weather was below zero and snowy. He spent cold hours riding the train and a

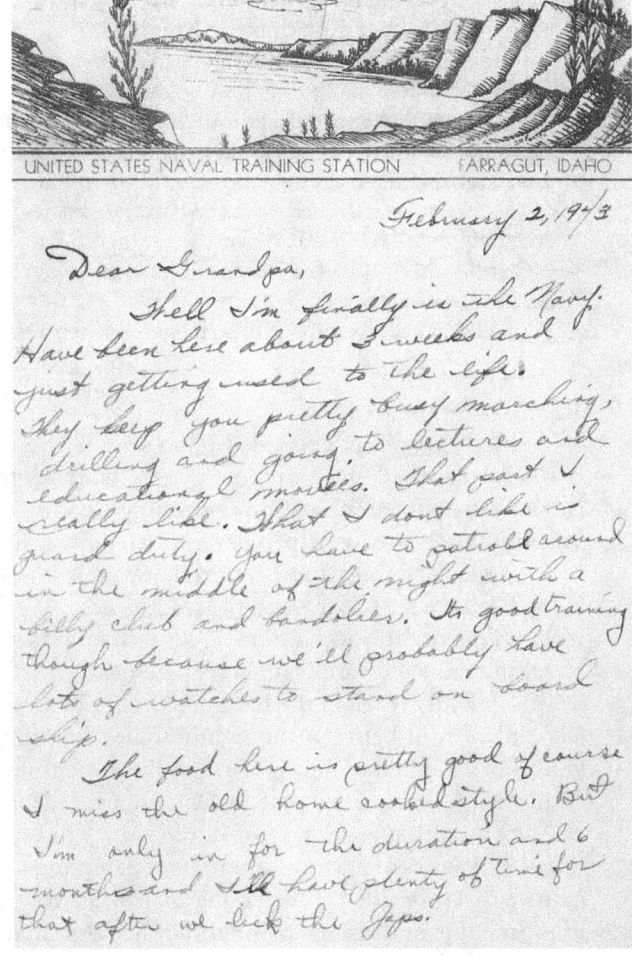

McDonald's letter home to his grandfather from boot camp (author's collection).

bus to the base, stood in lines, and waited for warmer clothing and a bunk roll. He was assigned to Company 10-43, Camp Waldron. For many of the new recruits it was the first time away from home. For the next couple of days, in the darkness of the barracks, sobs were heard from some bunks.

The first duty was to label all belongings. For laundry purposes the sailors' names had to be stenciled on all clothes (Lane). Regardless to which boot camp a new draftee went there was plenty of time to learn marching on the parade area, known as the grinder. Learning right from left and how to follow orders was necessary. Some of the camps had band music to accompany the marching. McDonald had been in the Boy Scouts with a scoutmaster who was an ex-Army officer, so he had some previous training in close order drill. He recalled lots of marching on the grinder and generally being treated like an idiot. After a few weeks at boot camp he wrote to his grandfather on February 2, 1943, three weeks before his nineteenth birthday (McDonald). He was already looking forward to coming home, a universal desire of all men in the service during the war.

> Dear Grandpa,
> Well I'm finally in the Navy. Have been here about 3 weeks and just getting used to the life. They keep you pretty busy marching, drilling and going to lectures and educational movies. That part I really like. What I don't like is guard duty. You have to patrol around in the middle of the night with a Billy club and bandolier. It's good training though because we'll probably have lots of watches to stand on board ship.
> The food here is pretty good of course I miss the old home cooked style. But I'm only in for the duration and 6 months and I'll have plenty of time for that after we lick the Japs.
> I went to church Sunday before last but wasn't able to attend last Sunday Services. They hold morning mass though and will try to attend them when we get off guard duty.
> Last week we marched with the band, had rifles and everything; it sure was fun and our company did pretty well. We've also learned the manual of arms and some drill exercises.
> I still kind of miss the freedom I had in civilian life and the money I made at the shipyard, but I'll get over that.
> Well that's all for now, will write again when I get time...
> Your grandson,
> Donald Jr.

Physical training depended upon season and location. Some of the training McDonald did at Farragut was done indoors due to the inclement weather. The nearby lake was frozen. During the appropriate season swimming, rowing whaleboats, running, and mock loading a 5-inch gun repeatedly helped develop strength and stamina (McDonald; Thoman; Metz).

A sailor had to learn how to roll and stow *all* of his belongings into a sea bag, including his bed. Where the sailor went, the sea bag went. World War II sailors carried a mattress, which replaced the traditional hammock. A mattress was safer than the hammock, which originated on sailing ships. Edward Dauplaise, the *Puffer*'s chief of the boat in 1945, who entered the Navy in 1936, vividly recalled the hammocks at boot camp: "It took some doing to climb up the 6 feet and inch in between the tightly folded hammock. Many nights I was awakened by the loud crashes of bodies falling down to the cement floor amidst many cries of pain and groans" (Dauplaise). Fortunately mattresses were provided on the submarines.

Learning the Navy way of doing things did not always come easy to some of the new recruits. Peter Keane, who went to boot camp in New York during a cold December 1943 and January 1944, recalled three young men who were going to run the Navy the way they saw fit—probably in the same manner they had dominated their neighborhood as kids. It was not uncommon for a group of young men to enlist and stick together during boot camp. Keane described how the gang was shaped up.

Our Chief straightened out three guys from New York City who thought they were going to run our barracks, boot camp, and the Navy! It only took two nights to do it by awakening them at 2 AM, empty their lockers; pack their sea bags and run a mile with them; come back and unpack the sea bags; put their gear in the locker; stand inspection and then go to bed around 4 AM. The second night they ran two miles with their hammock included with the sea bag. No more problems after this duty [Keane].

McDonald had a few months between high school graduation and enlistment. Not so for Andrew Jackson Thoman. Thoman recalled his first day at boot camp experiences in a letter he wrote in 2001.

Peter Keane (photograph courtesy of Peter Keane).

The night I graduated from Phoenix Union High School, June 1943, we left for the San Diego Naval Training Center. Upon arrival we were lined up like cattle in a chute and handed over all of our toilet accessories, which I had received the night before for graduation gifts. We then proceeded to the sheep shears and were shaved "BALD." The 4:30 AM reveille was a cry of disbelief. A lot of bad words echoed throughout the barracks. A mad scramble for toilets, wash basins, making up your bunk, Navy style, and mustering in formation for a march to the chow hall kept one alert. The chow was terrible, and I have never eaten "shit on a shingle" (some kind of goop spread over toast), or spam since I left the Navy.... Then came the series of shots, a medic on one side and a medic on the other. While you were watching the guy on your left, the guy on the right zapped you, some fainted on the spot. Others got the chill or cat fever as we were told [Thoman].

Thomas Metz wrote in 1976 about his two years of naval duty. His recollections were insightful and reflective. He described himself as "an inquisitive boy raised on a one-mule farm in Arkansas" (Metz). His boot camp experience started in January 1944. Six months later his training in San Diego was similar to Thoman's, yet he recalled some different details.

We lived at Camp Decatur in eight-man huts. While we were in quarantine, we were given shots and hair cuts. We learned how to store a mattress cover full of clothes in one sea bag. The Navy had no razors [interesting since they had taken Thoman's six months earlier] or toothbrushes to issue us and some of the boys didn't bring toilet articles with them. So they began to look really wooly by the time they received a razor from home. I took the razor I had been issued in July, 1940 by the Civil Conservation Corps. I carried this razor half way around the world and I am still using it today.

At the end of two weeks quarantine, we moved to permanent 150 man barracks at Camp Farrigut [not the one in Idaho] for four more weeks of training. This training consisted of close order drill, marching, more calisthenics, boating, class room lectures and pictures. We also took a test to determine what field of duty we would be best suited for. We had a few men in our company that were in their late thirties, and about fifty pounds overweight, and about six that were short and fat, those folks had trouble staying up with the company on the five mile marches.

We moved to Camp Paul Jones for our last two weeks of training. There we did more precision drilling and calisthenics, thirty minutes each morning before breakfast. We did competitive company parades. Sometimes we would stand at attention for an hour or more. I had heard about men in the military standing at attention for long periods of time, so before I reported for duty, I hung a watch beside a mirror and stood at attention for one and a half hours just to prove I could.

We marched about five miles to Pacific Beach to swim in the salt water pool. They had us drop feet first off of a twenty-eight foot high scaffold into eight feet of water and I went to the bottom. Then we swam under a life raft and through truck tires tied below the surface. I had done considerable swimming most of my life, but when I got to the top of that twenty-eight foot scaffold and looked down at the water, I almost "chickened" out. But when I saw the two life guards reach for me, I jumped off. After this swim, we had to march the five miles back to camp.

At camp we spent hours aiming an empty rifle at a target and snapping it; the Navy called this "snapping in." Later on we did go to the rifle range out in the country near San Diego. There we used 03-A3 Army rifles and fired them at targets 200 yards away. The 03-A3 Army rifles are the same ones the Army used during World War I. The Army used M-1 rifles during World War II, so the Navy inherited the older and slower bolt action 03's. The firing range officer explained that the Navy always stays one war behind on rifles.

We spent many hours working the five inch gun. This taught us how to aim and operate a medium sized Navy gun. The exercise also helped build up our muscles so we could do that kind of work for a long period of time.

At the close of basic training, an officer made us a short speech. The gist of what he said was, "Some of you are not coming home alive." For many of us, this was the first real introduction we had to the cost of war. Some of us have often been reminded of this cost in the remaining years of our lives [Metz lost a son in Vietnam] [Metz].

At the end of training Thoman recalled his rite of passage into the world of the drinking man.

Able-bodied seamen Donald McDonald (left) and Rod Dotson on leave from boot camp (author's collection).

After seven weeks of boot camp we were allowed to go on liberty. Some of us went to a movie with a pint of rum. Rum was our only choice as whiskey was no where to be found. I often wondered what happened to all of the whiskey at that time. Shots of hot rum out of a bottle were my last. A terrible hangover and the other side effects of too much to drink followed [Thoman].

After five weeks of training McDonald went on liberty with a friend he had made at boot camp, Rod Dotson, from Eugene, Oregon. They headed for the nearest town Coeur d'Alene, Idaho, for a movie and whatever contact they could make with the outside world. McDonald and Dotson had their pictures taken to record the event. McDonald sent one of the photos to his mother with the words, "We finally got our liberty and I thought I'd send you something." The pair attended torpedo school and submarine school together, but were assigned to different submarines.

For many young men who had grown up during the Great Depression, three square meals and a warm place to sleep were great improvements. The food was tolerable (Lane), although Thoman disagreed when it came to chipped beef on toast (Thoman). The naval cooks were by no means culinary artists, but at least there was always food on the table. Dauplaise recalled he went from a scrappy 119 pounds to a strong 135 pounds at graduation (Dauplaise). McDonald felt he was in the best physical condition of his life when he finished boot camp (McDonald).

Specialty School

The next step in the Navy was specialized training. Tests were given during boot camp, and each man had to put down four choices for future training that were appropriate based upon his aptitude test. Most men wanted to do something related to airplanes or electronics. Airplanes and radios in the 1930s were the latest technological developments that captured the imaginations of many young men. Many boys had built model airplanes and played with crystal radios. As a result McDonald's list looked like this: (1) aviation maintenance; (2) aviation ordnance; (3) aviation electronics; (4) torpedo-submarines. Naturally the Navy saw fit to give him his fourth choice, submarines. His next stop was Norfolk, Virginia, to Fleet Service School—Torpedoes and then on to submarine school. McDonald felt it was an "honor to be chosen" for submarine duty (McDonald).

At Fleet Service School the inner workings and proper maintenance of the torpedo were studied. A torpedo was one of the most complex weapon systems used during World War II. The school consisted of 10 weeks of intense study from April 4 to June 12, 1943. Also the "A to O Naval Manual" was studied. The manual consisted of 15 sections of seamanship and naval regulations (*ibid.*).

Three of the men in the class were lost: Richard Wells and Harvey Thommen on *Shark II* (SS314) on October 24, 1944; and Barry Geraghty on the *Swordfish* (SS 193) on January 12, 1945. Clayton Decker narrowly escaped from the *Tang* after it had been sunk by its own torpedo. Commanded by Richard O'Kane the *Tang* fired its last torpedo, which would have completed the most successful submarine patrol of the war. Unfortunately the defective torpedo broached and circled back toward the *Tang*, hitting the boat in the after compartments. With the use of an underwater breathing device, known as a Momsen Lung, eleven men attempted to escape, but only Decker and four other men survived the ascent to the surface from 180 feet. They joined the four surviving officers, who escaped from the conning tower. The nine men were picked up by the Japanese and survived the remainder of the war in a POW camp (O'Kane, pp. 326–340). Upon capture they were beaten and threatened with beheading. Postwar analysis credited the *Tang* with destruction of 13 vessels accounting for 107,324 tons of enemy shipping on the patrol. Upon his return from POW camp in 1945, Commander O'Kane was awarded the Congressional Medal of Honor by President Harry Truman.

Submarine Torpedo Class of "1943–20," picture taken May 22, 1943. *Front (left to right)*: Joe Hamilton, Clayton Decker, Cornelius "Monk" Moynahan, Charles Farmer, Ed Osborne, Wilton Wentworth, Dick Harden, Harold Swanson, Eugene Sieracki. *Middle*: Warren "Shanty" Sullivan, Chief William Cielakie, Rod Dotson. *Back*: Don Kersbergen, Lester Owens, Corwin Maupin, Harvey Thommen, Barry Geraghty, Donald McDonald, Bob "Dutch" Wanek, Robert "Buck" Buchanan, Jack J. Caroline, Wesley Tombleson, Van J. Horne. Not Pictured: Richard Wells (author's collection).

Submarine School

The selection process for submarine duty was very discriminating. All men were volunteers, but only about one in 10 men survived the grueling physical and mental screening. Howard Baird joined the *Puffer* upon its return from the war. He gave a vivid and colorful description of his February and March 1945 experiences at New London, Connecticut, in a 2001 letter. Baird's experiences were typical of the weeding out process.

> Screening began with a physical and a visit to a "shrink," apparently to make some dubious determination of one's ability to get along with others in confined quarters. And then the pressure tank. I do not remember anyone "chickening-out," of this test, but a certain Chief Petty Officer thought for a while that I may have been trying.
>
> To pass this test, the students, six or eight at a time, or as many as could be crammed into about a 12 foot two section steel tank, too small to stand upright, were subjected to air pressure pumped in to around 50 pounds per square inch, or the equivalent of 100 foot depth in water. Closed in and sitting on a wooden bench as air was pumped in, the building pressure on the ear drums was relieved by putting internal pressure on them while holding the nose, like descending in an aircraft. If you were unable to do so, and the pain became severe, we were to raise a hand, and the Chief, observing through a small glass port, would wave you into the first section of the tank, close the door and lower the pressure, to be literally jerked out with that certain "look" from the Chief.
>
> The doctor after examining my ears said, "Sorry, son we fractured your ear drums," and I was sure I was going to be kicked out of another branch of the service, to sneak home in disgrace. But, he added that it was not a puncture, just a break, caused by enlarged adenoids that could be corrected if I wanted to try again. With an enthusiastic, "Yes, sir," came a pat on the back from the Chief.
>
> Correcting the adenoid condition postponed my submarine school classes, but the Navy had no trouble keeping me busy, as they never did where Seamen 2nd were concerned, like scullery mess "cooking" and doing the steel-wool shuffle on barracks floors. But, the treatment (for the adenoids) was unique, at least by today's standards. Once a week for four weeks I reported to Sick Bay to lay on a table while a Corpsman, removing two metal rods with "nubs" on the ends from a lead jar, shoved them up my nostrils and started a timer. It was the method used in the '40s, and also with aviators, to shrink, or burn out, the hindrance with radium. Years later visiting a doctor for a sinus infection, he sort of shuddered when I related the experience.
>
> The second time through the pressure tank was a "piece of cake," even getting a kick from the thick "feel" of the air, at the equivalent of the 100 foot depth, when you ran your hand through it with fingers spread; just like under water.
>
> The 100 foot Dive Tower, a landmark at New London, and the Pearl Harbor submarine bases, came next, and although it was primarily designed to train for escaping from a sunken submarine, the requirement probably did some screening also.
>
> Locks, or chambers, accommodating about 8 students, were built into the sides of the water filled tower at 25, 50, and 100 foot depths. With the doors closed water entered, rising from chest to chin high, until the chamber pressure equaled the pressure to that within the tower. A door below the water level could then be opened for access to the tower. Wearing a Momsen lung, an underwater breathing device, the student would then duck under and exit the lock, grasping a knotted rope to ascend slowly to the surface, breathing and counting to ten at each knot. Rising from at least the 50 foot depth was required. Coming up from the 100 foot level was voluntary with pride and peer pressure assuring that we did.
>
> Finally came the day, the reprieve from classroom studies and practice in mock-ups, that were looking forward to ... our first day of diving on a submarine. We marched to the piers on the lower base with out notebooks and eight strips of paper, each indicating our station for dives to be made that day. There we assembled alongside a black, old looking and somewhat rust-streaked vessel only vaguely resembling the large, sleek, gray wolf of the seas, the

submarine of our studies. This was an "O-Boat," an earlier class of submarine from World War I, built in 1916 or 1917, reassigned to submarine school.

We entered through the conning tower and asking questions of the crew sought our assigned stations. My location said, "Motor Room," a compartment in the absolute stern of the boat, and completely under water even when on the surface. In those days, even though over six feet, I only weighed about 130 pounds, and as I passed through the Control Room, After Battery, and Engine Room to my station, one of the ship's company, apparently wishing to offer a novice sound advice, called out, "Hey Skinny, watch where you put those sharp elbows, these bulkheads are all rust."

With that lesson in safety in mind I ducked through the last water-tight door to enter the Motor Room, a compartment in which one can only crouch, perhaps no more than ten feet in length that tapered down to where the propeller shafts penetrate the hull. Outside of a bare light bulb the only machinery to "study" on this dive, as part of my learning, were the warm casings over the two electric motors, about two feet apart, upon which one might half-sit. Feeling a bit more than comfortably warm on my backside as the submarine submerged for the first dive of the day we were hardly under more than a few minutes when a siren sounded. Since all major activities in submarines are announced by various loud sounds, i.e., bells, honks and sirens, these were studied in class to be memorized. I quickly related the siren to the alarm of an impending collision. I was right, as the proper response in such an emergency is to close all water-tight doors and, the one to the Motor Room was slammed, in my face I might add.

The first thing to come to mind was an old sub-

The tower at New London, Connecticut, was used to simulate an emergency escape from a submarine as deep as 100 feet (photograph courtesy of the U.S. Navy).

marine movie I saw as a youngster where, to save the lives of as many in the crew as possible, a water tight door was shut dooming those behind it, as seen through a small glass port. There was a glass port in this door also, but I could see no sympathetic faces on the other side.

The second thought that came to mind was that our class of student submariners was being put through one more screening, or test, to see if we could "take-it." So, I settled back on my "hot-seat" to await surfacing and the chance to calmly move on to my next dive station. And, I was right again. Passing through the Engine Room I pretended not to notice the subtle, but interested glances below my belt to see if the color of my dungarees had darkened. I even added a touch of calmness by asking, "Hey, is the smoking lamp lit?" [Baird].

Chief Charles Spritz, the tough taskmaster of "Spritz's Navy" during World War II, was primarily responsible for the conduct of submarine trainees. Whenever possible Spritz reminded the recruits: "Around here there's only one daily prayer — you'll commit it to memory: 'O Lord, help us to keep our big mouths shut until we know what we are talking about!' and 'There is room for anything on a submarine — except a mistake'" (LaVo, p. 15). Peter Keane, who served on the *Puffer* after the war, described his impressions of Chief Spritz in early 1944.

My first memory of sub school was Spritz's Navy. I thought he was tough to work for, but in later life I realized what a job he had to do. He had to determine if us kids were fit for sub duty.
The *S-48* was at a pier and we had to clean it, inside and out. By inside I mean inside the forward buoyancy tanks. It was a dirty job. Stopping for lunch we came out looking like a bunch of bums, prompting Spritz to say we were a disgrace to the Navy and never would amount to anything. It then followed we were to get cleaned up, have lunch with a clean uniform and then go right back to work to the job we were doing in the morning. This lasted about 3 days and then some better duty came along [Keane].

Keane also related an incident that demonstrated Spritz could be protective of his charges.

I realized also later on that he must have had quite a bit of authority. One miserable might I had the 2 to 4 AM watch on the degaussing ship. It was raining hard, wind blowing and at the end of the pier you got soaked with the small waves in the Thames River. During my watch a jeep drove up and someone shouted for the watch. I immediately replied and after verifying it was Spritz he wanted to know what in hell I was doing out at the end of the pier. I explained to him this was how we were [instructed] to patrol it. Without another word he took off with his jeep and was back in about 10 minutes with the duty officer. In very plain and simple language he informed the officer that if he ever again on a night like this saw one of his [Spritz's] men having to walk a pier in this kind of weather there would be hell to pay and it would come from him. I was then instructed to walk the pier only as far as the conning tower on the sub [Keane].

With the completion of the arduous physical training, intense classroom learning, and Spritz's psychological testing, the men were sent to the boats. There was only one way to truly understand submarines— ride the boats. Much of submarine training was accomplished on the job. Assignments took various avenues: some men were assigned to new construction, boats still on the building ways; other men were assigned as replacements on boats in the war zone; and others were assigned to submarine tenders to serve on repair crews. Construction of new submarines was primarily taking place at Groton, Connecticut; Mare Island (San Francisco); Portsmouth, New Hampshire; and Manitowoc, Wisconsin. The next stops for the men directly headed for action were one of the following: Pearl Harbor; Perth, Western Australia; or Brisbane, Queensland, Australia. During the last two years of the war submarine bases or tenders were established at Midway and Guam, as the war moved closer to the Empire of Japan. McDonald was ordered to Perth, Australia.

2

Building the *Puffer* and the Bonding of the Crew

Submarines in Wisconsin

The history of the *Puffer* began in a Manitowoc, Wisconsin, shipyard in 1940, when the Navy Department contracted with the Manitowoc Shipbuilding Co. (MSC) for the construction of 10 submarines. Charles West, president of Manitowoc Shipbuilding Co., went to Washington, D.C., in 1939 with the idea of building small ships for the Navy. His shipyard was limited to small ships, because vessels had to reach salt water via the St. Lawrence Seaway and the Welland Canal, a series of locks 270 feet long and 14 feet deep. The other route to the sea was via the Illinois and Mississippi Rivers, where there was no length restriction, but the route was limited by a 9 foot draft (Nelson, p. 14).

Early in 1939 it was evident to West that war in Europe was inevitable. West knew that because of limited facilities in the shipbuilding industry some small ships were available for construction. West considered building destroyers; however, these ships drew 12 feet of water. The solution to the depth limitation was a floating drydock, which the Manitowoc Shipyard used for servicing boats. With the necessary plans West headed to Washington, D.C., but left there before the Navy could give him a concrete answer (*ibid.*, p. 17).

Later in 1939 war broke out in Europe and President Roosevelt declared a limited national emergency. The Navy was concerned that the submarine building capacity of the United States was not sufficient to support a long war. The Electric Boat Co. (EBC) was the only commercial source of submarine construction, and the Navy felt private competition was beneficial. The Navy approached EBC president Lawrence Y. Spear about the possibility of building more boats. Spear knew there would be more submarine construction than his company could handle. Spear called MSC's West and asked if he was interested in building submarines. West answered that he knew nothing about building submarines and was not interested (*ibid.*, p. 19).

In 1940 with the invasion of Western Europe by Germany the war escalated. Britain was attacked. President Roosevelt signed the Naval Expansion Bill in July 1940. The Navy Department knew submarine production would be strained to the limit. West was again asked to come to Washington to the Navy Bureau of Construction and Repair, where Rear Admiral

Manitowoc Shipbuilding Company workers (photograph courtesy of the Wisconsin Maritime Museum Collection).

Claude Jones asked him to build submarines. Jones assured West that EBC would provide the plans and necessary assistance (*ibid.*, p. 20). Lacking knowledge of the construction methods used to build submarines West told the bureau he would reply within a week. After study and conversations with EBC he was convinced Manitowoc could build the boats, and accepted a contract for 10 Gato class submarines at a cost of $2,850,000 each (*ibid.*, p. 23). The submarines were to be exact duplicates of the *Growler*, SS215. The contract was approved December 26, 1940 (*ibid.*, p. 27).

A full size wooden mock-up of a submarine was built at Manitowoc by the skilled carpenters of the MSC. Workers toured the mock-up to familiarize themselves with pipes, machinery, valves, and gauges (*ibid.*, p. 30). Manitowoc Shipbuilding Co. had previously built cargo ships, tankers, and ferries. Building submarines was a radical change in production. However, the fundamental procedure of welding joints required for the construction of submarines had been employed extensively in all previous MSC vessels. MSC was capable of superior welding, using an innovation known as down welding. Workmen were stationary while the plates to be welded moved under and away from them, always keeping the weld in clear view of the worker (*ibid.*, p. 30). MSC also built special cranes and a crawler to lift the sixteen sections and conning tower into place on the building ways (*ibid.*, p. 29). Some sections weighed 60 tons. A rush order for eight of these cranes was used to clear the destruction at Pearl Harbor. Because the Manitowoc River was too narrow for a conventional lengthwise launch, MSC had to use a tilted side-launch. This launch method was of concern to the Navy. Navy officials feared the boat would keel over as it slid sideways into the water. However, scale models convinced the Navy this launch method would not allow the submarine to roll over. The first submarine launched, the *Peto*, slid off the ramp of timbers April

30, 1942. The *Peto* rolled to 48 degrees, exactly as predicted by the model. A Navy observer commented that the method of launch was "undignified, but effective" (*ibid.*, p. 32).

The final and most important component of construction was additional skilled workers. Before the war MSC normally employed 500 workers (*ibid.*, p. 34). The combined population of Manitowoc and Two Rivers, Wisconsin, was 34,000, with about 4,000 additional people living on farms in the surrounding area. The submarine building process started in October 1940, and by March 1941, employment reached 1,700 workers (*ibid.*, p. 35). In the months ahead workers were recruited from the neighboring towns and farms. Farmers milked their cows in the daytime and welded on submarines at night. The peak of employment reached 7,000 plus workers which included 600 women trained as machinists and welders (*ibid.*, p. 36).

A national magazine paid tribute to West and his shipyard. The magazine reported the MSC apprentice course was tougher than a "Navy Shakedown Cruise." The result was custom trained shipbuilders. A naval inspector at the yard commented, "We lovingly call them 'Cheese-workers and cherry pickers,' but Lord what beautiful work they do" (*ibid.*, p. 37).

The first section of the first submarine, the *Peto*, SS 265, designating hull number 265, was placed on the building ways June 18, 1941 (*ibid.*, p. 41). When Pearl Harbor was attacked on December 7, 1941, the slogan "Uncle Sam Needs His Boats" was all the response the workers needed. By February 12, 1942, four submarines were already on keel blocks, which included the *Puffer*, hull number 268, the fourth MSC boat (*ibid.*, p. 42). Nine of the first 10 boats survived the war; the *Robalo* was lost. An additional order for 31 more boats was placed in 1943, however only 18 of those boats were built, and 16 of them saw war action. Three of the later MSC submarines were lost (*ibid.*, pp. 165–6).

Building the *Puffer*

The keel for the *Puffer* was officially laid down on February 16, 1942, as the first section of the boat was moved to the assembly area. The *Puffer* was the fourth submarine built in Manitowoc, hence the No. 4 on the photo.

As prefabricated sections were completed in covered sheds, they were brought to the building ways by crawler-tractors, lifted into position onto keel blocks, and welded to the adjacent section. The steel was $^{11}/_{16}$ inch thick and was produced in 15-foot lengths by a single mill, the Lukens Steel Company in Coatesville, Pennsylvania (Sasgen, pp. 11–12). By August of 1942 the *Puffer* started to look like a submarine.

Late in the construction phase the SJ radar was installed in the conning tower. From that moment on until the *Puffer* went to sea, an armed guard was posted adjacent to the new and highly classified piece of equipment. On October 9, 1942, as reported in the MSB employee newsletter, the *Keel Block*, the first flag purchased by the men on the work crew was raised over hull 268. As the crew hurriedly ate their lunches the company band, appropriately named The Submariners Band, began the noon ceremony with concert music. At 12:10 as the national anthem flowed out over the occasion the Stars and Stripes were raised. The assembled group rose to their feet, bared their heads, and watched as the colors slowly unfurled in the Wisconsin breeze. Upon completion of the anthem, John E. Thiell, vice president and secretary of MSC, gave a brief and stirring message to the workers, emphasizing the importance of their efforts—production of submarines (Flag Raising).

> You gentlemen, who have been working so diligently on this splendid vessel, have just purchased an American flag. I understand that this flag is to go out of here with the ship. This patriotic gesture on your part exemplifies the spirit that is back of the desire to complete these

The *Puffer* keel is laid — Section No. 1 is lowered into place. Note the censored detail of the structure. "No. 4" refers to the *Puffer* as the fourth submarine built at Manitowoc (photograph courtesy of the Wisconsin Maritime Museum Collection).

submarines in a hurry. It is an answer to the appeal for doing everything possible for increased production [Flag Raising].

Following the address the Submariners Band continued their concert until exactly 12:20. As the last notes echoed in the distance, the men returned to their assigned tasks. Nine months after the start of construction the *Puffer* was launched at noon, Sunday, November 22, 1942, splashed with champagne by Mrs. Ruth B. Lyons, the granddaughter of Chris Jacobson, Sr., the oldest employee of MSC. Charles West proudly stood next to Jacobson, his longtime friend and employee as the champagne hit the bow and Mrs. Lyon exclaimed, "I christen thee *Puffer*" (Nelson, pp. 37–38). According to the *Manitowoc Herald-Times*, Jacobson began working for MSC shortly after he came to Manitowoc from Denmark in 1880. Six of his sons also worked in various departments at the yards. The *Puffer* was the first Manitowoc boat launched on a Sunday. With an emphasis on production, the Sunday launch least interfered with normal construction operations (4th Sub).

Construction was completed during the next four months and the *Puffer* was put into commission on April 27, 1943. The completion date was 316 days ahead of schedule, a tribute to the workers at MSC (Nelson, p. 152). To see the interior of a submarine similar to the *Puffer* and tour the various compartments visit this Web site: http://www.maritime.org/

Two sections of the *Puffer* are joined on March 8, 1942 (photograph courtesy of the Wisconsin Maritime Museum Collection).

View from the bow with all sections joined on July 26, 1942 (photograph courtesy of the Wisconsin Maritime Museum Collection).

tour/index.htm. (By holding down the left mouse button and moving the cursor left/right or up/down, it is possible to get a 360° view of each compartment.)

The commissioning crew, known as plank owners, consisted of the following men. See the Glossary for the meaning of rates. V6 after the rate indicates a Naval Reserve sailor (USNR) who enlisted for victory plus six months. The other men were

The first flag flies over the *Puffer* (photograph courtesy of the Wisconsin Maritime Museum Collection from the *Keel Block*).

View of the *Puffer* from across the Manitowoc River on launch day (photograph courtesy of the Wisconsin Maritime Museum Collection).

The christening platform awaits Mrs. Ruth B. Lyons and other guests (photograph courtesy of the Wisconsin Maritime Museum Collection).

regular Navy. Roy "Tiger" Lyons was chief of the boat, the most senior enlisted man (National Archives, *Records Group 24*, henceforth referenced as RG24).

PLANK OWNERS — ENLISTED MEN

Last Name	*First Name*	*Service Number*	*Place of Enlistment*	*Rate Received*
Allen	Howard Ardell	329 10 26	Minneapolis MN	S2c
Allen	John Francis	223 63 68	New York NY	MoMM2c
Anderson	Robert Emil	250 45 32	Pittsburg PA	EM2c
Braley	Charles Frederick	341 70 65	New London CT	CY(PA)
Brockhausen	Charles William Jr	223 47 23	Brooklyn NY	QM1c
Burris	Marvin Monroe	355 97 08	Dallas TX	TM2c
Chambers	Wayne Marvin	321 28 74	Des Moines IA	MoMM2c
Clouse	Fred Wayne	628 16 91	Kansas City MO	TM3cV6
Corke	Robert Edward	647 16 61	New York NY	S2cV6
Creech	Bishop Boggs	634 13 65	Louisville KY	F3cV6
Deem	Jay Arden	668 43 38	St Louis MO	RT2cV6
Dufault	Ernest John	200 51 88	Manitowoc WI	CEM(PA)

2. Building the Puffer and the Bonding of the Crew

The side launch of the *Puffer* on November 22, 1942 (photograph courtesy of the Wisconsin Maritime Museum Collection).

Last Name	First Name	Service Number	Place of Enlistment	Rate Received
Dickinson	Master James	636 47 51	Macon GA	F3cV6
Gardner	Theodore Nash	234 37 46	Buffalo NY	F3cV6
Goin	James Warren	393 26 12	Portland OR	FC2c
Golden	Lawrence Joseph	283 26 70	Cleveland OH	MoMM2c
Gosselin	Victor Joseph	212 18 98	Portsmouth NH	SC1c
Graves	William	393 30 81	Portland OR	QM2c
Gutensohn	John Peter	368 30 94	Salt Lake City UT	MoMM1c
Haycraft	Geoffrey David	287 12 43	Manitowoc WI	CMoMM(AA)
Hayward	Herbert David	410 04 80	Kansas City MO	MoMM2c
Henger	Vincent John	250 58 16	Pittsburg PA	RM2c
Hetrick	William Herman	250 49 66	Pittsburg PA	MoMM1c
Huddleston	Walter Carter	644 39 21	New Orleans LA	S2cV6
James	Paul Daniel	652 44 71	Pittsburg PA	S2cV6
Jones	LaMar	660 19 18	Salt Lake City UT	TM3cV6
Kellum	Raymond Herlong	268 17 81	Jacksonville FL	GM2c
Kennedy	Robert Francis	622 45 19	Detroit MI	S2cV6
Kerls	Charles John	410 38 89	Quonset Point RI	MoMM2c

The on deck commissioning ceremony held on April 27, 1943. The event formally passed the *Puffer* from the Manitowoc Shipbuilding Company to the U.S. Navy (photograph courtesy of the Wisconsin Maritime Museum Collection).

Last Name	*First Name*	*Service Number*	*Place of Enlistment*	*Rate Received*
Kimbrell	William Warner	551 80 61	Jacksonville FL	S2cV6
Kutscherousky	Mike Elliot	355 80 51	Los Angeles CA	TM2c
La Freniere	Joseph Lewis	666 48 75	Springfield MA	S2cV6
Lefferts	Harry Edward	223 62 74	New York NY	F1c
Lennon	Francis Donald	375 65 05	San Francisco CA	TM1c
Liggett	James David	636 49 86	Macon GA	F3cV6
Love	Oliver Willard	346 76 77	Little Rock AK	TM2c
Lyons	Roy Damon	250 29 83	New York NY	CTM(AA)
Orbovich	Michael MacAllen	258 50 07	Baltimore MD	S2c
Patacsil	Felix	497 97 60	Manitowoc WI	St1c
Patsko	Demeter	250 38 55	Long Beach CA	Y1c
Patton	James Woodley Jr	342 21 06	Kansas City MO	Ck2c
Penzenik	William	283 35 14	Cleveland OH	F1c
Perro	John Louis	207 26 05	New Haven CT	MoMM2c
Pruitt	John Alden	274 68 64	New Orleans LA	StM3c
Rawls	Jefferson Weldon	624 90 26	Houston TX	S2cV6
Rhymes	Ralph Willard	269 77 73	Jacksonville FL	EM2c
Roberts	Raymond	646 13 01	New York NY	RM3cV6
Ross	Oliver Barron	291 49 03	Portsmouth NH	MoMM1c

2. Building the Puffer and the Bonding of the Crew

The commissioning crew, officers, and friends and wives. *Front row (left to right):* Ernest Dufault, William Pugh, Roy Lyons, Walter Mazzone, Frank Stoltz, Carl Dwyer, Lawrence Bernard, Cmdr. Marvin Jensen, Franklin Hess, Kenneth Dobson, unknown (kissing), William Shaw, Roy Waites, Edgar Washburn, unknown. *Second row:* Robert Anderson, John F. Allen, Mike Kutscherousky, Victor Gosselin, Raymond Kellum, John Perro, unknown. *Third row:* Harry Lefferts, Ladislaus Topor, Ralph Rhymes, Charles Kerls, Lawrence Golden, Wayne Chambers, Herbert Hayward, Raymond Voss, unknown, William Graves, John Vaughn, Joseph Zelaznicki. *Fourth row:* William Hetrick, unknown, Oliver Love, Norman Trudeau, Geoffrey Haycraft, Charles Braley. *Back row:* unknown, William Wilson, Marvin Burris, Jefferson Rawls, James Dickinson, Stanley Shanholtz (extreme back with tie), unknown, Charles Brockhausen, Harold Sander, unknown, Wilbur Warner, unknown, unknown, John Gutensohn, unknown, Russell Tidd (photograph courtesy of the Wisconsin Maritime Museum Collection).

Last Name	First Name	Service Number	Place of Enlistment	Rate Received
Sander	Harold Eugene	316 56 20	Omaha NE	EM1c
Sears	Philip Clayton	602 06 87	Baltimore MD	TM3cV6
Shanholtz	Stanley Sherman	371 68 12	Boston MA	CMoMM(AA)
Shaw	William Frank	359 90 04	Denver CO	TM1c
Shelton	Eugene Chester	291 64 17	Indianapolis IN	S1c
Smith	Clark Sam	620 63 34	Des Moines IA	S2cV6
Snyder	Harry Franklin	652 40 73	Pittsburg PA	S2cV6
Spalding	Robert Bruce	337 30 50	St Louis MO	PhM1c
Stafford	Vertis Allen	360 25 28	Houston TX	SC3c

Last Name	First Name	Service Number	Place of Enlistment	Rate Received
Steeley	Robert Samuel	296 00 33	Nashville TN	F3c
Stoltz	Frank Nicholas	385 10 84	San Diego CA	CRM(AA)
Tidd	Russell Ellis	204 48 05	Providence RI	S2c
Topor	Ladislaus	238 52 61	Mare Island CA	MoMM1c
Trudeau	Norman	201 76 62	Boston MA	EM2c
Unangst	William Kenneth	404 67 99	Philadelphia PA	F2cV6
Vaughn	John Anthony	291 46 33	Chicago IL	EM2c
Vincent	Leonard Russell	654 39 52	Portland OR	F2cV6
Von Sternberg	Donald Valiant	700 31 80	Great Lakes IL	SM3cV6
Voss	Raymond Henry	372 22 92	Denver CO	EM3c
Waites	Roy Durward	336 93 91	San Diego CA	EM2c
Warner	Wilbur Dudley	328 46 24	Manitowoc WI	MoMM1c
Washburn	Edgar Wheeler	706 67 52	New York NY	S2cV6
Wilson	William Earl Jr	311 93 42	Detroit MI	S2c
Zelaznicki	Joseph	410 31 59	Detroit MI	EM1c

The officers included Lt. Cmdr Marvin J. Jensen, USN; Lt. Franklin G. Hess, USN; Lt. Lawrence C. Bernard, USN; Lt. Carl R. Dwyer, USN; Ensign William M. Pugh, USN; Warrant Officer (Machinist) Kenneth L. Dobson, USN; and Ensign Walter F. Mazzone, USNR.

The bar at the commissioning party — the bar was staffed by the *Puffer* crew members Norman Trudeau, Ladislaus Topor and Harry Lefferts (photograph courtesy of Ladislaus Topor).

Test dives were conducted in Lake Michigan to a depth of 312 feet on May 6, 1943. Typical naval engineering practice designed sub hulls for one-and-a-half to two times test depth. Undamaged the *Puffer* could safely submerge to at least 500 feet, possibly deeper. Test models of the *Grouper* failed at 550 feet (Alden, *The Fleet Sub*, pp. 88–89). Other components of the pressure hull, such as pressure seals around gaskets could fail at lesser depths. During the test dive the *Puffer* accidentally surfaced underneath and hit the accompanying ship, the Coast Guard cutter *Tamarack*. The periscopes were slightly damaged and the cutter crew was undoubtedly frightened by the impending disaster. No damage was done to the *Tamarack*. A few crew members of the *Rasher* (SS 269) were on board during the test dive. It was the custom of familiarizing future crews with procedures as soon as possible (Sasgen, p. 21).

Mrs. William Pugh, William Pugh, Lawrence Bernard (all seated), and Marvin Jensen (standing, with arm in sling) on the perimeter of the dance floor at the commissioning party (photograph courtesy of Ladislaus Topor).

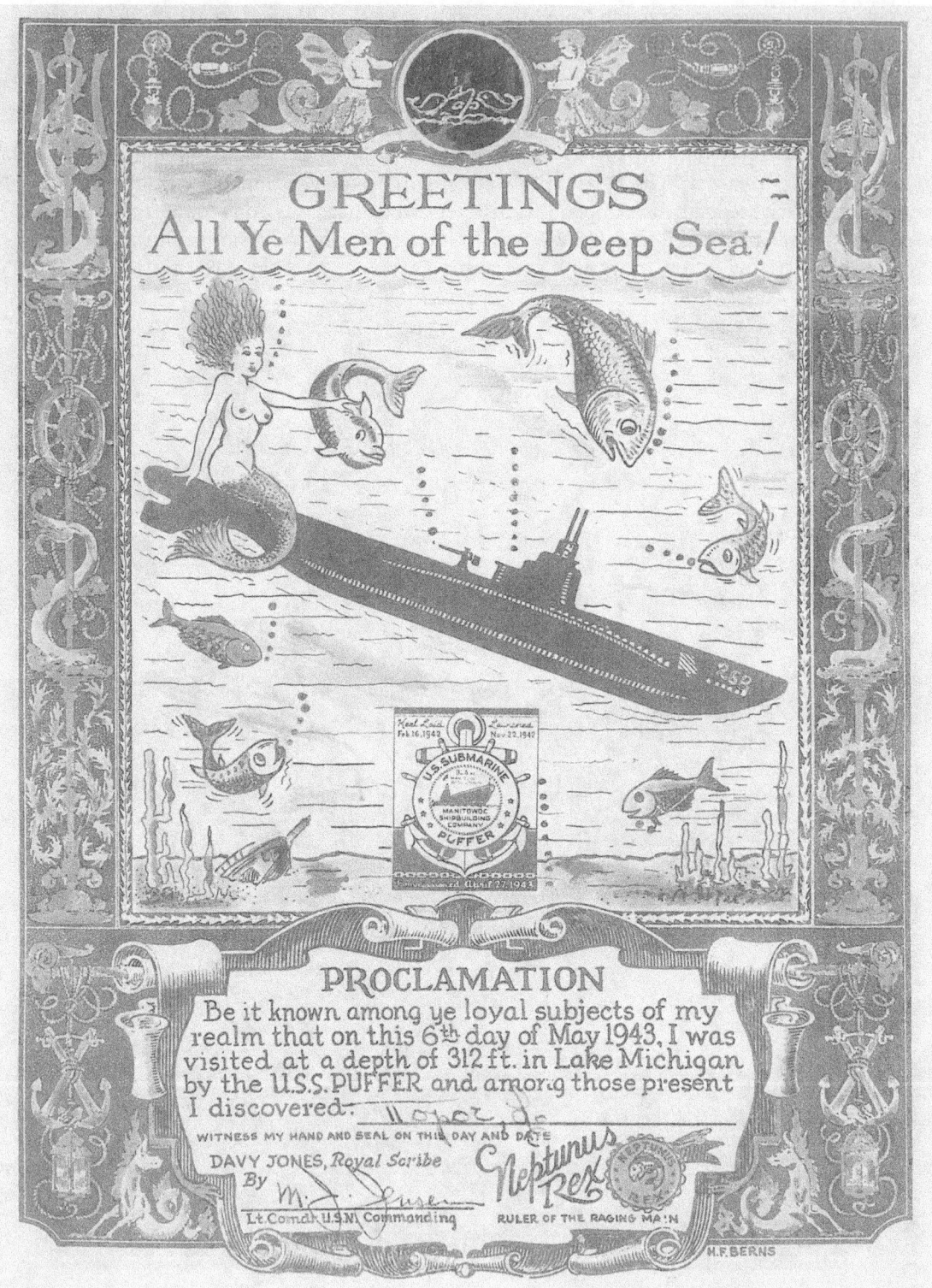

Example of a Test Dive Certificate given to each crew member. On May 6, 1943, the *Puffer* was tested to a depth of 312 feet in Lake Michigan (image courtesy of Ladislaus Topor).

The Bonding of the Crew

The future crew and officers of the *Puffer* began arriving in mid–1942. During the construction of the *Puffer* the crew members were able to see and learn about the many hidden systems of the boat—electrical, hydraulic, steering, depth control, etc.—as each was installed. Every man on a submarine must know the job of every other man on board and be able to perform it. "School of the Boat" was held daily above the Officers' Quarters in the shipyard. The students kept a notebook of the myriad tubes for the various systems on the submarine. Every crew member had to prove his knowledge to an officer in order to qualify. Only qualified sailors had the privilege of wearing the Silver Dolphins pin on their uniforms.

The local population treated the crew well. The sailors were readily accepted into the local drinking establishments, The Passion Pit, the lounge at the Hay Hotel or the Red Star Bar (Sasgen, p. 21; Topor). The Red Star had an Irish setter that delivered El Rojo rum (Topor). Ladislaus Topor, Demeter "Pat" Patsko, and Joseph "Zel" Zelaznicki frequented the bar often as a trio. All were over six feet tall and quite thin. Patsko practiced meditation, the reading of tea leaves, and astral projection. As a result the trio became known as the "Voodoo Doctors" by the bar patrons and among the crew. Their jukebox favorite, "Bolero," was nearly worn flat.

A few of the crew attended church and met some of the locals at the service. From that time on, the friendly Wisconsin people bought rounds of drinks for the *Puffer* gang. The young women of the area freely associated with the sailors at the various "passion pits" (*ibid.*). James Liggett recalled his days in Manitowoc fondly.

> After being in Manitowoc a few days we had the experience of meeting the most wonderful people in the world. Never again in my life will I experience the warm welcome and hospitality that was shown us by these wonderful people. Believe me—home was never like this! They took us to theaters, beer joints (nightclubs to some), bowling, anything we desired was ours, even into their homes. Brother, we never had it so good!

Testing of all systems, except torpedo firing, was conducted on Lake Michigan (photograph courtesy of the Wisconsin Maritime Museum Collection).

All I can say on my recollection is "Thank God for such wonderful tolerant people." A few of the boys (my shipmates) married some of the local belles, and to this day I say "Girls, you met the *Best*."

We really had ourselves a ball and the crew of USS *Puffer* was most receptive and appreciative. Our foster friends did all in their power to make their homes away from home. We got to the point where the merchants (especially the beer joint merchants) would trust us implicitly, but when we took off for overseas the "Exec" and "Old Man" made sure the bills were deducted from our future pay and forwarded to the trustworthy people. To make it short for Manitowoc, I am sure we left with a great love for these marvelous people and hope to this day we didn't leave a bad memory. If so, my deepest and most profound apologies [Liggett].

The single men were housed in an old Navy barracks. With 50 young men in a small area practical jokes were bound to happen. The boatswain's mate, "Boats," who was in charge of the barracks, had brought a bear with him from his circus days (Sasgen, p. 19; Trudeau). The bear was used to awaken hung over sailors such as Sam Smith at reveille. Smith nearly climbed the wall as the hot breath, wet nose and tongue of the bear stirred him from his slumber (*ibid.*). In another incident jokester Norman Trudeau dumped cold water on hotheaded Ray Kellum while he took his morning shower. Kellum stumbled out of the shower with soap in his eyes and threw a bucket of water on the first person he saw, the boatswain's mate. Fortunately he had a good sense of humor and laughed off the incident. Trudeau escaped discovery or "Kellum would have killed me and tied me in a knot" (Trudeau).

The food in the submarine service was the best in the Navy. During training and construction of the *Puffer* was no exception. Russ Tidd recalled the good food served by the cooks, who were brought to Manitowoc from some of the finest Midwestern hotels. It was the first time he had tasted coconut cream pie. Tidd, always hungry and looking forward to his next meal, recalled the *Puffer* was a good "feeder" (Tidd).

Life was not so easy for the black stewards. Black people were rarely seen in this part of Wisconsin. James Patton, a black officers' cook and steward from the Kansas City area, knew the rules of white society, but the officers' steward, John Pruitt, attempted to push the envelope. Patton, an excellent boxer, was forced to put Pruitt in his place when he too closely fraternized with the local women. Patton probably wanted to maintain a low profile and avoid trouble with the locals. Certainly some Wisconsin natives would have accepted the black sailors, but jealousy could quickly develop when women were involved. Patton, a Golden Gloves boxer as a youth, became part of the crew when he warded off an unfriendly bunch of townies that didn't like the *Puffer* crew in town, white or black (Mazzone).

Down the Mississippi River

The *Puffer* began the long journey to the South Pacific by first traveling from Manitowoc to Chicago on Lake Michigan. Liggett wrote, "As we left the breakwater a true sense of sadness reached not only my heart, but the hearts of a few other shipmates because this was 'it.' We were on the greatest adventure of our lives." The boat made a quick stop at Great Lakes Naval Training Camp so the newly inducted sailors could look at a submarine—and maybe volunteer for service on one (Liggett). The boat traveled from Manitowoc to Chicago along the shore of Lake Michigan. Commander Jensen in an interview recalled the details of the journey. The *Puffer* passed through the middle of Chicago via the Chicago River and Drainage Canal at dawn, passing under the many raised drawbridges. Two tugs, one on the bow and one on the stern, assisted the boat through the canal. The boat had passed through the heart of Chicago before it was light. The canal was patrolled by police craft throughout the passage (Kueh).

The next leg of the journey followed the Des Plaines and Illinois Rivers, where the *Puffer* entered a floating drydock at Lockport, Illinois. The *Puffer* waited four days for the Mississippi River tug, the *Minnesota*, that pushed the drydock down the river. Because of the high water on the Mississippi River caused by the melting snow, the *Minnesota* was delayed on its return trip from New Orleans (Nelson, p. 116).

Four days in one spot was enough time for some crew members to find trouble. Three of the crew headed for an office of a nearby gravel yard so Trudeau could call his wife and inform her they would be delayed arriving in New Orleans. Raymond Kellum and other crew members had been shooting at carp in the gravel pit with a .22 caliber pistol. The sanitary engineering officers that operated the locks asked Penzenik, Kerls and Trudeau if they had been doing the shooting at the fish. The officers were concerned because fuel tanks were nearby. The three crew members responded, "No, it was not us" (Trudeau).

No phone was available at the lock office, so the engineering officers volunteered to take the men to Lockport where they could make the phone call. Civilians typically went out of their way to help servicemen. Men back on the ship viewing the events from a distance concluded the trio were being arrested for shooting at the fish and informed Ensign Walter Mazzone (*ibid.*).

The sanitation officers dropped off the three at a nearby bar, but stayed in the car to listen to their favorite radio show, "Gang Busters." Trudeau made the call, but the three also picked up some beers for later. Upon their return to the boat, Warrant Officer Ken Dobson and Chief Electrician's Mate Ernie Dufault were on deck watch. The beer was left on deck and the three were sure they were in serious trouble. The three reported to Mazzone, and the confusion about the suspected arrest was cleared up, but he knew the bunch — he wanted to know where the beer was (*ibid.*). All ended well as Mazzone shared the beer with the trio. Mazzone remembered the "quiet" trip down the Mississippi River fondly. He became well acquainted with the men (Mazzone).

The tug finally arrived and the *Puffer* went down the Mississippi at the crest of the flood. The periscopes were removed and placed on the deck to provide clearance under the many low bridges that spanned the Mississippi River. Near St. Louis the tug captain tied up to sycamore trees ten miles outside of St. Louis to avoid visibility to the day traffic on the bridges (Mazzone). As the drydock approached New Orleans the current was running between 5 and 7 knots, which made "ship handling a novel experience" (Kueh).

Commander Jensen recalled the *Minnesota* captain, Lowell Sorrells, as quite a character, but an extremely good ship handler. His 22-year-old son, who had been with his father since he was 11 years old, assisted the captain of the tug. With the river pilot, Walter Hass, Jensen discussed books over lunch. He found the pair were fine people, but also to "have peculiar psychology and expressions" (*ibid.*).

The *Puffer* stayed in commission during its trip down the Mississippi to New Orleans. Some of the crew and most of the officers were given leave as the boat left Manitowoc. One such crew member was Jay Deem from Alta, Illinois. He headed for home to visit his parents and intended to catch the *Puffer* at it progressed down the Illinois River. With the four day delay at Lockport, he thought he had missed the boat, and headed for New Orleans on his own (Deem). Most of the remaining crew took several days leave upon arrival at Lockport and traveled separately to New Orleans, some with their wives. For Trudeau, who had been recently married, the journey to New Orleans became his honeymoon (Trudeau).

Ensign Mazzone and a few crew members stayed on board and did final work, such as touch-up painting of the interior hull. Manitowoc workers also accompanied the crew to do external painting. The rest of the crew and boat were reunited at the naval station at Algiers, Louisiana, across the river from New Orleans. Mazzone had grown up in California, so he enjoyed the springtime journey through the heartland of America, a part of the country he had never seen (Mazzone).

While in New Orleans some of the crew decided to get their ears pierced, similar to the China sailors on the crew. China sailors were stationed in the Philippine Islands prior to the start of the war and visited Chinese ports, such as Shanghai (Deem). In New Orleans the electricians mates were amused by throwing the breakers on the outside of the buildings, plunging the businesses into darkness (Sander). The various drinking and entertainment establishments were visited and good times were had by all (Trudeau). Mrs. Charles Brockhausen, wife of quartermaster Charles Brockhausen, related a story at the 1991 World War II Submarine Convention about Executive Officer Hess. Mrs. Brockhausen told of Hess's kindness. When the *Puffer* crew was quarantined on the boat in New Orleans, prior to leaving for the canal zone, Hess gave Mrs. Brockhausen a ride back to her hotel. Fifty years later that act of kindness was not forgotten (Polk and Sanders, video 1991). With the periscopes reinstalled, stores and torpedoes loaded, on June 13 the *Puffer* sailed for Coco Solo, Panama, at the eastern end of the Panama Canal. (Nelson, p. 114).

Final Training and on to Brisbane

A week later the *Puffer* safely arrived at Coco Solo, Submarine Squadron Three, a base under the command of Commander Jesse Hull. Upon arrival at Coco Solo a number of experienced torpedomen from Squadron Three were temporarily assigned to the *Puffer* to assist

The *Peto*, the first Manitowoc submarine, rides in the drydock. The *Puffer* and all other Manitowoc submarines were transported to New Orleans in this manner (photograph courtesy of the Wisconsin Maritime Museum Collection).

with the training and the test firing of dummy torpedoes (RG24). After three days at Coco Solo, where swimming was possible inside the shark nets, the isthmus was traversed. While passing through the Gatun Locks the men could hear the noise of parrots and monkeys in the jungle filling the air (Tidd).

Upon reaching Balboa on the Pacific Ocean side of the canal, the *Puffer* began four weeks of advanced training near the Perlas Islands. Daily operations in the Perlas Islands were primarily dummy torpedo firings. Other drills took place throughout the day such as emergency dives, and rigging for silent running. Training included drill and exercise, exercise and drill, repetition after repetition, until the crew and boat became extensions of each other and the crew members worked as a coordinated team. One mistake could cause a submarine to be lost (*ibid.*).

The blue surface of the Pacific was occasionally broken by the splash of a giant manta ray, whales, and other marine life. Evenings at the anchorage in the Perlas Islands were livened with the catch of Spanish mackerel by the crew, and by visits alongside the submarine by natives in canoes selling exotic fruits and souvenirs. Liberty was allowed at night. In the darkness of the evening the sound of Wilbur "Artie" Warner playing "Begin the Beguine" on the clarinet or John Allen playing the harmonica flowed from the open hatch of the after torpedo room or up through the main induction (Topor; Trudeau; Tidd).

On July 20 the *Puffer* set out on the monotonous nonstop run to Brisbane, Australia. The weather needed to cooperate for an uneventful trip. Two months earlier the *Pompon* was diverted to Auckland, New Zealand, to refuel after it met heavy seas. The *Puffer* encountered better weather, but arrived very low on fuel at Brisbane on August 21, 1943. Jay Deem, who had an ear pierced in New Orleans, arrived with something extra for the Australians. His ear and one side of his face had become infected with the yellow blisters of impetigo. Upon arrival in Australia half of Deem's face was painted with potassium permanganate, a purplish-colored medicine, and powdered with talcum. No Australian would come close to him, male or female (Deem). Through the serious and the humorous the crew had become comrades. The crew had grown to love the *Puffer*, always referred to as "her," and had turned the machine into a destructive force. In a few weeks their unity and training would be severely tested.

3

The Initial Officers of the *Puffer*

Commander Marvin J. Jensen

Jensen was born in Sheboygan, Wisconsin, July 8, 1908, only 25 miles south of Manitowoc. Both cities sit adjacent to Lake Michigan. He was raised there and graduated from Sheboygan High School. While in high school and the year after he had four years experience as a repairman for the Firestone Tire and Rubber Company in Sheboygan. He served in the Wisconsin National Guard from September 1925 to June 1926. Appointed midshipman from his native state, he entered the United States Naval Academy on June 14, 1927, and was graduated and commissioned ensign in the U.S. Navy on June 4, 1931. After graduation he was assigned to the Naval Air Base, Norfolk, Virginia, for elimination flight training for two months, and reported to the USS *West Virginia* for sea duty. He had engineering and gunnery duties on board that battleship from August 1931 until March 1932, after which he continued flight training at the Naval Air Station, Pensacola, Florida, for another four months (Jensen, "Biography").

During the period from August 1932 until July 1935 he was at sea on the USS *New York*, USS *Yarnall*, USS *Talbot* and USS *Wickes*, with engineering, commissary and communications duties, except for three months he spent in the Naval Hospital, San Diego, California, as a patient in 1934. From July 1935 until January 1936 he went to the U.S. Naval Submarine School, New London, Connecticut. For eight months he served on the World War I vintage sub USS *R-14* as engineer, commissary officer and communications officer. He remained at sea as first lieutenant and gunnery officer of USS *Plunger*, until June 1938, then returned to the General Line School in Annapolis. A year later he reported to the Bureau of Navigation, Navy Department, editing enlisted training courses. In 1940 he joined the commissioning detail of submarine *Thresher* as executive officer (XO). At the outbreak of the war Jensen was the XO and navigator in *Thresher*, then commanded by William L. Anderson, and continued in that position during that boat's first three war patrols until May 1942 (*ibid.*).

Jensen's experiences on the *Thresher* and mentoring by Anderson, as well as the reaction of superiors to Anderson's decisions, probably influenced Jensen's attitudes, decision-making, and actions during the First War Patrol of the *Puffer*. The *Thresher* underwent harrowing experiences from friendly fire and a Japanese depth charging similar to the *Puffer's* First War Patrol. Returning from a long pre-war patrol off of Midway in December 1941, a heavy sea had swept the bridge, hurling one of the *Thresher* lookouts to the deck. The lookout was in critical condition and Anderson was in a hurry to get the injured sailor back to Pearl Harbor for medical treatment. The *Litchfield,* an old four-stack destroyer, was escorting the *Thresher* into Pearl Harbor when the word came of the December 7 attack. The *Thresher* and the destroyer passed a United States naval task force steaming out to find the Japanese. Unfortunately the *Litchfield* joined the task force, and left Anderson to fend for himself. Anderson planned to submerge until dark and then surface to make his way alone to port (Blair, pp. 101–2).

As the *Thresher* submerged Anderson received a message from Admiral Tom Withers at Submarine Force Command not to separate from the escort under any conditions. After decoding the message, Anderson poked up his antenna and radioed for the escort to come back to the spot where he had submerged. After some time elapsed, Anderson spotted through the periscope a four-stack destroyer at the rendezvous point. He surfaced to again make himself known to the friendly escort, assuming it was the *Litchfield* (*ibid.*).

However, the destroyer was a different destroyer, the *Gamble,* converted to a light minesweeper (DM-15), which mistook the *Thresher* for a Japanese submarine. In the aftermath of December 7 every ship looked Japanese. The destroyer turned on the submarine and commenced firing with the 4-inch forward gun and intended to ram the *Thresher.* Anderson took the boat to 250 feet in record time and rigged for the expected depth charges. Anderson's attempt to contact the destroyer by sonar failed. Fortunately the *Gamble* was not carrying depth charges and left the scene, possibly in fear of a "Japanese" torpedo attack (*ibid.*).

With the *Gamble* gone, Anderson again poked up his radio antenna through the waves and informed Withers of the attack. Even after many attempts, Withers could not set up an escort with another vessel. That night Anderson desperately attempted to reach port again. The following morning Withers informed the *Thresher* that the Pearl Harbor entrance net was opened at a specific time, but each time the *Thresher* was driven off by friendly forces. Withers then directed the *Thresher* to a sanctuary where the boat was to remain submerged, but once again the *Thresher* was bombed — the first of many U.S. submarines that were attacked by friendly aircraft. During this perilous waiting period, the injured man died. Finally the escort USS *Thornton* appeared. After exchanging recognition signals, the badly shaken *Thresher* returned to Pearl Harbor and by midafternoon tied up next to the submarine tender USS *Pelias* (Roscoe, p. 21; Blair, pp. 101–2).

After repairs the *Thresher* left for the Marshall Islands on December 30, 1941, where three other boats were operating. The *Thresher* attacked a large freighter near Guam. Anderson fired six torpedoes, five missed, one hit. Anderson believed the ship had sunk, but had no proof. Once again on the return to base two days from Pearl Harbor, friendly aircraft bombed the *Thresher.* To add insult to injury, Anderson received a stiff critique from his squadron commander, Al McCann: "The percentage of time utilized in productive effort was too low." He criticized Anderson for being too quick to dive on night contacts, for firing six torpedoes, which were in short supply, at the freighter off Guam, and for not carrying out orders to reconnoiter Saipan. Anderson did get credit for a 4,500 ton freighter sunk. Postwar analysis was unable to verify the sinking. (Blair, pp. 116,121)

Anderson was the only one of the four officers to escape criticism by Withers. He criticized the other three commanders for varying faults ranging from firing three torpedoes at a minelayer, a vague patrol report, and not detailing the shortcomings of an aging boat. Despite the criticism, Withers decorated the commanders who reported sinking a vessel with the Navy

Cross, one step below the Congressional Medal of Honor. (Blair, p. 122) Jensen was awarded the Bronze Star Medal, with Combat V, and cited.

> For meritorious service as Executive Officer and Navigator of the USS *Thresher*, during that vessel's Second War Patrol against enemy Japanese forces in the Pacific War Area from December 30, 1941, to February 26, 1942. By his administration and technical ability, Lieutenant Jensen rendered invaluable assistance to the commanding officer in conducting successful attacks which resulted in the sinking of a 4,500 ton ship during a critical period of the war [Jensen, Citations].

The Third War Patrol of the *Thresher* sent the boat on the special mission of furnishing weather reports to support the Doolittle air raid on Tokyo. While waiting for the *Enterprise* and the *Hornet* to arrive on station from San Francisco, Anderson and Jensen received a severe depth charge attack. Anderson received an Ultra (intercepted decoded Japanese message) reporting at least four Japanese submarines were operating near Tokyo Bay. Though he took precautions, one of the Japanese submarines located the *Thresher* and fired two torpedoes which missed. On April 10, 1942, Anderson and Jensen attacked three freighters, firing three torpedoes at the first two, which missed, and one at the third. The third, a 3,000 ton freighter, *Sado Maru*, sank (Blair, pp. 214–5).

Immediately after sinking the *Sado Maru*, the *Thresher* was counterattacked by enemy patrol vessels. The three or four patrol boats pinned the *Thresher* down for 12 hours, delivering one of the worst depth charge attacks of the war up until that time. During the attack, depth control of the boat was lost and she plunged to 400 feet, 150 feet deeper than test depth. The boat was badly damaged, and Anderson considered returning to Pearl Harbor immediately. However, he stayed to support the Doolittle raid, radioing weather reports to the *Hornet*, which eight days later launched the first air strike at the heart of the Japanese homeland, Tokyo. When Anderson returned to Pearl Harbor, he stepped down from command and became the submarine repair superintendent at Mare Island. The badly damaged *Thresher* was sent to the yard for extensive overhaul and repairs (*ibid.*).

On the *Thresher* Jensen had received the awards and experienced the dangers of submarine command. He had also seen the professional dangers of failing to command successfully; however, he pursued submarine command. It was the duty and honor of an officer to place himself and his ship "in harm's way." There was absolutely no way to tell in advance if a new skipper would be aggressive and bold or passive. Early in the war two pre-war skippers could not handle the day-in and day-out strain of wartime command or depth charge attacks and suffered nervous breakdowns. What a skipper did, how he performed under pressure, how he dealt with the unexpected, was the result of deep inner motivation that could not be quantified or assessed in port or even while he was an executive officer. An aggressive XO might become a different person when weighted down by the loneliness of command, the responsibilities of a ship, and the lives of seventy-five other men. The Navy's solution was to give command to all that deserved it primarily based upon USNA graduation seniority, and see what happened. If the person failed to perform, then he was usually relieved after two patrols (Blair, p. 201). In November 1942 Jensen reported to the Manitowoc Ship Building Company as commanding officer of the *Puffer*.

Franklin G. Hess

Hess was born in Sacramento, California, on September 12, 1911. After attending Sacramento Junior College for two years he entered the USNA and graduated in 1935. His first duty was aboard the battleship USS *New Mexico* (BB 40) as a junior engineering officer for 14 months. He then served for another 15 months on the destroyer USS *Simpson* (DD 221) followed by a year as a staff officer at COMBATFOR (Command Battle Forces). As part of his continued development as an officer, Hess then served as 1st Division officer on the cruiser USS *Salt Lake City* (CA 25). To hasten promotion he attended Submarine School during the last half of 1939 and was assigned to the submarine USS *Nautilus* (SS 168) as the communications and assistant engineering officer (Hess, Bio Sheet).

Hess served in the *Nautilus* during the first eight months of the war. With the outbreak of the war in the Pacific, the *Nautilus* quickly joined the fight. On its First War Patrol, it was at the Battle of Midway. At the time the *Nautilus* was credited with "three torpedo hits on a 10,000 ton carrier" (Hess, Citations). Hess received a letter of commendation. Postwar analysis verified a hit on the aircraft carrier *Kaga* with a dud torpedo (Alden, *Successes*, p. D-13). On the second patrol, the *Nautilus* carried out the first of many special missions. The *Nautilus*, one of the largest submarines of the era, was well armed with large deck guns and had adequate room in which to transport troops. Carrying a detachment of the Second Marine Raider Battalion and in company of the sister submarine USS *Argonaut* the Marines attacked and captured the enemy held island of Makin (Hess, Bio Sheet).

In September of 1942 Hess reported to Manitowoc, Wisconsin, as executive officer of the *Puffer*, where he trained crew members and became familiar with the new fleet boats. Hess served as executive officer on the *Puffer* for three war patrols. For his efforts to save the boat during the First War Patrol he received a Bronze Star (*ibid.*).

He was given the command of the submarine USS *Angler* from July 1944 through December 1944. During that tenure of duty on two war patrols, the *Angler* was credited with sinking the 2,407 ton *Nanrei Maru*. He received a second Bronze Star and Letter of Commendation for his command of the *Angler*. For the remainder of the war Hess served on the submarine USS *Grampus* as a prospective commanding officer (PCO) (*ibid.*).

Postwar he commanded the submarine USS *Corporal* until March of 1947. For the next three years he served in Submarine Administration, Pacific Reserve Fleet (PACRESFLT), overseeing the Reserve Fleet at Mare Island, California. From July of 1950 to June of 1951 he was a student at the Naval War College, Newport, Rhode Island. For the next two years he served as a logistics officer on the Staff Command 7th Fleet and 1st Fleet. For his "resourcefulness and outstanding planning" for the naval forces involved in the Korean War effort, he again received a Bronze Star and Letter of Commendation (*ibid.*).

Hess served three years at Naval Operations (OPNAV), until August 1956, when he was given command of the USS *Winston* (AKA 94), followed by the USS *Pickaway* (APA 222), each for six months. He returned to the staff of Commander in Chief Pacific Fleet (CINCPACFLT), as assistant commander of ship logistics for two years. For three academic years he was a professor of naval science at the UCLA Naval ROTC unit. His final three years of naval duty were on the staff of Submarine Command—Squadron 12. He retired from the Navy on July 1, 1965 (*ibid.*).

Hess had married Sarah June Evans on June 12, 1937. He had three sons, Sanford (1939), Franklin C. (1943), and Daniel (1952). Three months of retirement was enough and Hess went back to work for the State of California, Division of Highways, San Francisco Office. In 1967 after 30 years of seeing the world, Frank and Sally bought their first home in Piedmont, California. In 1976 Hess retired from the State of California. He and his wife remained active at the Oakland Children's Hospital and Children's Home Society. Hess continued an active life with his wife, played golf, cared for his home and garden, and enjoyed his grandchildren. He died January 11, 1995 (*ibid.*).

Lawrence G. Bernard

Born and raised in South Dakota, he was appointed to the Naval Academy from that state. He was a varsity rower and intramural boxer. Upon graduation in 1937, he served two years on the battleship USS *California* (BB 44), after which he attended Submarine School in New London. From there he was ordered to the Asiatic Submarine Station in the Philippines for duty on the *S-39* where he served until the outbreak of World War II and on four war patrols after the outbreak of the war (Bernard, Service Record).

Just prior to the entry of the United States into World War II, the *S-39* patrolled off southern Luzon. On December 8, 1941, she moved into the San Bernardino Strait to impede Japanese mining activities. However, the escorts screening the minelayers kept the American submarine at bay with persistent depth charging. On December 11, the *S-39* endured a daylong pounding of depth charges. The *S-39* then turned to a more hopeful mission, cutting into the Japanese supply line. On December 13, the submarine contacted and attacked an enemy freighter, but again escorts interfered and the crew was prevented from a verified sinking. The *S-39* continued her patrol, unsuccessfully chasing other targets until December 20 when the boat returned to Manila (Gugliotta, pp. 88ff).

Increased enemy air activity soon rendered naval installations in the area untenable, and the *S-39* was ordered to Java to join what would become in mid–January 1942 the American-British-Dutch-Australian (ABDA) command. Conducting her Second War Patrol en route, the *S-39* arrived at Surabaya on January 24, underwent an abbreviated overhaul, and departed for the Third War Patrol (*ibid.*, pp. 119ff).

Operating in the South China Sea and Java Sea, the *S-39* reconnoitered Chebia Island, in search of British refugees from Singapore. Unsuccessful, the boat returned to the Java Sea

Commander Bernard, Caroline Bernard, and sons Lawrence "Lance" Bernard, Jr., and Alan "Chris" Bernard (photograph courtesy of Chris Bernard).

and, on March 4, sank the *Erimo*, a 6,500 ton naval tanker (*ibid.*, pp. 142ff). Two weeks later, the S-boat arrived at Fremantle, Australia, and by the end of April had moved on to Brisbane from where it departed on the fourth patrol on May 10. During the next four weeks, the sub reconnoitered designated areas of the Louisiade Archipelago, and then operated in the Solomon Islands (*ibid.*).

The *S-39*'s fifth patrol was delayed twice by mechanical failures of the engines and air compressors. After getting underway Bernard, the executive officer, became sick with symptoms similar to pneumonia. The *S-39* continued toward the patrol area, but a few days later Bernard's condition had worsened. Radio contact was made with headquarters. Bernard was taken to Townsville. En route the *S-39* was met by the HMAS *Bendigo*, which delivered him to the Army Hospital in Townsville. A few days later on August 14, 1942, the *S-39* ran aground and was lost. All crew members were rescued after spending a night knee deep in water on a reef in squally seas. The only possessions they saved were the clothes on their backs. The crew was returned to Townsville (Wikipedia *S-39*; Gugliotta, pp. 191ff).

Bernard next served in the Pacific as engineering officer on the First War Patrol of the *Puffer*. (Mike Kutscherowsky, a torpedoman on the *S-39*, was also reassigned to the *Puffer*.) He then served as CO of *R-2* in the Atlantic. At war's end he observed the surrender ceremony in Tokyo Bay from the deck of the submarine *Archerfish* (SS 311), where he was aboard as a prospective commanding officer (PCO) (Bernard, Service Record).

After the war, he continued his sea duty in submarines for three years' service as commander of the *Stickleback* (SS 415) and the *Brill* (SS 330). Next came three years of shore duty, followed by three additional years of submarine duty on the staff of Command Submarine Atlantic and as submarine division commander (*ibid.*).

In 1954 he reported for duty with the Weapons Systems Evaluation Group in the Office of the Secretary of Defense, leaving there in 1957 to command the *Howard Gilmore* (AS 16). This command was followed by duty as navy advisor to the commandant of the Air War College in Montgomery, Alabama (*ibid.*).

In 1961 he assumed command of Submarine Squadron Seven in Pearl Harbor. He next served as chief of staff of Command Submarine Atlantic, and then was Commander Submarine Flotilla One in San Diego. This was followed by duty in the Office of the Chief of Naval Operations (CNO) during which period he was promoted to rear admiral (*ibid.*).

In 1967 he returned to sea duty as Commander Submarine Flotilla Six with headquarters in Charleston and squadrons in Norfolk, Charleston, Key West, and Rota, Spain. He was proudly present in 1968 for the launch of the nuclear submarine *Puffer* (SSN 652). His final assignment was a second tour in the Office of the CNO. He retired in 1971. Decorations include the Silver Star Medal, Bronze Star Medal with Combat V, and two awards of the Legion of Merit (*ibid.*).

Following retirement, he and his wife, Caroline, traveled for the better part of a year, most of it in a motor home, throughout the United States. In 1972 they eventually settled in Sonoma County, California, a few miles outside the city limits of Santa Rosa. He was a member of the local chapters of the Navy League and The Retired Officers Association (TROA). He retained his interest in the Naval Academy and in his class affairs. He also served for many years on his local congressman's committee for the interview and selection of nominees for appointment to the various military academies (*ibid.*).

Rear Admiral Lawrence G. Bernard, USN (Ret.), died on March 29, 1997, at his home in Santa Rosa, California. At his request, services were private. He was survived by his wife of 58 years, Caroline; his sons, Lawrence G. "Lance" Bernard, Jr. (USNA '64), of Los Gatos, CA; Captain Alan C. "Chris" Bernard USN (Ret.) (USNA '65) of Evergreen, Colorado; and Jon M. Bernard (Naval OCS '69) of Foster City, California; and one grandson. In 1969 Bernard and all three of his sons were officers in the Navy. Chris commanded the Ohio class SSBN *Henry M. Jackson* and later the Trident Refit Facility at Bangor, Washington (*ibid.*).

Carl R. Dwyer

Dwyer was born on June 9, 1915, in Edgerton, Kansas. Raised in Ponca City, Oklahoma, he graduated from Ponca City High School, attended Oklahoma State and graduated from Oklahoma University Junior College. Carl entered the Naval Academy in 1934, was a member of the Ninth Company and active in track and cross country, editor of *Reef Points* and on the staffs of the *Log* and *Lucky Bag* (Dwyer, Biography).

Upon graduation in 1938, he was ordered to the cruiser USS *Louisville*, and then the battleship USS *Texas* until June 1940 when it departed on a midshipman cruise. He studied at the Naval Gun Factory until he reported to the Submarine School in New London. Upon graduation from Submarine School in December 1940, he was ordered to the submarine *Saury* (SS 189). When World War II started, the *Saury* opposed the Japanese entry to the Philippines at Lingayen Gulf in western Luzon province, but was plagued by unreliable Mk XIV torpedoes. Dwyer was promoted to lieutenant in June 1942 (*ibid.*).

The *Saury* withdrew to Albany, Western Australia, in July, 1942 for a refit. Problems with torpedoes were already suspected by various submarine commanders. Admiral Lockwood made arrangements with Admiral Fife to conduct another test on the Mk XIV torpedoes, after the Bureau of Ordnance (BuOrd) questioned the validity of an initial test made a few weeks earlier (Gannon, p. 84). BuOrd blamed the commanders for various faults. Four Mark XIV torpedoes were fired by the *Saury* at a net from a range of approximately 900 yards. The three torpedoes that hit the net were set to run at 10 feet, but pierced the net at 21 feet. Fife concluded, as had been seen in the earlier test, the Mk XIV ran 11 feet deeper than designed. After blaming the skippers for various inadequacies related to the use of the torpedoes for eight months, a few weeks later BuOrd verified the problem (Blair, p. 277). Problems with the Mk VI magnetic exploder were not considered at this time. As the future weapons officer of the *Puffer*, these tests were extremely important for Dwyer to have observed.

Dwyer was then ordered to Manitowoc, Wisconsin, to commission the *Puffer* (SS 268) as the gunnery officer. He made eight war patrols in the *Puffer*: two as the gunnery officer, two as the executive officer, and four as the commanding officer. He was awarded the Navy Cross, Silver Star, Bronze Star and Secretary of the Navy Letter of Commendation for that service. Upon relief in 1946, he was ordered to the Naval Academy as an instructor in electronics, then command of the *Requin* (SS 481), and back to the Naval Academy in electrical engineering until 1951. He then commanded the destroyers USS *Fiske* and USS *Rooks*. From 1953 until 1964, while at sea he commanded Destroyer Division 132, Destroyer Squadron 23 and was on the staff of the Commander Amphibious Forces Pacific. Ashore, he served several tours in the Office of the Chief of Naval Operations and Navy Material until his retirement in 1967. After a brief stint with the Stanwyck Corporation, he served as deputy comptroller in the Office of Budget and Reports until his second retirement in 1981 (Dwyer, Biography).

Carl and his wife, Katherine Wood O'Toole, spent many pleasant years with their family in South Bethany Beach, Delaware. His wife of 58 years died in 2002. Captain Carl R. Dwyer died quietly at the Casey House in Rockville, Maryland, on May 6, 2004. He was survived by his three children, Katherine Everngarn, John Dwyer, and Margaret Lutsky, all of the Washington, D.C., area. Burial with full military honors was in Arlington Cemetery on July 14, 2004 (*ibid.*).

William M. Pugh II

Born in Delaware in 1920, Pugh entered the Naval Academy from that state after a year at Duke University. In December 1941 he reported to the battleship USS *Mississippi*. Later that year he began a long career in submarines aboard the *R-4* in Key West. While there Pugh married his hometown sweetheart, Doris Mears, before moving to New London for Submarine School. He then reported to Manitowoc to take part in the construction and commissioning of the *Puffer*. His awards included two Silver Star medals while on the *Puffer* and the Legion of Merit (Pugh, Biography).

After three years of submarine warfare during World War II in the Pacific, he served during peacetime another three years on the *Tusk* in the Atlantic. He then studied at the Post Graduate School at Annapolis, finishing at UC-Berkeley with a degree in petroleum engineering. He served as executive officer on the submarine *Sennet* and commanded the *Medregal*. That command was followed by three years as head of a joint staff in London where he was responsible for the petroleum supply for U.S. Forces in Europe and the Middle East (*ibid.*).

Naval War College was followed by additional submarine duties, including command of Submarine Division 81 and then command of the Submarine Squadron 14 rear echelon in the early days of the SSBN (nuclear submarine) force buildup, a period of intense activity in new construction acceptances, missile firing tests, overseas base establishment and SSBN deployments. Command of the submarine tender USS *Holland* in Rota, Spain, and Submarine Development Group Two in New London prepared him for duty as deputy director of anti-submarine warfare programs in the office of the Chief of Naval Operations, from which he was selected for flag rank. Subsequently intelligence community assignments were followed by four years as Commander Naval Base—New York, and the assignment of five collateral duties, including command of the Military Sealift Command—Atlantic (*ibid.*).

He retired in 1974 after a heart problem developed. Pugh found another career in the business world, becoming a vice president of TRACOR, Inc., a strong contributor to Navy anti-submarine warfare technology, and finally as president of Hydronautics, Inc., a scientific testing subsidiary of TRACOR, Inc (*ibid.*).

He moved to Great Falls, Virginia, in 1974, where he and Doris were later joined by the families of their three children, Bill Jr., Diane and Dana, including nine grandchildren. A loving son, brother, husband, father, grandfather and friend, he also played an active role in support of his local Episcopal church. William Pugh died in Great Falls on July 7, 1996, after battling cancer for over a year. His memorial service and burial were conducted at Arlington National Cemetery (*ibid.*).

Walter Mazzone

Mazzone was born in 1918 in San Jose, California. He took part in boxing and developed an interest in human physiology as a high school student. He completed a BA degree from San Jose State in biological science in 1940. Uncle Sam called on him in 1941 and he attended Officer Candidate School at Notre Dame and Columbia universities for a semester each. He went directly to Manitowoc and assignment on the *Puffer* as an ensign. He completed two war patrols on the *Puffer* and was then transferred to the submarine *Crevalle* for the remainder of the war (Mazzone, telephone interview).

Following the war he completed another bachelor's degree in pharmaceutical chemistry and served in the Medical Service Corps at Balboa Naval Hospital. During the Korean War he served at Yokosuka Navy Base as a pharmacist. From 1953 to 1958 he was at Brooklyn, New

York, as chief of purchasing for the Armed Services Medical Supply Division — managing the supply of blood and drugs for all branches of the armed services. In 1958 he went to the submarine base at New London, Connecticut, as the physiological officer for underwater research. He was officer in charge of submarine medicine and worked on such projects as Sea Lab I, II, and III. During his tenure at New London he earned a master's degree in environmental physiology from Harvard University in 1964. He assisted Harris Steinke, another *Puffer* vet then in charge of the diving tower, develop an improved submarine escape device. The Navy refers to it today as the Steinke Hood. Mazzone tested the hood in an ascent from 318 feet. In 1966 Mazzone left New London for San Diego to assist on the Deep Submergence Systems Project, which trained aquanauts, as technical officer. He returned to New London in 1969 and retired from the Navy in 1970 (*ibid.*).

Mazzone continued to work in underwater technology for the next 34 years, working for the Civil Service Naval Oceans System Center and International Science Applications (ISA). He and his wife live in San Jose. They have a son who is a captain in the Navy, currently serving as operations officer at the naval base in Bremerton, Washington. A grandson is a lieutenant on the USS *Virginia*. Mazzone has been an active member of the World War II Submarine Veterans (*ibid.*).

Kenneth Dobson

Dobson was born in Michigan in 1913 and graduated from Decatur (Michigan) High School. He joined the Navy in 1934. After completing boot camp and Class "A" School he served on the destroyer USS *Hull* (DD 350) for two years. He was discharged from the Navy in November of 1940, and rejoined shortly thereafter to attend Submarine School. He served on the *O-4*, which was re-commissioned for training purposes at New London. He and his wife were married there in 1941. He then went to the *R-13* in Key West, Florida, where the Navy conducted sonar school. As the warrant officer with minimal seniority on the *R-13*, he was sent to new construction in Manitowoc and the *Puffer* in 1942 as assistant engineering officer (Dobson, telephone interview).

After the war Dobson served at the San Diego submarine reserve training center in the *S-34*. In 1947 he was stationed at the submarine base in Kodiak, Alaska. He served as the engineering officer on the oil tanker the *Monongahela*, making deliveries between Pearl Harbor, Guam and the States. He retired from the Navy in 1956. He attended Seattle University from 1956 to 1960 and earned a mechanical engineering degree. He worked for Boeing Aircraft from 1960 to 1971, and then for Honeywell Corporation, doing deep sea mining, until his retirement in 1978. He returned to Boeing for another 6 years. He and his wife had five children and live in Seattle. He has been an active member of the World War II Submarine Veterans (*ibid.*).

4

The Political, Physiological and Psychological

Torpedo Politics

At the beginning of World War II in the Pacific, the role of the submarine was very different from what evolved in the months that followed. Naval theory of the 1930s was a remnant of World War I. American naval theory, called Plan Orange, was centered on big ships, battleships, and big decisive battles, similar to the battles of World War I (Blair, pp. 46–47). The Japanese accepted the same theory and Pearl Harbor was their answer to a decisive big ship victory (Blair, p. 85).

However, the long term economic requirements of warfare had been overlooked by both the Japanese and American naval planners. They had forgotten the lessons of World War I. Early German U-boat attacks had minimal effect on the economy of Great Britain during that war. Moral indignation and self-imposed rules limited the effectiveness of the German blockade of England (Blair, p. 39). A desperate Germany struck back in 1917 without restrictions on submarines, and nearly isolated the British Isles from the rest of the world (Blair, p. 41).

At the outset of World War II unrestricted submarine warfare by Nazi Germany was repeated from 1939 until 1942 with a similar result. U-boats isolated Great Britain from its empire and raw materials. U-boats sank thousands of American and English freighters, some within sight of the American coastline (Blair, p. 72). In contrast, in the United States Navy of 1940 the submarines were seen as support boats for the big ships. Submarines performed scouting and special missions, but were not yet envisioned as a key element of a long-term war effort (Blair, p. 76). The Japanese saw little threat from submarines, and had not developed effective anti-submarine techniques to guard their freighters.

Unrestricted warfare was ordered immediately after Pearl Harbor, but the faulty use of American submarines during wartime evolved from unrealistic training exercises in the pre-war era (Blair, p. 125). With the destruction of the battleships at Pearl Harbor, Plan Orange was dead, and the newly developed fleet submarines suddenly had a new role (Blair, p. 106). However, it was believed the development of sonar, aircraft, and deadly depth charges and bombs made the submarine easy prey after an attack on an enemy ship (Blair, p. 67). The only way to make a safe attack was using sonar from a great depth; the periscope must never be exposed. Such daring maneuvers as a daytime or night periscope attack, or a night surface attack were deemed as nearly suicidal (Blair, p. 84). Such beliefs lead to extreme caution within the submarine command.

When wartime came, it took many months and many personnel replacements to change the mentality of the submarine command. By mid–1943 the older officers were for the most part replaced with younger and more aggressive commanders. Early in the war intercepted secret Japanese messages often sent submarines after fast, headline grabbing targets, such as battleships. With extreme luck the slower submarines could sink the faster warships, but this was not their most significant contribution. Wars were won by economic destruction as well as by the destruction of battleships (Blair, p. 19).

During the first 18 months of the war the effectiveness of the submarine commanders was undermined by the Bureau of Ordnance (BuOrd), an isolated and self-protective branch of the Navy. BuOrd developed the torpedo in use during World War II in the peacetime of the early 1920s. The torpedo had two methods of detonation: direct impact with the side of a ship or by detecting a change in the earth's magnetic field created by the target ship. The magnetic method required the torpedo to closely pass under the keel of the ship. Theory predicted that the explosion below the keel would break the back of the ship, inflicting much greater damage than a direct impact on the side of the ship (Gannon, p. 77). As a result a single torpedo could sink a ship as compared with three with side impact. Use of the magnetic exploder would conserve torpedoes. Even as late as May 1943 the supply of torpedoes was a "very urgent" problem and commanders were encouraged to conserve torpedoes (Gannon, p. 88; Blair, p. 278).

Ralph W. Christie, a 1915 graduate of the USNA, was closely involved with the development of the magnetic influence exploder. In 1922 and 1923 Christie pursued postgraduate work in ordnance engineering at the Massachusetts Institute of Technology. The $25,000 development of the magnetic exploder, known as project G-53, was carried out under the tightest secrecy. Only a handful of people in the BuOrd with a "need to know" were aware of the project, and none within the submarine command. Christie performed very unrealistic tests to verify the capability of the magnetic exploder or the keel breaking effect theory. In his defense, the Navy provided only one vessel as a test target. Earlier both the Germans and the British had abandoned the use of the magnetic exploder as unreliable. (Blair, pp. 54–55.)

In general the self-contained BuOrd had done very little wartime-like testing on the Mark XIV torpedo. BuOrd was convinced the torpedo was flawless. Submarine commanders suspected otherwise after a few months' use. In July 1942 Admirals Lockwood and Fife conducted tests at Albany, Western Australia. The first problem was discovered and begrudgingly verified by BuOrd a few weeks later: the depth setting of the torpedo was faulty. The torpedo ran 11 feet deeper than indicated by the settings on the torpedo (Blair, p. 277). It was believed with the depth problem corrected, which had made the magnetic influence exploder ineffective, torpedoes would no longer pass harmlessly under the enemy ship.

Other problems still plagued the torpedoes. The Mark XIVs continued to pass harmlessly under targets, prematurely explode, or impact the side of the enemy ship without exploding. In spite of these observations by submarine commanders, due to the limited supply of torpedoes, the BuOrd insisted on continued use of the magnetic exploders. The problems surrounding the torpedo influenced the morale of the entire submarine force, especially the officers. Gannon, in *Hellions of the Deep*, the most detailed study of torpedo development and use during World War II, wrote about the frustrations of the submarine commanders.

> As 1942 eased into 1943, morale steadily sagged. Today one can read memoirs filled with stories of daring submarine attacks, brilliantly executed, that failed because of malfunctioning torpedoes. The stories still ring with bitterness [Gannon, p. 87].

Some skippers decided to deactivate the exploder's magnetic aspect. Most failed to report that they did so, and swore crews to secrecy, for tampering with equipment is, in theory, an offense punishable by court-martial. Some who did let Command know of their actions received severe admonishments (*ibid.*).

Finally, in June 1943, Admiral Nimitz was convinced the device was faulty and ordered deactivation of the magnetic exploder in all Pacific Fleet units under Lockwood's command (*ibid.*, p. 89). But commanders continued to report multiple duds bouncing off the sides of Japanese ships. Additional tests discovered the contact exploder design was also defective. The firing pin mechanism, aligned perpendicular to the long axis of the torpedo, jammed upon impact with an enemy ship. With this problem diagnosed in September of 1943, finally by the spring of 1944, submarine commanders had a reliable torpedo (*ibid.*, p. 92).

Submarines under the command of Ralph W. Christie, commander of submarines leaving from Fremantle, Western Australia, retained the magnetic exploder until at least the end of 1943 (*ibid.*, p. 89). Christie had been instrumental in the development of the magnetic exploder 20 years earlier, and would not abandon its use. In a December 9, 1943, letter to Capt. Allan R. McCann in the Office of Naval Operations he touted the performance of the torpedoes equipped with the magnetic exploder on the Second War Patrol of the *Bowfin* "with the most difficult conditions of weather, seas and enemy pressure" (Christie, McCann letter). Christie wanted the patrol given wide publicity to bolster confidence in the device. At the end of December Christie was ordered by his superior to deactivate the Mark VI exploder. Submarines leaving from Brisbane, Australia, which included the *Puffer* for the First War Patrol in September 1943, were under the command of Admiral James Fife. However, the *Puffer*'s First War Patrol Report (WPR) indicated the torpedoes on board the *Puffer* maintained magnetic exploder capabilities.

BuOrd concluded after the war that the problems with the magnetic exploder were a combination of simple mechanical problems and inadequate understanding of the earth's magnetic field. The mechanism was designed to detonate by detecting a very small change in the vertical component of the earth's magnetic field. Premature detonations generally were caused by induced electrical voltages, often the result of water leakage around the magnetic detonator housing. The flow of the spurious electricity created an unwanted variation in the surrounding magnetic field, enough to detonate the torpedo (Gannon, p. 89). In mid–1943 the sensitivity of the detector was reduced (McCallum), causing additional premature detonations. Near the equator, where many of the submarine attacks occurred, the magnitude of the vertical component of the earth's magnetic field was very small. As a result it was impossible for the device to discriminate between variations in the magnetic field caused by a ship's hull, induced electrical voltages, or variations within the earth's magnetic field (Gannon, p. 89).

The Physical Environment

Most submarine crew members never were on deck during training or war patrols. Night and day lost meaning — the routine became four hours on duty, eight hours off. Only lookouts and officers were allowed above deck. Lookouts were rotated every hour, but it was usually within the same group of non-rated or third class petty officers. When submerged, lookouts typically manned the bow and stern planes. Torpedomen, motor mechanics, electricians and others who manned other equipment within the boat usually stood their watches below deck. Few men were allowed on deck so that crash dives to avoid detection by enemy ships or airplanes were done quickly (Tidd; McDonald).

It was a rare occurrence, usually in the black of night, when anyone else was allowed on the deck. Some skippers might allow a man suffering the ill effects of continual confinement on the after deck of the conning tower (aptly named the cigarette deck) for a quick smoke (Johnson). The closest most men came to getting on deck for a gasp of fresh air was handing the garbage up through a hatch, passing the dripping weighted bags hand over hand along the cramped passageways and up the ladders to the deck. There some lucky sailor scrambled out onto the deck long enough to throw the bag overboard, and then scampered back for another bag until all were disposed. McDonald enjoyed looking up at the blue or star filled sky through the hatch in the after torpedo compartment. It allowed him to breathe fresh air and maintain a connection with the outside world (McDonald).

During battle stations when the submarine was submerged and depth charged by enemy escorts, the conditions deteriorated to the edge of sustaining life. Men waited silently for the next depth charge. The only illumination was from the red battle lights or flashlights. If the holddown continued for many hours, red battle lights were turned off to conserve energy, and lanterns or flashlights were used (Dobson). In the near total darkness, the temperature rose to 120 degrees in parts of the boat, sweat bathed everyone in an oily diesel film. Humidity rose to 100 percent from an already high level. Bulkheads and men clammily perspired. To maintain silence men walked around in stocking feet in the inches deep condensation on the decks, and ate with their hands (Williams), if they felt like eating at all.

No one talked, unless necessary, and then in a whisper. Any noise might be heard by the listeners above. Men avoided drinking so they would not need to urinate, in fear the sound on the stainless steel bowl would be heard. "God help the man who dropped a wrench or a fork" (*ibid.*). The silence and darkness allowed some men's imaginations to run wild. Lying in their bunks to conserve oxygen became a curse. There was too much time to think. Sleep was impossible. Racing minds listened for the next click of a depth charge detonator, and wondered if it would be the last sound they would hear (Brown).

Oxygen was gradually replaced with expelled carbon dioxide (CO_2). CO_2 absorbent helped reduce the carbon dioxide concentration, but could not regenerate the used oxygen. Oxygen was released into the boat from the low pressure air banks. Hydrogen gas was present. Flash fire explosions of the hydrogen became a potential problem (*ibid.*). After 48 hours of submergence, the only sleep available was permanent "sleep."

The long and short term effects of these environmental conditions affected the mental condition of the men. The day-to-day environment that existed on a submarine affected the physiology and mental state of most men, some more than others, but not usually to a debilitating level. In World War II the 38 hour submergence of the *Puffer* during the First War Patrol was the extreme example of these conditions. No other American submarine endured a longer submergence. After 38 hours in a low oxygen environment the effects became devastating on some men.

The stress of battle stations exacerbated the already unnatural conditions. While submerged and attacking an enemy ship or under attack, all men were at battle stations for as long as the conflict endured. During battle stations and long submergence more severe factors affected the physical environment, which in turn altered the psychology of the men. These factors included no sleep, increased temperature and humidity, reduced oxygen (hypoxia) and the stress induced by frequent adrenaline rushes. Many of these factors have similar compounding effects. Not every man responded the same because of general physical condition, physiological differences related to body type and heredity, and individual personality traits.

Lack of Light

The malady that affected most of the crew on a daily basis was lack of natural light. Lack of sunlight for extended periods of time can alter the mood of some people. Research in Scandinavian countries has discovered as the winter approaches and the days get shorter, some people experience a form of depression called Seasonal Affective Disorder (SAD). Heartbeat, blood pressure, breathing, hormones, enzymes and other bodily functions rise and fall in a 24-hour pattern called the circadian rhythm. Decreased exposure to sunlight alters some people's circadian rhythms and leads to SAD. An estimated 25 percent of the population suffers from mild winter SAD, and about 5 percent suffer from a more severe form of the disorder. SAD is an extreme case of the winter blues (NMHA).

Symptoms, such as anxiety, irritability and a general loss of interest or motivation are common with SAD. Extended periods below the deck of a submarine probably induced SAD-like symptoms in some crewmen. Exposure to light and other external cues are necessary to reset internal clocks and keep people in sync with the natural cycles of day and night. In an effort to artificially maintain day and night, in the latter part of the war, submarines were equipped with sun lamps above a couple of bunks, a crude tanning bed. Men were encouraged to bathe in the artificial sunlight, but few did (*ibid.*).

Sleep Deprivation and Irregular Sleep

As a result of having no daily exposure to regular sunlight, day and night lost meaning. Some men were able to maintain natural sleeping habits of 7 to 8 hours, but most did not. The constant activity on the boat made deep sleep impossible. Men would catch a few hours of sleep whenever possible or be overcome with fatigue. Meals did not always coincide with usual sleep patterns. Some boats reversed days and nights, because the boat was usually surfaced during the night. As a result most crew members were in varying states of fatigue. Frank Mays recalled, "I was always tired. I never slept well" (Mays).

Sleep is essential for the body and mind to function properly. However, it is possible to function at lower levels of performance after extended periods of time without sleep. Sleep deprivation is one of the most common causes of reduced mental functioning and physical exertion becomes difficult. An unwillingness to stand up after sitting or lying down for an extended period of time is common. Carrying heavy objects becomes impossible, as does gripping things for a long period of time (BBC, *Sleep*).

Research by Eve Van Cauter, Ph.D., at the University of Chicago Medical School, explained the physiological mechanism for the physical symptoms. The conditions and subjects of the study closely mirror those of the men on a submarine. The results showed that after being deprived of sleep (limited to four hours of sleep for 6 nights), the men's bodies (ages 18 to 27) metabolized glucose less efficiently. Levels of the stress hormone cortisol were also higher. Elevated cortisol levels have been linked to the development of memory impairment and may impair recovery from physical activities (Spiegel).

Other symptoms of sleep deprivation are a decreased ability to cope with stress and emotional oversensitivity. Small noises motivated one person in a sleep deprivation study to have a desire to strangle the source (a small child) and he had to leave the room. A person's ability to perform tasks doesn't appreciably change when a person is sleepy. The *willingness* to perform any task is severely diminished. The need to feel motivated is torture. All around lethargy is an accurate description of the symptom (Frank).

The ability to perform exacting physical tasks is impaired. People who drive a car after being awake for 17 to 19 hours perform worse than those with a blood alcohol level of 5 percent. Yet another study found that people who get too little sleep may have higher levels of stress, anxiety and depression, and may take unnecessary risks (CNN, *Sleep*). Shorter sleep periods and greater indications of daytime sleepiness were related to negative moods such as anger, stress, pessimism, and fatigue (Frank).

Perception of Time

Recent research shows that our bodies contain clocks that measure intervals from fractions of seconds to minutes and even longer circadian clocks that measure daily intervals. The perception of time is fairly stable, but it is influenced by special environmental circumstances. When a person's *internal* clock changes, the perception of the passage of *external* time changes. If a person's *internal* clock runs fast, then the perception is that *external* events are happening very slowly. Conversely, if a person's *internal* clock runs slowly, then the perception is that *external* events are happening more quickly.

One condition that can influence the perception of time is excitement level. Excitement or stress speeds up the internal clock so a person perceives time is externally moving more slowly. John Brodie, an NFL quarterback, described the sensation. "Sometime, for example, time seems to slow way down, in an uncanny way, as if everyone were moving in slow motion" (Dossey, p. 170). On a submarine, during the excitement of battle stations, a similar excitement level could have occurred. Events would have appeared to be occurring slowly. External time was actually moving more quickly.

The limited or nighttime red light environment of the submarine conning tower was very similar to a photographic darkroom where total absorption in the process is required. Developing film and printing pictures is a very time sensitive activity. The author's personal experience indicates external time moves much faster than perceived when in a detail oriented, darkened, time sensitive environment. The tracking of an enemy vessel, firing torpedoes and picture-taking during an attack create a very similar environment in which time would slip by more quickly than perceived.

Heat and Humidity

The combination of heat and 100 percent relative humidity inside a submerged submarine was extreme. The following chart shows the apparent temperatures for combinations of heat and humidity (University of Virginia, *Apparent Temperature*).

The apparent temperature is a measure of the relative discomfort due to combined heat and high humidity. It was developed by R.G. Steadman in 1979 and is based on physiological studies of evaporative skin cooling for various combinations of ambient temperature and humidity. The apparent temperature equals the actual air temperature when the dew-point temperature is 57.2 degrees F. (14 degrees C). At a higher dew point, the apparent temperature exceeds the actual temperature and measures the increased physiological heat stress and discomfort associated with a higher than comfortable humidity (*ibid.*).

Apparent temperatures greater than 80 degrees F. are generally associated with some discomfort. Values approaching or exceeding 105 degrees F. are considered life threatening, with severe heat exhaustion or heatstroke possible if exposure is prolonged or physical activity high. The degree of heat stress varies with age, health, and body characteristics (*ibid.*). Thin people with a high skin surface area to volume ratio are able to lose body heat more easily and generally fare better under such conditions.

Apparent Temperature

Relative Hum. (%)	Real Temperature (°F.)													
	70	75	80	85	90	95	100	105	110	115	120	125	130	135
0	64	69	73	78	83	87	91	95	99	103	107	111	117	120
5	64	69	74	79	84	88	93	97	102	107	111	116	122	126
10	65	70	75	80	85	90	95	100	105	111	116	123	131	
15	65	71	76	81	86	91	97	102	108	115	123	131		
20	66	72	77	82	87	93	99	105	112	120	130	141		
25	66	72	77	83	88	94	101	109	117	127	139			
30	67	73	78	84	90	96	104	113	123	135	148			
35	67	73	79	85	91	98	107	118	130	143				
40	68	74	79	86	93	101	110	123	137	151				
45	68	74	80	87	95	104	115	129	143					
50	69	75	81	88	96	107	120	135	150					
55	69	75	81	89	98	110	126	142						
60	70	76	82	90	100	114	132	149						
65	70	76	83	91	102	119	138							
70	70	77	84	93	106	124	144							
75	70	77	85	95	109	130	150							
80	71	78	86	97	113	136								
85	71	78	87	99	117	140								
90	71	79	88	102	122	150								
95	71	79	89	105	126									
100	72	80	90	108	131									

Temperatures during the First War Patrol of the *Puffer* ranged from 110 to 125 degrees (Blair, p. 500). Until the installation of air conditioning on submarines temperatures of 100 degrees F. and humidity of 100 percent were not unusual for boats submerged for 12 to 16 hours in tropical waters (Alden, *The Fleet Submarine*, p. 48). First War Patrol veterans recalled the extreme heat, but cannot recall an actual temperature reading they observed (Deem; Dobson; Tidd; Topor; Trudeau). They realized it was hot, but were too busy to note the temperature. A real temperature of 100 degrees with a relative humidity of 100 percent produces a deadly apparent temperature, off the chart shown above. Dr. Joel Stager, an exercise physiologist at Indiana University, likened such an environment on a submarine to a pressure cooker. Without some loss of body heat a person in such conditions for an extended period of time would literally be pressure cooked. With the surrounding temperature in excess of body temperature, there is little ability to lose internal heat by sweating, radiation, or convection — only conduction, direct contact with a cooler object, would allow the person to survive (Stager).

Apparent temperatures in a range of 90 to 110 degrees F. cause heat cramps and possibly heat exhaustion. Dehydration is a major contributing factor to heat related injuries. In a dehydrated state a person becomes weak, dizzy, profoundly exhausted and can have problems thinking clearly. Feeling nauseous, being drenched in sweat, having dark urine with a strong odor, and muscle cramps are also warning signs of dehydration. Drinking a substantial quantity of fluids with some small amount of salt helps treat early dehydration. Too much salt is not good, causing an imbalance in body electrolytes (Williams; OutDoorPlaces.com, *Heat*).

Apparent temperatures in a range of 110 to 130 degrees F. can cause heat exhaustion. Heat exhaustion is the next step beyond simple dehydration. Losing fluid and salt through perspiration or replacing them in an imbalanced way can lead to dizziness and weakness. Body temperature might rise, but not above 102 degrees F. Because of a large loss of body fluid, the circulatory system can collapse, causing a sudden drop in blood pressure, which can lead to unconsciousness. Increasing fatigue, severe cramps, weakness, inability to think properly or exhibiting strange behavior, drenching sweats, dilated pupils, and nausea are all warning signs of heat exhaustion. A person with more severe heat exhaustion can have cold, pale, clammy skin, be agitated or disoriented, and can complain of profound thirst (*ibid.*).

Apparent temperatures in excess of 130 degrees F. can result in heatstroke, the final level of deterioration. In some cases extreme heat can upset the body's thermostat, causing body temperature to rise to 105 degrees F. or higher. In the final stages severe heat exhaustion induces symptoms of lethargy, confusion and ultimately unconsciousness (*ibid.*).

Hypoxia and Carbon Dioxide Poisoning

These two conditions typically coexisted on a submarine. As oxygen levels fell, carbon dioxide levels increased. Normal air contains about 21 percent oxygen and about 0.03 percent carbon dioxide and 79 percent nitrogen (Noble, p. 135). Normal breathing delivers oxygen to the cells via the blood and carries away carbon dioxide and water vapor. The movement of oxygen to the blood and waste products from the blood occurs in the lungs (*ibid.*, p. 163). As carbon dioxide levels increase in the blood due to an external change in content of the air, the human body responds by increasing respiration and heart rate. As a result more oxygen is delivered to the body to sustain it (*ibid.*, p. 140). Extreme factors on a submarine, such as a high body temperature and increased air pressure, help oxygen transport to the cells (*ibid.*, p. 167) and a high level of water vapor (humidity) in the air tends to more readily remove CO_2 from the lungs (*ibid.*, p. 137).

If the air contains higher levels of carbon dioxide than normal, the absorption of oxygen within the lungs is hampered. The blood no longer can carry the required level of oxygen to maintain the cells of the body. At levels of 5 percent and above carbon dioxide in the lungs the exchange of oxygen and carbon dioxide fails. Under these conditions death will occur in a matter of minutes. Hence there is an extreme need on a submarine to keep carbon dioxide levels well below 5 percent (Harris). In a submarine where CO_2 is building up there may be plenty of oxygen, but it is intensely uncomfortable, and a person feels like dying (*ibid.*). Because it is heavier than oxygen, carbon dioxide tends to sink to a lower level than oxygen. As a result lower submarine compartments would generally have a higher concentration of CO_2 and less oxygen; the higher compartments, such as the conning tower, would tend to have a greater concentration of oxygen.

Frank Golay, an officer on the *Puffer* during seven war patrols, described the physical effect the buildup of carbon dioxide had on him, long before CO_2 reached the deadly 5 percent level.

> Our first long day submerged — the faint headache behind the eyes as the CO_2 content begins to approach the critical three percent early in the afternoon and we hoard our oxygen and CO_2 absorbent for a real emergency — the hours on the periscope drag by waiting for the sun to set and the enveloping darkness to settle — the throbbing pain spreading thru your head until to be able to surface and gulp in the fresh air seems to be the end of existence ... and to stand alert on the bridge as they "blow up" seeing if you can possibly breathe deeper than ever before [Golay].

The most dangerous symptom of hypoxia is a lack of self awareness that abilities and behaviors are adversely affected. The brain center that could warn a person of decreased physical efficiency is first affected. The person even enjoys a misguided sense of well-being or euphoria. Although Golay reported headaches, generally there are few warning signs that signal alertness is deteriorating. Increased age, drinking, use of drugs, and lack of rest all increase the susceptibility of the body to hypoxia. Continuous exposure to mild hypoxia for periods of more than four hours, similar to that on a submarine, can produce fatigue as well as deterioration in concentration, problem solving skills and general efficiency (Mountain High; Transport Canada).

As oxygen supplies dwindle or are blocked by increasing CO_2, lassitude and indifference are appreciable. There is additional dimming of vision, tremor of hands, clouding of thought and memory, and errors in judgment. Frequent personality changes, emotions, insight and judgment are profoundly affected. Cyanosis (blue discoloring of the fingernails) is usually observed. In the later stages of hypoxia a person becomes disoriented, is belligerent or euphoric, and completely lacks in rational judgment. Frequent personality changes continue, with fits of volatility, complete impairment of judgment and insight, lack of inhibition, and loss of willpower. The effects of hypoxia progress from euphoria and increased boldness, to reduced vision, confusion, short term memory loss, inability to concentrate, impaired judgment, slowed reflexes, and finally loss of consciousness. Night vision is especially diminished, which could result in misread instruments and maps in a darkened submarine (Mountain High; Transport Canada).

Hypoxia interacts with other stressors. Just as a lack of light does, acute hypoxia can disturb the normal circadian patterns, especially those related to the regulation of body temperature. Men in a hot environment could shiver as if cold. Hypoxia can also contribute to sleep disturbances, making restful sleep more difficult (Bosco, p. 316).

Adrenaline

Distress (bad stress) is a reaction to some type of internal or external stimuli which prompts physiological and psychological changes in the human body. These changes are complex, but all involve a group of basic body responses which developed in the course of human evolution, primarily to meet situations of physical danger. Such situations trigger the body's fight or flight response. However inappropriate these responses are in certain social, emotional or occupational situations, they still occur. Usually the responses are of short duration (Noble, pp. 55–56). If the effects continue to persist for hours or days, it can lead to mental and physical problems (Twilight Bridge, *Survival*).

Each individual has different reactions to the same stressor depending on how the event is interpreted or internalized. Some people relish change and stress; others fear it. A great deal of stress has to do with the degree to which a person needs control of events. People who have less need to control their environment tend to experience less stress. Many people are not aware of being under stress. Some are frequently under so much stress that they assume the feeling is normal. This is especially true for those individuals who are not aware of their emotional responses. There is no single symptom that can identify stress. Some physical symptoms of stress, like high blood pressure and heart disease, are life threatening while others, such as headaches and insomnia, are not. Along with these physical symptoms an entire plethora of emotional symptoms occur, varying from general irritability to loss of libido (Dewey; Twilight Bridge, *Symptoms*).

Short-term physical symptoms, caused by a release of adrenaline, occur as the body adapts to a perceived physical threat. These symptoms are signs that the body is ready for the explosive action that assists survival or high performance: dry (cotton) mouth, cool skin, cold hands and feet, increased sweating, rapid heartbeat, faster breathing, tense muscles, feelings of nausea, diarrhea, and a desire to urinate (*ibid.*).

In a short-term survival event adrenaline aids in a physical fight-or-flight situation, but has negative effects in situations where a direct physical response is not required or not possible, such as would occur on a submarine. Adrenaline interferes with clear judgment and impairs a person's ability to take the time to make good decisions; it interferes with fine motor control; and it damages the positive frame of mind needed for high quality work by narrowing attention, damaging self-confidence, promoting negative thinking, disrupting focus and concentration, and making it difficult to cope with distractions. An adrenaline response consumes mental energy in distraction, anxiety, frustration and temper. This energy should have been devoted to other, more immediate tasks (*ibid.*).

Long-term physical symptoms occur when the body is exposed to adrenaline over an extended period of time. One of the ways adrenaline prepares a person for action is by diverting resources (blood and oxygen) to the muscles and away from the areas of the body which carry out body maintenance. When exposed to adrenaline for a sustained period, one's health may start to deteriorate. One or more of the following symptoms may appear: insomnia, change in appetite, sexual disorders, aches and pains, and frequent colds and other illnesses such as asthma, back pain, digestive problems, headaches and feelings of intense and long-term tiredness (*ibid.*).

Internal symptoms of long term stress usually impair a person's ability to think clearly and rationally about problems. Inability to think clearly can cause the following internal emotional problems: worry or anxiety, feeling out of control or overwhelmed by events, confusion and an inability to concentrate or make decisions, and mood changes such as restlessness, helplessness, impatience and irritability, hostility, negativity, frustration and depression. Externally the behavioral symptoms of long term stress are overreaction and reacting emotionally, increased use of alcohol and cigarettes, relying more on medication, yawning, talking too fast or too loud, fiddling and twitching, nail biting, grinding teeth, drumming fingers, and pacing (*ibid.*).

Two mainstays of most sailors, cigarettes and coffee, contain nicotine and caffeine. Nicotine causes a rapid release of adrenaline (Frankenhaeuser) and coffee intensifies the effect of adrenaline (DrugEducation.net, *Caffeine*). Reaching for a cigarette or cup of coffee while under stress only worsens the situation by reinforcing and intensifying a loop of downward spiraling negative symptoms. Caffeine also interferes with work performance (*ibid.*) and nicotine is associated with less stamina and reduced motor skills (Frankenhaeuser).

Summary

The crew of any submarine, and especially the *Puffer* during the First War Patrol, was affected by many negative environmental conditions. Most men suffered from lack of light, sleep difficulties and fatigue. During battle stations adrenaline affected their mental state and their perception of time. High temperatures and humidity caused various states of dehydration and heat exhaustion. Deteriorating oxygen and increasing CO_2 made physical exertion difficult, if not impossible for some men. Men with the cardiovascular systems of long distance runners may have been able to overcome the effects of hypoxia.

The mental state of the crew was greatly influenced by their physiological state, which was most affected by hypoxia, build up of CO_2, dehydration and adrenaline. Men who had some regular exposure to daylight, such as the lookouts and officers, may have been in a better mental state. Men who kept doing something and didn't lie down maintained the willingness to continue, and were less affected by the negative side effects of adrenaline and hypoxia. Continued physical activity helped delay the physical effects of the deteriorating environment — it dissipated adrenaline, and as a result helped maintain a positive mental outlook. Concentrating on a task occupied the mind and prevented thoughts from wandering toward the negative.

5

The First War Patrol Beginnings

Repairs and Rest at Brisbane

On August 21, after the month-long journey, the *Puffer* arrived at Brisbane. On August 23 and 24 the *Puffer* was pulled out of the water at the South Brisbane Dry Dock to repair the silver solder fittings in the No. 2 air bank located in the No. 2 Main Ballast Tank. The repairs were preformed by the USS *Fulton,* a submarine tender. Leaks in the air banks would prevent the ballast tanks from being blown dry and the *Puffer* could not resurface. All repairs to the *Puffer* were completed by August 28 (War Patrol Report, henceforth referenced as WPR).

General Douglas MacArthur had his offices on the top floor of the Lennon Hotel in Brisbane. The *Puffer* crew was allowed into the hotel. Russ Tidd recalled the availability of "big plates of white meat chicken sandwiches and pitchers of beer" served in the dining room. He humorously recalled, however, that he did not rub shoulders with "Dugout" Doug. During the week the boat was under repair, the crew went to a rest camp of small cottages erected in Newtown Park, within the nearby town of Toowoomba, Queensland. Toowoomba was about 75 miles inland from Brisbane (Tidd).

There was an effort to get Americans out of Brisbane to the quieter Toowoomba. In Brisbane bloody clashes had taken place between Australian and American soldiers stationed there in mid–1942 (Barker, p. 189). Although the Americans were welcomed as heroes for stopping the Japanese advance, Australians were insanely jealous of Americans (*ibid.*, p. 192). As a result returning Australian soldiers were not shy about beating the hell out of Americans. Tidd recalled that while the crew was in Brisbane, the soldiers they came in contact with "were mostly of the female gender, and like most of us, young also" (Tidd). Jay Deem, with half a purple face infected with impetigo, couldn't get a date, even with his face powdered (Deem).

At Newtown Park pickup softball and touch football games occupied the time of the crew. There were horses to ride and beers to drink (Tidd). Harold Sander recalled seeing the unusual flora and fauna of the Land Down Under such as koala bears and kangaroos (Sander). As usual Liggett found trouble with a boomerang. "(I was) curious about their damn boomerangs. First time I threw it, I hit some kid in the head. I sure am glad this mother thought a lot of the Yanks at that particular moment" (Liggett). The downtown area of Toowoomba was within walking distance. The local Australians were friendly and hospitable, even to the point of inviting American servicemen to lunch or dinner, and in a few instances

The First War Patrol — September 7, 1943 (Darwin), to October 18, 1943 (Darwin) — 5,537 nautical miles in the patrol area. The *Puffer* arrived at Brisbane from the Panama Canal Zone and after minor repairs sailed to Darwin to begin unrestricted warfare against the Japanese fleet in the areas of the Banda Sea and the Makassar Strait. The *Puffer* returned to Darwin for temporary repairs and then proceeded to Fremantle for more thorough repairs. The lone sun flags show an attack on a merchant vessel (map artwork by Nancy Webber).

they attended church together. In contrast, some of the more adventurous crew explored the bars and brothels of Brisbane, Elsie's and the Killarney near Fish Lane in South Brisbane. There were horse races in Brisbane for the gamblers in the crew (Tidd).

After a week the fun was over. On August 28 and August 30 the *Puffer*'s crew preformed repeated practice approach maneuvers with HMS *Stuart,* tested sound equipment, and re-established the training level of the crew. Crash dive evasive tactics for aircraft contacts were practiced, as well as depth charge training exercises, with live depth charges. It was standard training to use live depth charges to prepare officers and crew for the incredible loudness and shock wave of the explosive device. The Navy wanted to convince the submarine sailors depth charges were not death charges—in most situations (WPR).

As the *Puffer* sailed from Brisbane to Darwin for refueling a recurring defect plagued the engines. After lengthy runs on the surface the outboard exhaust valves failed to close numerous times on dives. Salt deposits formed on the valve seats in a thick hard scale. During refit the USS *Fulton* crew adjusted the valve seats, but that work did not remedy the problem. The failure of the valves allowed salt water to flow down into the diesel engines, which would cause serious damage. Manually removing the scale allowed the valves to close normally, but was not always a practical solution (*ibid.*).

The creativity of the engineering officer, Lawrence "Moose" Bernard, and the crew found a solution. If the valve seats remained cool, then evaporation and salt deposits would not form. By modifying the exhaust valve body water jacket, the valve seats were kept cool and no deposits formed. After the modification surface runs of 18 hours or more were possible without salt buildup. Submarines in 1943 were still undergoing refinements and were by no means perfect. Frequently on the spot jury rigs had to be invented and completed by the crew to overcome potentially fatal defects. Gasket design was another major flaw that would soon haunt the crew of the *Puffer* (*ibid.*).

The First Attack

On September 7, 1943, the *Puffer* left Darwin. After traveling halfway around the world, and four months after commissioning, the *Puffer* was finally headed for its assigned patrol area. The *Puffer* headed north and entered the Banda Sea from the Timor Sea through the eastern islands in the Dutch East Indies (today Indonesia). The first area of patrol was south of Ambon (see map), a Japanese hub of aircraft and shipping about four degrees south of the equator (*ibid.*). Daytime temperatures exceeded 100 degrees F. and the humidity was oppressive. The midday sun was almost unbearable. Fortunately most of the daylight hours were spent submerged. On the surface the temperature of the sea water was like bath water, which kept the interior of the boat like a sauna.

The officers and crew fell into the exhausting routine of four hours on duty and eight hours off. Also part of the daily routine was the "School of the Boat," which continued for the benefit of the seaman who had not yet qualified in submarines (*ibid.*). In case of an emergency all crew members had to understand and able to perform all duties and skills. Tests had to be passed for advancement. Rarely did anyone get a good "nights" sleep (Mays). In the tropical climate with limited laundry facilities available, the vinyl covered bunks became odiferous and slippery with sweat.

Between September 8 and 15 contacts were made with Japanese patrol vessels, small ships and aircraft, but no attacks were made. Even though no attacks were made, evasive actions, diving and surfacing, and call to battle stations kept the adrenaline flowing for both officers and crew. It was not a week of relaxation. On the afternoon of September 16, a contact was made with a medium sized freighter coming out of the fog near the entrance to Ambon. The target was identified as a camouflaged tug; torpedo tubes 1, 2, 3, and 4 were made ready. The tug began smoking profusely (WPR).

It was decided by the officers that the target was a Q-ship. A Q-ship was specially designed to lure submarines to attack, possibly even feigning damage with excessive smoke. Many other sub commanders had reported contact with Q-ships. Blair attributed all of these contacts as "figments of uneasy imaginations." The first Q-ship was actually put into commission by the Japanese in January of 1944, the *Delhi Maru*. The Japanese hunter was equipped with sonar, additional watertight compartments, depth charges, and hidden armament and guns (Blair, p. 534). Although not a true Q-ship, it still may have been a trap.

On September 17, on the surface and moving westward from Ambon, the *Puffer* radar picked up a darkened ship at a range of 8000 yards, closing the distance rapidly under a brilliant moonlit sky. The Officer of the Deck and Quartermaster Charlie Brockhausen identified the ship as an enemy submarine. The *Puffer* submerged and continued the approach. Sonar contact was lost. Events that unfolded a couple of hours later led the skipper to believe it was not a submarine, but a protective patrol craft rendezvousing with an incoming convoy (WPR).

At approximately 0230, with the assistance of radar, Executive Officer Hess spotted two ships illuminated by a nearly full moon with the #1 periscope. After weeks of nothingness, the sight probably sent a charge of electricity through his body as adrenaline was released. His heart rate quickened. He calmly reported the sighting to the skipper and the fire control party. His report brought the captain to the conning tower and sent the officers and qualified enlisted men to all the key stations in the conning tower and the control room below (Rindskopf). The officer of the deck cleared the bridge and Jensen took the *Puffer* down to periscope depth (WPR).

In the conning tower Carl Dwyer manned the torpedo data computer (TDC), and the most skilled sonar operator took over the equipment (Rindskopf), probably Frank Stoltz or Ray Roberts. The TDC was an analog computer which relied upon accurate observations of speed, course and range (distance) to the target vessel. The range to the target was estimated through the periscope by estimating the height of some part of the target above the surface of the water, using ship identification books. Range could have been measured with the SJ radar, but was possible only while on the surface or at radar depth, which exposed the upper portion of the periscope shears. Radar was a great aid, but the signal could also be detected by the Japanese and therefore sacrificed the element of surprise. Jensen felt he might give away his position by using radar (WPR). The course and speed were determined by the tracking team (Rindskopf).

In the control room the tracking team went into action, assembled around the 30-inch by 30-inch plotter which produced a track of the *Puffer* as it received course and speed data from the gyro compass and pitometer log, respectively (*ibid.*). The two Japanese ships were identified as a 7,500 ton naval auxiliary and a 5,000 ton freighter. Both were headed toward Ambon, currently at an estimated range of 5000 yards. No escorts were visible; however the ships were "zigzagging independently and radically." Jensen directed the *Puffer*'s speed and course. The naval auxiliary was chosen as the first target (WPR).

"Battle stations torpedo" was ordered by the captain. That order brought Jim Goins, a fire control technician, who assisted Dwyer on the TDC and communicated with the torpedo rooms. Bernard was in the control room overseeing depth control and trim. The tracking team plotted the target's range and bearing from the numerous periscope observations taken by Hess as the *Puffer* closed the range. From the plot data the target's course and speed were determined, which were verbally relayed to Dwyer on the TDC. A series of hand wheels below the dials enabled the TDC operator to input the target's range and bearing, the observed angle of the target's bow, and its calculated course and speed from the plotting party. The TDC automatically received continuous course and speed data for the *Puffer*. The TDC also continuously updated the target's position, range, and angle on the bow, which were compared with subsequent periscope observations. If differences resulted, target course and speed inputs were refined until the observations and the TDC agreed on the target's position (Rindskopf).

When agreement between the observed and the calculated values occurred a tracking solution had been obtained. The TDC angle solution, the gyro angle setting for the torpedo, had been continuously relayed to the torpedoes in the tubes so that at the instant of firing each underwater missile would turn in the required direction to hit the target. It was not necessary for the submarine to be pointed toward the target (*ibid.*). After tracking the target for twelve minutes, Jensen gave the command to "Fire!" and a spread of three torpedoes was fired from the bow tubes toward the naval auxiliary at a range of 1750 yards, approximately one mile (WPR).

Quickly shifting to the other target, the range, speed and course of the second target were dialed into the TDC. Two minutes later three more fish were on the way toward the freighter. Since no explosions were heard at the time the torpedoes should have struck the target Jensen swung the boat about to use the stern torpedoes. Ninety seconds later a series of six explosions were heard. The crew cheered. Periscope observations of the auxiliary revealed a small port list and sound reported all screws stopped. The periscope was shifted to the position of the freighter and the bridge appeared to be sinking rapidly. Within another 90 seconds the freighter was gone (*ibid.*). After many months the crew believed they had accomplished the deadly task for which they had been trained.

Two minutes later the sound crew listening on hydrophones heard heavy screws started again. Periscope observation indicated the auxiliary was steaming away at about 7 knots toward Ambon. During the next ten minutes a sub chaser was spotted directing a red searchlight on the water in the direction where the freighter had been attacked. Sound picked up fast screws, indicative of a sub chaser on the port side. Two depth charges were heard, but were not close. The *Puffer* went deep to get under a layer at 260 feet (*ibid.*). A layer was the boundary where a cold mass of water from below met the warm surface water. The difference in the water temperatures caused the water densities to differ. As a result the sound waves created by Japanese sonar reflected off the cold layer. The signal could not reflect off the submarine below and hence locate the submarine.

After 45 minutes the screws from the Japanese sub chaser were no longer heard, and Jensen came to periscope depth. Nothing was sighted, so the *Puffer* surfaced. With a 45 minute head start, daybreak only 90 minutes away and Ambon only 50 miles away, Jensen decided pursuit was unwise. He cleared the area at high speed. For the rest of the daylight hours the *Puffer* submerged and later in darkness surfaced to recharge the batteries (*ibid.*). Morale had been boosted by the apparent success, but the postwar evaluation could not verify the sinking of a 5,300 ton cargo ship or damage to a 7,500 ton transport (Alden, *Successes*, p. D-75). Intercepted Ultra messages reported an attack at this location (4-20S, 127-20E), but no hits (Allied Claims). The explosions heard were probably the end of torpedo run explosions. The Japanese ships had disappeared over the horizon; they had not been sunk.

Bad Weather and Disaster

The next four days Jensen conducted surface patrols and training dives as the boat moved northward through the Molucca Sea. Rounding the northeast corner of Celebes, on September 22 the *Puffer* began to patrol westward along the tanker shipping route between Balikpapan, Borneo, an oil port, and Palau, a forward base of the Japanese. The next destination was the Makassar Strait, the narrow expanse of water between the islands of Borneo and Celebes. The only vessels observed for the next week were sailboats, some of which Jensen suspected were Japanese spotters reporting American activity. On September 28 Jensen believed he patrolled off Balikpapan, but was unsure of his exact position because of overcast skies, rain,

5. The First War Patrol Beginnings

and poor visibility all day. Jensen observed that the Japanese ships were hugging the coastline which made attacks difficult. He decided to move northward again into the narrowest portion of the Makassar Strait. He hoped the narrowness of the mouth of the Makassar Strait might force the tankers into an attackable position. With no luck he continued to move north along the east coast of Borneo to Tarakan (WPR).

The nasty weather continued during the evenings, which is typical for the tropics during this part of the year. Early in the morning on October 4 with good visibility and a glassy sea, contact was made with a 7,000 ton (or more) passenger freighter, with no escort and not zigzagging. The freighter was a sitting duck. Unfortunately the target evaded Jensen. The target changed course and headed down the Tarakan Channel, an area where a submarine could not easily follow. Jensen commented in the WPR, "This one was a tough one to see get away after going so long without getting so much as even a 'nibble' at a worthwhile target" (*ibid.*) Submarine duty was often 30 minutes of excitement and 2 weeks of waiting — often without a positive result. Recklessness by a commanding officer could result in death. Patient aggressiveness was a trait necessary to command, have success, and live to tell about it.

For the next two and one-half days the weather was overcast, making it impossible to accurately fix the position of the *Puffer*. During World War II there was no Global Positioning System (GPS). Ship position had to be determined from star positions measured with a handheld sextant. In addition there was a strong current in the area moving the *Puffer* northward. Jensen continued to patrol off Tarakan on October 5, but the 7,000 ton maru did not leave the protection of the channel. As darkness fell over the water the *Puffer* surfaced and headed east toward open waters to recharge the batteries and the compressed air tanks (*ibid.*).

Around 12:45 A.M. on the night of October 6 disaster struck. With the *Puffer* moving forward at 9 knots the boat struck a reef. The sudden stop threw men from bunks and unsecured items became projectiles. Even though the fathometer was reading 1350 fathoms, the *Puffer* stopped on top of a pinnacle (*ibid.*). Modern maps show a reef about 5 miles across at latitude 04-10.5N and longitude 118-44E, the location the *Puffer* was stranded. A submerged pinnacle was slightly exposed at low tide. (A great Internet tool to view a satellite or map image of a location given in the text by a latitude and longitude is located at maps.google.com — convert the minutes of the location (the numbers after the dash) to a decimal by dividing by 60. The above location would be entered as 04.175N 118.733E — press "Search Maps" and zoom in or out as needed using the roller button on the mouse.)

The charts available to the Navy during the war were sometimes based on 200 year old Dutch and English maps. If the course of the boat had been a mere quarter mile south, the reef would have been avoided. The officer of the deck (OOD) immediately backed emergency and ordered ballast tanks blown. The boat was running partially flooded down to present a lower profile and to make detection more difficult. However, the *Puffer* would not budge off the reef (*ibid.*).

For the next hour and forty minutes the officers and crew desperately attempted everything to get the boat off the reef, short of throwing over the kitchen sink. Torpedoes were disarmed and prepared for jettisoning (*ibid.*). Before the torpedoes were unloaded, Ken Dobson convinced Commander Jensen to blow 10,000 gallons of fuel from #1 fuel tank — the fuel tank closest to the bow of the boat (Dobson). All ballast tanks and reserve fuel tanks were blown, dumping 9,000 gallons of fuel. Fresh water was shifted to aft tanks. The towing pendant was thrown overboard. During these attempts to lighten the boat, the engines were continually backed and alternated to twist the hull of the *Puffer*. There were plans for scuttling the boat (WPR). Charlie "Scurvy" Brown, the cook, recalled nervous crew members stole all the knives from the kitchen and handguns from the small arms lockers. The knives and guns would be used to fight the Japanese if they attempted to board the boat or take the crew captive (Brown).

Russ Tidd, tongue in cheek, commented he wanted to make sure that he had his dress blues in case they were close to a liberty port. Rifles and machine guns were removed from the lockers. If the boat was discovered by a Japanese patrol, Ray "Gunner" Kellum and the deck gun crew were ready to fight off boarders (Tidd).

William "Foxy" Hedrick suggested to Commander Jensen that they haul the anchor aft, throw it overboard, and pull it back in, hoping it would snag on something and the force would drag the boat off the reef. Jensen responded, "I don't think so." All men were moved aft. Preparations were finalized to dispose of the forward torpedoes. Mike "Punchie" Kutscherousky, the muscular boxing champ of the China Fleet, was on a line and felt the boat start to move (Deem). Kutscherousky was a veteran of the *S-39*, which had been lost after running aground (Gugliotta, pp. 83–84). He must have felt jinxed as history repeated itself. Fortunately the falling tide and backing full power catapulted the *Puffer* free (WPR).

The boat did not float free; gravity pulled the *Puffer* down off the reef. A tidal force computer simulation of the time, date, and nearby location to the *Puffer* predicted that within an hour the tide would have started to rise again. The tide would not fall again for another four hours, which would have left the submarine an easy target as daylight approached. The rising tide might have floated the *Puffer* free before the routine Japanese air patrols from Tarakan or Balikpapan made short work of the stranded boat and crew.

Commander Jensen noted the current was northeasterly, which pushed the boat farther north than expected. Once clear the fathometer read 100 fathoms. The most significant damage was to the port sound head. The boat still had one ear with which to listen, but direction determination was more difficult. Jensen cleared the area at high speed in order to distance the *Puffer* from the huge oil slick on the water's surface. The violent action of the props had also stirred up phosphorescent algae, in the dark another easily seen sign of ship activity that would give away their location. Ballast was redistributed in the tanks to put the boat back into diving trim. At 0532 the ship was able to make a dive and escape as daylight approached (*ibid.*).

Jensen submerged and moved south again to the narrowest part of the Makassar Strait. For the next two days the *Puffer* remained submerged during the day and surfaced at night to recharge the batteries. Any tankers headed for Balikpapan would be intercepted. The strategy proved effective (*ibid.*).

6

The Depth Charging of the *Puffer*

The Dangerous Escorts

For the third day on October 9 the *Puffer* submerged at 0525 off the northern entrance to the Makassar Strait lying in wait for enemy ships headed for Balikpapan or Tarakan. Within three hours the sound operators reported pinging directly to the north. The *Puffer* headed in the direction of the pinging and made visual contact with the masts of a zigzagging target moving at 14 knots. Minimum range attainable was 10,000 yards. An exact identification of the small ship could not be made at the time, but it was suspected to be an escort for another ship trailing behind. Jensen took the *Puffer* in the opposite direction of the escort and hoped to find the trailing ship (WPR).

At a distance escorts appeared similar though the periscope and commanding officers usually identified them as a *Chidori*. Rarely were convoys escorted by true destroyers. With a shallow draft, 300 plus feet long, the *Chidori* class destroyer and other classes of Japanese destroyers were generally well-armed vessels with 5-inch deck guns, sonar, radar, excellent torpedoes, 36 depth charges, and capable of in excess of 30 knots. But the Japanese were not planning for a defensive war on December 7, 1941. As a result the Japanese Navy had a limited number of destroyers, not enough to perform routine escort duties for all the convoys, and the Japanese were forced to use various types of vessels as escorts. Sub-chasers, about half the length of a destroyer, were the best of the escorts. They were capable of 20 knots, had 4-inch deck guns, and carried 36 depth charges. Typically the Japanese used converted minelayers, captured Dutch vessels, minesweepers, netlayers, and various other small craft to escort their vital convoys. The Imperial Japanese Navy commandeered over 200 small merchant ships and refitted them as sub-chasers for escort purposes near Japan (Hackett, *Kusentei!*). Regardless of their size or original design, submarine commanders respected the escort's effectiveness in harassing and sometimes sinking submarines. The following song by a crew member of another Manitowoc boat lamented the ability of the *Chidori* torpedo boats to locate submarines with sonar pings and lay down potentially deadly depth charges.

Pinging Pete Chidori

(To the tune of *Pistol-Packing Momma*)

Off Muroto Zaki, we were having fun;
Along came Pete Chidori,
And now we're on the run.
Oh, lay that pattern down, Pete!
Lay that pattern down!
Pinging Pete Chidori, lay that pattern down!
Click Click — BANG!
Click Click — BANG!
Click Click — BANG!
— Anonymous, USS *Pompon* (SS 267)

Although Jensen referred to the escort in the WPR as a *Chidori*, the escort was a 184 foot sub-chaser. Japanese records identified the escort as *Sub-chaser No. 4*. The Japanese documents reported that on October 7, 1943, Sub-chaser No. 4 (SC #4) arrived at Tarakan, and left the same day to perform anti-submarine sweeps and escort duty for approaching Japanese vessels in the area. On the morning of October 9, SC #4 was sweeping the Makassar Strait's north mouth in preparation for the arrival of an incoming ship (Somerville, *Submarine-chasers*).

At 1040 the masts of the arriving maru were sighted through the *Puffer*'s periscope. An attack approach was begun. The target was identified as a "very large merchantman, with no additional escort in sight." The ship was later identified in the ship identification catalog as looking most similar to the *Kinryu Maru*. During the next 30 minutes Commander Jensen maneuvered the boat to within 1,750 yards of the target. With the target passing almost directly across the course of the *Puffer*, a spread of four torpedoes were fired from the bow tubes, using both contact and magnetic detonation systems (WPR).

It was impossible to fire six torpedoes from the bow tubes, because the lower two tubes had been damaged when the submarine ran aground a few days earlier. Six torpedoes would have been judged excessive for a freighter at this time in the war. Command rules to conserve torpedoes dictated two or at most three torpedoes were necessary to sink such a vessel. Jensen was extravagant with four (Gannon, p. 88 footnote). Jensen stated, "Target apparently sighted wakes shortly before torpedoes hit and started turning away. The first two torpedoes hit both aft. The third and fourth torpedoes passed astern and ahead, respectively" (WPR). It was rare for all torpedoes to hit a target. To compensate for errors made in judging the range, speed and course of the target, torpedoes were fired in a spread. As a result some fish might miss ahead or behind the target, but some would find the target.

Based upon wartime Japanese ship movement records, the merchantman was the *Kumagawa Maru*, a 7,508 ton cargo ship recently converted to a tanker (Alden, *Successes,* p. D-82). The *Kumagawa Maru* was the former *Nichiyo Maru*, completed in March 1934. After the two hits the *Kumagawa Maru* was dead in the water and took a list of at least 50 degrees. The entire ship was covered in smoke. Jensen "believed the ship would sink rapidly, nevertheless commenced swinging to bring the stern tubes to bear in case follow up shots were necessary." Executive Officer Hess and Commander Jensen continued to observe the damage to the freighter. Then photographs were taken through the periscope to verify the damage, and hopefully a sinking vessel (WPR). Although the *Puffer* had two periscopes, only one could be used from the conning tower. William Pugh was taking pictures through that periscope (Brown). At the urging of Carl Dwyer, who was concerned about the location of the escort, Jensen checked for the *Chidori* (Dwyer). Nothing was seen on low power (1.5x magnification)

Kumagawa Maru (photograph courtesy of the U.S. Navy).

through the periscope. The scope was changed to high power (6x); no escort was visible. Vision through the periscope was not always perfect; lenses fogged over and water dripped down onto the lenses. At long range the small profile of a sub-chaser was extremely difficult to see in a sweeping periscope (Mazzone).

The Japanese tanker had not sunk rapidly. In the WPR Jensen mentioned the damaged ship actually reduced the list. He stated, "Apparently the vessel was running with very little fuel aboard which permitted it to use empty fuel tanks for correcting list. When last seen the list was about 10 degrees and the stern was settling" (WPR). Although the ship externally appeared as a cargo vessel to Jensen, it was actually an empty oiler. Correcting the list was accomplished by pumping the flooding water into the many empty storage chambers of the tanker.

Japanese records indicated the freighter was recently converted from freighter to tanker and was on its way to Balikpapan to take on a load of crude oil (Alden, *Successes*, p. D-82). Oil was badly needed by the Japanese war effort. The Borneo crude was of such high quality it could be burned in diesel engines without refining. If the tanker had been loaded, the volatility of the crude would have destroyed the ship. At 1119, two more torpedoes were fired from the stern tubes. These torpedoes proved to be defective. One was a dud and the other prematurely exploded about 400 yards from the *Puffer* (WPR).

Torpedoes that exploded prematurely were typically detonated by water leakage around the magnetic generator, which induced an electrical voltage and caused the influence firing mechanism to malfunction under its extremely small voltage tolerances (Gannon, p. 89). Jensen stated, "The premature and 'dud' fired nine minutes later unquestionably cheated us of a sure sinking and gave the destroyer a starting point from which to track us" (WPR). Duds were typically caused by the torpedo hitting the target at a 90° angle causing the firing pin mechanism to jam (Gannon, p. 92). In a worse scenario than the *Puffer*'s, on July 24, 1943, the *Tinosa* (SS 283) spotted a target, the *Tonan Maru III*, the largest tanker in the Japanese Navy. *Tinosa*'s skipper fired a spread of 6 torpedoes, none of which exploded, followed by 9 more duds fired one at a time in a period of 21 minutes. Christie dismissed the incident as a fluke, even suggesting sabotage (Christie, McCann letter). The *Tinosa* safely cleared the area five minutes after a destroyer escort was sighted, firing its last two duds just before making its escape to deep water (Gannon, p. 91). The *Puffer* was not so lucky.

The *Puffer* had ample time to fire more torpedoes, but for some reason Commander Jensen hesitated. Ken Dobson recalled the situation.

The bow tubes had been reloaded by that time and we were turning around to bring them to bear and at the same time taking pictures through the conning tower periscope of the ship we had hit. Remember that only one periscope could be used from the conning tower [Dobson].

Jensen did too much "fancy" maneuvering of the boat for the shots from the bow tubes and the subsequent attack never took place (Dobson). Electricians mate Harold Sander, cook Charlie Brown and others felt too much time was spent taking photos and not enough time paying attention to the position of the escort (Sander; Brown). The target was stationary; as a result the TDC setup was relatively simple. Torpedoes were in relatively short supply, and using additional torpedoes may have been viewed as excessive by Jensen's superior, Admiral Ralph W. Christie (Gannon, p. 88 footnote).

SC #4 received a distress call from the *Kumagawa Maru* at 1105 (Somerville, *Submarine-chasers*). At 1119 Jensen first mentioned the escort; he wrote the escort was "closing the scene fast" (WPR). A sub-chaser was capable of 20 knots, so "closing the scene fast" was an accurate description. The *Puffer* could make only 9 knots submerged and that speed would have drained the batteries in less than an hour. It was impossible to escape the escort using speed. Damage to the sonar head during the grounding a few days earlier required the sonar to be manually directed and further limited the ears of the *Puffer*. Sonar was least effective when pointing aft toward the subs own props, the direction from which the initial depth charging would take place. The 1119 WPR entry continued, "The maneuvers for another attack continued" after the escort was spotted. "Commenced maneuvering for another stern shot and favorable track" (WRP). Jensen wanted to send the seemingly unsinkable tanker to the bottom.

At 1125 three distant depth charges were heard. These charges were attributed to the tanker in the WPR. The crew of the tanker also commenced firing small caliber guns in the direction of the *Puffer*'s periscope. The *Puffer* was over a mile and a quarter from the motionless maru and fortunately these gun shots did not damage the periscope. However, this action helped direct the oncoming escort to the location of the *Puffer* (WPR).

Jensen may have misread the distance to the escort through the periscope (Dwyer; Mazzone). Hess typically manned the periscope during attacks, but during the picture taking and observation of the damage, Jensen also had been using the scope. Such an error would overestimate the range of a ship by a factor of 4, low power (1.5x) vs. high power (6x). If Jensen believed the escort was a *Chidori*, the quarter size image of *SC #4*, a vessel half the length of a *Chidori*, would have appeared even more distant.

At 1128 with the *SC #4* bearing down on the *Puffer*, Jensen "commenced clearing scene, when sound heard pinging and fast screws getting closer" (WPR). Pinging would have started when the sub-chaser's captain felt his boat was within 1,000 to 2,000 yards of the submarine (Japanese Underwater Sound Gear and Methods, p. 4). Because Jensen was still maneuvering for another attack, the periscope may have been sighted from time to time by the sub-chaser or the tanker crew continued to direct the escort to the last known position of the *Puffer*, greatly hastening the locating of the *Puffer*. Jensen also stated the tracks left by "the premature and 'dud' [torpedoes] ... gave the destroyer a starting point from which to track us" (WPR). Within 15 minutes *SC #4* detected the *Puffer* at 1143 at a range of 1100 meters (Somerville, *Submarine-chasers*).

Caught at Periscope Depth

Two minutes later at 1145 six depth charges went off very close overhead (WPR). Nine depth charges were dropped in the first salvo (Somerville, *Submarine-chasers*). *Puffer*'s miscount probably resulted from pairs of depth charges exploding simultaneously. Jensen described the damage done by the depth charges.

> [The depth charges] rocked the boat like a sailboat in a typhoon, let water in hatches and the Conning Tower door, backed sea valves off seats, blew out plug in casting for sea valve to Maneuvering Room water closet allowing considerable water to enter the After Torpedo room. Apparently sprung rudder and stern planes as evidenced by increased noise and overloading motors. Starboard sound head thrown out of alignment. Blew gaskets out of engine air induction and ship's ventilation supply outboard valves. Miscellaneous cork and glass flew around. Went deep [WPR].

If a hatch was unseated by depth charges, the compressed hatch gasket typically formed gaps when reseated, allowing water to come into the boat. Commander Jensen emphasized this point as a major defect (*ibid.*).

Dwyer recalled the shock dislodged the after conning tower door off its seal far enough to wet his back side as he manned the TDC (Dwyer). External inspection later would reveal damage was done from the deck gun, located forward of the conning tower, aft to the stern planes and rudder. Ken Dobson's battle station was in the control room. He was sitting between two electricians mates that controlled the main motors in the maneuvering room. They all bounced a foot in the air as the depth charges exploded around the boat (Dobson). Liggett, in the control room, recalled his predicament.

> My battle station aboard was on the trim manifold in the control room. I recall as we took the first close depth charges the packing came loose from one of the overhead valves above the manifold. As I was pumping (or flooding from one tank to another) a steady stream of water is hitting me directly on top of my head. I thought, "Damn it, this is the Chinese torture — not the Japs." But anyway, we didn't have much time at that particular point to think! [Liggett].

The sun and saltwater bleach-blonde lookouts William E. "Willie" Wilson and Russell Tidd, nicknamed "The Gold Dust Twins," were at their submerged battle stations, the bow and stern planes (Tidd). Years later at the 1991 World War II Submarine Veterans Convention, Dwyer gave credit to those two men for saving the boat from going into a fatal uncontrolled plunge to the bottom (Polk and Sanders, 1991). Flying glass from the depth gauges had imbedded in Tidd's bare chest, but he continued to man his station (Tidd). For the next 30 hours Tidd, Wilson, and a dozen other men rotated around the control room from the stern planes to the bow planes, and the helm (Tidd; Deem). To elude the Japanese with no hydraulic power the rudder and dive planes required manual operation to change directions. Without power, a right or left full rudder command to evade depth charges totally exhausted a man. Thirty turns of the wheel were required for each change in direction (Tidd; McDonald). Later under the reduced oxygen conditions the job became extremely taxing.

Pharmacist's Mate Robert Spalding had more than enough work to tend to the crew and officers. Spalding had served with the Marines on Guadalcanal, and had seen severe wounds (Spalding). There were no serious physical injuries, but the next 30 hours were an effort to prevent dehydration, heat stroke and mental malaise as the physical environment deteriorated. Tidd and Deem recalled "Doc" Spalding gave out an occasional teaspoon of whiskey or medicinal brandy for "bracing" (Tidd; Deem).

Substantial battery power had been used during the maneuvers for the torpedo attacks on the tanker, making impossible the maximum battery life of 48 hours. The batteries had to be saved for essential tasks. To conserve the batteries the air conditioning was shut off as the *Puffer* went deep. The postwar historian strongly criticized the decision to shut off the air conditioning. That analysis felt the high temperature was the primary physical factor which led to the decay of morale and the inability of the crew to perform (Voge). However, shutting off

Robert Spalding, the pharmacist's mate during the First War Patrol (photograph courtesy of Kelan Spalding).

the air conditioning was a standard part of silent running (Mazzone). Air conditioning was initially installed to improve the habitability of the boats operating in tropical regions (*The Fleet Sub,* p. 48), but also became important for cooling added electronic equipment such as radar (Mazzone).

The *Puffer* probably went to between 350 and 400 feet initially, because depth charges were still described as "very close" (WPR). For most of the war the maximum depth of Japanese depth charges was 300 feet (Gannon, p. 153). Depth settings recommended to Japanese anti-submarine vessels later in the war were 100 feet if periscope is sighted and continues exposed; 300 feet when submerged; when detected by echo-ranging, 200 to 300 feet depending upon conditions; and later in the war 400 to 500 feet when the sub was in a "stopped" condition (Japanese Underwater, p. 15). Depth charges below a submarine could damage the ballast tanks, which would make it impossible to surface. At 1155 there was a lone depth charge reported by Jensen, but not mentioned in the records of *SC #4* (WPR). It may have been rolled by the *Kumagawa Maru*.

At 1210 four more charges were dropped at staggered depths. Even though the *Puffer* was deep and nearly silent, the *SC #4* had no trouble pinpointing the location of the boat. Jensen hypothesized how the Japanese detected the boat so easily.

> We apparently are leaving an oil slick or air bubble wake or both because the attacking ship never loses us for a second and stays directly astern, gradually eases up and then attacks from directly overhead [*ibid.*].

It was later determined the slow flooding of the main induction was leaving a trail of bubbles as the air squeezed around the ruptured gasket on the exterior of the boat (*ibid.*). Some crew members guessed the attack had blown a hole in the air banks and escaping air bubbles were ascending to the surface (Brown). Damaged compressed air banks would have been a more serious problem than a flooded induction. With no compressed air, blowing the ballast tanks would be impossible, which would not allow the *Puffer* to surface.

Jensen also noted, "Current is throwing the ship around considerably making evasive maneuvering very difficult" (WPR). Modern oceanographic studies of the Makassar Strait in mid–October have shown the water flow at similar depths to the *Puffer*'s can be as much as 2 to 3 knots from south to north (Ffield). At this time the *Puffer* was probably moving only about 1 knot forward relative to the surface, while heading in a southerly direction. However, relative to the water flowing in the opposite direction, the *Puffer* was moving at around 3 to 4 knots. Although the current was making evasive action difficult, the relative speed and direction of the water to the boat, and the increasing up angle on the bow due to the aft flooding gave the *Puffer* improved ability to maintain some amount of lift and depth control, much like an airplane taking off into the wind. Without the current, added revolutions per minute, and an up angle the *Puffer* would sink. The current "probably saved our lives" (Dobson).

Normal silent running would have required 40 revolutions per minute (rpms) of the propellers, but the angle of the boat required 60 rpms to prevent it from sinking. Such a screw speed would produce a forward speed of about 1.5 knots (*ibid.*). However the added drag of the up angle reduced it to nearer 1 knot. The increased rpms hastened the discharge of the batteries. During the next 30 hours, as the batteries deteriorated and the screw speed slowed, the current moved the *Puffer* backwards to the north and east, all the while making handling difficult. The pump design was inadequate below 400 feet, which added to the unstable buoyancy and depth control of the boat. Dobson explained the situation.

> At 400 feet depth we would ordinarily pump off ballast to compensate for the reduction in displacement due to the water pressure (which compressed the hull of the boat). At any rate we were heavy and the trim pump could not discharge against the sea pressure. We had to use a rise angle of twelve to fifteen degrees and a speed of about 60 rpms to keep from sinking [*ibid.*].

The Japanese recorded an attack of seven depth charges at 1247, almost exactly an hour after the first attack (Somerville, *Submarine-chasers*). This attack was not included in the *Puffer*'s WPR. At 1250 the Japanese record also indicated a loss of contact with the *Puffer* and the escort's commanding officer was unsure of the results of the attacks. At 1340 Japanese sonar contact was regained with the *Puffer*. Six more depth charges were dropped at 1342 (*ibid.*). Jensen reported five more depth charges described as "very close" (WPR). Almost two hours later at 1525 there were two more depth charges. Jensen again noted that it was "impossible to shake this fellow. The manner in which he keeps on us in uncanny" (*ibid.*). Exactly an hour later, at 1625, six depth charges were dropped. The Japanese claimed dropping seven (Somerville, *Submarine-chasers*). Jensen noted the first two were "extremely close" (WPR). SC #4 was replenished with four depth charges from the *Kumagawa Maru* and dropped two of the charges at 1753 (1745 according to the *Puffer*'s WPR) for its seventh and final attack (Somerville, *Submarine-chasers*). Thirty-seven depth charges had been dropped, but the Japanese captain was still unsure of the effectiveness of the attacks (*ibid.*). Dobson described the effect of the attacks on the crew and the interior of the *Puffer*.

> A good deal of the time we were relying on those battery operated lanterns. Even the ordinary bulbs that were in pendants were going out from the shock. The noise inside the ship was indescribable. Most people saw a sheet of flame come in through the stern tube and into the motor room about three feet. That is just not physically possible. It may just have been their brains rattling around in their skulls. The gas bubbles from the charges ... were close enough that they made water roar through the superstructure. I thought a piece of deck grating had come loose and was flopping down the deck. But none was missing so I guess it was a dud depth charge [Dobson].

Harold Sander, EM2c, also saw the flames come in around the packing glands, which surrounded the propeller shafts (Sander). Retired rear admiral E. S. McGinley, an expert in submarine damage, suggested an explanation for the flames.

> The hot, explosive gases from the depth charge's expanding gas bubble may have at times penetrated around hull fittings. When the gases hit the atmosphere of the submarine which contained oxygen (albeit at a reduced amount), it probably caused the momentary flames [McGinley].

Something rolled or was dragged across the deck. It may have been a dud depth charge or a grappling hook (Dobson). The Japanese had previously tried snagging disabled submarines with a grappling hook (Submarine Veterans). At 1820 another anti-submarine vessel joined the harassment of the *Puffer*. It had been nearly seven hours since the initial depth charges were dropped. Salvage operations were initiated by the Japanese to get the damaged ship into a safe port, and an additional anti-submarine vessel, *Sub-chaser No. 6* (*SC #6*), arrived to take over the attack (Somerville, *Submarine-chasers*). This vessel was probably dispatched from a base at Balikpapan or Tarakan, two Japanese anti-submarine strongholds. Jensen mentioned some confusing sounds on the surface at 1825, seven hours after the attacks started (WPR). The unidentifiable sounds were probably produced by the salvage efforts on the damaged tanker.

The movements of *SC #4* indicated that after assisting *SC #6* in anti-submarine activities, it accompanied the damaged tanker *Kumagawa Maru* to Balikpapan, while in tow of a third ship, the *Shoyo Maru* (Somerville, *Submarine-chasers*). The WPR mentioned only three Japanese vessels overhead. However, when interviewed, Mazzone insisted there were numerous Japanese ships present (Mazzone). Ultra reports of intercepted Japanese radio messages reported the arrival of two smaller escorts, *Auxiliary Sub-Chasers 37* and *41* (Somerville, *Submarine-chasers*). Mazzone's recollection was verified by the Japanese records. For a time six ships were present: a stationary tanker and a tow ship; two sub-chasers hunting the *Puffer*; and two auxiliary sub-chasers scanning the area for additional submarines.

After an hour of quiet: click, click, bang! Click, click, bang! Click, click, bang! Click, click, bang! And another click, click, bang! At 1852 five more depth charges were dropped by *SC #6*; fortunately the depth was too shallow, but the blasts were still directly overhead (WPR). The long hourly intervals between depth charges were unnerving. The mental harassment of the attacks was severe.

> We could hear the escort coming like a fast train passing you at a crossing. We could hear the first depth charges hit the water and we could hear the detonator click. We would time the first charge and wait for the other depth charges.... Sometimes the escort would drop six charges, sometimes two or three, sometimes none. This would play on our nerves more than any other thing [Brown].

Then silence again, except for the sound of the screws of the ships overhead. On the surface the sun was setting. The *Puffer* had been submerged for over 13 hours. Invisible carbon dioxide was beginning to build up in the darkness of the hull. Men started to complain of headaches. Nerves were on edge. The *Puffer* could do nothing except stay deep and take evasive actions.

Heat and Humidity Rise

According to the postwar historian, with the air conditioning shut down to conserve the batteries, the temperature in the maneuvering room reached 125° F (Voge). As a result of the up angle of the boat, and hot air's tendency to rise, the forward torpedo room and the conning tower were even hotter. The other byproduct of breathing was water vapor. The decks and bulkheads, cooled by the external water, became clammy with condensed moisture. These bulkheads were the only cool places in the boat. The postwar historian wrote the crew "spent all the time they could, huddled around anything that was comparatively cool, hunched against an uninsulated portion of the hull or wrapped around an exposed circulation water pipe." The report continued, "rivulets of sweat would form and follow right behind a towel rubbed over a man's body" (*ibid.*). These rivulets were not sweat, but condensation on the men's relatively cooler skin. Paradoxically, the report also mentioned some men shivered as they moved from compartment to compartment (*ibid.*). The most likely cause of the chills was not fever, but hypoxia, which caused a loss of the body's normal thermoregulation mechanism. Deem sat on the floor of the radio shack and put on a jacket in an attempt to stay "warm" (Deem).

The flooding in the after portion of the boat continued (WPR). "The bucket brigade struggled against the mounting water in the motor room bilges and against extreme fatigue" (Voge). Stewards Patton and Pruitt came through the boat with lemonade to quench the thirst of those manning their stations and the bucket crew. Pruitt assured the men it was not yet their time to go. Their actions boosted the morale of the crew (Topor). The postwar historian identified the symptoms of dehydration and inability to ingest liquids by some.

> The liquids available for drink, fruit juices coffee or water, soon reached room temperature. Frequently swallowing these liquids induced vomiting, yet thirst was so great the men were constantly drinking, vomiting, and then drinking again [Voge].

The entire crew did not suffer from vomiting, but some sickness did take place (Tidd; Trudeau). Hypoxia and heat exhaustion both can cause nausea. Undoubtedly some men were dehydrated. No one was hungry. Dobson related that someone brought him a cup of hot coffee which helped "cut the cotton" in his mouth. A piece of apple pie tasted like straw (Dobson). Cotton mouth was caused by dehydration, adrenaline and anxiety. Topor mentioned a bluish color to the water. Liggett also wrote about problems with the water supply that may have caused the nausea for some if they drank from the condenser and the creative efforts of Patton to alleviate the terrible physical conditions of the crew.

> Our water supply was contaminated with copper sulphate, as the tube from the condenser in the forward engine room to the fresh water tanks in the after battery room (crew's mess) must have been bent. So, no water to drink....
>
> During all this mess we're in: no water; no air; can hardly breathe, who comes along but our officer's steward, and seeing the plight the men are in, he returns with a bag of hard Christmas candy. He gave each of the men a few pieces, and believe it or not, it worked. It not only brought the saliva to our mouths, but also satisfied our hunger — temporarily [Liggett].

If in fact the water supply was tainted with copper sulphate, it would explain the reason why some crew members who drank water vomited. Side effects of ingesting the compound include abdominal pain, nausea and vomiting (International Labour). The glucose in the candy gave the men a small amount of energy to carry on and a pleasant taste in their mouths to hide the stench in the boat.

CO_2 absorbent was spread. The absorbent only reduced the CO_2 in the air; it could not replace the oxygen. Brown recalled the men in the forward torpedo room stretched a sheet between the bunks and put the CO_2 absorbent on top, creating a makeshift air filter. In the process of spreading the absorbent, Charles Kerls was temporarily blinded by CO_2 absorbent when it splashed in his eyes (Brown). While lying on the mess room table with his eyes covered, Kerls grabbed the arm of Trudeau, who was headed for the forward battery. Kerls said, "I can hear him coming, here he comes again." Kerls heard the turning props of their tormentor (Trudeau). The prop sound and the expectation of more depth charges, whether dropped or not, grated on the men's nerves. Men looked up into the darkness of the boat and moved their heads to follow the sound of the props passing overhead. They wondered what was next — more depth charges or worse.

Sinking Deeper

Nine hours after the initial depth charges at 2100 the flooding had caused the submarine to tilt with a twelve degree up angle. Depth control continued difficult in the strong current. The main induction was completely flooded. The 12 tons of water added to the problem of depth control. However if the main induction was flooded, the tell tale bubbles no longer burst on the surface. The water in the after torpedo room continued to rise. It became necessary to blow the safety ballast tank to maintain depth control (WPR). Jensen lamented the noisy trim pumps, which would give away the location of the boat.

> [The] trim pump is worthless. If only the people in the Bureau [of Engineering] who say an adequate trim pump will come in due time were here now, I'm sure they would stop at nothing to correct the serious military defect immediately [*ibid.*].

At 2240, about three hours and 40 minutes after the last attack, six more depth charges were "extremely close." The air leak in the after torpedo room must have been large enough to spot the bubbles on the surface, or the sonar operator on the *Sub-Chaser No. 6* was very talented. Jensen noted, "The hull is certainly taking it. A most deep felt 'well done' to the welders of the Manitowoc Shipbuilding Company and the Supervising Officer and officials." In the same entry he blasted the Bureau of Ships again: "[The] electric motors in the bilges are flooding out. Design *must be changed* to re-locate auxiliary motors from the bilges" (*ibid.*).

Due to the excess weight of the flooded induction tube and inability to pump off ballast, the *Puffer* slid down to a depth greater than 500 feet, 200 feet deeper than test depth. Five hundred thirty-five feet was recalled for the depth in the control room, which would place the after torpedo room 35 feet deeper, or at 570 feet with the 12 degree angle (Trudeau). Chief Electrician's Mate Frank Stoltz wrote on the back of a *Puffer* photo the boat was as deep as 650 feet (Stoltz). Jay Deem recalled that the depth gauge indicator had rotated well beyond the 450 feet maximum shown on the gauge and stopped when indicator hit the 0 depth rest on the other side of the gauge (Deem). "We were tested in Lake Michigan to 312 feet, and were forced down to 525 feet by our boy on topside" (Liggett). The external pressure of the extreme depth made the leaks worse as the boat settled deeper and deeper.

For the previous ten hours, throughout the numerous depth charge attacks, William "Foxy" Hetrick, MoMM1c, led the effort of the motor macs, electricians and torpedomen in moving water forward from the after torpedo room to the forward bilges using a bucket brigade (WPR). Even though the water became waist deep "Butch" Lennon, ranking torpedoman in the aft room, kept his crew at battle stations for the entire 38 hours (Tidd). Without the bucket brigade's effort the sub would have continued to drop by the stern. Eventually the additional weight would have taken the boat to the bottom. There was nothing that could be done to alleviate the flooded induction until the boat surfaced. Jensen complimented Hetrick as "doing a seemingly tireless job keeping [the] bucket brigade going and cheering on the entire crew." Jensen also singled out Chief Radioman Frank Stoltz for praise. Jensen said Stoltz "on the one remaining sound head which had to be trained by hand was particularly outstanding and made it possible to continually maneuver the ship to the best advantage during the depth charging" (WPR).

6. The Depth Charging of the *Puffer*

At midnight, in spite of evasive maneuvers and silent running, the Japanese anti-submarine vessels were still tracking the *Puffer*. Jensen described the anti-submarine attacks.

> One would listen and the other ping, both on station on the quarters. A number of rehearsal runs were made, screws being heard throughout the boat, but no depth charges. During these dry runs rapid pinging was heard, and it is believed he was running his fathometer while crossing [our position] [*ibid.*].

The Japanese records indicated difficulty maintaining contact with the *Puffer* in the evening hours. Finally at 0115 on October 10 the last six depth charges were dropped. For the next eleven hours, the sub-chasers attempted to locate the *Puffer*, but without dropping additional depth charges (Somerville *Submarine-chasers*). The suspense of the dry runs was as unnerving as the actual depth charges. The postwar historian summarized the terror of the depth charging.

> Suspense was the hardest thing to bear. The officers state that because of this, the ordeal was harder on the men than it was on the officers. The officers, when on watch, were in the conning tower or control room. They then knew the proximity of the enemy, the state of the battery, what was being done to evade and in general were busy in some manner or other. On the other hand, men not engaged in some useful task could only sit and think, and frequently lacked information. To remedy this, officers occasionally went through the boat and told the men what was happening. The use of the public address system was annoying to many and a feeling existed that the noise of it might disclose the location of the submarine. The conning tower telephone talker described what was happening to the other talkers on the fire control telephone circuit. This was the best method of spreading the word and later became the standard practice.
>
> The universal advice the men would give to anyone else who might have to go through a similar experience is "Find something to do to keep busy." To idle men, it was unbearable to realize that an hour or so had gone by since the last attack, and another would soon be due [Voge].

The adrenaline rush of the initial depth charges did not wear off as the Japanese continued to harass the *Puffer* for 24 hours. Each time pings and screws were heard, additional adrenaline was released into the blood of the men, except possibly those men with the steadiest of nerves or those that concentrated on a task. The prolonged exposure to the adrenaline was physically and mentally debilitating. It initially induced euphoria and later a negative mental attitude. Men who remained physically active dissipated the negative effects of the adrenaline with their muscular activities. The bad physical and psychological effects of the external torture were intensified by the deteriorating internal environmental conditions of hypoxia, and increased heat and humidity. Some men were able to function, others continued to deteriorate. Even military discipline could not overcome the multiple physiological and psychological effects that afflicted the men.

The postwar historian described the deteriorated mental state of the men as day one became day two of the ordeal.

> Then to hear the screws on the approaching vessel, the pinging of her echo ranging as she deliberately and methodically probed for the submarine, finally the rush of racing screws, and the shattering detonation of a salvo of depth charges carried the suspense to a maddening pitch. Both officers and men seem to have reached the conclusion that they would never come out of it. The persistence with which the enemy located and relocated the submarine forced them to this conclusion [*ibid.*].

Waiting It Out

The postwar historian described the physical state of the men after 30 hours submerged.

Breathing was very difficult and headache was severe. An officer (Engineering Officer Bernard) making the rounds from control room to after torpedo room had to stop and rest several times on the journey. A good many of the men were in a state of physical collapse. From the stupor in which they sank, it became impossible to arouse them to go on watch [*ibid.*].

Bernard's son said his father told him the physical exhaustion of the men was accurately described. According to Liggett the trips through the boat took an added toll on Bernard.

One of our officers was six feet tall or better [Bernard] ... every time this officer came through the forward hatch, he would straighten up, ramrod stiff, and start to march through the engine room. Bracketed from the overhead between the bottom of the motor was a drain plug. Invariably as he went under the motor, he creased his skull [Liggett].

The air was so laden with carbon dioxide it was impossible to light a match (Trudeau). Ensign William Pugh labored through the boat and released oxygen into the compartments. This oxygen was in small tanks in each compartment and was supposed to be used to charge Momsen lungs, the emergency escape breathing devices. With the use of the oxygen, if the boat could not reach the surface, there was no possibility of an emergency escape. Some of the men were so desperate for a smoke they used the oxygen flow to light and enjoy a last cigarette. The hydrogen level from the discharged batteries was approaching the explosive level (Brown). The low oxygen level probably prevented the explosion. Venting available air from pressurized tanks into the boat increased the air pressure in the boat, which aided the exchange of oxygen and carbon dioxide in the lungs (Stager).

Not only was the air depleted of oxygen, but a stench permeated the air. Some men had vomited. Fear and stress caused increased mobility of the digestive tract. Because of the external noise and bubbles created, it was impossible to flush the "head" and dispose of the human waste. The odor of a sewer pipe filled the boat. On the previous morning of October 9 the evening meal of twenty-four Australian rabbits had been removed from the freezer. By the afternoon of October 10 the "rancid smell" of the deteriorating meat greatly added to the foul smell (Brown).

At 1225 of the second day, 25 hours after the first depth charge attack, the pings of the Japanese sonar died out. For eleven hours, since the last charges were dropped, the crew had hung on. The bucket brigade continued to ferry water forward. Hypoxia was taking a toll on the men.

Breathing was most difficult and headaches severe in spite of all that could be done to revitalize the air. Due to tension, bad air, heat, humidity, hard work on [the] bucket brigades, etc. the crew were practically out on their feet, but carrying on like veterans [WPR].

The postwar historian made the connection between the physical and the mental. Anger, belligerence and lack of rational thought resulted from sleep deprivation and hypoxia.

The physical conditions were severe and had much to do with the mental reactions. Both officers and men state the first mental reaction was anger. They were mad at everything and anything. They were particularly mad at themselves for allowing themselves to be caught in such a situation. They cursed themselves for being such fools as to serve in submarines. They cursed the enemy for their persistence. They spent much time day dreaming about what they could do to the torpedo boat above them — discussing such fantastic ideas as discharging acid around the ship to eat holes in the hull [Voge].

The crew suggested the Japanese skipper had a psychology degree from an American university. The men hypothesized he was timing the attacks to grate on the men's nerves, approximately every hour or two. The men conjured up another explanation and guessed that the ship the *Puffer* had torpedoed was the last of a convoy, and the escort captain was taking out his frustrations on the *Puffer* (Allen). These myths probably originated at the same time as the other fantastic scenarios that occupied the idle minds of the *Puffer* crew. The euphoric effect of hypoxia undoubtedly influenced the minds of the crew to invent such stories and later curse the situation as the effect induced negativity.

The historian prognosticated that many years later, "There is no doubt but the necessity of taking a beating without being able to fight back made a lifetime impression on the minds of the men" (Voge). John F. Allen confirmed that prediction for one man. In an interview at the 2001 World War II Submarine Veterans Convention in St. Louis, he vividly described his fear during the 30 hour nightmare. It was still etched in his mind. Allan was a young man toughened by the Great Depression who had run away from home at age 16. He joined the Merchant Marine and transferred to the Navy when World War II started (Allen).

After the war Allen was a police officer in New York City's Hell's Kitchen. He told an illustrative story about his police service that contrasted the lingering fear on the submarine with the sudden action of police duty. While investigating a domestic dispute, a large drunken man attacked him with a knife. He blocked the attack with his raised left arm. He reached for his gun with his right hand, but was unable to get the gun out through the pocket of his winter coat as the hammer snagged the opening. John was forced to shoot through the coat (*ibid.*).

Help arrived a few minutes later. The arriving officers had to make Allen aware that his left arm had been slashed and his coat pocket was smoldering from the gunshots. When the shooting was investigated he was asked, "Why did you shoot the man six times?" Allen replied, "Because the gun only had six bullets." He pointed out that the fear on the *Puffer* during the First War Patrol was a fear where no immediate response was possible. The pent up fear drove some men to the brink and a few over the edge (*ibid.*).

"In the afternoon of the second day things seemed to be hopeless, but we still held on" (Dobson). One crew member climbed the escape hatch ladder in an attempt to exit the boat. The tormented soul would hit his head, fall down, and then get up and tried the same futile escape again and again (Tidd). Liggett confirmed, "Another man went berserk and wanted to go out the crew's quarters hatch" (Liggett). One crew member lost all mental orientation and acted as if he was back on the farm chasing chickens. Another crewman threatened others with a wrench if they made the slightest noise. He was restrained with ropes (Topor; Tidd). The postwar historian similarly reported one crew member became acutely "allergic to noise, a squeaky pair of sandals," which was enough to nearly instigate a fight (Voge). Jensen wrote, "Four men suffered from nervous strain during depth charging but seemed alright two days later" (WPR). Typically such men were relieved from their torment with an injection of sedative by the pharmacist's mate or in a less kindly manner with a crack on the head with a wrench. "One of our men went blind with fright and made us promise to help him out and over the side if need be" (Liggett).

Decision Time

Human physical and mental fatigue were not the only problems. Power in the batteries was fading. The specific gravity of the battery electrolyte was so low it could no longer be read on the hydrometer. Lanterns were used to conserve energy. For the most part the boat was in darkness, except for the eerie glow of the red emergency lighting in some compartments and

Ensign Walter Mazzone with the damaged deck gun in the background (photograph courtesy of Walter Mazzone).

the flash of lanterns (Dobson). Trudeau credited Robert Anderson (EM2c) for telling a heroic white lie. Even though the batteries were nearly dead, Anderson replied to inquisitive crew members, "Don't worry, we've still got juice in the batteries" (Trudeau). "The batteries were so low in the end you could have drunk the acid, it was almost water" (Deem). The lie gave a small glimmer of hope to the crew.

6. The Depth Charging of the Puffer

In the early hours of Sunday morning, totally exhausted from the physical labor, Trudeau fell asleep holding a picture of his new wife (Trudeau). A few hours later around 1300 a meeting took place among the officers, and according to the postwar historian, the crew was also involved (Voge). A decision had to be made; time was running out. Adequate oxygen to maintain consciousness would be gone in a few hours. Previously other submarines had been held down for 24 hours—the limit of Japanese persistence early in the war. The *Puffer* had been chased for 25 hours, and submerged for 32 hours. Maybe the Japanese were really gone, maybe not. The choices were: 1) surface now and escape or fight it out; 2) scuttle the ship and avoid capture (proposed by a few); 3) wait it out until dark.

The worst case scenario was probably assumed, that their adversary on the surface was a *Chidori*. The first choice was not considered for long because the *Puffer* had a lone 3-inch artillery piece, no match for a *Chidori*. Some of the younger officers wanted to fight it out; the older officers wanted to wait it out. Fortunately the increased boldness associated with hypoxia or youth was overcome by the reason of the older officers. The deck gun duel with the *Chidori* was not seriously considered for any length of time (Tidd). A deck gun action would have been totally futile. The list to port due to the flooding of the main induction would have prevented accurate firing of the gun. Unbeknownst to the officers, the breech cover of the deck gun was damaged by the depth charges, rendering the gun useless. The damage was visible in the photo (Mazzone). Jensen reported aiming the gun was difficult after prolonged submergence (WPR). The deck wood became swollen with water, making rotation of the gun difficult on its mount. After 32 hours below the surface the wood was undoubtedly swollen.

The second choice was considered by a few men. The men were aware of the torture in POW camps, especially used on officers. Howard Allen, the baker, argued some men would survive in a POW camp; flooding the boat left zero chance for survival (Deem). Because the pinging had stopped for about an hour and another piece of good luck was discovered the third choice became most attractive.

The current pushed the *Puffer* northward as the batteries died. The same current had created a layer under which to hide. In the narrow northern entrance to the Makassar Strait huge masses of cold water can be pushed northward and upward from the ocean depths during October (Ffield). These flows typically created a temperature layer around 450 feet, weaker than the layer usually found at a lesser depth, but still well defined. Mazzone concurred a layer was present. The phenomenon hid the *Puffer* from the *Chidori*. Ernest Dufault, chief electrician's mate, claimed discovery of the layer on the bathythermograph. Dufault claimed Jensen in his excitement had promised him a Silver Star for the discovery (Dufault). Jensen noted the decision that the crew "decided to hang on at all costs until darkness at which time we would have to come up to surface directly—regardless" (WPR).

Jensen spoke to the crew. To paraphrase Jensen's comments over the intercom as recalled by crew members, "I've done all I can do boys. If you know how to pray, pray." (Deem; Trudeau). Commander Jensen retired to his cabin, handing over the situation to Hess, Bernard and Dwyer until the boat was ready to surface. Jensen commended these three officers.

> [Their] high degree of professional knowledge and ability and was in no small measure responsible for successfully getting the ship off the reefs and successfully controlling damage, leaks, and depth control during the long depth charging. The CO is convinced that the work of these experienced officers made the difference between saving and losing the vessel. Their suggestions and untiring efforts were always sound and correct [WPR].

Many did pray, even those who had never done so before in their lives—or at least their lips were moving (Deem). Edgar "Wash" Washburn's son told of his father's prayer, asking for a chance to return to his home town in New Jersey, where he would allow God to take his life by stepping in front of a trolley car. Washburn didn't want his parents wondering what had happened to him (Washburn). The son of Robert Kennedy recalled his father said little about the submarine service, but recalled the words of Jensen had "a devastating effect on the morale of the crew." If the commander had given up, what else could they do? Kennedy roused one man from prayer and told him to close a valve, with the encouragement, "God helps those who help themselves" (Kennedy). In addition to the officers, pragmatic enlisted men like Kennedy and others were also responsible for saving the *Puffer*.

The postwar historian wrote, "Toward the end, stations were manned by volunteers, and by men who had the stamina and the will to move and think. Many of the others were past the stage of caring what happened" (Voge). Men would have been ordered to lie down to conserve oxygen. Unfortunately in a low oxygen environment, once a person lies down, it was very unlikely he would get back up. It was mentally painful to do so. Liggett wrote, "We had used up all our oxygen bottles and were on our last 5# tin of carbon dioxide absorbent when the 'Old Man' says, 'The Hell with it, let's go'" (Liggett).

Surface! Surface!

The order to put on life jackets was given by Jensen over the intercom immediately prior to surfacing (Mazzone). If the engines could not be fired up or the flooded induction caused the boat to capsize, it would be necessary to abandon ship. Waiting at deep submergence was terrible, but a known quantity. The unexpected events that would occur on the surface might be worse: capture, capsizing, and possible death.

The postwar historian felt this order had a devastating effect on morale (Voge). The donning of life jackets merely coincided with a realization that the Japanese destroyers waited on the surface to end it all. To some men the prior words and actions of the commanding officer may have made his order to put on life jackets a symbolic surrender. In stressful situations, timing and tone were more important than the content of the communication. If another officer had given the command, the previous prayerful and fatalistic attitude may not have been associated with Jensen's order. It was also possible the postwar historian confused the life jacket event with the captain's earlier fatalistic prayer statement, of which no mention was made. Most crew members thought nothing special of putting on life vests (Mazzone). In some of the crew's negative mental state scuttling the *Puffer* or its sinking was inevitable. Extreme oxygen depletion caused a negative mentality. Their brains could only conclude there was no hope.

John Allen broke out of his locker three cans of pineapple juice and passed them around (Allen; Voge). The *Puffer* was caught in its own trap, the narrowest passage of the Makassar Strait. It was no longer necessary to save anything "for when things got worse" (Voge). Ensign William Pugh was ready to give away the $100 in his locker. He had no need for it. He was also preparing to destroy sensitive documents as soon as enough air was present to burn the paper (Deem). Other men were ready to fight it out. If the Japanese were still waiting on the surface, there would be no surrender.

With the remaining battery power the *Puffer* slowly crawled upward from 550 feet, and by 1830 had ascended to 250 feet below the surface (WPR). The postwar historian reviewed the complex situation.

> *Puffer* was then in very difficult trim, and to have attempted to come to periscope depth might involve loss of control. Safety tanks, negative, auxiliary tank, and after trim had been blown dry and had pressure in them. There was a 12 inch pressure in the boat already which practically precluded venting these tanks into the boat. They stuck it out until 1910 when they sur-

faced direct from deep submergence into the bright moonlight, 37 hours and 45 minutes after diving [Voge].

With no charge left in the batteries the *Puffer* was committed to at least 6 hours on the surface, "come what may" (WPR). Upon surfacing the boat had a 15 degree list to port from the tons of water flooding the induction. It took a couple of minutes to get the conning tower hatch open. It was opened slowly to let the pressure in the hull equalize with the outside world. Opened quickly the rush of air pressure in the boat would have ejected a man out of the hatch like a cork from a champagne bottle. Dobson recalled, "As the conning tower hatch was opened the control room fogged up so badly you couldn't see across it." Quartermaster Charlie Brockhausen carefully opened the hatch and emerged first. Next the officers of the deck and lookouts went out the hatch (Dobson).

Battle stations surface, repel boarders, was the order. Lookouts Wilson and Tidd climbed the periscope shears and anxiously started to scan the horizon. Kellum's gun crew was ready for action. Men mounted, loaded and readied 50 cal. machine guns and a 20mm and 40mm cannon on the conning tower. Men armed with Thompson submachine guns and small arms were ready to repel boarders. Initially two engines were put on propulsion; the other two engines were put on battery charge (*ibid.*).

The forward torpedo room hatch was opened second. For the moment the Japanese vessels were gone (*ibid.*). Unfortunately there was a near full moon rising higher in the eastern sky. As luck would have it, the *Puffer* was in the shadow of a large bank of clouds that formed in the evening tropical sky as the evaporated ocean water condensed in the cooler night air (Mazzone). The boat was not yet out of danger; SC #6 was still looking for the *Puffer*.

Initially the fresh air made the stench worse (Trudeau). The two open hatches supplied enough air to get one of the diesel engines running and revived the crew. The engines pulled fresh air through the boat, evacuating the odor of 38 hours. Fresh air in the lungs of the exhausted men never felt so good. Within an hour the induction tube was drained of the tons of water and the bilge pumps had adequate power to remove the water. This process took what seemed like an eternity (Dobson). Liggett described his part in getting the boat back in operational condition and the excess water out of the boat.

> Next was to get the ship in shape to keep going. The main induction was flooded and I was on my station in the forward engine room. The bilges were plugged and the water was up to my chin, by closing my eyes and ducking down, I could feel the drain and keep it unplugged. As I came up for air, our engineering officer (Bernard) asked if I wanted a sandwich. Man, I was starved! He brought me one and just as I took a bite, someone opened the main induction. I never tasted anything so good — a salt water sandwich [Liggett].

From the position of the attack on the tanker the current had moved the *Puffer* east about 10.4 miles and 5.8 miles north. After about 15 minutes on the surface the intermittent sweeps of the radar returned a signal. *SC #6 was* still looking for the *Puffer*. Fortunately the sub chaser was still listening for the *Puffer* in the attack location. "Then our enemy was spotted on the horizon and we went four [engines] full power on propulsion" (Dobson). Liggett wrote, "The stinker is setting a couple of miles to the rear of us, so we pour on all four mains and shag" (Liggett). But Jensen wanted no smoke from the engines, which might attract the attention of the enemy (Deem).

Evasive action was aided by going north and east with the current around the northern coast of Celebes Island, away from the chaser. Jensen hid the *Puffer* between the darkened land mass in the distance and the patrol boat, presenting only its stern toward the enemy. The escape course of the *Puffer* presented a minimum silhouette to the Japanese lookouts (WPR). Some officers argued for zigzagging, others a straight line rapid retreat (Deem). On full power the *Puffer* could match the sub-chaser's top speed of 20 knots. Just when power was needed most, one of the four diesels failed and produced a loud noise — a noise that might be heard by the enemy.

> The #2 engine in the forward engine room developed a noise we couldn't identify. We gagged the injector. Without fuel there was no chance of a catastrophic failure ... and kept going. It turned out to be a sticky injector. All was well. When he was out of sight we went back to two each on propulsion and battery charging [Dobson].

The postwar historian contended that the men physically recovered relatively quickly, but nervousness of the men continued for the next few days.

> After surfacing and getting out of danger they recovered physically with great rapidity. Within twenty four hours they were normal physically. For days however they were very nervous. If the diving officer wanted to cycle the vents, he had to pass the word quietly through the boat before hand. The noise of opening the vents, without primary warning would bring every man out of his bunk standing [Voge].

Dobson wrote, to the contrary, no one had much of an appetite for a day or two. He finally had a piece of Howie Allen's apple pie and coffee, "the best he ever tasted" (Dobson). Mechanically the boat was back in trim by 0450 of the next day. The *Puffer* had managed to elude the Japanese for eight hours. The boat was able to make a trim dive and no serious leaks were found (WPR).

Jensen wrote, "Stayed submerged to rest crew and steady down. Decided the boat could not undergo another attack." At 1800 the *Puffer* surfaced to recharge batteries. On October 12 Jensen informed Command of Task Force 71 that the *Puffer* was returning (WPR). The next day the crew received a radio message that stated the Japanese claimed the *Puffer* was sunk with all hands lost (Deem).

The next few days were spent submerged during the days, and repairs continued. The *Puffer*'s return followed much the same path as the first part of the war patrol, hugging the coastline of Celebes, sailing south through the Molucca Sea, the Ceram Sea where a plane contact was made, the Banda Sea, and finally the Timor Sea and on to Darwin (WPR).

Some of the first patrol crew probably suffered from post traumatic stress syndrome, then known as battle fatigue. There were bar fights in Darwin among some crew members, which may have released their frustrations, but that was not unusual (Allen). "At that time no one talked about it, [we] just muddled along and did what needed to be done. Some drank; some had other ways to get rid of the bad memories." These were events that were best "forgotten" (Tidd).

According to his son, Executive Officer Hess considered the events of those 30 hours a defining moment in his life (Hess). After escaping death John Solak, who boarded the *Puffer* as it pulled away from the quay in Brisbane, felt the rest of his life had been a gift (Solak). Washburn did not return to New Jersey and get run down by a streetcar (Washburn). Ray Roberts, who was undergoing chemo therapy treatments when interviewed in 2004 said, "I can't live forever, I was lucky once already; I survived the First War Patrol" (Roberts). In my last telephone conversation with Carl Dwyer in March 2004, his words of wisdom were, "Be lucky." He felt he had been lucky the rest of his life after escaping the horrors of the First War Patrol (Dwyer). The *Puffer* would be lucky numerous times in the future.

The *Puffer*'s Return

At 1545 on October 17 the *Puffer* reached Darwin and received over 35,000 gallons of fuel and 6000 gallons of fresh water (WPR). Admiral Christie had beer flown to Darwin at altitude so it would be cold when it arrived (Tidd). Schnapps was also included in the cargo (Liggett). A naval engineer determined the hull was safe and accompanied the *Puffer*. The next morning the *Puffer* was underway to Fremantle and badly needed repairs. For the next six days the *Puffer* proceeded on the surface, except for occasional training dives. On October 24, the boat returned to the safety of Fremantle (WPR).

Blair described Christie's initial reactions based upon his diary. However, other events during the 38 hours also were acknowledged.

> When *Puffer* came into port, Christie had nothing but praise for the ship and her captain. He wrote in his diary that "strength of character ... skill and experience and knowledge, the excellent state of training, saved the ship.... A brilliant job carried through by guts determination and the inspired example of the Commanding Officer.... Christie's staff, meanwhile, conducted a thorough investigation of the episode. Those taking testimony then discovered the extent to which Jensen had lost control of the crew.
>
> In view of this and other factors, one *Puffer* officer suggested that the wardroom and crew be scattered to other boats. This was done, in part; Jensen was relieved of command, becoming an assistant to Murray Tichenor (Christie's Chief of Operations), but Hess remained as exec [Blair, p. 501].

The author was not able to find a person that was interviewed by Christie's staff (Mazzone; Dwyer; Dobson). The matter was probably handled at the highest levels. Possibly Jensen, Bernard or Hess made the suggestion to scatter the officers and crew. Four crew members snapped under the pressure. Jensen had not instilled confidence among his crew with his words, but there was not a general loss of control of the crew. Christie's staff may have inferred a loss of control from the involvement the enlisted men played in the final decision to evade, scuttle, or wait it out until dark. There may have even been some yelling as men expressed their opinions. Most of the men by this time were flat on their backs, and unable to lose control. Men were unable to stand watch because they could not, not because they would not (Tidd).

Regardless a change of command was probably in order. The bond of mutual trust and confidence between the crew and skipper was no longer present. Walter Mazzone recalled the grumbling started after the *Puffer* ran aground a few days earlier. The 37 plus hours of submergence and depth charging deteriorated any remaining feelings of confidence the crew had in Commander Jensen. In the book *War in the Boats — My WWII Submarine Battles*, Capt. William J. Ruhe, then an officer on the *Crevalle*, described Mazzone's recollection of the situation.

> Walter Mazzone had been transferred to the *Crevalle* from the *Puffer* after she'd taken a frightening and punishing depth charging at the hands of several Japanese destroyers. The thirty-seven hours of relentless antisubmarine attacks against the *Puffer* had made his skipper so terrified and morose that he'd become a "useless pussy cat" during the depth charge attacks and caused the crew's morale to be shot to hell.
>
> Despite being one of those chosen to leave the *Puffer*, Mazzone, a light heavyweight boxing champ from San Jose State, showed no signs of having been fazed by the experience. To Walt, having a submarine leaking badly, bottomed, out of oxygen, and with a skipper immobilized and unable to make decisions, was just part of the "war in the boats." And the retelling of his ordeal was full of chuckles and Italianate gestures [Ruhe, p. 196].

Possibly, considering Jensen's previous depth charging and bombing experiences on the *Thresher*, and the similar events that transpired on the *Puffer*, he lost the confidence necessary to command a submarine. P.G. Nichols, Christie's chief of staff, indicated Jensen was "all shook up" after returning from the First War Patrol (Blair, Research Notes). Jensen may have suggested his own reassignment.

Awards

In correspondence from Admiral Ralph Christie to Captain Homer Graf, chief of staff, Commander Seventh Fleet, on February 15, 1944, Christie expressed his disappointment that all requests for awards for the *Puffer*'s First War Patrol had been turned down.

> The action of the Board of Awards that no recognition should be given to the officers of the *Puffer* is a very great personal disappointment to me. Everyone here concerned felt that Jensen's performance of duty under almost hopeless odds was superb [Christie, Graff letter].

Compared with the investigation of Christie's staff as reported by Blair, these remarks reflect a different attitude. Christie must have changed his mind about Jensen between October and February. The Board of Awards reconsidered at a later date. Commander Jensen was awarded the Silver Star for his First War Patrol on the *Puffer*.

> For conspicuous gallantry and intrepidity as Commanding Officer of the USS PUFFER during the First War Patrol of that vessel in enemy controlled waters. Directing his ship courageously and with exceptional skill throughout twenty-four hours of intense enemy depth charging attacks, he maintained his vessel at periscope depth and pressed home his attacks boldly and with heroic aggressiveness, destroying a valuable enemy merchantman. Although his submarine sustained severe damage during the vigorous engagement, he nevertheless returned her safe to base under her own power, thereby saving one of the important units of the Fleet for further service [Jensen, *Biography*].

If Jensen had remained mentally positive during October 9 and 10, he might have been given a Navy Cross. With the shadow that hung over Jensen, the other officers and crew were also belatedly given awards of a lower status than they probably deserved. Hess and Bernard were awarded Bronze Stars. Dwyer, Stoltz, and Hetrick were each given a Letter of Commendation. Dufault got nothing (Dwyer, Ship's History—Awards). Bernard's Bronze Star citation for the First War Patrol credited him with helping save the *Puffer*. Hess's citation was very similar.

> For distinguishing himself by heroism and intrepidity in action against the enemy. During the First War Patrol of the U.S.S. PUFFER, as executive officer, while that vessel was being severely depth-charged by a skillful and determined enemy, on 9–10 October 1943, his attention to making repairs of damage and to organizing damage and control parties, enabled the commanding officer to devote his entire attention to evading the depth-charge attacks being made by enemy surface vessels. His efforts during and after the depth-charging, contributed materially to the safe return of the U.S.S. PUFFER to her base. His actions and conduct were in keeping with the highest traditions of the Navy of the United States [Bernard, Naval Historical Center].

For the remainder of the war Jensen's skills were well utilized. For a year Jensen was assistant for submarine operations on the staff of Commander Submarines, 7th Fleet, and received a Letter of Commendation from the Commander 7th Fleet.

> For distinguishing himself by excellent service as Assistant Operations Officer on the Staff of Commander Submarines, SEVENTH FLEET and Commander Task Force 71 during the period of November 1943 to November 1944. He demonstrated great mental alertness in directing of the complete submarine operations of this Force, and was in large measure responsible for the successful interception of two large enemy task forces which were bound on a mission to surprise and frustrate the offensive operations of our forces in the Philippine Islands [Jensen, Naval Historical Center].

Jensen's analysis of Japanese ship movement patterns helped position American submarines in favorable locations to intercept Japanese vessels. He remained in the Pacific until the end of hostilities in August of 1945 with duty on the staff of Commander 7th Fleet (Jensen, *Biography*).

7

The Second War Patrol

Distorted History

Blair described the passing of command to the new skipper, Frank Gordon Selby.

> Command of the *Puffer* fell to Gordon Selby, who had been exec on the first patrol of the *Billfish*. For Selby, *Puffer* was a big challenge. Later he [Selby] wrote, "I didn't have time to think about much of anything but training since I had a 50 percent turnover in officers, and in crew. And it was not only 'training' but 'retraining' since I felt it necessary to change attack procedures and various other things for psychological reasons" [Blair, p. 501].

The record shows much less than a 50 percent turnover in officers after the first patrol. Lawrence Bernard was supposed to stay on the *Puffer*, but was replaced four days before the start of the Second War Patrol (WPR; Mazzone). Bernard had been taken off the *S-39* a year earlier with pneumonia like symptoms. His breathing problems returned after the extended submergence of the *Puffer*. Selby had only one new officer. Excluding the change in command, the *Puffer* received one out of six new subordinate officers. Lt. Stiles Morrow Decker replaced Bernard as engineering officer (WPR). Franklin Hess, Carl Dwyer, William Pugh, Walter Mazzone, and Kenneth Dobson remained. In reality the suggestion to scatter the wardroom was ignored and greatly exaggerated. The loss of control of the crew by the officers previously mentioned by Blair was also likely greatly exaggerated.

The postwar historian suggested a mythical bond as the reason for sending a large part of the crew to other duties.

> The common experience of such an ordeal knits them together in such a bond that no one else can penetrate the inner circle. Men who subsequently made several patrols on *Puffer* were still not members of the gang, if they hadn't been through THE depth charging [Voge].

Selby's sentence quoted by Blair in the opening quotation was structured in such a way that it was easily interpreted to mean at least 50 percent of the enlisted crew was transferred. In the nearly 30 years that passed between 1943 and the early 1970s, Selby may have read and believed the two earlier histories (Voge; Rosco, p. 278) of the *Puffer* and confirmed the inaccurate transfer assumption back to Blair as fact. Selby may have been recalling his collective experiences from war patrols two through five. If the postwar historians interviewed Selby in 1945 or 1946, his recollections may have been inaccurate as the events of numerous war patrols on the *Puffer* merged in his mind. John Allen, interviewed by Blair, estimated a 25 percent turnover in the crew, but Blair ignored his recollection (Blair, *Notes*).

Corrected History

A complete analysis of the crew transfers of the *Puffer* was derived from the muster roll rosters (RG24). The chart below clearly shows the transfer of the crew after the First War Patrol was very typical when compared with the next four patrols commanded by Selby. On the

Fourth War Patrol the number of crew members persisting from the First War Patrol finally dropped below 50 percent; 30 original crew members were still on the *Puffer*. As late as the Eighth War Patrol 12 crew members remained from the original crew. Crew sizes grew and became more stable in later war patrols as the supply of men exceeded demand on the boats, hence the larger crews on the sixth and seventh war patrols of the *Puffer*.

COUNT OF CONTINUING CREW MEMBERS

	Patrol Number (Crew count)						
	1 (71)	2 (72)	3 (71)	4 (71)	5 (71)	6 (76)	7 (83)
Continued on:							
Second War Patrol	51						
Third War Patrol	37	50					
Fourth War Patrol	30	41	48				
Fifth War Patrol	25	30	35	49			
Sixth War Patrol	21	26	32	43	59		
Seventh War Patrol	17	24	28	36	51	66	
Eighth War Patrol	12	18	20	29	38	51	67

Muster roll rosters show that only 20 out of the 71 enlisted men left the *Puffer*, about 29 percent. Seven of those 20 men returned to the *Puffer* on the Third and Fourth War Patrols. Fifty-one of the *Puffer*'s crew continued on the Second War Patrol (*ibid.*).

Jobs still needed to be done; the new crew members were as important to the survival of the boat as "THE" First War Patrol crew. Donald B. McDonald (S2c) joined the crew on the Second War Patrol for the remainder of the war. He was welcomed to the forward torpedo room by Fred Clouse (TM2c), William "Willie" Wilson (S1c), and Russell Tidd (S1c). He did torpedo training as Mike "Punchy" Kutscherousky's (TM2c) understudy. There was no talk about the First War Patrol; it was the Silent Service. After a year and a half, McDonald still knew virtually nothing about the First War Patrol. Wilson did not talk about it during seven war patrols; he did not ask about it. McDonald suspected the crew had been ordered not to talk about it, but he found no mystic bond among the crew (McDonald).

Selby wrote in the *Personnel Section* of *Puffer*'s Second War Patrol his opinion of the crew and new crew members.

> The crew conducted themselves like the veterans they are. No commanding officer could ask for a finer group of men to work with. It is considered remarkable that only two or three of the crew were still showing any signs of the nervous ordeal they underwent on the previous patrol. These men will be left in for a rest.
>
> Of the seventeen new men who came aboard without previous war patrol experience all but two fitted into the crew very nicely. The high caliber of firemen received was particularly noticed. The two mentioned are not temperamentally qualified for submarine duty and will be so designated [WPR].

Selby's endorsement spoke highly of the first patrol crew, verified the small number of new men who came aboard for the second patrol, and debunked the mystic bond myth.

Opposite: The Second War Patrol — November 24, 1943 (Fremantle), to January 12, 1944 (Fremantle) — 3,328 nautical miles in the patrol area. After refueling at Exmouth Gulf and traversing the Lombok Strait, the primary areas of patrol were the Makassar Strait and the western reaches of the Philippine Islands, especially the approaches to Manila. The flags indicate where attacks were made. The rising sun flag shows an attack on the Imperial Japanese Navy; the lone sun flags show an attack on a merchant vessel (map artwork by Nancy Webber).

Fifteen of the new crew members were welcomed and "fitted into the crew nicely." The scattering of the crew was highly exaggerated and most likely the loss of discipline by and of the crew was also exaggerated by the original historian and Blair.

Even though the muster rolls were available to Blair and more recent authors, the transfer of the *Puffer* crew has persisted as reality. William Tuohy, Pulitzer Prize winning author, in *The Bravest Man — The Story of Richard O'Kane & U.S. Submariners in the Pacific War,* also relied heavily on the Voge text in 2001. Tuohy paraphrased the original text and revived the breaking up of the crew.

> The Force Command concluded that when a submarine had been through such an ordeal the crew should be broken up; otherwise newcomers would be considered "outsiders" by those who went through THE depth charging [Tuohy, pp. 168–71].

The myth was repeated in 2006. In an extremely well documented text Michael Sturma in *Death at a Distance — The Loss of the Legendary USS Harder* concluded the *Puffer* transfers had occurred. Sturma wrote, citing Blair and Roscoe, "The *Puffer*'s captain was subsequently relieved of command and more than half of the crew reassigned to other submarines" (Sturma, p. 99).

In *USS Pampanito: Killer-Angel* published in 2000, Michno paraphrased Roscoe's account of the first patrol. His account lead a reader to believe the entire crew of the *Puffer* was sent to other boats or duties.

> In fact, after the depth charging *Pampanito* took, it was possible that her entire crew might be redistributed. Such was the experience of the USS *Puffer* (SS 268).... After studying the situation, submarine command determined that when a boat had gone through such an experience, its crew should be disbanded and sent to other boats. The sharing of the ordeal welded the men together in a mystic bond, and no newcomer would ever be able to penetrate the circle, for he had not gone through the experience [Michno, p. 113].

The *Puffer*'s crew, the *Pampanito*'s crew, and no other crew underwent a complete dispersion during the war. The continued historic inaccuracy that the officers and crew of the *Puffer* were dispersed must not continue. This myth, which has been propagated by various authors, casts a shadow on the heroic actions of the officers and crew members who saved the *Puffer*. Their actions should no longer be questioned or diminished.

New Crew and Boat Repairs

The following enlisted men left the *Puffer* after the First War Patrol. Some of these men went to relief crew duty, permanent assignment on the submarine tenders, back to the U.S. for new construction, or transferred to other submarines (RG24).

Crew Transferred after the First War Patrol

Name	Service #	Rate Arr.	First WP	Second WP
Brown, Charles Edwin	321 59 01	SC3c	SC2c	TRAN
Creech, Bishop Boggs	634 13 65	F3cV6	F2cV6	TRAN
Dickinson, Master James	636 47 51	F3cV6	F3c	TRAN
Flournoy, James Arvell	268 57 67	S1c	19-Jul-43	TRAN
Forest, Raymond Francis	234 31 29	S1c	19-Jul-43	TRAN
Gardner, Theodore Nash	234 37 46	F3cV6	F3c	TRAN
Guthrie, John Wise	300 49 87	TM3c	22-Jul-43	TRAN

Name	Service #	Rate Arr.	First WP	Second WP
Haycraft, Geoffrey David	287 12 43	CMoMM	CMoMM	TRAN
Justus, Leonard Everett	291 80 81	S1c	9-Jul-43	TRAN
Kerls, Charles John	410 38 89	MoMM2c	MoMM2c	TRAN
Kimbrell, William Warner	551 80 61	S2cV6	S1c	TRAN
Lennon, Francis Donald	375 65 05	TM1c	TM1c	TRAN
Rhymes, Ralph Willard	269 77 73	EM2c	EM2c	TRAN
Roberts, Julian Alonzo	272 23 31	EM1c	19-Jul-43	TRAN
Roberts, Raymond	646 13 01	RM3cV6	RM3c	TRAN
Shanholtz, Stanley Sherman	371 68 12	CMoMM	CMoMM	TRAN
Vaughn, John Anthony	291 46 33	EM2c	EM2c	TRAN
Von Sternberg, Donald Valiant	700 31 80	SM3cV6	SM3c	TRAN
Voss, Raymond Henry	372 22 92	EM3c	EM3c	TRAN
Washburn, Edgar Wheeler	706 67 52	S2cV6	S1c	TRAN

NEW CREW MEMBERS

Name	Service #	Rate Arr.	Date Arr.
Akeman, Robert Bruce	300 57 76	S2c	7-Nov-43
Allen, John Chester	360 09 28	QM3c	7-Nov-43
Bartorelli, Ralph Antonio	202 94 88	S2c	24-Nov-43
Bollman, Eric Peter	555 58 73	RT2cV6	9-Nov-43
Cochran, Robert Hugh	617 89 20	F1cV6	9-Nov-43
Coggins, Donald Grey	656 99 31	MoMM2cV6	7-Nov-43
Czatynski, John	243 95 99	EM2c	7-Nov-43
Evans, Leonard Dale	291 85 26	FC2c	7-Nov-43
Fleming, William Phillip	671 60 14	S2cV6	7-Nov-43
Funk, Leonard Gerald	279 78 34	MoMM2c	7-Nov-43
Garner, William Elmer	650 35 92	F1cV6	7-Nov-43
Kronberg, Lloyd Joseph	655 59 73	S1cV6	7-Nov-43
Lane, John Nelson	225 10 12	RM3c	9-Nov-43
Lankerd, Charles Eugene	372 50 72	F1c	7-Nov-43
McDonald, Donald Bernard, Jr.	386 54 45	S2cV6	9-Nov-43
Pieper, Alfred Leroy	316 96 21	S2c	7-Nov-43
Prisby, Henry Bernard	622 24 82	EM3cV6	7-Nov-43
Schley, Earl Stephen, Jr.	602 27 27	F1cV6	7-Nov-43
Smith, Henry Nelson	615 50 22	EM3c	24-Nov-43
Steinke, Harris Eugene	372 46 98	SM3cV6	7-Nov-43
Wiseman, Charles Emerson	613 18 20	S2cV6	9-Nov-42

Seventeen of the twenty men were fresh from submarine school with no war patrol experience. McDonald was one of those men. Those who were coming from sub school had endured a long trip. First there was a train trip from New London to San Francisco by way of Chicago. McDonald met Charlie Wiseman on the train; he was also headed for Australia and the *Puffer*. The highlight of the stopover in Chicago was a cab ride to the location of the St. Valentine's Day Massacre. After another long train ride, Wiseman and McDonald arrived in San Francisco and boarded the *U.S.A.T. Sea Pike* for the three week cruise to Brisbane, Australia. The cruise cured the seasickness of many a neophyte Navy man. As the ship crossed the equator, Polliwogs were properly initiated as loyal Shellbacks into the Domain of Neptunus Rex. The initiation usually consisted of drinking from a rubber glove, mild electric shocks and bowing down before a costumed Neptunus Rex (McDonald).

The next leg of the journey was a 3,000 mile rail trip across Australia. The Australian railroads were not of standard gauge, so as the passengers crossed the border from one Australian state to another, everyone and everything was transferred from one train to the next. Sailors carried all their belongings in sea bags, which contained uniforms and their bunk mattress. There were no dining cars on the Australian trains. Meals were eaten at various stops along the way and served by the Australian Army (McDonald). The Aborigines watched from a distance and descended upon the garbage bins as the train departed. The contents of the garbage barrels were literally thrown into the air and the contents devoured. Upon reaching Perth, the beef and pork fed Americans commented if they never saw mutton stew again, it would not be too soon (Stoy).

Sleeping was difficult on the hard, wooden seats in the trains. Some daring men slept in the narrow overhead luggage racks. After a four day journey, the new recruits arrived at Fremantle-Perth on November 8, 1943. McDonald thought the first night was great; he was able to sleep in a soft, stationary bed at the submarine base. Next day it was off to the *Puffer*; no more plush accommodations. McDonald's nearest overhead bunkmate was a 3,200 pound torpedo (McDonald). He was assigned a bunk in the forward torpedo room and was to train with "Punchy" Kutscherousky. "Punchy" was an ex-professional boxer who came out with fists flying at the sound of any bell, exercised while on board the submarine, and ate garlic to maintain his health. An easygoing man outside the ring, Kutscherousky had been the All-Asiatic Submarine Fleet boxing champion prior to the war (Gugliotta).

After the pounding the *Puffer* took during the First War Patrol, extensive repairs and modifications were made. The periscopes were replaced and installed so that both could be used from the conning tower. The improved "T" hatch gaskets were not yet available. As a result the main induction gaskets, which were completely blown off, could be repaired only to Manitowoc specifications. If the deck or conning tower hatches had completely lost the seal gasket, the *Puffer* would have been lost. The noisy pumps were not replaced. All the troublesome air bank silver solder joints were broken and replaced with a superior joint, called a Walworth fitting. The sonar heads damaged during the grounding were repaired while the ship was drydocked from October 30 to November 3. Many gauges had to be replaced or recalibrated. The work was completed on November 13 by the crew of the USS *Pelias* (WPR).

The New Commander

On November 8 Lt. Commander Willard R. Laughon, a prospective commanding officer assigned to Christie's staff, relieved Commander Jensen as commanding officer. Laughon conducted deep dive and training exercises testing the repairs to the boat and training the new crew until a permanent commanding officer could be found. On November 16, Lt. Commander Frank G. Selby arrived in Fremantle and assumed command of the *Puffer* (*ibid.*). A few weeks later Laughon would be chosen to command the *Rasher* (SS 269) (Sasgen).

Selby was a 1933 graduate of the USNA. He entered the Submarine Service in 1938 and served on the USS *Pike* and the *S-28* as executive officer between October and December 1941. During the initial months of the war Selby had made two war patrols with Creed Burlingame on the *Silversides* as executive officer (Selby, *Biography*). Burlingame had won the Navy Cross twice for these patrols, credited with four sinkings and 25,000 tons on the first patrol, and 3 more and 15,000 tons on the second. Postwar analysis pared these credits to 1 for 4,000 tons and 2 for 9,800 tons, but still very respectable patrols for early in the war. Selby observed about Burlingame, "A guy with his ideas has to be good" (Casey). Selby received a Bronze Star as diving officer on the *Silversides* (Selby, *Biography*).

Under Burlingame's tutelage in 1942 Selby experienced an aggressive commanding officer and combat in Japanese Empire waters. Selby nearly met his maker during a surface gun action versus a sampan. In extremely rough waters off the coast of Japan, *Silversides* attacked a bobbing sampan with the deck gun. Two deck gun crew members were washed overboard. The first couple of 3-inch shots were hits, but went cleanly through the wooden vessel's hull doing minimal damage. As the distance between the two boats closed, it appeared the sub might ram the sampan. The closeness made the artillery action more difficult in the turbulent waters. At approximately 200 yards the Japanese let loose with a quick burst from a concealed automatic weapon. The first rake hit the 3-inch gun crew. The number one loader was severely injured; the number two loader was killed instantly. Selby, who had been on the deck, dodged behind the fairwater of the conning tower just as a slug hit the other side. Directly in front of his forehead a slug partially penetrated the steel plate and knocked paint chips into his face. Small arms fire from the *Silversides* cleaned the deck of the sampan and the 3-inch gun hit the sampan aft below the water line. The *Silversides* had prevailed, but the loss of life and burial at sea of a fellow shipmate was a somber occasion for all (Casey, pp. 302–5). Tempered with a healthy respect for small vessels, Selby brought the aggressiveness of Burlingame to the *Puffer*.

The *Silversides* operated so close to the shore of Japan that Commander Burlingame and the crew became familiar with the daily lives and scenes of Japanese life, even to the point of observing the comings and goings of a specific household. Targets were many, but hard to see at night against the green background of the Japanese hillsides. *Silversides* was successful in sinking a tanker and a Japanese submarine. Selby also saw ships that got away. Similar events occurred on the *Puffer* while Selby was commanding officer. But such was the everyday life of a submarine commander: lots of waiting, some successes, and some failures (*ibid.*, pp. 306–11).

> One that got away from us that I shall always remember. We were only vaguely aware of her. Not until she was almost on top of us could the captain be sure that he was looking at a ship at all and not some play of the wind in the foliage ashore. We had made an approach, but since it had been impossible to make out what we were approaching, we couldn't judge her speed. And when finally we saw her, bulking up like a block of houses in the gloom, we were in a position from which we couldn't fire. She went by us, towering over us, one of the biggest ships I ever saw — loaded I suppose, with troops and supplies for the Southwest Pacific. She was over and then she was gone. We felt pretty low about it for a long time. A little more light, a little more luck and we'd have piled her right up on somebody's front lawn. But the luck wasn't there.... Not that night [*ibid.*, p. 309].

Selby then served as executive officer on the *Billfish* for one unsuccessful patrol and was held in reserve as a prospective commanding officer (PCO) (Selby, *Biography*). The *Puffer* command situation required the use of Selby. Selby was prematurely gray and was nicknamed "The Great White Father" by the crew (McDonald). The premature gray hair may have resulted from his earlier experiences on the *Silversides*. Selby was cut from the mold of the younger, more aggressive submarine commanders and was a big change from the previous commander (Tidd; Topor).

Departure for Subic Bay

Due to the transfer of Lawrence Bernard four days before leaving on the patrol, Lt. Decker, USNR, came aboard as engineering officer. Between November 14 and 23 sound tests, deep dive and anti-submarine training exercises were conducted under the supervision of J.H. Haines, commander of Submarine Division 16 (WPR). On November 24 a couple of last minute additions were made to the crew, Bartorelli and Smith (RG24). The *Puffer* pulled away from the quay at Fremantle and was underway for the assigned patrol area with good wishes and good hunting from Admiral Christie. The *Puffer* was assigned to patrol the area near Manila, an area of much Japanese activity. The same day more anti-submarine training exercises were conducted and the simulated night surface pursuit of an enemy vessel (WPR).

November 25 was Thanksgiving. The crew was treated to an all-American Thanksgiving dinner of turkey and dressing with all the trimmings. Training dives and exercises continued en route to Exmouth Gulf, where the fuel tanks were topped off. By early morning on November 30 the *Puffer* was near the entrance to the Lombok Strait — a narrow stretch of water between the islands of Bali and Lombok, heavily patrolled by the Japanese. Although there was some doubt as to the exact location of the boat due to the bad weather and to a lack of star shots for 36 hours, SJ radar confirmed their location. Selby waited for the cover of night. At 1918 the boat surfaced and ran at full speed through the darkness. At 2200 radar picked up a contact, but Selby was able to evade what was believed to be a patrol boat. At 2345 the passage through the narrow gauntlet was completed, and the open water of the Flores Sea lay ahead. For the next eight days the *Puffer* traversed nearly 2000 miles: passing through the Makassar Strait, the Sibutu Passage, the Sulu Sea, and the Mindoro Strait toward the approaches to Manila, the Philippine Islands. The only contacts made for the next two days were small vessels and possibly a submarine (*ibid.*).

The First Attack

Early on the morning of December 9 the *Puffer* was patrolling 20 miles from Capones Island, near the entrance to Subic Bay, in the light of a three-quarters moon. At 0255 radar contacted a ship at a range of 20,000 yards directly ahead. Selby put the target astern and went to full speed, tracking the ship as they both traveled in the same direction, gradually letting the contact close the range. Selby described the action in the War Patrol Report.

0300 Radar picked up two more targets on about same bearing at 17,000 yards and 18,000 yards. Moon was due to set at 0345 so decided to stay out ahead to track zig-zag plan and speed and then attack on the surface in the dark. Quartermaster [Brockhausen] in the lookout platform could see dim outlines of three large ships on horizon and possibly three or four smaller ships. Slowed and speeded up as necessary to keep closest contact at a range of 15,000 yards or over while tracking. Tracked nearest contact first on course 165°, speed 11, and then picked up a zig to the left to 135°. Thought the situation was well under control when at...

0325 Radar picked up another contact at 9,600 yards on port quarter. Could see one ship on this bearing but about 30 seconds after the contact a steady red light showed up. I believed this to be a port side light at first but realized it was too high up for a side light. The range was closing so went ahead full on 4 engines and swung to starboard to 150° to put him astern and open out. The moon at this point had sunk behind a low cloud on the western horizon giving the convoy a dark background and leaving us pretty well silhouetted on a light background. I wanted to swing left slowly and take advantage of the high, dark land background north of Subic Bay in an attempt to lose him and then circle around to attack the convoy from the port side. He apparently had no intention of letting us get a decent background for he kept drawing out on the port quarter and closing the range. At 7,000 yards I could make him out dimly and at this point he flashed his steady red recognition signal again. The rate of change of range decreased slowly down to 6,800 yards and then the range started decreasing rather rapidly, this in spite of the fact that we were making 18 knots. I was convinced then that he had us spotted cold and that we could not outmaneuver him on the surface, so at...

0340 Submerged. I did not feel that I had enough information or that I could see him well enough through the periscope to get off anything more than a wild shot so went to 200 feet. At...

7. The Second War Patrol

0345 He dropped four depth charges in succession none of which seemed very close. [Dwyer's comment, recalling the First War Patrol, was, "Oh hell, here we go again" (Deem).] Heard no echo ranging at any time. Sound picked up screws on starboard bow but lost him again in a couple of minutes when the I.C. motor generator failed and we lost power on the power training gear. Shifted to hand training in the forward torpedo room but could get no contact.

0354 Single depth charge farther away.

0415 Got the I.C. motor generator back, sound gear and gyro, and started back up in an attempt to regain contact with the convoy.

0429 At 140 feet put power on the bow planes and simultaneously received a depth charge closer than before. Coincidence I believe but disconcerting. Went deep again.

0515 Came to periscope depth on course 270°. As it gradually got light enough to see, spotted *Chidori* class MTB or similar vessel astern of us in toward the beach about four miles, 90° starboard angle on bow, lying to. Also saw two columns of smoke from the convoy on true bearing 160°, apparently headed in the direction of Manila. On next look at MTB he had a 90° port angle on the bow. Ten minutes later I could not find him and never saw him again.

0555 Thought our luck had changed when I spotted a black column of smoke from the direction of Subic Bay which tracked on a westerly course. Closed for two hours at standard speed. Began to get suspicious that something was haywire when he began to track course 120° which headed him directly for the beach. Also I could now see tops of two high masts which seemed too close together and a little of the top of a superstructure in addition to the continuous black smoke from his stack.

0822 Got my first look at the target and was not too surprised to see that he was a built up sampan, probably the same one *Crevalle* reported. Broke off approach. Estimated draft of 6 or 7 feet and heavy swells make firing at a target of questionable value seem inadvisable. Took southerly course for the rest of the day [WPR].

Almost six hours of intense effort resulted in a jolting depth charge and no torpedoes fired. This set of events was not unusual. A heightened sense of anticipation was often followed by disappointment. However, there were always more Japanese ships.

Frustration Again

On December 12 at 1839 the *Puffer* surfaced in the light of the full moon and began patrolling 50 miles outside of Manila Bay. At 0155 on December 13 the SJ radar made contact with a ship at a range of 21,000 yards. Here was Selby's description of the action. It is a good example of the unpredictable nature of submarine warfare. Selby candidly commented on his thoughts, mistakes and afterthoughts during the entire contact (*ibid.*).

0415 Submerged. With generated range 14,000 yards, picked him up in periscope. With generated range 6,000 yards, 45° port angle on the bow, course 115°T, could make him out as a large two stacker, HORAI MARU type AP. Went ahead full to close track. On next look with the generated range 5,000 yards, he had zigged toward us and the angle on the bow was 5° port. Headed toward him and prepared to fire a "down the alley" shot in case he did not zig.

0517 Angle on the bow 20° port. Came to course for a 60° port track, 1,000 yard torpedo run. On raising the periscope for what I thought would be the final set-up, he had zigged toward us again and was presenting a zero angle on the bow. He looked big as a barn and in view of the fact that we hadn't had a really reliable range since diving an hour before, I was afraid he was much closer than our generated range of about 1,900 yards. Decided to take a final bearing and fire "down the alley" with a 40° right gyro angle, hoping to get a hit and slow him down.

0523 Fired four torpedoes and started down to 100 feet to avoid being rammed. 51 seconds after firing heard first torpedo explode. One minute later heard a second explosion which sounded more like a depth charge. It must have been a depth charge or an internal explosion as any of the other three torpedoes would have had to hit much sooner.

Sound tracked the target's screws still coming in on us and then finally heard them stop. They started up again on our port quarter but were reported by our number two sound man as "fast screws coming toward us." This caused me to delay getting back to periscope depth although I had seen no escort previously. A check by the number one sound operator indicated that they were the target's screws and had slowed to 72 r.p.m. from their previous 100 r.p.m.

Back at periscope depth I could see the target fairly clearly in the early morning light, range about 5,000 yards, angle on the bow 160° starboard and carrying about a 5° port list. Commenced chasing at full speed to overtake him. For about five minutes we were closing the range slowly and then he speeded up again and began pulling away from us. Continued to chase for about 15 minutes hoping his damage would slow him down but he continued to open the range. In retrospect I wish I had fired two long range shots at him, but I felt so sure that I was going to be able to close the range that I didn't think of it soon enough.

As he drew away he seemed to be settling down by the bow but not so much but what he should have been able to make the remaining distance to Corregidor without too much trouble.

0700 Lost sight of target and changed course to 280°T [*ibid.*].

These opportunities served well to train the crew in live action situations. The problems helped Selby and the rest of the officers refine their roles, and their communications and tracking skills during the approaches. At the time the second approach seemed to be successful— some damage appeared to have been inflicted on the enemy ship. However as was often the case, postwar analysis could not verify damage to the 9,200 ton freighter as claimed. An intercepted Japanese Ultra message stated the *Teiko Maru* reported torpedo tracks at this time and location, but no damage (Alden, *Successes,* p. D-100). Two months later the *Teiko Maru* crossed paths with the *Puffer* again.

Waiting for Action

The next seven days were uneventful; no ships were spotted, only a lone aircraft contact. The Philippine Islands—Taiwan—Japan was a route often used by Japanese shipping. Patience and persistence were required to avoid recklessness. Shortly after midnight on December 20 a small boat was sighted. It was tracked for a number of hours, and in the early morning hours the crew went to battle stations (WPR).

0335 Radar contact bearing 026°T, range 20,000 yards. Put main engines on propulsion and commenced tracking. Target tracked on steady course 180°T at 9 knots. Went ahead of target and with range at 16,000 yards could not pick him up visually. As he had a land background and ours was not very good, felt we might be sighted so at...

0432 Submerged. With generated range 13,000 yards came up to 40 feet but could neither see target nor get radar contact.

0500 Regained radar contact at 10,000 yards from 40 feet depth. Target had changed course to 150°T. Closed track at full speed slowing for periscope observations.

0525 Picked up target in periscope. He seemed to be very small considering that we had picked him up at 20,000 yards on radar but thinking that early dawn light might be fooling me, made ready four bow tubes. Continued closing. Bearing indicated that he had slowed considerably. As it continued to get lighter there was no question but that he was a small ship and at...

0600 I could see clearly that the target was about a one hundred ton sampan, but a most peculiar one. He had *two* higher masts aft and a fairly large deck house — possibly built up. Having no camera aboard [probably because of the problems on the First War Patrol], but an excellent amateur artist [possibly Kennedy], I let him have a look from which he made a quite accurate sketch. In light of following events, I believe that this ship was almost certainly a radar decoy. His masts or deck house must have been specially energized in some manner or otherwise it is fantastic to have picked up a sampan of that size at 20,000 yards by radar. He had me fooled completely for I was ready to fire when the torpedo run was 2,500 yards—only the improved visibility of oncoming daylight saved us from wasting four torpedoes and giving away our position. I do not think I would be fooled next time for certain aspects of the radar pip gave him away. Will mention this under A/S measures.

0615 Came to reverse his course, 330°T, to see if anything was coming in behind him.

0637 Secured from battle stations.

0640 Sighted smoke bearing 341°T and went back to battle stations. Small sampan similar to one sighted at 0050 passed on course about 180°T, range about 6,000 yards. The number of columns of smoke continued to increase until it was evident that it was a large convoy.

0728 Sighted masts and stack of right hand ship and commenced approach on him. Looked like the convoy was coming in from seaward on course 090°T having just made a landfall.

0735 Picked up echo ranging on sound gear and shortly thereafter sighted destroyer ahead of target on parallel course and about a mile closer to me. Decided to try and get escort first if possible so took good look at destroyer stacks and drafts in recognition manual, ONI 14.

0743 Took cut. Bearing 160°T, distance 10.5 miles from Salanguin Island, just north of Subic Bay.

0751 Convoy changed course to right to about 180°T. Destroyer was apparently holding his course toward beach so gave up idea of shooting at him for the time being and commenced approach on largest ship I could see, which was about fourth from the right flank.

0607 Destroyer had swung right and had a 10° starboard angle on the bow, relative bearing 139°. Temporarily secured approach on freighter and got set up on destroyer. As the angle on the bow increased I could see that it was a two-stack destroyer, large stack forward, smaller stack aft, with tripod foremast and mainmast. Closest resemblance was to HATSUHARU Class (Page 73) although it could have been SHIGURE (Page 75) or ASASHIO Class (Page 77). He continued regular echo ranging and at...

0816 With the range 2,000 yards he shifted to hand keying and gave several short pings followed by a long one. As the pings were beamed on us, considered that he had made contact, so at...

0817 Commenced firing early with 75° starboard track, a generated torpedo run of about 1600 yards and a gyro angle of 170°.

0817-15 Checked bearing.

0817-34 Fired fourth torpedo.

0818-10 Heard explosion and looked. Hit aft—about 30 feet of his stern was gone.

0818-26 Second hit just forward of bridge was probably magnetic as I could see column of water on both sides of the ship. Seemed to lift whole ship up momentarily but did not break it. She settled back and commenced sinking by the stern. Took a quick sweep around to locate the rest of the convoy. The sweep took about 30 seconds and when I came back to the destroyer there was nothing left of her except about 15 or 20 feet of bow sticking up at almost a 90° angle.

We were now in the happy position of having gotten rid of the only escort in sight; three ships were coming right down the groove on course still about 160°T in a rough line of bearing about 300°T from the nearest ship, about 1000 to 1500 yards between ships; and a fourth (the right flank ship—easternmost) was headed at us with a zero angle on the bow, range about 4,000 yards. I could see a fifth, sixth and seventh and the smoke of an eighth; could not get much idea of their courses.

0820 (About) Lost depth control. This disappointing loss of depth control has been subsequently thoroughly investigated and faults found corrected to the extent that I am satisfied it will not happen to us again.

0825 (About) One of the ships dropped a depth charge. The sound operators were giving me continuous sound bearings of the targets as they crossed our bow from starboard to port but it didn't seem wise to fire by sound as I felt sure they must by this time be maneuvering.

0830 (About) Got to periscope depth and held it at standard speed. Another depth charge as the periscope went up. At that point everything was past but two ships, only one of which it was at all possible to get in on. Got set-up on him with a 70° port angle on the bow, range 5,000 yards. Closed at full speed until the torpedo run was 4,700 yards and decided to fire a full salvo from the bow tubes to cover more possible errors at range.

0836 Another depth charge. Couldn't see who was dropping them.

0841 Commenced firing bow tubes.

0841-16 Took check bearing. TDC was checking perfectly.

0841-30 Almost simultaneously with the firing of #4 a premature exploded. Fired #5 and held up #6 for another check bearing. The smoke and wall of water from the premature completely blotted out the target and as I swept to the right looking for it I discovered where the depth charges must have been coming from. Another destroyer, smaller than the first (my fleeting impression was a CHIDORI) was headed at us at high speed, range about 2,000 yards. He must have been originally way out on the outboard flank as this was the first I had seen of him.

0844 Started deep and rigged for depth charges. There had been one explosion shortly after the premature and at this time there were two more. They could have been torpedo hits or they could have been depth charges. I think it possible that we got one or two hits even with the high range because the TDC set-up checked so well. On the other hand all torpedoes may have missed — I don't have enough data to do any more than state the possibilities. The ship I fired at was an AK, similar to the SYUNKO MARU or ITALY MARU.

0846 to 0942 Received 18 depth charges about half of which were single and half in pairs. None were close and only one was near enough to shake the ship up any. It was as a matter of fact, the most ineffective depth charging I have experienced to date considering that, he knew from our premature and our torpedo wakes just about where we were. I suspect that having his colleague sunk dampened his ardor somewhat. We took the most evident escape course, 270°T, and did not have to vary it over 20° either side to keep him astern.

0942 to 1415 Continuous pinging astern which finally died out.

1540 Came to periscope depth. Nothing in sight.

1852 Surfaced. Decided to run west for three hours at 12 knots and then head north to spend the next day giving all hands, including myself, a rest from battle stations. In addition the SJ radar mast and pitometer log needed repairing and the gyro compass needed routine servicing [*ibid.*].

Postwar analysis confirmed the sinking of the 820 ton destroyer *Fuyo* in Subic Bay. There was no confirmation of the damage or sinking of the freighter, which postwar was identified as the *Gozan Maru* (Alden, *Successes,* p. D-101). The premature explosion of the torpedo was most likely caused by a malfunctioning magnetic trigger, which was still in use by Christie commanded boats. Tidd succinctly summed up the situation when he stated, "Those damn torpedoes!" Similar to the First War Patrol, the premature explosion again directed a hidden escort toward the *Puffer*. Unlike the First War Patrol Selby was able to quickly evade the escorts.

No Christmas Presents

For another week contacts were nil. The *Puffer* patrolled traffic lanes between Manila and Taiwan. Heavy seas and poor visibility made navigation near the coast hazardous. Early on the morning of Christmas Eve a contact was made with a craft near Cape Bolinao, Philippine Islands. The craft was small and could not be picked up on radar. It pursued the *Puffer*. After a couple of hours of running at 18 knots the probable PT-type boat was lost. Selby noted one crew member suggested it was Santa Claus trying to catch them to deliver packages. The next two days were spent patrolling in the direction of Manila. Selby noted, "Spent two hours at 150 feet on Christmas Day for turkey dinner and entertainment by local talent over the 1 MC system" (WPR).

Over the last couple of weeks, about every seven days some type of convoy passed along the route between Manila and the Japanese held territories to the north. December 27 was no exception.

> 1207 Sighted smoke bearing 105°T. True bearing changed to northward so came to 000°T on approximate normal approach course. Bearing gradually became steady and then began to draw south so came to 120°T. As the range decreased, three columns of smoke were visible and finally the masts and stacks of several ships. Angle on the bow was 90° starboard, true course 190°T, estimated range 18,000 yards, and it looked very much as if they were headed to pass northward of Lubang Island and on down to Palawan Passage.
>
> 1515 Counted six ships and one CHIDORI class escort echo ranging. The whole group looked very much like the convoy we had attacked on December 20th, less two of their MARUS and the destroyer escort.
>
> 1545 Sighted a KATE flying low over convoy.
>
> 1345 to 1530 This outfit fooled me with a gradual change of course to the right from 190°T to 320°T. Every time I looked at them, except once (70°), they had a 90° starboard angle on the bow. I didn't have enough battery to run full speed on a parallel course but ran at standard speed between looks planning to track their zig plan and speed and close at night. In retrospect had I not turned north originally or had I run at full speed for about half an hour, I would have been able to get into firing position. As it was I got in to a 4500–5000 yards torpedo run on the last ship. Rather than fire at this range, I decided to wait for one more zig to the right and, if this didn't materialize, to track them further and close at night. They zigged but it was slowly to the left.
>
> As it was only two hours until sunset I did not anticipate any trouble in closing on them; and, as the night was due to be dark, it looked like an ideal set-up for a night surface attack. I intended to surface when their range had opened sufficiently and commenced the chase during the remainder of daylight using the periscope to keep visual contact on their masts. However, at...
>
> 1646 Sighted the KATE again astern of us bearing 120°T so remained submerged.
>
> 1805 True bearing of smoke was 290°T and we had determined the base course to be approximately 280°T heading just south of Macclesfield Bank.
>
> 1855 Surfaced and commenced chase at 15 knots on course 285°T working up to 18 knots as battery charge progressed.
>
> 2330 Had not made contact and it was evident that they must have made a radical course change at dark. Came right to 000°T to cover base course change which would take them just north of Macclesfield Bank, then, having reached interception point without contact at...
>
> *28 December*
> 0000 Came to course 193°T to intercept them had they changed course to pass north of the Dangerous Ground. Had no further contact with the convoy. Ran out of southern and western limits of area and as I had no further hope of contacting this convoy, headed back north toward Manila on the surface maintaining a periscope watch.
>
> 1730 Headed toward Mindoro Strait in accordance with revised orders [*ibid.*].

Happy New Year

Another convoy had escaped, but the new orders were promising. Orders were usually changed as a result of an intercepted Ultra message, which foretold the movement of a convoy. Four days later on January 1, 1944, a convoy was contacted as the *Puffer* moved south toward the Sulu Archipelago. This group of islands separates the Sulu Sea and the Celebes Sea and stretches between the southern Philippine Islands and the northeast corner of Borneo. It was a shallow sea lane that was traversed by ships headed for the occupied Japanese islands to the south of the Philippines. The first day of the New Year was a good one for the *Puffer*, maybe too good. A dangerous night surface attack ensued.

0020 SJ radar contact on ship bearing 180°T, range 18,000 yards. Put contact astern and commenced tracking at full speed. Altogether, the radar contacted three large ships and two smaller ones intermittently. This convoy tracked on from 045°T to 055°T on the route from Basilan Strait to Cebu heading to pass about six miles from Madalag Point, thence, probably on to Apo Island, and from there to Cebu. The night was dark but fairly clear except inshore where there was a dark background formed by a haze around the land. Decided to work around from their port bow to the starboard bow and take advantage of this haze for firing.

0220 On starboard bow of convoy, slowed and commenced approach. It appeared at this point that the ships were in column with an escort ahead on the port bow and one astern. We had ten torpedoes in the tubes and one in the rack forward so decided to approach for about a 110° track on the leading ship, fire three torpedoes at him, shift to the second target, fire three at him with about a 60° track, and save the stern tubes for the third target or any other opportunity that presented itself. When the range was down to 6,000 yards I could just make out the dark outlines of two of the three big ships. Headed to keep the first ship slightly on the port bow while adjusting our speed to get a position about 2,000 yards off the track.

When about 2,300 yards from the track I was beginning to see the second ship well enough to realize that it was not in column but on the starboard quarter of the first and that the original scheme would not work as planned. Before I had time to concentrate much on this new development the control party reported a target bearing 035° relative, range 4,000 yards. I thought they had accidentally shifted targets and it took a few moments to find out that they were still on the original target. I got a quick look at it and could see the silhouette of a destroyer with about a 60° starboard angle on the bow. Had the Officer-of-the-Deck watch that while we swung slowly to the right to shoot at the original target.

Our target now apparently spotted us for he made a sharp turn to his starboard to give a small angle on the bow and then for some unaccountable reason turned back toward his original course and gave us about a 60° starboard angle on the bow.

0303 Commenced firing bow tubes. Coincidental with this the second target altered course to the right and headed directly at us. Held our course until #3 was fired, in the meantime building up speed. Swung right with full rudder at full speed to put second target astern. Saw two torpedo tracks pass just ahead of our target and a bright orange flash followed by heavy black smoke as the third one hit him forward of the bridge. Somewhere in the above interval radar had picked up and reported 6 to 10 new contacts from our port quarter to our port bow. To quote the assistant approach officer and radar operator [Jay Deem], "The screen looked like a picket fence."

The second target had at this time continued his swing to starboard and was heading across our stern while the third had now shown up headed directly for us from slightly on the port quarter, closing rapidly. Decided to shoot the stern tubes down his throat in an attempt to slow him down and then swing to starboard and shoot the remaining three torpedoes forward at the second target. The second escort had now shown up between #2 and #5 and looked like he was headed for us.

Here the control party and I unknowingly came to a parting of the ways. I thought they understood my intention to fire at the ship directly astern but they were busy tracking the ship on the starboard quarter by radar.

0507 Fired the stern tubes. About a minute after firing there were three explosions in succession which each shook the ship. I focused on the ship astern for some sign of the hits or of his opening out in range but there was none. What with the escort closing, the ship astern still apparently closing, 8 or 10 contacts astern and on the starboard quarter which I couldn't see and all of them overdue to open up with their guns, it didn't look like we could maneuver our way out on the surface. Also, we were headed directly for the beach on 078°T, our last radar range on land having been 12,000 yards.

0510 Submerged and swung left 90°.

0512 Could hear the screws of a ship passing overhead as we passed 80 feet.

0513 Depth charging started as we were going deep.

0515 to 0518 Five depth charges fairly close but not dangerously so. Only three more charges were dropped in the next half hour.

While the set-up is a freak one we must have put three hits into the ship on the starboard quarter. The details of this firing are contained in the attack data for Attack 5 along with a Norman Bel Caddes sketch of the action drawn up from our known track and ranges and bearings of all three of the ships at various times.

The ship we presume to have hit looked, at close range with a large angle on the bow, like an aircraft carrier or converted carrier. This was the Officer-of-the-Deck's independent impression also. He had a single mast and stack forward immediately aft of the bridge. The silhouette in ONI 14 which he looks most like is that of the seaplane tender CHIYODA (Page 59) without the hangar deck aft. In view of the fact, however, that I didn't see any gun turrets and that he didn't open up on us (he should have been able to blast us out of the water if he had been on his toes as he got in to 900 yards by radar at one time) I am inclined to believe that he was a tender for all the small ships that we contacted by radar and that the whole outfit was traveling at the slow speed of 7 knots for the benefit of these small ships.

0353 Last depth charge.

0400 Screws faded out.

0440 Picked up three sets of distant screws aft.

0530 With daylight just breaking came to periscope depth. Sighted masts of small ship aft and then as it got lighter the masts of two more. One seemed to be lying to while the other two maneuvered around indiscriminately. They were, or appeared very similar to, the 450 ton minelayer of the TSUNAME Class on Page 161 of ONI 14. They may have been three of our many small ship contacts. Could see some kind of a small object astern one of which looked like it was being towed.

0705 The three mine layers formed column and steamed off on a northeasterly course.

0748 Heard what sounded like a terrific underwater explosion at a great distance. Nothing visible through the periscope. Continued working out to westward for rest of day.

1856 Surfaced and set course for northwest entrance to Basilan Strait [*ibid.*].

The *Puffer* earned the distinction of inflicting the first damage of 1944 on the Japanese. Although only damage was claimed on the freighter and the seaplane tender, postwar analysis awarded the sinking of the 6,707 ton *Ryuyo Maru* to Selby and the *Puffer*. The *Ryuyo Maru* had left Wasili, Halmahera Island (between Celebes and New Guinea), on December 28 bound for Manila with 88 passengers. One passenger and six crewmen lost their lives (Somerville, 1991). Damage to the seaplane tender was not confirmed. If there had not been communication problems among the tracking team members, the attack may have been more successful. The events that transpired made it clear that while under stress the communication and coordination of attack procedures by the tracking team were still being refined. For another two days the Basilan Straits of the Sulu Archipelago were patrolled (WPR).

Deck Gun Action

Leaving the patrol area, on January 4, 1944, the *Puffer* headed south for the return passage through the Makassar Strait. Late in the evening of January 6 the *Puffer* neared the Lombok Strait and exchanged recognition signals with another submarine headed north, the

Crevalle. After the moon had set at 0316 on January 7, the *Puffer* proceeded at high speed on the surface through the Lombok Strait. By 0510 the passage was completed, and the *Puffer* remained on the surface, continuing toward Fremantle. Around noon the last action of the second patrol took place (*ibid.*). Selby described the contact with a sometimes dangerous small craft.

1205 Sighted ship bearing 287°T, distance about 7 miles. Turned away to put him astern while observing his actions through the periscope, decided he was a large fishing vessel or patrol boat and commenced closing to investigate. With the range closed to 4100 yards I could not see anything to identify him as definitely Japanese but could see that his superstructure aft was amply high to conceal a three inch gun or larger.

1326 Fired a shot across his bow as a signal for him to heave to. He turned away smoking heavily as he increased speed. We had been watching a thin vertical object in the water which appeared intermittently about four ship lengths to his left. It could have been a fishing stake, a periscope or the mast of a ship over the horizon but when the Quartermaster was positive he saw it raised and lowered twice in succession I decided to believe it was a periscope until proven otherwise. Rather than continue on into what could have been a very neat trap I decided to work to the northward of him so I could approach both him and the periscope (?) with a zero angle on the bow. After turning fired 15 rounds at 3500 yards range (one possible hit aft). While maneuvering for position, renewed badly fogged pointer's telescope with a spare and bore sighted gun using horizon and his masts as reference marks.

1433 After another false start finally exploded periscope bogey by running one down at full speed and determining to my own and the crew's satisfaction that there were 8 or 10 fishing stakes around.

1447 At a range of 3000 yards finally saw a Japanese flag painted on his side and opened fire again. He was tracking at eight knots.

1453 Had fired 29 rounds, hit him about 15 times, and was in to 900 yards when he hoisted a white rag from his forward boom. Ceased fire.

1457 White flag disappeared. Resumed fire, fired three rounds and the flag reappeared, Ceased fire.

1500 Commenced maneuvering to go alongside approaching from his port quarter. We had shot out his flag on the starboard side but could see another painted on his port side as we approached it when about 100 yards from him observed someone throwing papers over the side so fired a burst with the 20 MM over his masts as a warning. He had apparently been throwing them in when we were on his starboard side for there were many more papers floating around than we had seen him throw in.

Decided not to go alongside as he was pretty well shot up and on fire aft and his forward boom was swinging wildly from port to starboard as he rolled. Signaled to Jap standing with his hands raised to get into the water and collect papers. He collected a big handful and we pulled him aboard with a heaving line. We then tried to signal to two others on deck to get everyone off the ship. At the first wave two of them dove in and came swimming over. They were Javanese so we pulled them aboard, tied a heaving line around the youngest and most agile and sent him back in the water for more papers.

The youngest Javanese could understand a little English and indicated that there were 16 more men aboard of which two were Javanese, the rest Japs, and that none would get off the ship. The Javanese indicated the Jap we had as the captain and the Jap himself, although he professes not to understand English, bowed a couple of times at the word captain and pointed to himself.

1532 We had the Javanese out on the heaving line getting more papers and were still trying to get the rest of the crew to get off when our number one sound operator reported screws at 175° relative. He took a second check and was so positive of the contact that he was ready to get an r.p.m. count. We pulled in the Javanese as we got underway again at full speed. We had now been in the vicinity about four hours; the enemy submarine bogey was back with us, and we were only 100 miles from Lombok Strait, so I decided it was high time to sink him and get clear.

It took two more runs and 31 more rounds to sink the ship. Made both runs at high speed for our protection in view of the possible sub contact. Slowed on the first run long enough to drop our inflated rubber boat with canned provisions, a can opener and water. Figured the survivors would have sense enough to get off the ship and make for the raft. Apparently they did for we counted about eight in the water as we approached the second time.

1625 The ship sank. The young Javanese, one Abdul Hamid, identified it as the NANSING MARU, number 16, out of Surabaya. Resumed base course and speed. Placed all prisoners under guard although the two Javanese are apparently very happy to be aboard, Abdul professing a distinct dislike for the Japs and great friendship for the Americans and Dutch. The pharmacist's mate treated the older Javanese for several superficial wounds, one required a stitch, and the Jap for very minor abrasions. Unfortunately, the Jap has some ailments in his nether regions which appear to be a result of his own misconduct and not our action. He is being kept segregated as a probable venereal case [*ibid.*].

From the repeater compass in the forward torpedo room, the Japanese captain gestured he knew where the *Puffer* was headed (Deem). The compass was disconnected. Ray "Gunner" Kellum and "Pappy" Love guarded the Japanese captain with a large knife and a ready .45 pistol strapped to his side (Liggett). As an addition to these events, Leonard Funk, the tender of the washing machine, was given the duty of washing the clothes of the captured men. The rumor had been started that the Japanese commander had a horrible, exotic disease that could be contracted from his clothes. Or maybe it was just hatred for the Japanese, but Funk refused to wash the clothes. Funk was then in trouble with the officers for not following orders, but when he finally washed the clothes, he was temporarily shunned by the crew. Nobody wanted to catch the disease he supposedly carried (Funk).

Kutscherousky, a fitness fanatic, was impressed with the physical strength of one of the Javanese boys. He was able to lift a 20 pound sledge hammer with an extended arm ten times (Tidd). The Javanese boys were put to work, but missed their home cooking.

> The Java boys sure did a good job on the boat. Man, you never saw bright work so polished in all your life. Even the engine room decks were a sight to behold — they glistened. The only problem was food. We stopped a small boat in the Indian Ocean and "Big Dealed" some rice for our guests. Then they were contented [Liggett].

When the *Puffer* returned to Fremantle Admiral Christie and other staff members greeted the boat. Marines removed the prisoners. The Sub Command was anxious to hear the details of the damage inflicted upon the Japanese. McDonald and other crew members were moved by the band on the quay playing "Waltzing Matilda," the national song of Australia. McDonald had survived a war patrol and had performed his duty. He had earned his Silver Dolphins. A feeling of pride of duty filled the crew (McDonald). There were no heroes among them, but collectively they had done a heroic deed. And now they had two weeks liberty to recover from the stress of a war patrol and mentally prepare to do it all over again.

Selby received a Silver Star for the Second War Patrol. The citation stated, "Skillfully maneuvering his ship to avoid severe enemy countermeasures and to press home his attacks, he aggressively struck at hostile surface vessels, sinking a 1,368 ton destroyer and a trawler, and damaging four ships totaling 31,051 tons" (Selby, *Biography*).

8

The Third War Patrol

New Crew Members and Training

The crew changes after the Second War Patrol numbered 21. Dickinson, Guthrie, Kimbrell, Roberts, and Voss returned from relief crew work. 16 other men joined the crew of the *Puffer* for the first time. Roy Durward Waites (336 93 91— EM2c), who had been on the commissioning crew, was temporarily assigned to the *Puffer* from the relief crew, but did not make the war patrol (RG24).

Crew Transferred after the Second War Patrol

Name	Service #	Rate Arr.	Second WP	Third WP
Chambers, Wayne Marvin	321 28 74	MoMM2c	MoMM1c	TRAN
Czatynski, John	243 95 99	EM2c	7-Nov-43	TRAN
Deem, Jay Arden	668 43 38	RT2cV6	RT1c	TRAN
Dufault, Ernest John	200 51 88	CEM	CEM	TRAN
Fleming, William Phillip	671 60 14	S2cV6	7-Nov-43	TRAN
Goin, James Warren	393 26 12	FC2c	FC1c	TRAN
Golden, Lawrence Joseph	283 26 70	MoMM2c	MoMM1c	TRAN
Graves, William	393 30 81	QM2c	QM1c	TRAN
Hensley, John Howard	256 43 61	F2cV6	F2c	TRAN
Hetrick, William Herman	250 49 66	MoMM1c	MoMM1c	TRAN
Kellum, Raymond Herlong	268 17 81	GM2c	GM1c	TRAN
Kutscherousky, Mike Elliot	355 80 51	TM2c	TM1c	TRAN
Lankerd, Charles Eugene	372 50 72	F1c	7-Nov-43	TRAN
Lyons, Roy Damon	250 29 83	CTM(AA)	Hon Disc	TRAN
Perro, John Louis	207 26 05	MoMM2c	MoMM1c	TRAN
Pieper, Alfred Leroy	316 96 21	S2c	7-Nov-43	TRAN
Sears, Philip Clayton	602 06 87	TM3cV6	TM2c	TRAN
Stoltz, Frank Nicholas	385 10 84	CRM(AA)	Ext Enl	TRAN
Szysko, Michael	210 65 58	SC1c	SC1c	TRAN
Topor, Ladislaus	238 52 61	MoMM1c	CMoMM	TRAN
Trudeau, Norman	201 76 62	EM2c	EM2c	TRAN
Wilson, William Earl, Jr.	311 93 42	S2c	S1c	TRAN

New and Returning Crew Members

Name	Service #	Rate Arr.	Date Arr.
Bauersfeld, James Robert	608 86 03	EM3cV6	3-Feb-44
Camp, Gerald Maurice	410 67 41	SM1c	3-Feb-44
Corcoran, Frank Howard, Jr.	647 33 81	MoMM2cV6	3-Feb-44
Darrah, Charles Anthony	244 06 06	TM2c	31-Jan-44
Dickinson, Master James	636 47 51	F3cV6	25-Jan-44
Fallon, Merritt Dayton	228 11 89	CTM(PA)	3-Feb-44
Guthrie, John Wise	300 49 87	TM3c	3-Feb-44
Henry, Melvin "B"	624 77 40	S2cV6	25-Jan-44
Kimbrell, William Warner	551 80 61	S1c	25-Jan-44
Lemar, John Edward	607 49 76	F1cV6	3-Feb-44
Maloney, Herber Earl	650 44 47	S1cV6	3-Feb-44
Martinson, Kenneth Russell	665 12 72	RT2cV6	3-Feb-44
Mathis, Charles Howard, Jr.	268 19 31	CMoMM	3-Feb-44
Roberts, Raymond	646 13 01	RM3cV6	25-Jan-44
Robertson, Eugene Carlisle	381 29 43	EM1c	3-Feb-44
Sasso, Anthony Patrick	706 15 44	F2c	4-Feb-44
Schmidling, Charles Jentz	223 74 91	FC2c	4-Feb-44
Stoy, Glenn Earl	283 22 58	GM2c	3-Feb-44
Switzer, Donald Raymond	411 18 66	MoMM2cV6	3-Feb-44
Thatcher, Roy Orlando	329 27 16	S1c	3-Feb-44
Vogan, Merle Francis	648 06 41	F1cV6	25-Jan-44
Voss, Raymond Henry	372 22 92	EM3c	25-Jan-44

Two new officers joined the *Puffer*, Ensign Lawrence Picone and Lt. Frank Golay. Picone had recovered from an accident during training for the Naval Air Corps, re-enlisted for Officer Candidate School and upon completion volunteered for the Submarine Service. Picone initially served as commissary officer, the typical assignment for the most junior officer, and then as communications officer. He served as J.O.O.D. with Pugh, and credited Pugh with excellent training (Picone). Golay was another "90-day Wonder" who had been a math teacher in Kansas prior to the war. He had seen previous duty on surface ships before volunteering for submarines. Golay assisted Decker with engineering duties, a responsibility Golay grew to dislike (Golay, letters). Picone left after the sixth war patrol, but Golay stayed on the *Puffer* through the end of the war and beyond.

While repairs were made the officers and crew were given the usual two weeks leave. On January 26, the officers and crew returned from recreation. The day was spent stowing provisions, personal belongings, taking care of laundry and checking job orders. The next day was used for testing all the machinery and equipment on the boat, training new lookouts to clear the bridge, diving, and solving torpedo control problems utilizing the TDC on an adjacent ship. Selby wrote, "The details of these two days are mentioned only because it was felt that the extra day spent as above resulted in our getting a great deal more benefit from subsequent training operations than if we had commenced operations on the day immediately following our return to the ship" (WPR).

The day after returning from leave was not a good day to begin training, because many of the men were either hungover or had been up most of the night. Carl Dwyer said, "The first day out a Jap in a dingy with a pea shooter could have sunk us" (Dwyer). The second day was all business and the crew knew the expectations. The anti-submarine (A/S) training—

evasive maneuvers, silent running, and live depth charge experiences—prepared the new crew members for what to expect during counterattacks. The *Puffer* was in excellent mechanical condition. Selby wrote in the war patrol report about the training and excellent refit.

> January 28–February 2: Conducted independent exercises and training exercises. A deep dive was made during the independent exercises. Training exercises included day, surfaced and submerged, night approaches, surfaced and submerged, the firing of three exercise torpedoes, radar tracking, A/S training and a short range firing run with the three inch gun following a battle surface.
>
> The refit given this ship was excellent, it was clean and livable when we moved aboard, the

work was one hundred percent accomplished, and most important of all the great majority of the overhauled machinery operated satisfactorily. Our operating period was noticeably free of the multitude of minor repairs, adjustments, and completing of uncompleted work items which, in my previous three experiences, have invariably followed a refit. All credit is due to the officers and men of the refit crew and the submarine Repair Unit and appreciation is hereby expressed for a fine job carefully supervised [WPR].

On February 4 at 1300 the *Puffer* was again underway to conduct unrestricted submarine warfare against the enemy in the South China Sea. Later in the day A/S runs and day and night torpedo approaches were conducted with the destroyer USS *William B. Preston* (*ibid.*).

February 5 through 7 consisted of additional training dives and torpedo fire control exercises as the *Puffer* moved up the west coast of Australia to top off the fuel tanks at Exmouth Gulf, known as "Potshot" (*ibid.*). The nickname was taken from the code name of an abandoned plan to make Exmouth Gulf an advance base earlier in the war (Blair, p. 285). The next four days more training dives were conducted as the boat headed for the Lombok Strait (*ibid.*). James Liggett, known as the "Oil King" on this run, wrote of what appeared to be an act of sabotage or at best shoddy work. The situation later required some creative patrol adaptation on the part of Selby.

> I was elected as "Oil King" on this particular run, and brother what a mess! After taking aboard fuel and lube oil we took off on our patrol. We stopped at Pot Shot on the northwest coast to top off our fuel tanks, then proceeded on patrol. After about 1500 miles, we noticed our fuel consumption was too great. We put into a secluded area at night and checked the main stop valve to the receiving line. Sure as hell — under the seat of the valve there was a piece of soft lead. We were losing oil, going all this time and never realizing it. Man, what a blow! We knew there was sabotage going on, but like everyone else, we were sure it wouldn't happen to us. Another experience in life chalked up [Liggett].

Lombok and Makassar Straits

The *Puffer* arrived at the entrance to Lombok Strait early on the morning of February 10, and submerged for the remainder of the day. Traversing the strait was best done in the dark of night. At 0035 Selby wrote, "Clouds and rain squalls covered approach. Entered Lombok Strait as clouds and rain squalls cleared leaving us in the romantic beams of a full bright moon" (WPR).

The romance was short lived. Within two hours four small patrol boats were spotted at the northern end of the Lombok Strait at an estimated range of 4000 yards, about 2.25 miles. These vessels were not picked up on the SJ radar. Selby evaded on the surface by pulling away at flank speed. Within 30 minutes contact was lost with the patrol boats. At 0530 Selby submerged the *Puffer*, as he decided to run through the Makassar Strait mostly submerged during the daytime and on the surface at night to avoid detection (*ibid.*).

By February 14 the *Puffer* had reached the northern entrance to the Makassar Strait, very close to the same location as the First War Patrol ordeal. With a clear sky and bright moon, Selby ran the narrow sea lane submerged. Selby lingered in the strait for one day of submerged patrolling. Contact was made with a tanker and escort, but Selby was unable to close the range

Opposite: The Third War Patrol — February 4, 1944 (Fremantle), to April 4, 1944 (Fremantle) — 3,704 nautical miles in the patrol area. The primary area of patrol was in the South China Sea against the Japanese vessels traveling the Manila to Singapore sea lane. The lone sun flag indicates an attack on a merchant vessel (map artwork by Nancy Webber).

to less than 10,700 yards. Harassed by aircraft he gave up the chase. Selby headed the *Puffer* northward through the Sibutu Passage and around the northeast corner of Borneo, then west toward the cities of Miri and Kuching. Oil was refined at Miri. Kuching was the largest city on the north side of Borneo. Both cities were focal points for Japanese troop and cargo ships going to and from Singapore. No contacts were made for the next four days (*ibid.*).

Invasion Scare

On February 19 the boat entered the assigned patrol area near Singapore. While patrolling northeast of Singapore in the early evening darkness of February 20 the *Puffer* made contact with a large convoy. Submarine Command likely directed Selby to the location because of intelligence gained from an Ultra message. The American submarine *Permit* (SS 178) had reported the task group leaving Truk. Selby described the high speed events.

> 1955 Radar contact at 9800 yards bearing 003°T followed by three more contacts on approximately the same bearing. Commenced tracking on four main engines at seventeen knots.
>
> Convoy was zigging from about 220°T to 270°T making good a base course of about 250°T to take them between Soebi Besar and Great Natuna Islands. Three of the first four ships sighted were very large, their superstructure having the triangular appearance of battleships or cruisers. The fourth was considerably smaller and appeared to be a destroyer escort. The night was too dark and the horizon too hazy to make out any definite type characteristics on the large ships but the overall silhouettes were those of men-of-war and not freighters, tankers, or transports. Also, I am convinced that none of the three were aircraft carriers as they did not show the long, straight, horizontal line of a flight deck that shows up on carriers at night. The final speed of eighteen and a half knots at which we tracked them tends to verify the visual identification of men-of-war.
>
> In the very early stages before I realized they were making high speed I hoped to get ahead at seventeen knots, maintain position, and get in at least a partial battery charge prior to attacking. As a matter of fact we actually gained eight degrees in true bearing up until 2200, due to their zig zagging. At that time with the convoy on our starboard beam at 13,000 yards they steadied on course 225°T and we commenced to lose true bearing. Went to full power, only 18.3 knots by pit log as fairly heavy swells were slowing us.
>
> In the meantime at 2132 radar picked up six more small ships in the formation. The disposition as plotted by radar ranges and bearings on a mooring board showed the three large ships in column, distance 1000 yards, a roving screen ahead, one 2000 yards on the port beam of the second ship, one each on the port and starboard quarter of the third ship and three about 2000 yards astern sometimes in column and sometimes in open order. It is possible that there may have been one or two screens on the starboard side that radar did not pick up.
>
> 2535 Went to battle stations and made all tubes ready. It was evident that we could not gain by further chase as we were losing true bearing so decided to attempt to close the last three screens at full power.
>
> *Monday, 21 February*
> 0010 Commenced closing.
> 0025 With minimum range 7,200 yards, angle on the bow 145° port and range commencing to open out broke off the attack. Decided not to send contact report yet as I expected other traffic in this vicinity and desired to remain undetected for a few more days.
> 0045 lost radar contact on last large ship at 25,000 yards [*ibid.*].

The ten ship convoy contained the battleship *Nagato* and a collection of nine other men-of-war. Built in 1920, the *Nagato* was the first battleship in the world equipped with 16-inch guns. On February 1, 1944, the Japanese began the evacuation of Truk Island. The battleship

Nagato departed Truk for Palau with a task group which included the battleship *Fuso*; cruisers *Suzuya*, *Kumano* and *Tone*; and destroyers *Isokaze*, *Tanikaze*, *Hamakaze*, *Urakaze* and *Akizuki*. The logs of the *Nagato* reported that their lookouts sighted an enemy sub at 04-16N, 108-40E, which was probably the *Puffer* (Hackett).

Glenn Stoy, a new gunner's mate who had seen duty on the American battleship *Mississippi*, recorded the events in his diary.

> Cruising off the N.W. coast of Borneo waiting for a convoy reported in this area, submerged at 0620, surfaced at 1950, sighted three ship convoy which we ran abeam of in an attempt to head them off, but they were too fast and so we lost them; it was here we stumbled into a huge Jap task force though we were unable to make an attack due to their speed; we sent word to Radio Perth of its presence in these waters which caused quite a stir, as it was thought this force was on its way to attack the Australian mainland, but it ended up in Singapore we learned [Stoy].

The radio message concerning the convoy was not sent until February 23 (WPR), so the three days delay no doubt made the Australians concerned about the current location of the task force. It was a rare opportunity for Selby, but in order for a submarine to sink a battleship, the paths of the submarine and battleship must converge, and then a lot of luck was necessary. At 20 knots top speed on the surface, a submarine was not capable of running down a 30 knot battleship, even while it zigzagged.

A Second Chance

The remainder of February 21 was uneventful as the *Puffer* continued to patrol along the Singapore-Manila traffic lane. The next day while patrolling on the station at 0710 masts and smoke were sighted by the lookouts, with an estimated range of 15 miles. The east bound convoy was moving at about seven knots, well within the speed capabilities of the *Puffer*. However, this part of the South China Sea was very shallow — a dangerous area to attack with limited escape possibilities. In the process of tracking the initial convoy, the *Puffer* made contact with another west bound ship of much greater interest (WPR).

Japanese ship movement records indicated a convoy of eight vessels and one escort, the destroyer *Kuretake*, left Manila on February 16 and arrived safely at Miri (northern Borneo) at 0700 on February 21. However, prior to the convoy's arrival at Miri, the *Teiko Maru* and the 3,887 ton tanker *Kikusui Maru* left the convoy at 0400 and headed directly for Singapore without escort (Somerville, 1987). The speed of the *Teiko Maru* was limited to that of the slower tanker — about 8 knots. The decision by the Japanese commanders to make the unescorted run to Singapore proved fatal. The Japanese may have assumed American subs would not operate in such shallow water. Selby described the contact with the initial convoy of medium and small freighters, and subsequent contact eight hours later with the larger transport *Teiko Maru*. As luck would have it, his choice to pursue the convoy around the northern coast of Soebi Besar island led to the *Teiko Maru*.

> 0720 (*SHIP CONTACT #5*) Sighted top of bridge, stack and mast of a small destroyer escort.
> I now have two choices: (1) Commence an end around immediately with a view to attacking in twenty-two fathoms (132 feet) of water at the entrance to Koti Passage; or (2) commence a run at high speed back around the northern tip of Soebi Besar and thence south to pick them up in daylight as they came out of the eastern entrance to whichever passage they used. If I chose the first plan and their course took them through Sarasan Passage instead of Koti, I wouldn't be able to get in for an attack without accepting twenty fathom water containing numerous shoals and small islands even if I could get ahead in time. I chose the latter plan as

I could make it around to the other side of the passage with three hours of daylight remaining where the water was from thirty to thirty-seven fathoms deep and clear of navigational hazards.

0735 Started around islands at 17 knots, tracking convoy as we left it. On the closest look I had the ships all appeared to be medium or small freighters, single mast forward and aft with stack amidships.

After 8 hours of running on the surface at...

1545 Picked up smoke of our convoy in direction of eastern entrance to Koti Passage. Slowed to ten knots to commence tracking. Was taking a series of bearings on the islands for a fix when at...

1554 (SHIP CONTACT #6) The high lookout reported two ships bearing 320° relative. Swung the periscope to that bearing and saw two stacks, masts and superstructure of a camouflaged transport with what looked like a yacht trailing astern. Target angle on the bow 20° port.

1556 Submerged, hoping we hadn't been sighted and commenced approach. Target was zigzagging at intervals of six minutes and less giving us alternately port and starboard angles on the bow, so that practically the whole approach was conducted at full speed except for periscope observations. Planned to fire four at transport and two at escort from bow tubes but target made big zig across our stern in final stages of approach.

1702 Got final set up for a stern tube shot, following the zig away. Target course 320° T, speed ten, angle on the bow 102° port, torpedo track 110° port, range 2575 yards, torpedo run 2800 yards. Target's course and speed was checking so well on the TDC that I decided to fire two at the transport using a twelve foot depth setting and two at the escort with a six foot depth setting using periscope offset for spread.

1704-21 Fired #7 at transport.

1704-30 Fired #8 at transport.

1704-35 Got set up on escort.

1704-52 Fired #9 at escort.

1705 Fired #10 at escort and commenced swinging left at high speed to bring bow tubes to bear [WPR].

The *Teiko Maru* spotted a periscope at ninety degrees to port, then two torpedo tracks were discovered. The maru immediately began to turn. One torpedo was avoided but at 1807 (1707 *Puffer* time) the other torpedo struck the No. 2 tank on the port side. Flooding immediately occurred and the injured vessel took a twenty-five degree list. Consequently abandon ship was ordered (Somerville, 1987).

Selby's description of the sinking continued.

1706-16 Heard explosion and looked. Hit the transport halfway between bow and forward stack which threw a column of smoke and debris about two hundred feet in the air. Both ships still holding their course. Hauled down periscope immediately to avoid being sighted at high speed. Continued to swing.

1706-28 Second explosion. Very dull sounding and much quieter than first.

1707-11 Noises like sharp crack of gun fire or torpedoes hitting ship without 1708-46 exploding heard by sound operators and some personnel in conning 1711-46 tower.

Presume it was gunfire since the times do not check with the times of firing the last two torpedoes. The noise at 1707-11 could have been #10 hitting the escort without exploding (a dud). No gunfire was observed.

Second hit on transport was not observed but I feel quite positive that the second torpedo hit her in the stern as she was almost dead in the water on next look, had 10° list to port and was swinging to the left apparently with no steering control, the escort had reversed course and was showing his stern to us. Took several quick ranges to be sure the transport was not opening the range and then commenced closing her.

8. The Third War Patrol

As we approached I could see some lifeboats already in the water, more being lowered and all sorts of gear being thrown over the side. As the ship continued to swing slowly to left showing us a 150° port angle on the bow, I could also see a cargo net or series of cargo nets strung along the port side extending down to the water, I could not tell from this range and angle whether they were being used to abandon ship or not but presumed they were. Continued closing and, since the escort was still headed away, commenced taking pictures.

1720 It began to look as if the ship was not going to sink from the damage already sustained and also I thought I saw one of the propellers commencing to thrash the water so prepared to fire two more. Target had now swung to give a 120° port angle on the bow [WPR].

At 1825 (1725 *Puffer* time) the Japanese records reported that "two more torpedoes rushed in from aft, they both smashed into No. 5 tank, again on the port side. *Teiko Maru*'s speed fell away" (Somerville, 1987).

1724 Fired #1 tube.
  1724-07 Fired #2 tube.
  1725-30 #1 hit about a quarter length in from the bow.
  1725-37 #2 hit about a quarter length in from the stern. Ship began to sink slowly by the stern and at the same time to roll over on her port side. Obtained a series of about twenty-five still pictures including the last two hits and her final death struggles up until the time she sank with a big explosion aft at 1735.

I have been unable to identify this ship from any of the data we have aboard on two stack Japanese or Allied ships. I noticed, too late to be able to get close enough to read it before she sank, that she had her name in big block letters on the port bow, while I could not read them I counted nine or ten letters. I could only see the one word-there being no sign of the usual "MARU" after it. I am inclined to believe it was one of the American, French, Dutch or Italian ships taken over by the Japanese at the beginning of the war. Other characteristics besides her two stacks and two masts were four sets of kingposts from her forward mast to the beginning of her superstructure, one set at her after mast, a big number painted on her after stack and zigzag camouflage in a vertical plane. Her length of 520 to 530 feet was determined by measuring the angle subtended between her bow and stern (4°) immediately after the fourth torpedo was fired at her. Range of 2250 yards determined by torpedo run and angle on the bow was about 120° port although 93° port was used on the TDC. My estimate of the tonnage is that she was 10,000 tons minimum. A length versus tonnage comparison with the ASAMA MARU class gives her 15,000 tons, She was well loaded for she was riding low in the water when we first fired at her. I believe the pictures taken will provide the means of positive identification.

The escort was painted white, had a single stack aft and gray zigzag camouflaging in a vertical plane. He looked like either a big yacht or a very small freighter. Estimated tonnage 800–1000 tons. During the whole attack he made no effort to depth charge us but worked his way around to the far side of the transport and about three or four miles distant. Believe he is in two of the pictures.

All men in the life boats were in white but whether this was their underwear or some sort of a fatigue uniform I couldn't make out. There were about nine or ten life boats in the water, two of which had only one man each in them. None of the boats seemed particularly crowded. [Japanese records reported the survivors were later rescued by small naval craft and arrived safely at Singapore on February 24 and 25.]

I decided not to make any further attempt to close the escort [actually a tanker] and attack him with torpedoes primarily because I felt sure that the two fired at him set at six feet had passed under him. Nor did I feel that he was worth risking our ship by attacking him with a three inch gun on the surface in sight of land. I pulled away submerged on the assumption that (1) the pictures and information I had should be sufficient for identification, (2) that our convoy would be warned if we headed in their direction on the surface, and (3) that A/S measures in the form of a plane or destroyer should be forthcoming shortly from the beach.

On pages 106–109: The sinking of the ***Teiko Maru.*** At the time the vessel was the third largest merchant ship sunk by American submarines (photographs courtesy of the Golay family).

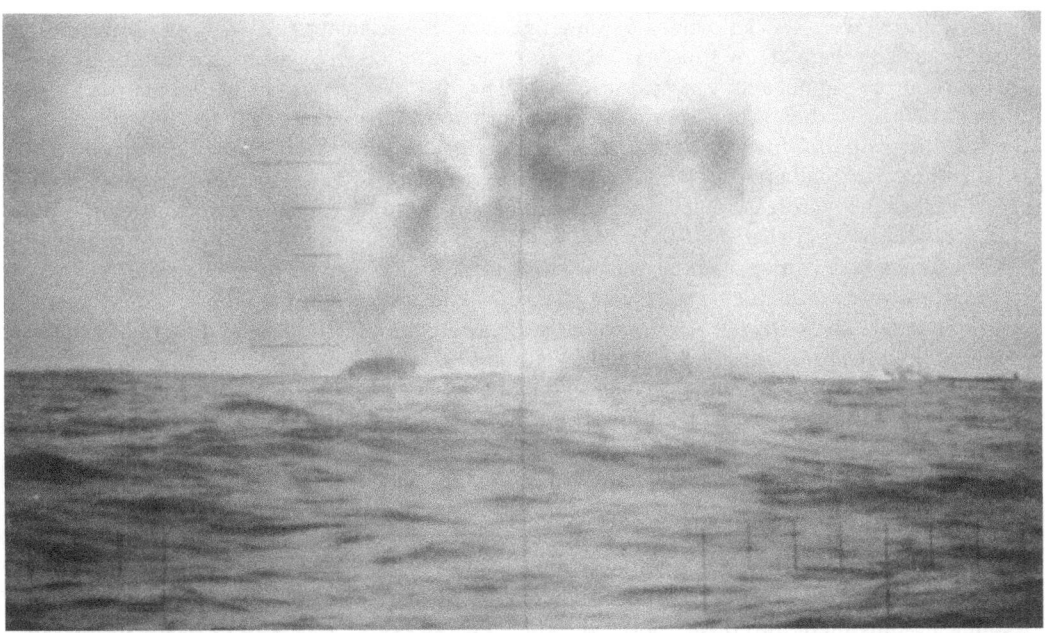

1847 (*SHIP CONTACT #7*) Sighted a WAKATAKE class destroyer [probably the escort *Kuretake* arrived from Miri] with a twenty degree starboard angle on the bow headed across our stern, range about 5000 yards. Went to battle stations while watching to see if he was going to close us.

1901 Destroyer commenced echo ranging. Maneuvered to keep him astern as it gradually began to get dark.

2020 He seemed to be getting closer with his pinging but it was nearly dark so surfaced and pulled clear on battery for about ten minutes before starting the engines. No contact by SJ Radar at forty feet or on the surface so he must have been a good six miles away. Took course to close estimated track of convoy.

2114 SJ Radar contacted our convoy at 15,000 yards. Commenced tracking and working for position ahead while charging batteries. Convoy was apparently on the alert for they were zigzagging radically on base course about 095°T, speed nine knots. In addition, whether purposely or accidentally they were remaining in a dense black rain cloud and managed to stay in it the rest of the night. In comparison our background without any moon looked like broad daylight. The escort, which I assumed to be the same small destroyer that we had sighted with them in the morning was all over the place, ahead, astern, on the bow, on the beam, and at one time, during the latter stages, was about 8,000 yards out on the port quarter.

Wednesday, 23 February

0005 With the battery charge completed and having gained a position 12,000 yards on their port bow, angle on the bow fifteen degrees port, was ready to attack. Our good luck of the previous day seemed to desert us with the beginning of a new day for from here on frustration reigned supreme. To make a long story short I started in on attacks three times and completed none of them.

On the first I swung left to come in at full speed with a larger angle on the bow. Half way around radar contacted two small boats 340° Relative at 3100 yards with the range closing rapidly. Swung right slowly in an attempt to circle around them and still come in on the convoy. Net results was that I had lost so much bearing by the time I got clear of them that I had to work up ahead again.

On the next attempt, the same two boats were contacted by radar again at 2700 yards. Tried circling outside them again but seeing that this wasn't going to work tried to circle inside them toward the convoy. Was enjoying a fair amount of success in losing them this way (maximum radar range on them at any time was 5200 yards) when the convoy which now seemed to be on a base course of about 120°T, zigged toward us. Decided to take this opportunity to work across to their starboard bow, completely lose our two small contacts and take advantage of the better background. That was unsuccessful because they began to work to the right again coming around eventually to 130°T.

To make the picture complete I should add here that in order for them to clear Point Sirik on Sarawak, Borneo, (Lat. 2-45N, Long.111-20E) and continue on to Miri, they would have to make good a base course of about 080°T. The southwesterly heading they were now working around to was heading them into the bay between Point Datoe and Point Sirik and into pretty shallow water. The water we were running in was from 25 to 50 fathoms and they were beginning to head for soundings of 13, 16 and 19 fathoms.

The third and final attempt was made without the two small radar contacts which had been heckling us. We were heading in at full speed, all tubes ready, range 7800 yards, angle on the bow estimated at 45° port, when a steady white light was shown on our starboard beam. Had the radar train on that bearing and got a range of 5300 yards closing rapidly. It was, judging by the size of the radar pip, our escort whom we had temporarily lost. Swung left to put him astern. The quartermaster on high lookout saw another ship send some blinker and another one show a steady white light. Whether it was a signal for a routine course change or a change due to our being sighted I don't know but at any rate they came to course 150°T and held it, this course heading them into the harbor at the port of Sarawak. A check with the chart showed that we would have to use up practically all of the remaining darkness and get into fifteen fathom water to attempt another attack. Our presence in the vicinity was known from the sinking, the convoy was alert and either suspected or knew we were chasing them, I wanted to get into minimum thirty fathom water prior to daylight and their calling out of the dogs, so at...

0528 Secured from battle stations and a disappointing and anti-climactic chase after our sinking of the previous afternoon which had put all hands in high spirits. The past twenty-four hours operations had cost us 5005 gallons of fuel.

0641 Submerged after clearing the area forty miles to northward.

1943 Surfaced and set course for a point 150 miles northwest of Great Natuna Island on the Singapore-Manila-Empire traffic route. Since our presence in the area was known decided to send message concerning the men-of-war sighted on the night of the twentieth and morning of the twenty-first, the sinking of the transport on the twenty-second and the approximate location of the convoy in the USS BLUEFISH area [WPR].

Postwar analysis gave the *Puffer* credit for sinking the *Teiko Maru*, a 15,105 ton troop transport (Alden, *Successes,* p. D-118). As Selby guessed the ship was a captured French liner, the *D'Artagnan*. At this time in the war the merchant ship was the third largest sunk by a submarine (Blair, p. 615). The *Teiko Maru* was carrying 906 passengers. Japanese records reported 201 casualties and 800 tons of cargo went to the bottom. Survivors were later rescued on February 24 and 25 and taken to Singapore (Somerville, 1987).

Jay Deem was given a peek through the periscope and noticed the white uniforms of the passengers. He and other crew members speculated that the Japanese troops on board were headed to Singapore for shore leave (Deem). Sound man Jack Lane wrote, "I had the pleasure of listening to her go down on the QB sonar gear and could hear water rushing into the various compartments as she sank" (Lane).

A Dangerous Destroyer

On February 24 Selby took the *Puffer* back north, toward Great Natuna Island, where the patrol had taken them a few days earlier. By now Japanese anti-submarine activity in that vicinity should have cooled off. For the next two days patrolling continued in the same area—most of the daylight hours were spent submerged and on the surface at night. While patrolling on the surface, on February 26 another convoy surprised Selby and the *Puffer* crew (WPR).

1048 (*SHIP CONTACT #8*) A five ship convoy with one destroyer escort popped out of a low lying haze which had been present all morning. Range about six or seven miles. They consisted of one transport, which from that distance looked to be larger than the one sunk on the twenty-second, at least two tankers and two other ships which were either freighters or tankers. They came on us very suddenly and unexpectedly in spite of the fact that a watch was being kept with #1 Periscope for five minutes out of every fifteen. Some idea of the suddenness with which they appeared can be gathered from the fact that the officer on the periscope had just completed one sweep of the horizon and picked them up on his second round. Their hulls were plainly visible from the bridge and were picked up by the lookouts about the same time they were seen through the periscope.

I knew that it was very probable that we had been sighted also. If we hadn't been, it was safe to open the range to track. If we had been and they weren't sure what we were I knew it would be a dead give away to dive, so I elected to open out at high speed. As we started opening out they first reversed course and then, a few minutes later, turned to starboard presenting a 90° starboard angle on the bow on a southerly heading. I couldn't be sure that their actions were evasive, but if not it was a most peculiar zigzag plan. There was no question but what they had been all set to proceed between Great Natuna and Soebi Besar Islands for they were right on the edge of the entrance.

1120 I could just barely see them and was positive they couldn't see us now, so submerged. Commenced closing on their last true bearing of 094° hoping that we were undetected and that they would continue on through.

1145 (*SHIP CONTACT #9*) Sighted a destroyer headed at us with a zero angle on the bow, estimated range 10,000 yards. Turned right to open the distance to the track and went to battle stations.

1147 He was still headed directly at us. Made ready all tubes, depth setting six feet. Would have felt a bit more confident about being able to hit him with some magnetic torpedoes.

1155 Picked up his pinging on sound gear. As he approached I could not determine what class he was but afterward by checking ONI 14 decided from his single stack and broken deck forward of the bridge that he was a mine layer. There does not seem to be a picture of his exact type in the identification pamphlets. He gradually swung left as he closed and we slowly swung left at one-third speed to keep set up for a stern tube shot. His echo ranging seemed to be directly on us. Only twice did he sweep around. I was determined to let him have all four tubes aft if he got within range or started in for an attack for there was the possibility that he might have a deep enough draft to be hit by a torpedo set at six feet, whereas otherwise he might have a free afternoon of depth charging. However at...

1311 He steadied on course 225° T and at...

1315 He secured echo ranging. His echo ranging didn't fade out. It just plain stopped.

The whole exhibition smelled very suspiciously as if he knew exactly where we were and very calmly proceeded to keep us down while keeping out of torpedo range. The closest he got to us was 4600 yards.

Having last seen the convoy on a southerly heading I began to suspect that he had swung through this passage to keep us down while they went through Koti Passage to the south. On that assumption I headed south so that if they should still try to come through here I ought to see them and at the same time heading for a spot from which we could make a run to their 2100 E.P. [estimated position].

1800 Surfaced in order to be able to arrive at their estimated 2100 position south of Soebi Besar Island and through Koti Passage.

2100 Arrived at their 2100 position and patrolled the rest of the night without contact. In reconstructing the above events, I believe that they sighted us about the same time we sighted them. Then either recognizing us as a submarine or suspecting that we might be one, they headed for the coast of Borneo where they either took refuge or went through the eight to ten fathom Api Passage hugging the coast [*ibid.*].

No Contacts and Return to Fremantle

Selby had used a large quantity of fuel in the unsuccessful chase. On February 27 Selby devised a plan to conserve fuel. He moved slowly northward to a spot about 100 miles northeast of North Natuna Island and did a minimum of movement at minimal speed. He hoped the Japanese ships would come to him. For the next 17 days the *Puffer* hung around with no contacts, except for other American submarines, *Ray*, *Raton*, and *Bluefish*. As a result of the fuel conservation, coupled with the fact that the moon was on the wane, Selby requested and was given a five day extension to the patrol. He investigated the Singapore-Saigon traffic along the shallow water off the east coast of the Malay Peninsula, near Pulau Tenggol (then known as Pulo Tenggol Island). There were no contacts except with Japanese aircraft, which precipitated two crash dives on March 23 (*ibid.*).

After nearly a month of inactivity on March 24 the long journey back to Fremantle began. The path took the *Puffer* through the Karimata Strait, on the west coast of Borneo, then into the Java and Bali Seas setting up the transit of the Lombok Strait on March 26. The usual Japanese patrol boats were in the vicinity to harass the often used passage. The passage of the Lombok Strait took four hours and some excitement ensued (*ibid.*). Selby wrote of the two nervous passages.

Friday, 24 March
0620 Submerged 60 miles from entrance to Karimata Strait.
1937 Surfaced and commenced transit of Karimata Strait.

Saturday, 25 March
0555 Submerged in 16 fathoms of water.
0603 Sighted black object through periscope and went to battle stations. It was still too dark to make out what the object was.
0645 Finally made out sails of what appeared to be a typical Chinese junk. This boat was on a southerly course as we were, but practically becalmed. It remained in sight the rest of the day, its bearing drawing forward and aft alternately as it got an occasional breeze. We closed to about 5000 yards range to get a better look at it and take some pictures. In my estimation the junk was not worth sinking. If Japanese, it did not have the customary flag painted on it; if native and being used by the Japanese, it was too old, dilapidated and slow to conceivably improve the Japanese shipping situation.
1914 Surfaced 50 miles east of Discovery East Bank and set course to commence passage through Java Sea.

Sunday, 26 March
0605 Submerged 60 miles northwest of Bawean Island.
1905 Surfaced and set course to pass 10 miles south of Great Masalembo Island.

Monday, 27 March
0555 Submerged 15 miles southwest of Great Masalembo Island. Sighted numerous small sailing sampans during day.
1902 Surfaced and set course to pass north of Kangean Islands.

Tuesday, 28 March
0557 Submerged 15 miles east of Sekala Island.
1941 Surfaced and set course for Lombok Strait.

2257 Land contact by SJ Radar on small island off northwest side of Lombok Island. Commenced passage through strait.

2310 (*SHIP CONTACT #11*) Sighted small ship followed by SJ Radar contact on it at 2500 yards. Maneuvered around it at high speed.

This was the first of six patrol vessels encountered during the passage. Visibility was to our advantage as there was no moon, a varying amount of surface haze, and the land background of Bali and Lombok to make use of in evading. All contacts were encountered from the northern entrance to the middle of the strait and tracked on courses from 060°T to 090°T at about 9 knots. The first four we saw in addition to contacting them by radar. The fifth and sixth we did not see. The sixth was apparently the largest as we could track it out to 7000 yards, whereas the other five were all lost on radar at about 4000 yards. I do not believe that any of these vessels sighted us as none of them tracked in such a manner as to indicate they were chasing us. Also, in each case we were able to keep a dark background behind us.

It took us four hours to complete what is normally a two hour passage at our speed of 18 knots — not surprising since our track shows us spending almost as much time on easterly, westerly and northerly courses as on our base course of 200°T. The crowning blow was a half hour spent in evading three tide rips in formation as we approached the southern exit. When first picked up by radar at 1200 yards dead ahead we also spotted them from the bridge. They were dead ringers for three PT boats kicking up high bow waves. After turning away from these gruesome phantoms three times with tubes #9 and #10 ready to fire to scare them off our track, and having once cleared the bridge to dive, finally decided to head at them and pass them at full speed. We got through all right. Due allowance must be made for the fact that we [editorial we] were a bit "contact happy" after our previous six bona fide contacts [*ibid.*].

Selby received a Letter of Commendation for the Third War Patrol. The citation stated:

With great daring and consummate skill [he] launched a series of brilliantly executed torpedo attacks which resulted in the sinking of a 15,105 ton enemy transport. The aggressiveness and determination displayed by [him] in sinking this valuable enemy ship are outstanding and worthy of much praise [Selby.].

After the Third War Patrol, Executive Officer Hess left the *Puffer* for assignment as commanding officer of the *Angler*. During the Second War Patrol Hess had taken McDonald through the boat when he was ready to qualify for his Silver Dolphins. He recalled Hess as a very nice man and officer. At times his demeanor and soft voice reminded him of a church's pastor (McDonald). Hess loved to play cribbage. As a gesture of respect and fondness for Hess, upon his departure the *Puffer* crew made a cribbage board for him. Note the gold and silver .22 caliber shells for pegs. John Gutensohn was Hess's best competition and was awarded a fifth of whiskey for his skill by Hess (Deem). Hess's son, Dan, still uses the board.

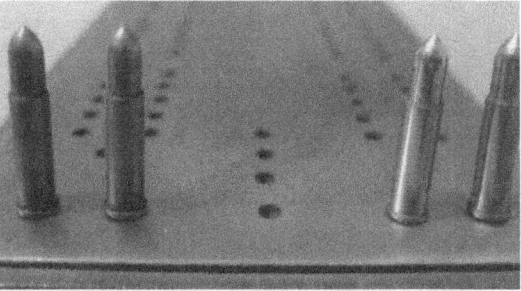

Cribbage board given to Lt. Commander Hess by the officers and crew (photographs courtesy of Dan Hess).

9

R & R at Perth and Fremantle

Companionship and Craziness

The Perth-Fremantle area was affected by the influx of the American submarine sailors. The Australian social environment was much more unrestrained than most cities in the United States. Prostitution was legal, the beer was much stronger than American beer (Barker, p. 195), and the wartime mentality gave a wide berth to the actions of American servicemen.

Calvin Hamilton, Sam Smith, and Donald McDonald (left to right) during rest and recuperation (author's collection).

The etching *Shore Leave* by Paul Cadmus (1904–1999) pictured sailors on leave in New York City. Even though not in Australia, the artwork captured the wild mentality of sailors on liberty (image courtesy of Carleton College, Northfield, Minnesota).

Many of the Americans took advantage of the wide open laws and the open arms of the Australian women. It was not unusual for Australian women to have two or three American boyfriends, timed so that only one was in port while the others were at sea (*ibid.*, p. 155). Wartime stress, uncertainty of survival, and the hormones of young men lead to sexual relationships and unwanted pregnancies. Some marriages took place, although it was highly discouraged (*ibid.*, p. 171).

At the other extreme some submariners left the big city for quieter surroundings in smaller towns south of Perth. McDonald and Jack Lane headed south to the small towns of Pinjarra and the beach town of Bunbury (McDonald; Lane). Some men sought out Australian women for friendship only. Many were welcomed as sons by their parents and treated to dinners and hospitality (Barker, p. 83). Somewhere in the middle of the celebration spectrum, other men ended up drinking too much and doing humorous, yet harmless acts. Jay Deem enjoyed riding a rented horse along the beach; however on one occasion he rode a horse into a bar after a too many beers. Other sailors "carrying a little too much left rudder" attempted to return to the boat over the mooring lines, with wet results. One dairy minded sailor bought a cow and tried to bring it back onto the boat (Deem).

Sam "Certifiable" Smith was a fun loving guy. At the King Edward Hotel one of his fellow shipmates convinced the manager of the lounge that Sam was an excellent singer and before he enlisted had performed at the Palmer House in Chicago. Sam was coaxed to the stage in an inebriated state and belted out a few bars of "Pistol Packin' Mama" before he was given the hook. As with this incident, most of the antics of the sailors were relatively harmless (McDonald).

Some of the crew members went panning for gold or on kangaroo hunts. Robert Polk recalled going with Jack Lane, Harris Steinke, and John Perro on a 'roo hunt after the Fourth War Patrol. They hired a taxi to take them into the country near Bunbury. Due to the shortage of gasoline, the taxi was powered by charcoal. The first target was an Australian rabbit. The rabbit didn't have a chance from the 30 rounds from Steinke's Browning Automatic Rifle. Through the peep sights of the carbines the 'roos, bounding from side-to-side, proved more difficult targets. After the Americans expended dozens of rounds, the Australian guide said, "Oh Yanks, what a waste of ammunition." He gave a shrill whistle, the 'roo froze, he dropped the animal with a single shot, and saved the scarce shell brass for another reload. For the price of the hide he delivered the meat to the hotel, and the men had more 'roo steaks than they wanted to eat (Polk).

The Extreme

A less than harmless incident involved a *Puffer* sailor. The episode was reported in the Perth yellow press, *The Mirror*, a newspaper prone to exaggeration. As reported by *The Mirror* some of the daughters of the city leaders were involved in a wild party. A wild scene was described.

> In Mount Street, Perth, that's [where] the war's most notorious sexual escapade took place. Whether invented or merely reported by the local scandal sheet, the *Mirror*, the story of women's breasts dangled in champagne, and a nipple bitten off by an American, was quickly and widely believed, not only throughout the metropolitan area but, within twenty-four hours, in both Geraldton and Albany, thanks to the miracles of the "bush telegraph." According to Syd Harvey, the women who partied with such intensity were not prostitutes, any more than were those the Yanks brought to his club, but the "pick of the town." This was an assessment broadly in line with memories of more sedate women, who watched, with a mixture of disapproval and envy, the sensuous dancing of young girls of "good family" in the tight confines and loose atmosphere of American-dominated cabarets and ballrooms [Barker, pp. 157–8].

Deem recalled a radio message sent to the *Puffer* while on patrol in the war zone. From time to time he was allowed to decode messages, a task usually done by officers. Deem found the contents of a message that contained an unusual request from a high government official in Perth. Deem indicated that such a message on behalf of a civilian was highly unusual and the official involved must have been very influential. Although Deem did not recall the name of the *Puffer* sailor, the radio message demanded the return of the crew member to Perth to answer for the incident described in *The Mirror*. Deem's recollection indicated the events in the newspaper were not totally invented and probably had some basis in fact. On a more personal note, Deem had the tragic circumstance of decoding the message from the Red Cross that notified him of his father's death in Illinois (Deem).

The Tragic

Two weeks were adequate time for rest and recreation, and during that respite most of the crew members kept out of serious trouble. However, transfer to a relief crew meant a longer stay in the city, as long as two months or more. Two men that left the *Puffer* for the relief crews after the Third War Patrol were involved in tragic situations. The two men were William Penzenik and John Pruitt. John Pruitt (StM2c) was transferred to the tender *Orion* on April 19, 1944, and Submarine Division 161 for duty. On May 9, 1944, he caught a cab to Roe Street in Perth for liberty with a number of fellow sailors about 3:00 P.M. Unfortunately Pruitt was involved in an altercation that would end his naval career. They arrived at the King Edward Hotel and during the next few hours drank heavily at various bars. During the binge Pruitt met another steward named Goode, and they entered a nearby alley to share a bottle of gin (Pruitt, Court Martial Document No. 128932).

The recollection of events after this time differed. Pruitt claimed he left Goode in the alleyway and went to find something to mix with the gin. When he returned he found Goode, who appeared to have been in a fight during his absence. In the scuffle Goode had lost his hat and wanted to retrieve it. So the two of them, with several other steward mates trailing behind, went down the alley again. Goode proceeded to get in a fight over the hat with an old man. Pruitt claimed that with the help of the others he pulled Goode off the old man, who was bleeding from a knife wound. All of the men left the area to avoid detection by the Shore Patrol and returned to their respective tenders (*ibid.*).

During the court-martial the judge advocate painted a different picture of the events. He contended that Pruitt was the only man in the alley and that he also verbally abused another sailor, Robert Wells, and his girlfriend, Lavinia Mestichelli. Wells and Mestichelli were going to the movies. It was alleged by the judge advocate that Pruitt was the aggressor, knocked down Wells, and was about to strike him with an axe when she stopped him. At this point Pruitt fled, but returned a few minutes later, assaulted the old man, Angelo Mestichelli, the young lady's father, stabbing him several times as they fought in the alley (*ibid.*).

The prosecution presented seventeen witnesses to strengthen the case against Pruitt. Pruitt was aided by only two witnesses: Franklin Hess, the executive officer on the *Puffer*, as a character witness; and Eddie Gordelle, a steward from the *Raton*, who supported the innocence of Pruitt. The court was unconcerned that Ulysses Reed, another sailor who might have strengthened Pruitt's claims, could not be produced. Reed was on a war patrol and was unavailable. No effort was made to find Goode, the man Pruitt identified as the assailant. The judge advocate dismissed Goode as a fabrication by Pruitt (*ibid.*). Claude Goode existed and was a steward on the *Gar* before he was transferred to the tender *Pelias* (Knoblock, p.111). Goode was a friend of Pruitt and Pruitt would not put the finger on his friend as the assailant. Pruitt reasoned if he himself was innocent, then he could not be convicted. However, such was not the case.

By current standards the case against Pruitt was weak. Eyewitnesses were unsure of exactly who did what when. Wells identified Pruitt in a lineup that even the judge advocate admitted was poorly done. The Mestichellis could not identify Pruitt. None of the other stewards that testified for the prosecution identified Pruitt as the perpetrator of the stabbing (Pruitt, Doc. No. 128932). The lack of definitive testimony from these men, who may have been protecting Pruitt, themselves, or another friend, was likely construed as protecting a guilty man.

The Australian government had their own color problem, the Aborigines, and generally did not want black Americans from any branch of the service in Australia. The stewards were a very small number of the total naval presence in Perth and were largely accepted in clubs and restaurants, more so than back home in the States (Barker, pp. 177–8). Unfortunately the prejudices that existed in America were brought with the Navy to all corners of the world (Knoblock, p. 99). Whether guilty or not, the Navy probably felt pressured by American-Australian politics to find someone guilty. Pruitt was involved one way or another and was a good candidate as the guilty party. He was sentenced with a reduction in rate, a bad-conduct discharge, and five years in prison (Pruitt, Doc. No. 128932).

The other tragic situation was that of William Penzenik. Penzenik had also been transferred to Submarine Division 161 for tender duty. On June 8, 1944, he and a friend, Emmert Ziegler (not of the *Puffer*), went on leave in Fremantle. They first stopped at the National Hotel and had a few drinks between 2:40 and 3:15 P.M. A few drinks meant four schooners of beer and a shot of whiskey. The pair then moved to the Savoy Club until around 5:15 P.M., where Penzenik had another seven schooners of beer. Then they checked out the Palace Lounge and United Service Hotel where they had another schooner of beer. At the Palace Hotel Ziegler bought a bottle of wine. At around 6:00 P.M. the pair headed down the street with the wine and sat down on the top step of the entrance to Trinity Church. Ziegler admitted they were both intoxicated (Penzenik, Court Martial Document No. 103998).

Australians knew that Americans were well paid. The American equivalent of a seaman was paid the wage of an Australian captain. Submarine sailors received pay-and-a-half, which by comparison made them extremely well paid. The difference in pay gave the Americans a great advantage over the Australian servicemen in dating the Australian women, and the Australian men resented the Americans for it (Barker, pp. 144–5). While Ziegler and Penzenik began to share the bottle of wine, two Royal Australian Navy sailors, William G. Reynolds and Arthur R. Flores, walked down the street. According to Reynolds' testimony both were drunk, having recently consumed two whiskeys and nine beers. According to Ziegler, "The Australian sailors asked us for a drink." Then he told them, "You fellows are all alike; why don't you shove off?" Americans resented being asked for handouts (Penzenik, Doc. No. 103998).

A few words and too much alcohol was all it took to escalate the situation. Reynolds and Ziegler met halfway down the 14 steps; Flores went completely up the steps and hit Penzenik as he stood up. Penzenik was knocked back to his seated position by the blows. Flores turned and went down the steps toward the other pair now fighting in the street. Apparently Ziegler got the better of Reynolds, and turned to Flores standing at the bottom of the steps. According to a witness, Flores was smoking a cigarette with his hands in his pockets. Ziegler was heard to say, "I can't hit you while you have a cigarette in your mouth." Penzenik recovered, walked down the steps, and hit Flores from behind in the jaw, which spun him around. Penzenik hit him two more times, Flores fell and hit his head on the pavement causing a concussion. Flores died five days later after two operations to reduce the pressure on his brain from internal bleeding. The surgeon testified his skull was abnormally thin (*ibid.*).

Penzenik was found guilty of voluntary manslaughter. Legally it did not matter who started the fight or that all parties involved were heavily intoxicated. Such conditions were considered during sentencing. Voluntary manslaughter carried a maximum sentence of 10 years. He was sentenced to three years in prison, reduced in rate, and was given a bad-conduct discharge. In August of 1944 T.L. Catch, judge advocate general of the Navy, reduced the period of confinement to one year (*ibid.*). For many years Penzenik fought with the Navy to remove the bad-conduct discharge with no success. Upon his death in 1984 he was not allowed military honors at his burial. No American flag was allowed to cover his casket (Penzenik, Charles).

As a footnote to the incident, the mother of Arthur Flores wrote a letter to the American Consul in 1945.

I'm writing to obtain information regarding one of your lads who was sentenced in August 1944 for killing my son the previous June.

My son Arthur Reginald Flores who was a member of the R.A. Navy died on June 12th 44 as a result of being attacked by William Penzenik, a U.S. Naval rating.

At first I was very bitter towards him for taking my boy away from me, and although the loss is still great I feel as though I should forgive this boy for what he did, as I know he wasn't in his right frame of mind when it happened. So do you think it possible for that boy to be released, as I feel sure he has learned his lesson by now.

He also must have a Mother who loves him dearly and is anxious to have him free. I know how I'd feel if I were in her position, and it's mostly this thought that brings me to writing this letter. I feel too that my son would want me to forgive this boy, so I'd be very grateful if you could get him released. If he must finish his sentence would it be possible for me to write to him. If so would you be kind enough to forward me his address. I could then tell him he has been forgiven. Could I possibly have his mother's address too [Penzenik, U.S. Consular Reports].

Unfortunately none of the above requests were made. Recently the author provided the transcript of the trial to Charles Penzenik, William's son, and he shared it with his mother, Mrs. Elaine Penzenik. They knew little about the events, but knew something had made William bitter with the Navy. The above letter was shared with the Penzenik family by Avis Nelson-White, a wartime friend of a *Puffer* crew member. Ms. Nelson-White indicated Charles was very pleased to finally receive the letter, and that it would make a big difference to his mother. In a telephone conversation with Mrs. Elaine Penzenik, she related that although her husband was bitter with the Navy, he continued a lifelong friendship with another *Puffer* vet, "Foxy" Hetrick. The two attended numerous submarine veteran events in Ohio and Pennsylvania (Penzenik, Elaine).

Comparing the sentences handed out to Pruitt and Penzenik for their respective crimes, the sentences were grossly disproportionate. Penzenik served one year for manslaughter and Pruitt received five years for assault with a dangerous weapon. The victim of Pruitt's crime was an Australian civilian, Angelo Mestichelli. There lies the difference. The Navy wanted to show the Australian government that all criminal acts against civilians would be dealt with severely, especially if committed by a black serviceman.

10

The Fourth War Patrol

New Crew Members

Twenty-three men left the *Puffer* and twenty-three replacements came aboard. Some of the replacements had served on the refit crews during the third patrol (RG24). Russ Tidd was supposed to transfer to the *Flyer* but was delayed by the civil trial of Penzenik as a possible witness (Tidd). He ended up on the *Nautilus* (SS 168). Penzenik's misfortune was a fortunate turn of fate for Tidd; the *Flyer* was lost in a subsequent war patrol. Two good friends, Spalding and Graves (who had left after the Second War Patrol), were reunited when Spalding was transferred to the *Lagarto*. Both men were lost with all hands in January 1945 when the boat was sunk. The wreck of the *Lagarto* was located off the coast of Thailand in May 2005 in about 250 feet of water.

CREW TRANSFERRED AFTER THE THIRD WAR PATROL

Name	Service #	Rate Arr.	Third WP	Fourth WP
Bollman, Eric Peter	555 58 73	RT2cV6	RT1c	TRAN
Clouse, Fred Wayne	628 16 91	TM3cV6	TM2c	TRAN
Corke, Robert Edward	647 16 61	S2cV6	TM3c	TRAN
Funk, Leonard Gerald	279 78 34	MoMM2c	MoMM2c	TRAN
Garner, William Elmer	650 35 92	F1cV6	MoMM3c	TRAN
Gutensohn, John Peter	368 30 94	MoMM1c	CMoMM(AA)	TRAN
Guthrie, John Wise	300 49 87	TM3c	3-Feb-44	TRAN
Henry, Melvin "B"	624 77 40	SC3cV6	4-Feb-44	TRAN
James, Paul Daniel	652 44 71	S2cV6	EM3c	TRAN
Kennedy, Robert Francis	622 45 19	S2cV6	S1c	TRAN
Liggett, James David	636 49 86	F3cV6	MoMM2c	TRAN
Maloney, Herbert Earl	650 44 47	S1cV6	3-Feb-44	TRAN
Mathis, Charles Howard, Jr.	268 19 31	CMoMM(AA)	3-Feb-44	TRAN
Penzenik, William	283 35 14	F1c	MoMM2c	TRAN
Pruitt, John Alden	274 68 64	StM3c	StM2c	TRAN
Rawls, Jefferson Weldon	624 90 26	S2cV6	EM3c	TRAN
Robertson, Eugene Carlisle	381 29 43	EM1c	3-Feb-44	TRAN

Name	Service #	Rate Arr.	Third WP	Fourth WP
Schmidling, Charles Jentz	223 74 91	FC2c	4-Feb-44	TRAN
Shaw, William Frank	359 90 04	TM1c	CTM(AA)	TRAN
Spalding, Robert Bruce	337 30 50	PhM1c	PhM1c	TRAN
Tidd, Russell Ellis	204 48 05	S2c	TM3c	TRAN
Vincent, Leonard Russell	654 39 52	F2cV6	MoMM2c	TRAN
Warner, Wilbur Dudley	328 46 24	MoMM1c	MoMM1c	TRAN

NEW AND RETURNING CREW

Name	Service #	Rate Arr.	Date Arr.
Alexander, John	225 12 58	F1c	19-Apr-44
Allen, Carroll Louden	930 56 92	StM2cV6	19-Apr-44
Bowden, Thomas Albert	376 20 12	S1c	19-Apr-44
Cassidy, Bernard Folsom	212 61 45	S1c	19-Apr-44
Chamberlain, Roland Joseph	400 62 71	TM1c	19-Apr-44
Deem, Jay Arden	668 43 38	RT2cV6	19-Apr-44
Engborg, Frank Thomas	206 76 65	EM1cV6	30-Apr-44
Goin, James Warren	393 26 12	FC2c	19-Apr-44
Golden, Lawrence Joseph	283 26 70	MoMM2c	19-Apr-44
Gordon, Allen Harold	356 69 63	TM3c	29-Apr-44
Hannon, James Wesley	382 59 33	SC3c	25-Apr-44
Hensley, John Howard	256 43 61	F2cV6	19-Apr-44
Hetrick, William Herman	250 49 66	MoMM1c	19-Apr-44
Hopkinson, Alfred Harry	222 98 51	CPhM(PA)	19-Apr-44
Kellum, Raymond Herlong	268 17 81	GM2c	29-Apr-44
Owen, Lawrence Joseph	234 42 44	F2c	19-Apr-44
Perro, John Louis	207 26 05	MoMM2c	19-Apr-44
Polk, Robert Edgar, Jr.	656 56 30	EM2cV6	29-Apr-44
Sanders, John Wiley	645 08 12	S1cV6	19-Apr-44
Sears, Phillip Clayton	602 06 87	TM3cV6	19-Apr-44
Shiflett, John Lawrence, Jr.	659 72 33	S1cV6	19-Apr-44
Topor, Ladislaus	238 52 61	MoMM1c	29-Apr-44
Troop, Ralph Thomas	860 92 26	S1cV6	19-Apr-44

Repairs and More Repairs

Intended work on the sub included overhaul of two of the four main engines, cutting down the bridge to reduce the silhouette, conversion of #4 ballast tank to a fuel ballast tank (giving the boat additional range), realignment of both sound shafts, complete overhaul of the SD radar equipment to improve its performance, and installation of the PPI (Plan Position Indicator) display for the SJ radar. All the above items were accomplished with the exception of the installation of the PPI display. Refit was completed on April 21, 1944 (WPR).

Radar gave American submarines superiority over Japanese ships. SD air search radar was the earliest radar installed and warned subs on the surface of approaching airplanes within a distance of 6 miles. That distance gave a submarine about 60 seconds to submerge from an airplane approaching at 300 miles per hour. Early SD radar did not rotate and therefore gave limited directional information. The improved SD radar could sense airplanes at a greater distance, but still had limited directional capabilities. Excellent lookouts were essential. Rotational SV radar came later in the war, which gave superior distance and directional information of approaching aircraft (Alden, letter).

By the middle of 1942 a rotational type of offensive radar was being installed in new submarines. It was called SJ radar. Accurate direction of the enemy was read from a rapidly changing numeric display, which displayed a number from 0 to 360 as the radar antenna turned. The rotation could be stopped to focus on a single target and accurately read its bearing. Range was determined on the A-scope from a scale across the bottom of the screen; the farther to the right the pip or spike, the greater the distance; the taller the pip the larger the

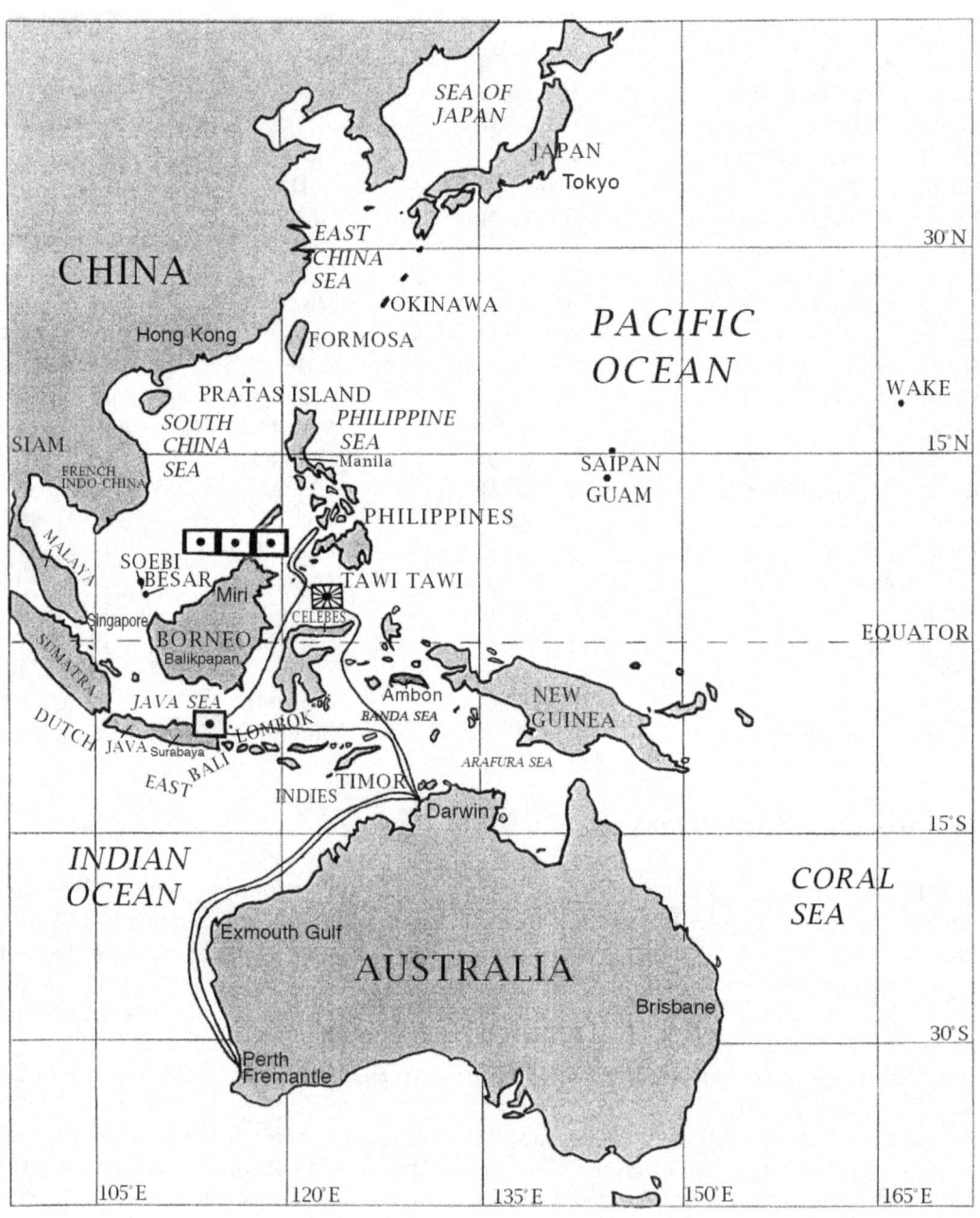

target. SJ radar could be tuned to near (10,000 yards) and distant (40,000 yards) sweeps. Early in 1944 SJ radar was vastly improved by the addition of the PPI display. The PPI display placed the sub at the center of the display and simultaneously gave both range and direction of a target with a glowing dot on a cathode ray screen, exactly like modern radar. Relative positions of multiple targets were easily visible on the same screen, which made attack plans more efficient (*ibid.*; Blair, p. 448).

On the *Puffer* the SD radar, although completely checked and tuned, still gave unsatisfactory range performance. The radar situation undoubtedly troubled Selby. He wanted the PPI display, but it was not available. Number 1 and #2 periscopes were interchanged to put the attack periscope forward and #1 was again replaced (WPR).

During April 22 to April 30 the *Puffer* engaged in training operations. Selby conducted sound tests, deperming (demagnetizing the boat to make it less sensitive to mines), deep dives, day and night practice approaches, surfaced and submerged, and fired three exercise torpedoes. On April 30 the *Puffer, Rasher,* and *Angler* conducted simulated, coordinated attack exercises on a single ship convoy, escorted by two ships. The exercises with the other two submarines prepared for the future use of wolf packs, multiple submarines attacking a convoy. Communication problems had to be ironed out. Selby felt, "When larger convoys are available and all submarines have a PPI unit this training will be of much greater benefit" (*ibid.*).

On May 1 and the next two days the *Puffer* and the *Rasher* continued valuable training exercises. Old and new lookouts, sound operators and radar operators needed training. In addition third and fourth officers had an opportunity to practice approaches. Selby had previously lobbied for a study to determine the ability of radar and humans to see submarines under various conditions. During the training with the *Rasher*, he determined that under a half moon overhead the *Rasher* could be seen at a range of 9000 yards, over 5 miles. However, the *Rasher* was invisible to both radar and human eyes while making a submerged radar approach, which required about 10 feet of the upper portion of the conning tower to be exposed. Sonar picked up the *Rasher* at 2,500 yards (*ibid.*).

On May 3 Selby continued to test the capabilities of the SD radar. He wanted empirical evidence; his life and the crew's lives were at stake. Visual contact was made with a Catalina (PBY) at about 12 miles. Radar was unable to detect the plane, flying at between 500 and 1000 feet, until within 3.5 miles. Selby requested by signal blinker that the plane go to 2000 feet when it left. At this altitude radar was barely able to reach out to nine miles, and then it was doubtful a radar operator would have seen it without prior knowledge. Selby was "convinced that our SD radar as a whole is a lemon or that the new type of 'M' antenna is far inferior to the old type" (*ibid.*). These tests of the radar's capabilities allowed Selby to determine how much trust could be put in these new gadgets. It was obvious to him that radar still needed the assistance of eagle eyed lookouts.

As the day progressed there was more bad news. The master gyro was not working properly. While testing the 3-inch deck gun, the sight was found to be badly fogged. Replacement parts were requested for delivery and repair at Darwin. The next day was no better; the SJ radar was out of commission as well as the pitometer log (the speedometer). Without accurate readings from the pitometer and master gyro, TDC calculations for the *Puffer*'s speed and

Opposite: The Fourth War Patrol — April 30, 1944 (Fremantle), to June 21, 1944 (Fremantle) — 5,915 nautical miles in the patrol area. The *Puffer* stopped off at Darwin for repairs and then performed lifeguard duty for the first bombing of Surabaya. The *Puffer* headed north via the Makassar Strait to Tawi Tawi and the southern reaches of the Philippine Islands in an attempt to thwart a growing Japanese force in the area. The flags indicate where attacks were made. The rising sun flag shows an attack on the Imperial Japanese Navy; the lone sun flags show an attack on a merchant vessel (map artwork by Nancy Webber).

position were incorrect. Another message was sent requesting repairs at Darwin. Early in the morning on May 8 the *Puffer* arrived at Darwin. The above defects were fixed. In addition the refrigeration units, the after TBT (Target Bearing Transmitter) on the bridge, a device used for sending the bearing of an enemy target directly to the TDC; and the communication system to the bridge were repaired. After taking on 35,000 gallons of fuel, the *Puffer* was underway at 1743, headed north toward Timor (*ibid.*).

Lifeguard Duty

The first assignment for the *Puffer* was lifeguard duty, the rescuing of downed American pilots carrying out the first air strike against the Japanese on Surabaya. During the next 9 days the *Puffer* stealthily moved northward and crossed the barrier east of Timor and then moved west into the Banda and Flores seas, avoiding detection by anti-submarine vessels and airplane patrols. Selby had hoped he might make contact with a convoy running between Ambon and Surabaya or Makassar City, Celebes and Surabaya. At 0527 on May 17 the *Puffer* was in position lying to (stationary) on the surface in an awash condition (decks just above sea level) off the coast of Surabaya. On the surface, in daylight, and stationary was a dangerous position for a submarine. In addition the water depth in the area was less than 200 feet. The next three days were busy days. Selby described the dangerous and frustrating events that occurred during lifeguard duty. The situation evolved into more than saving pilots (*ibid.*).

> 17 May
> 0009 to 0235 Contacted ten sailboats visually and by radar.
> 0415 On station.
> 0455 Submerged for trim dive.
> 0527 Surfaced and commenced lying to in awash condition on station. Keeping a close lookout particularly in direction of Soerabaja [the Dutch spelling for Surabaya].
> Decided to remain on the surface so that aviators heading for our approximate spot would have a chance to see us and land or crash near by. Believed that Japanese aviators would be too busy with the striking force to see us.
> 0800 Sighted low cloud of smoke rising through haze in the direction of Soerabaja.
> 0805 (Aircraft Contact #4) Sighted two formations of carrier planes which approached us from the direction of the smoke cloud and then headed in a general southerly direction. I could see at least six planes attacking one of the formations but there were probably more that I didn't see as the whole show was about 15 miles from us and rapidly disappearing.
> 0815 Heard voice calling "Help, help, help" on the aircraft frequency. I had been watching our planes closely for any sign of trouble but had seen none fall out of formation or head our way so had no idea where to look at this time.
> 0830 Received message from carrier informing me that there were three survivors in a rubber life boat in the harbor.
> 0853 Sent message to carrier requesting true bearing and distance of survivors from our station.
> 0900 Received message giving location of survivors in Soerabaja outer harbor. This message repeated several times.
> 0923 Amplified message stating crew of VTB was attempting to get out of harbor in rubber boat.
> 0929 Their chances looked mighty slim. If the Japs didn't pick them up, the southeast wind would probably blow them in the direction of Madoera [now Madura] Island. Aside from the obvious impracticability of entering Soerabaja harbor in the daylight on the surface, shallow water would prevent approaching their position (Lat. 07° 12.5'S, Long. 112 50'E) any closer than 14 miles either on the surface or submerged. Decided my only course was to remain on station,

keep a look out for them and listen for any more distress calls or messages until at least the time limit of the operation order which was 1230.

Sent message to carrier informing them that I could not penetrate the harbor but would watch for the men.

1002 Sighted masts of a trawler type vessel bearing 270°T and headed in direction of Soerabaja.

1005 Submerged to avoid detection. The smoke cloud in the meantime continued to rise and spread out over Soerabaja. A second smaller column of smoke had commenced to rise to the right of the larger. Later in the day I measured the number of degrees the smoke cloud subtended in height and width and estimated that it was about 20 miles wide and 4 miles high — 21 degrees high at 40 miles.

1155 A/S vessel clear, surfaced and commenced lying to with decks awash. Many sailboats in sight, none closer than five miles. For a while I entertained the idea of pulling alongside one of the sailboats in an attempt to get them to sail into harbor and look for the aviators. However, memory of my previous unsuccessful experience in attempting to talk to two Javanese prisoners (PUFFER Second War Patrol), one of whom had gone to Dutch schools and could read and write, made me decide to give up as not worthy enough of success to warrant the chance of detection. I could vision confused Javanese sailing into Soerabaja and picking up some Japs to come out and find out what we wanted.

1245 Received coded message giving us the further information that the aviators might have taken over a native sailboat to get out. If this were true and they sailed towards Zwaantjes (the Dutch chart name) Reef Light, this being the best landmark in line with our position, I figured they could be in that vicinity about 1800 with the fresh southeasterly wind blowing.

1309 Submerged and commenced heading toward above light.

1330 Burned secret letter concerning task force operation.

1944 Surfaced about eight miles west of our assigned point and commenced patrolling east-west line.

2035 Decided to put up a visual signal which would direct aviators to us if they were in vicinity. Took the light diffuser off the Aldis Lamp and spotted the beam straight up in the air for five seconds.

2037 Sighted a white light in toward beach on bearing 190°T which seemed to flash twice. Headed in this direction at 10 knots.

2125 No contact and no further sight of light so reversed course and returned to station. Commenced patrolling east and west line extending five miles west of our station. Had decided on questioning lookout who saw the light that it was high on the beach. It would have been difficult if not impossible for the survivors to reach any such location at this time. Decided to approach all sailboats encountered during night and signal them with red light attachment for binoculars.

18 May

0010—0040 Sighted anti-aircraft fire, tracers, searchlights and flash of explosions in direction of Soerabaja. Assumed our land based bombers were attacking as it looked too real for a drill.

0227 Sighted more AA fire, tracers, searchlights and explosions in direction Soerabaja.

Up until this time we had contacted four sailboats, approached to within 400 to 600 yards of them, and sent series of "V's." None made any response or any attempted to close us. I knew from a previous test conducted with the RAY that this light can be seen and read at 2,500 yards. The following radar contact and subsequent attack prevented our continuing to search any longer for these survivors. Felt bad about not finding them as I can well imagine their disappointment if they worked their way out to our vicinity the next day and found us gone.

0430 (Ship Contact #3) In Madoera Strait, Lat. 07°30' S, Long. 113°25' E, SJ radar contact bearing 153°T, range 14,250 yards. Pip one inch high indicated large target which would have been picked up at anywhere from 20,000 to 25,000 yards except for the fact that the SJ was tuned to a close sweep due to the presence of many small sailboats. Put four main engines on propulsion and commenced tracking. Target on course about 270°T, speed 10 knots, close to Java beach.

0505 Had reached a position 70° on the target's starboard bow on parallel course, range 12,000 yards. Visibility conditions were not good for a surface attack as the night was clear, a bright quarter moon was rising in the east and the first gray streaks of dawn were showing.

On the other hand navigational hazards prevented getting ahead for a submerged attack. We were in 31 fathoms [186 feet] of water, the target in 12, Endrachts RK, a ¾ fathom spot, was 20 degrees on the starboard bow distance 14,000 yards and the next seven miles on our westerly course the water shoaled off to 18 fathoms [108 feet]. Beyond this there were 13 more miles of 18 fathom water before reaching the ¾ fathom water of Soerabaja outer harbor. In addition I wasn't too sure he wasn't following a swept channel or about to enter one.

In view of the above decided this would be our only chance to attack and that the very good possibility of his sighting us and turning away would have to be accepted.

Starting in at full speed aiming for a 115° starboard track at 3,000 yards range, using TBT bearings and radar ranges.

0506 Slowed to 10 knots to make ready tubes #1, #2, #3 and #4.

0510 Tubes ready, resumed full speed, 17.5 knots.

0513 (Ship Contact #4) Sighted escort on starboard quarter of target range 5,200 yards. Made ready remainder of tubes depth setting four feet.

0514 (Ship Contact #5) Sighted sail boat coming down starboard side of target. He gave us a nice break for when the range to the escort had closed to 2,500 yards, he passed between us. The escort swung around and headed for him either to avoid collision or to investigate him. I think he may have sighted both of us about the same time and picked the wrong customer. He was a trawler type patrol boat. Why he hadn't seen us sooner I don't know for we could see him very clearly. He drew aft rapidly. During this period kept radar on escort and TDC on target.

0520 Had quite a thrill for a few minutes here as both the Officer-of-the-Deck and I decided without doubt that our target was a flat top. He certainly looked like it at this range — about 7,000 yards. (Ship Contact #6) At this time sighted another and larger escort ahead of target slightly on starboard bow.

0524 Range 4,000 yards, target subtended about one-third of the field of my binoculars, two and one-half degrees, giving him a length of about 500 feet disregarding angle on the bow. It was apparent now that he was an AP or AK with a single stack, well deck fore and aft, composite superstructure and riding high in the water — could see his counter stern. His amidship superstructure being about the same height as his bow and stern had given us the impression of a continuous flat top at a distance. Could not make out his masts at any time.

0525 Slowed to 12 knots and came right 15° for small gyro angle.

0527 In position, Lat. 07° 36.2' S, Long. 113° 12.5' E, target course 280°T, speed 10, angle on the starboard bow 115°, torpedo track 135° starboard, range 2,450 yards.

0527-00 Fired #1.
0527-13 Fired #2.
0527-25 Fired #3.
0527-39 Fired #4.

0528 Came left with full rudder and went ahead flank.

0529-11 Heard and saw one explosion forward of the bridge which sent up huge black column of smoke.

0529-22 Heard and saw second explosion on stern of target — another column of black smoke.

0529-25 Heard and saw third explosion on target's stern which was a brilliant yellowish orange color. This was not a torpedo but a depth charge on his stern or an internal explosion.

About a minute later his stern disappeared and the bow and rest of the ship seemed to be at an up angle of about 30°. About another minute later I could see nothing but black smoke where he had been and radar could no longer get a pip on him. I believe he sank in about two minutes. Radar lost his pip at 5,000 yards whereas it had previously had contact during tracking at over 16,000 yards.

From my observations the closest identification I can make is the ZUIYO MARU class, 7,360 tons, page 126, ONI 208 J (revised). This ship is listed under "potential naval value" as an AO with an oil carrying capacity of 73,000 barrels, so he may have been an empty stack amidship, tanker coming into Soerabaja to load. He was riding high in the water. My length estimate was verified by the Officer-of-the-Deck who was on the target continuously with the TBT. When the target filled half the field of his glasses the range was three thousand yards, giving a length of 550 feet. Other observations were verified by the Officer-of-the-Deck, quartermaster and one lookout who was assigned to the target.

There are a number of ships 450 to 500 feet long, 6,000 to 7,000 gross tons in ONI 208 J who fills this general description. Had I been able to determine his mast sequence I could be more positive of the identification. I have no doubt that salvage operations will be commenced very shortly since he sank in about 12 fathoms (72 feet) of water and was only a mile from the 10 fathom curve.

0533 Had come to course 082°T to put escort astern and head out of Madoera Strait — 70 miles to go. Radar had two targets; smaller escort on port quarter who was dropping back rapidly and the larger escort dead astern who was dropping back very slowly — range 5,000 yards.

Radar lost the small escort at 5,300 yards and one lookout saw him heading in the direction of the target's smoke. The escort astern slowly opened out to 5,530 yards and then his range commenced to remain constant. I still couldn't tell what he was other than that he had the general appearance of a small man-of-war. Radar pip identified that he was smaller than a destroyer — probably a minelayer.

I had hoped to get out of sight before he found out which direction I was going but it was too light and too obvious to him that an easterly course was our only way out.

0543 Range still 5,530 yards. Could see him quite plainly now and from the smoke he was putting out he appeared to be making about 130% MEP. We weren't making anything under 100% ourselves.

I decided here that the expenditure of a few torpedoes was warranted in an attempt to scare him off our track as I still had 20 miles to run to get into 35 fathom water and expected eventually to be forced down by planes.

Made ready tubes #9 and #10 for long range shots with a four foot depth setting.

0545-15 Fired #9.

0545-35 Fired #10.

0553 Range opened to 5,560 indicating he might have altered course slightly for these two torpedoes although it was not apparent visually.

0555 Manned SD radar, rigged ship for depth charge attack and commenced reload of tubes #9 and #10 with Mk 18 torpedoes; bow tubes had been reloaded previously.

0609 Sun rose.

0625 Range still 5,560. All ballast tanks had been given an extra blow, safety and negative were blown dry, we were making 272 RPMs on the shafts and the pitometer log was clocking 18.5 knots.

A four inch gun aft would have pulled us out of this spot very nicely. Considering the number of experiences our submarines have had in not being able to outrun this very common type of escort and patrol boat, I believe serious consideration should be given to mounting four inch guns both fore and aft if they can be obtained. Two ready lockers on the deck aft of the conning tower holding twelve rounds apiece should furnish sufficient ammunition to discourage this kind of a chaser.

0626 Fired #7 tube at him (high power) after carefully feeding continuous periscope bearings and radar ranges into the TDC for about three minutes. The torpedo was observed from the bridge and through periscope to run hot, straight and normal down the port side of the target about 300 yards off his track. After a run of about 3,000 yards the torpedo broached and continued the rest of the run on the surface. Target turned slightly to starboard and the range opened to 5610 yards.

0631-00 Fired #8 tube. Target had a slight port angle on the bow. Torpedo was observed to run hot, straight and normal on an apparent collision course with the minelayer and smoking heavily. This one nearly got him. About the time he spotted it and turned slightly to port to let it run down his starboard side, the torpedo broached, made a 90° right turn and came in on him for a 90° starboard track. The Nip swung hard left, was heeling hard over and presenting an 80° starboard angle on the bow, when the torpedo again broached, turned hard left and headed for him again at an estimated range of 300–500 yards. It eventually passed fairly close astern of him on its original course. I would not be surprised if this skipper turned in a report on a new type American acoustic torpedo when he got through talking to himself.

0632 Range 6,010 yards and he was headed back at us again. However, we had gained 400 yards. Although I didn't think of it at the time, if I had it to do over again I believe I would fire a salvo of two circular runs—one set to circle to the right and one to the left. I think this would worry him more and give better results per torpedo expended.

When he swung hard over to avoid the torpedo, could see that his high forecastle deck was painted orange and the rest of his hull a dirty brown color. He may have been partially through a navy yard overhaul when called out for duty. This silhouette view identified him as a coastal minelayer of the CMc 13-31 class similar in appearance to the NATSUSHIMA class with a deep well just forward of his bridge.

0635 (Aircraft Contact #5) I was beginning to think we were actually going to be able to pull clear on the surface when we sighted a "RUFE" 10° on the starboard bow, distance about 11 miles, elevation 2,000 feet and crossing from starboard to port on a northerly course. Radar reported contact at 10 miles as we watched him slowly crossing the bow hoping he would continue on his way.

0640 He turned toward us and, when the range had closed to eight miles, I submerged and came hard left for a 90° port track on the escort. Made ready tube #9, only, as difficulty had been experienced reloading the MK18's and this was the only tube reloaded.

0648 Lat. 07° 31' S, Long. 113° 40' E, TDC set-up checking, angle on the bow 60° port, torpedo track 90° port, range 1950 yards, torpedo run 1,600 yards, target speed 18.2 knots, depth setting four feet, fired #9. Sound heard torpedo running hot, straight, and normal.

0648-30 Heard first explosion and looked. There was a large column of water between us and the stern of the target which may have been either a premature or an aircraft bomb. I am inclined to believe it was a bomb as the explosion had a sharper sound than a torpedo explosion. It was considerably closer to him than to me and as we started down he was swinging right. I believe the torpedo missed either due to passing under him, because the final check bearing had not quite been cranked into the TDC when we fired, or because it prematured.

0649-0651 Seven more bombs and depth charges were dropped—none close. Went to 200 feet (bottom at 259 feet), rigged for silent running and set course 080°T at two-thirds speed, four knots.

0659 Target made a good echo ranging run up our port side and crossed our bow but dropped no depth charges although he was very close. From here on he never got close again. We were able to keep him astern with slight change of course on the base course of 080°T as his pinging gradually got further away. We had a sharp thermocline at 180 feet which was probably helping us.

1205 Came to periscope depth. Nothing in sight.

2007 Surfaced and set course 090°T heading for new patrol station in northern Makassar Strait and Celebes Sea in accordance with dispatch orders received earlier in the day.

19 May

0045 Changed course to 135°T while sending dispatch concerning failure to find downed aviators and sinking of ship in Madoera Strait.

0125 Radar operator noted interference from another radar which was typical of our submarine SJ radars. We were now on course 020°T heading toward the southern approach to Makassar Strait.

0206 Radar interference closer and on starboard beam. Believed it to be RATON who was about due to have passed through Lombok Strait and be heading for the Java Sea.

0355 (Ship Contact #7) Radar contact 120°T, range 6,000 yards. This was in direction of previously noted interference. Turned away and slowed to check his actions. He apparently had made contact about the same time and turned away, for the range opened rapidly.

0400 Lost contact. Resumed base course.

0426 Contact again at 050°T, range 6,300 yards. This time maintained course and speed (17 knots). Contact remained on steady bearing long enough to track him at same course and speed and then commenced to drop back. Decided he wanted to drop aft to pass across our stern so held course and speed. If he was enemy I was going to have a chance to see him first as he was going to be silhouetted on a clear eastern horizon at daybreak.

0530 Sighted Sekala Island bearing 325°T at about 12 miles.

0535 Sighted submarine bearing 120°T. Recognized it as one of ours so sent recognition signal twice. No answer.

0545 Sighted object bearing 250°T. Assigned lookout to watch submarine while attempting to identify new contact.

0549 Other submarine submerged.

0550 Having been unable to recognize the new target and not being absolutely positive the other submarine was friendly, I submerged.

0610 Recognized new target as a small sailboat. Decided to surface and pull clear. Submarine's refusal to answer recognition signal was probably due to the fact that the sailboat, which he had probably not identified either, would have seen his answer.

0627 Surfaced and zigzagged off at full speed.

0748 Submerged for rest of day.

1708 Surfaced, proceeding toward Makassar Strait. Received dispatch orders to conduct offensive reconnaissance patrol off southeastern approaches to Tawi Tawi Bay commencing night of 21 May. Task force consisting of three battleships, three heavy cruisers, one light cruiser, destroyers and possibly carrier anchored there.

20 May

0612 Submerged 30 miles south west of Cape Mandar. In order to reach my new station on time I either had to run through the bottleneck off Cape William in the daytime on the surface or through the northern entrance to Makassar Strait itself. Decided on the latter. Sighted five sailboats during the day.

1836 Surfaced and set course for Makassar Strait at full speed.

2051 SJ contact 312°T, 3,200 yards. Not sighted but probably sailboat. Avoided.

2244 SJ contact 030°T, 3,650 yards. Avoided, lost contact at 5,100 yards. Could have been a small patrol boat as the radar pip was slightly larger than the previous contact. Did not investigate either of these contacts as they were obviously small and valuable time would be lost [ibid.].

Glenn Stoy summarized the action from the enlisted man's perspective.

Fired four torpedoes forward getting two hits, two "fish" firing at the escorts with no hits, tanker blew up, split in two and sank, one escort gave chase, we stayed on the surface to outrun him, fired two more "fish" at him so he wouldn't get too brave, we were slowly outrunning him when a damn Jap patrol plane was sighted, we were forced to dive and rig for depth charge, which were not long in coming, we were lucky enough to find a layer though and lost the slant-eyed bastard after about six depth charges, surfaced at 2010, first blood for this patrol, but we're out for more [Stoy].

Although unable to rescue downed flyers, the *Puffer* did sink the *Shinryu Maru*, a 3,181 ton freighter built in 1918. Japanese records recorded the *Shinryu Maru* was returning empty to Surabaya after delivering an army unit and ammunition to Bima, Sumbawa Island. As the freighter attempted to evade, three of the *Puffer*'s torpedoes found their mark — one in the bow, one under the bridge, and the third in the No. 4 hold. The freighter flooded quickly and sank in two minutes. Twelve passengers, five army gunnery soldiers, five lookouts and 11 other crew were killed. No damage was recorded to the minesweeper that chased the *Puffer* after the attack on the freighter (Somerville, 1991).

Tawi Tawi — Carrier Carrier

For the third time under Selby's command the *Puffer* headed up the Makassar Strait. He avoided the small contacts on the way to Tawi Tawi (5-10N, 120-00E), where intelligence had reported many large targets. Tawi Tawi was a small island at the southern end of the Sulu Archipelago, which extends from the southern Philippine Islands toward Borneo. The Japanese were gathering men-of-war there for the inevitable battle the Allies would mount to retake the Mariana Islands and later the Philippines. The super-battleships *Yamato* and *Musashi* had arrived on May 14 along with the light aircraft carriers *Chitose* and *Chiyoda*. Numerous other light aircraft carriers and destroyers were also arriving to form the "Van Force" in defense of the Marianas (Hackett, *IJN Yamato*; Tully, *IJN Chitose*).

Stoy wrote in his diary, "Have sighted two aircraft carriers escorted by at least ten first line destroyers coming out of Tawi Tawi harbor" (Stoy). Deem recalled Selby coming over the 1MC (the all submarine speaker system) with a message, "This is a great opportunity for us to destroy 1000's of Japs and 100's of airplanes, with the possible loss of less than 100 men." Of course the "100 men" were the crew of the *Puffer*. Deem thought at the time, "What a damn fool" (Deem). Selby described the dizzying attack on the aircraft carriers in the war patrol report.

22 May
  0347 Visibility very poor. Reversed course as Bongao Peak had not been sighted and position was doubtful. Slowed to three knots.
  0401 Reversed course to north.
  0511 Submerged to commence approach to Manuk Manka Island south of Tawi Tawi Bay.
  0545 Sighted Bongao Peak bearing 355°T, distance 50 miles. Set course for point three miles southeast of Manuk Manka Island to have a look into Tawi Tawi Bay.
  0640 (AC #6) Sighted Type "JAKE" twin float observation plane bearing 270°T on easterly heading.
  0904 (AC #7) Sighted about 70 fighter planes in the general direction of 120°T flying at various altitudes on various courses.
  0912 Sound picked up fast screws bearing 070°T. Ship contacts #8, #9, #10, #11 and #12, occurring from this time until 0955 were respectively destroyer, aircraft carrier, aircraft carrier, destroyer, and destroyer. The bearing of the screws was drawing quite rapidly to the northward. I could not see anything but aircraft, until at...
  0925 Sighted destroyer on true bearing 043°, range 7,000 yards, angle on the bow about 60° port. A minute or so later, the long low flat top of a carrier showed up astern of the destroyer and on the same course.
  The sea was glassy calm, the sky clear and visibility excellent. Went to 90 feet and commenced an approach at full speed on the normal approach course hoping for a zig toward us. While slowing to take a look sound reported more fast screws on the starboard quarter. I chose to ignore these for the present to concentrate on closing the carrier whose angle on the bow was now 90° port. Went deep and went ahead full again. On the next look the carrier was practically out of sight so took a look on starboard quarter. What I had taken for granted as

another destroyer escort turned out to be another carrier and two destroyers, angle on the bow about 10° starboard, range about 3,000 yards, one destroyer ahead on the starboard bow and one trailing astern slightly on the port quarter. By the time I ducked the periscope, got a set up on the TDC and put the periscope back up, the first destroyer and carrier were past. By the time I changed the depth setting on the stern tubes from 10 to 6 feet, the last destroyer was past. The carrier passed 500 yards or less astern and the leading destroyer must have passed right over our stern. The general effect was similar to the dazzling speed with which the participants in a Walt Disney comedy sizzle past and disappear in a cloud of vapor.

The other carrier had now reversed course and, as I started another approach on her, I suddenly realized that I would get nowhere chasing them frantically and that I might as well sit tight, watch closely, and await my best opportunity. This I did, taking a course that would put us approximately between them. Carrier #1 looked similar to the identification picture of the HOSHO or HITAKA. Although I know the AKAGI was sunk at Midway, Carrier #2 was much more similar to the AKAGI or KAGA than any other carrier pictures we have aboard. The three outstanding features of this carrier that stick in my mind are (1) mass of framework forward supporting the flight deck (this immediately brought to mind the squib in ONI 41 (Nip Notes) which says concerning carriers "And bow or stern approach to some, suggests a Nagasaki slum"—-that was the general idea); (2) the flight deck extended practically all the way to the bow; (3) I did not see any superstructure, so any there was must have been small or easily removable for aircraft operations.

Both carriers were discharging their planes.

1013 The smoke from Carrier #2 commenced to hold a steady bearing so assumed he was heading toward or away from us—none of the three ships of this group were in sight.

1015 Could definitely see leading destroyer and carrier with small port angle on the bow. Took normal course.

1024 Range 2,700 yards, angle on the bow 30° port.

1024-30 Range 2,300 yards, angle on the bow 33° port. With the carrier on course 060°, speed 20 and torpedo run about 1,400 yards commenced firing.

1025-20 Fired #1.

1025-30 Fired #2,

Firing bearings were way ahead of TDC bearings so speeded target up to 25 knots and cranked the range in to 1,000 yards.

1025-39 Fired #3.

1025-48 Fired #4.

Bearings still not checking. Zigged target left to 040° and decreased range to 600 yards—he looked that close.

1025-57 Fired #5.

1026-05 Fired #6. The bearings were checking on the last two shots. The actual set up at firing by later plot was target speed 30 knots, angle on the bow 108° port, torpedo track 137° port, range 660 yards, and torpedo run 800 yards. My error was in the ranges. I used 50 feet from the flight deck to the water line, whereas 40 was probably more nearly correct. Also, I don't think I was seeing all the way down to the water line until we fired and at that time I was giving bearings only.

I should have used considerably more spread than I did. It just didn't look possible to miss with any of the torpedoes at that range, however, and I tried for a kill. I spread with the periscope starting just inside his bow and spreading the six along his entire length. Only fast and cool headed work on the part of Lieutenant William K. Pugh, II, USN, on the TDC got us a possible hit with the fifth torpedo.

Immediately after firing #6 took a quick look for the trailing escort. He was about 2,500 yards on our starboard beam, zero angle on the bow. We had come up to 63 feet on firing so he undoubtedly had us spotted. Flooded negative and started deep.

1026-43 Heard one explosion. A later plot of the correct set up and a check of the time of torpedo run indicated that this was #5 hitting. Our plot also showed that #6 could have hit on a 1750 track but no explosion was heard. I could classify the hit by #5 torpedo as "probable." The explosion was heard throughout the ship except for the Conning Tower and Control Room. The only person in either of these places who heard the hit was an officer whose sole duty was the recording of the times of all explosions heard. Since this explosion occurred while negative tank was being vented, it is probable that the noise of the venting air drowned out the noise of the explosion for all others. The times of the hit as recorded in the Control Room, Forward Torpedo Room and After Torpedo Room all checked.

This was most disappointing as he looked so close that it seemed the torpedoes had to hit. There is the possibility, of course, that he was in too close for the first torpedoes to arm.

1028-35 Close depth charges just after destroyer screws passed over us said we were passing 100 feet. Shook some cork loose, knocked the rudder angle indicator out of commission and apparently lifted the hull supply and main induction valves off their seats enough to partially flood them for we started getting salt water down the drains at that time. This was the only close depth charge.

It is possible this was an aircraft bomb. One of the amazing things to me about this whole action was that we were able to remain in the vicinity of the carriers from 0912 until 1025 without having a plane sight us. Every time I put the periscope up there were five or six planes visible close aboard — some passed low overhead flying toward the periscope and others came up from behind gaining altitude as they passed overhead. They appeared to all be forming up subsequent to taking off and were probably too busy to look for subs. There was only one plane on deck of the carrier we fired at and he was in a take off position. I could see the plane handling crew well enough to see them start pointing at the torpedo tracks after about three torpedoes had been fired.

1030-40 to 1032-05 Ten depth charges.

1032-05 to 1034-52 Four depth charges.

1036-50 to 1039-15 Four depth charges.

1053-17 One depth charge. This ended the depth charging, but it was only the beginning of the hunting.

1054 to 2305 Five destroyers conducted a systematic search. Lost them twice during the afternoon when they got too close, by using evasion tactics which the Commanding Officer of the Dutch destroyer TJERK HIDDES had previously recommended as being most confusing to an echo ranging search group. These tactics will be discussed under "Evasion Tactics" in case they may be of value to anyone else. I, for one, am sold on them. (Evasion Tactics: I commenced steering a constant helm zig zag course sixty degrees to the right and left of the base course at four knots. After seven or eight times I slowed to three knots and slowly circled off to a new base course.)

Tried to get up three different times but was picked up each time by a listener who apparently called the whole pack over again. I really didn't have much hope of getting up until the next night.

About 2200 located the current listener on our port bow and believe I threw him off the scent with a complete 360° turn. Don't understand why they didn't use more depth charges unless they are short — they were close enough several times. I feel that they knew when they were close to us for they would send double pings to check their echoes and tune their drivers a kilocycle or so each side of 17.2 kcs.

2305 Surfaced with SJ radar out of commission and commenced pulling clear.

2325 SJ radar back in commission, no contacts.

23 May

0524 Submerged for all day dive about 50 miles southeast of Tawi Tawi Bay. Repaired rudder angle indicator and dried out motor of MK 18 torpedo which had flooded. Heard eight distant depth charges during the day.

1815 Surfaced and headed for chain of islands along southern side of Tawi Tawi Bay in order to obtain a good fix and get into position for a look inside the bay early in the morning [WPR].

Stoy wrote about the wild and vexing events of May 22 through the early morning of May 24 in his diary. Although he wrote the approach on the aircraft carrier was by sound only, it was not. That may have been the original plan, but Selby took numerous quick looks through the periscope to set up the torpedo attack and Pugh made adjustments as each pair of torpedoes missed. The WPR mentions far fewer depth charges. Stoy's depth charge count was more likely accurate, since submarine crews liked to count everything.

> May 22 — Cruising off the southern coast of the Tawi Tawi island, in the northern Celebes Sea, submerged at 0530, battle stations at 0830 have sighted two aircraft carriers escorted by at least ten first line destroyers coming out of Tawi Tawi harbor, the carriers planes are practicing landings and take-offs, which is certainly going to make this tough, started the approach and will have to fire by sound as we can't risk having the 'scope sighted by one of the planes, here goes! Fired six torpedoes forward and immediately started for the depths, rigging for depth charges like mad as they are already coming down around our ears; pretty sure one or two hits on the flattop, well we're down at 300 feet taking one helluva beating, don't think they'll ever run out of ash cans, tried getting to the surface twice but they are still up there waiting for us, been down 18 hours now started using oxygen and CO_2 absorbent, have a layer over us which is the only thing saving us, finally made the surface late at night and got out of there in a helluva hurry, that fresh air smells good, hope we don't have to go through that again, well over a hundred depth charges. Cruising in the Celebes Sea recuperating so to speak; a little more blood for the yellow emperor.
>
> May 23 and early morning hours of May 24 — Cruising in the Celebes Sea, have steadied up on a northern course are heading back to Tawi-Tawi, submerged at 0530, heard depth charging quite a ways off, someone else is taking a beating, surfaced at 1820, contacted two Jap destroyers and played a spine tingling game of "hide and seek" with them before we finally lost them [Stoy].

Selby had candidly described his errors in the WPR in hopes other commanders would not make the same mistakes. Selby's description of evasive techniques he had learned from the Dutch might save other submarines. He seemed very much a student of submarine warfare, willing to learn and share his thoughts. Pugh was manning the TDC for the first time; on the previous patrols Dwyer had operated the TDC. Dwyer was in Fremantle during this patrol. Luck and skill had been with the boat to escape the numerous escorts.

The events that played out over the 70 minute period of time were the greatest opportunity for Selby and the *Puffer* that would occur during the entire war. Selby must have felt like a quarterback with two receivers wide open in the end zone, while being rushed by multiple linebackers. The excitement level probably was too great and affected his ability to think, analyze and perform at peak performance. As Selby described it, "the general effect was similar to the dazzling speed ... in a Walt Disney comedy" (WPR). His ability to concentrate on important details was probably impaired by 70 minutes of adrenaline. The evasive action of the Japanese carrier, made possible by the alert lookouts, undoubtedly also helped thwart the attack.

Postwar analysis of Japanese ship movements determined the aircraft carrier *Chitose* was the target of the *Puffer*. One torpedo exploded in the prop wake. No damage was done (Tully). The *Chitose*'s lookouts saw the torpedo wakes off her port quarter and were able to turn away to starboard, evading the torpedoes. Four of the torpedoes passed ahead of the carrier and one exploded prematurely (Somerville, 1991). As much as Selby and the crew hoped one of the explosions had found its mark, it had not. The destroyer *Yukikaze* has sometimes been credited as damaged in this attack; however, this damage was self-inflicted when the ship nicked a propeller on one of the many reefs while chasing the *Puffer* (Tully).

Tanker Tanker

For the next week the *Puffer* continued to patrol the vicinity of the Sulu Archipelago, moving north and west through the Sibutu Passage (5-00N, 119-30E) and along the northern approaches to the Sibutu Passage in the Sulu Sea. Then the *Puffer* moved north and east toward the western tip of Mindanao Island of the Philippines. The next day the boat reversed course and headed back toward the Sibutu Passage. For another week the *Puffer* patrolled off the northern entrances to the Sibutu Passage, a waiting game as Stoy referred to it. There were numerous aircraft contacts and calls to battle stations, which turned out to be only minor game. On June 4 the *Puffer* moved north toward Kulassein Island (6-19N, 120-33E) via North Ubian Island (6-9N, 120-26E) in the shallows of the Sulu Sea (WPR).

After a late night exchange with some natives, the *Puffer* arrived near Kulassein Island early on June 5. At 0756 the first target came over the horizon and the crew went to battle stations. Selby described the events of a successful submerged attack.

4 June
0530 Submerged for patrol off Pearl Bank.
1655 Surfaced and set course for a point about 10 miles north of Kulassein Island.
2040 Sighted North Ubian Island.
2218 Sighted three outrigger canoes in moonlight. Had one pull alongside to see what information I might be able to get out of them. Could not get any information either by sign language or Pidgin English except that they most emphatically didn't like the Japanese. Traded two pounds of rice for one fish, one pineapple and some breadfruit.

5 June
0055 Sighted Kulassein Island.
0756 (Ship Contact #20) Sighted through periscope the masts of three large ships and the tips of the masts of two escorts, one on either side, bearing 057°T, estimated range about 30,000 yards.
0800 Went ahead full on four mains and to battle stations for tracking. Desired to obtain zig plan and base course prior to submerging for attack. As they appeared to be following along the chain of islands, their base course had to be about 220°T.
0826 In position ahead on their estimated base course of 220°T with the convoy itself bearing 020°T, submerged for attack.
0851 Picked up the three tankers by periscope.
0908 Picked up pinging on sound gear.
0913 Escorts in sight through periscope still keeping station on port and starboard flank of convoy.
During the half hour in which we tracked them on the surface they appeared to be in a line of bearing about 000°T-180°T and zigzagging about 70° to the right and the left of the base course. After picking them up, submerged, however, they had commenced making very small zigs showing an angle on the bow of not more than 20° either side. One possible explanation for this is that they had just made a landfall on Kulassein Island and were preparing to go south through the passage east of Pangutaran Island. All three tankers appeared large, the largest being the inboard or southerly tanker and the other two almost as big. Their draft indicated that they were partially loaded. It would seem that they would normally be empty headed in this direction unless they were going into Tawi Tawi to give their remaining load to the task force.
0926 Made ready all tubes, depth setting eight feet. Intended to fire the forward tubes in two salvoes of three each and use the after tubes on the tankers or escorts as the situation permitted.
0931 Fourth tanker seen about two miles astern of the first three.
0938 In position Lat. 6° 32' N, Long. 120° 40' E, six and one-half miles due north of the

western tip of Kulassein Island. Center tanker was headed at us with zero angle on the bow, right hand target (my right) was presenting a starboard angle and the left hand target a port angle and also the farthest away.

Chose right hand target for the first three bow shots. Target course 220°, speed 14, angle on the bow 35° starboard, torpedo track 0° starboard, torpedo run 720 yards, own course 062°T, speed 3, TDC checking perfectly, single ping range of 1,100 yards checked exactly with generated range.

0940-00 Fired #2 tube.

0940-10 Fired #1 tube.

0940-18 Fired #3 tube.

During the firing, continuous periscope bearings of the MOT [middle of target] were fed to the TDC by periscope. The fire control man assigned to set spread had not heard a previous order I had given that he was to set the spread. Since I normally spread with the periscope he assumed that I was doing so this time. Consequently all three were fired to hit, and fortunately all three did.

After firing #3 immediately shifted to the center tanker who still had a zero angle on the bow and got a quick set up. Before I could fire, however,

0940-28 First torpedo hit.

0940-35 Second torpedo hit.

0940-42 Third torpedo hit.

Took a quick look at the first target and was in time to see the second one hit while smoke and debris from the first hit was still in the air. All had hit forward of his bridge, and he had burst into heavy flames forward. He was stopped and already commencing to sink by the bow. The third one hit after I had swung back to the middle target and just as we fired #4. Those three torpedoes were respectively a 900 lb. torpex head, a 1000 lb. torpex head and a 900 lb. torpex head.

Got final set up on middle tanker, zero angle on the bow, course 212°T, speed 14 knots, range 1,130, torpedo run 820 yards, own course and speed unchanged.

0940-42 Fired #4 tube.

0940-50 Fired #5 tube.

Checked fire. Target had commenced to swing to the right probably due to having seen the explosions on #1 target. He couldn't have done anything to please me more for it gave a 30° port angle on the bow and obviated the necessity of my having to go deep to avoid being rammed.

0941-10 Fired #6 tube.

Both escorts were well clear and still holding their courses. We had come up to 58 feet now so had to go ahead full.

0941-20 Heard and saw one torpedo hit about a quarter length in from his stern.

0941-32 Heard second torpedo hit but the periscope was vibrating so much that I couldn't see the target distinctly. Like the first tanker he immediately burst into flames aft on the first hit.

0941-36 Heard third torpedo hit. Had managed to get started down about a minute later so slowed. Got going down too fast and got to 75 feet before we could check it.

0944 Got back up to periscope depth. Nothing was left of the first target but floating debris. One particularly large piece of wreckage looked like the top of his bridge or a large hatch cover.

Found the second tanker back on my port quarter burning fiercely aft and his stern just about to go under and now an amazing sight greeted my eyes. The third tanker, which I had ignored in my concentration on #1 and #2, was just abaft my port beam and listing about 10° to port. One of the torpedoes fired at #2 target had hit him apparently. Subsequent plot indicated that the most likely occurrence was that #4 torpedo which was fired down the throat to hit #2 target missed to the left and #3 tanker ran into it. #5 was spread one-half degree to the right which was probably the hit I saw on the stern of #2 tanker. #6 torpedo was fired with a new set up and probably hit the MOT or somewhere abaft it.

The escorts, two minelayers, were now closing in, though not too close yet. #4 tanker had turned hard right and was on a northerly course about 6,000 to 8,000 yards from us. Got a quick set up on #3 tanker but the range was 4,000 yards so shifted to #2 target again. Although he appeared to be sinking by the stern I figured one more hit would really finish him. Got a set up for a stern tube shot with a MK 18 torpedo. Target speed zero, angle on the bow 120° port, range 1,040 yards, torpedo run 1,000 yards, and at...

0944-26 Fired #8 tube after feeding continuous bearings into the TDC for about 10 seconds to be sure he wasn't moving. Commenced watching the escorts again. The escort which had been on the starboard flank of the convoy was now headed almost directly at us—his angle on the bow 10° starboard and range about 3,000 yards. One escort was of the *Yukikaze* destroyer class or very similar to it but I did not get a good enough look at the silhouette of the other to identify it—probably the same class.

0945-28 Heard #8 hit. Looked at the target and saw the smoke from the hit. His stern was now under and his bow coming out of the water at an angle.

0945-40 Ten depth charges in rapid succession—escort about 2,000 yards away still headed in our direction. Started deep and rigged for depth charging.

0946 to 0948 Sound heard crackling noises typical of a sinking ship breaking up. Both operators are familiar with this sound as they had occasion to listen leisurely to a sinking ship on our last patrol.

0950 to 0952 Eleven depth charges. Commenced evasion at 300 feet.

0953 Four depth charges.

0956 Four depth charges.

0958 Ten depth charges.

1005 Escorts commenced echo ranging.

1008 Three depth charges.

1010 to 1014 Eleven fairly close charges but not close enough to do anything but shake the ship a little—no damage.

1025 to 1030 Eight depth charges.

1120 Commenced easing up to periscope depth to look the situation over.

1153 At 100 feet they had either heard us or coincidentally dropped three more. Started back down.

1212 Four more charges, fairly distant.

1217 Three distant explosions.

1229 Could hear screws and pinging of one escort on each quarter.

1229 to 1605 We seemed to gradually draw away from the escorts—our speed had been constant between three and four knots.

1605 Started up for a look—two distant depth charges—sounded like they were reading our minds. Continued on up slowly while hearing more pinging.

1704 Distant explosion.

1717 First periscope observation.

1727 (Ship Contact #21) Sighted masts of one escort much closer than I thought either of them were—about 9,000 yards. Changed course to keep him astern.

1910 Surfaced and set course north in bright moonlight.

1920 (Aircraft Contact #26) Sighted exhaust of a plane on starboard bow. He didn't seem to be coming in for an attack so hoped he hadn't seen us. He had, however, for he started circling slowly around us. He sent out letter "U" three times waiting for an answer each time. He didn't get one as we were busy trying to get the signalman up to the bridge. He gave up on the "U" and started to send "0." This looked very much as if he had made the foolish mistake of trying out both the challenge and the reply on us. I commenced sending "U" at him trying to imitate a frantic signalman on a JAP surface ship. We came to a deadlock here for he answered back with "U." I now took up sending "0's" trying to further confuse him into thinking we had all the signals.

This would have been a fairly risky procedure except for the fact that we could see him clearly and I was sure he couldn't come in on a bombing run before we could get down. After a couple of minutes he sent "NONO." That had me stymied so I sent no answer. I was hoping he would shove off so we could get our battery charge in and return to the scene of the firing but about this time he cut his run and started gliding in. This looked like an investigation run and not a bombing run. I didn't wait to find out. Submerged as SJ picked him up at 1,600 yards.

1927 One bomb.

1930 Second bomb.

2015 Planed up for a look. All clear on periscope and SD radar.

2025 Surfaced. Decided not to return to the vicinity of Pangutaran Island as we were now located and I anticipated that he would direct surface craft to our position. Resumed battery charge and took a westerly course heading for Cegayan Sulu Island.

As nearly as I can identify the tankers the largest was very similar to the NUZISAN MARU, page 235, ONI 208 J (revised), 9,527 tons, the second and third similar to the SAN CLEMENTE and SAN RAMON MARU, page 284, 7,300 tons, and the fourth I did not see enough of to be able to identify it. There are some 20 other tankers in the recognition manual capable of making a cruising speed of 14 knots about half of which have profiles similar to the tankers attacked. These are all 9,000 and 10,000 ton tankers having cruising speeds of 16 and 17 knots.

There are a couple of other points to be mentioned with regard to this attack. First, I believe I missed an opportunity to put two more hits into Tanker #3 which I passed up because of his excessive range of 4,000 yards. I have thought it over considerable since and I believe I was in low power on the periscope when I took that range. Also, the range was difficult to take due to his heavy port list. I was using top of mast to deck. Secondly, though we got seven hits with seven torpedoes, the maximum expectancy was only five. One accidental hit and failure to spread the first target gave us the two extra hits. Also I am strictly cognizant of the fact that the fire control error of failing to spread the first three might have cost us three misses. Only the short range and the fact that the problem was checking so well on the TDC insured our hitting.

Two native sailing canoes were in the vicinity and must have observed the entire action.

6 June

0030 Sent message concerning the action of the previous day, number of torpedoes left, and that we were off station.

0641 Submerged with Cegayan Sulu Island in sight for all day dive.

1917 Surfaced and headed toward northern approach to Sibutu Passage.

2200 Received orders to return to Darwin via Sibutu Passage, Celebes Sea, Molucca Passage and east of Timor for possible reload [WPR].

Stoy described the action from his perspective.

Commenced our approach, in position, fired six torpedoes forward at 0845 and were greeted with the beautiful explosions of six hits, they were not asleep as the depth charging has started already, we came about and fired one more "fish" aft which was also a hit, in doing so two of the tankers were observed to sink while the third was in a severely damaged condition, depth charge attack has increased considerably and we were forced to go deep, after being held down for eleven hours by a constant and fairly accurate depth charge barrage we managed to surface and find they had given us up and shoved off, but we were immediately challenged by a Jap float plane, in stalling for time we returned the same challenge he sent us and before he got wise to us and started his bombing run on us we were on our way down, but when he dropped his bombs they were still close enough to shake the hell out of us, after being down about fifteen minutes it was found the batteries were just about exhausted, so we would have to surface and shoot it out with him, but upon surfacing we found he had lost us in the dark and that was the last we heard of him, charged batteries underway on a southeastern course [Stoy].

Japanese sources verified the *Puffer* credit for sinking two tankers of 7,951 tons and 4,465 tons—respectively the *Ashizuri Maru* and the *Takasaki Maru*. The *Takasaki Maru* was formerly the British *Shinhwa*, seized by the Japanese at Kuching, Sarawak (Borneo), in January 1942. The two tankers left Balikpapan on May 12 bound for Saipan. Both carried 3,700 kiloliters of aviation gasoline. They successfully delivered the aviation fuel to Saipan and left on May 28 bound for Yap Island, escorted by coastal defense vessels *Kanju* and *Miyake*. The two tankers successfully delivered aviation personnel and equipment to Yap on May 30. Escorted by the same two coastal defense vessels, on June 1 the empty tankers departed for another load of aviation fuel from Balikpapan (Somerville, 1991). The *Puffer* terminated the supply chain of gasoline, materials and personnel on June 5. The damage to the third tanker was not verified.

Mechanical Troubles

Although not mentioned in the war patrol report, motor machinists Ladislaus Topor and Herbert Hayward performed a maintenance duty which earned them a Bronze Star. In a 2004 letter Topor explained the situation.

Ladislaus Topor receives the Bronze Star (photograph courtesy of Ladislaus Topor).

We encountered a small Japanese naval force. In the ensuring approach one of the destroyers spotted us and initiated a depth charge attack. Three additional destroyers joined the party and all had a merry time dropping depth charges. By night fall we finally eluded them. Our batteries were low, so we surfaced. Lit off #1 and 2 mains [engines] but immediately shut them down due to the muffler noise and sparks. Since the destroyers were still in the vicinity we did not dare to light off #3 and 4. I was the engineer Chief in charge of main propulsion, so the Capt. questioned me on the probable cause of the commotion.

The diesel mufflers were water quenched. This helped muffle the noise and cool the exhaust. The racket and sparks indicated that the mufflers were damaged. Requested and received permission to go topside and verify my prognosis. Found #1 and 2 mufflers ruptured. #2 indication of damage, unable to inspect #4 totally. However the "donkey" (small 8 cylinder auxiliary) muffler seemed intact. Returned below, advised the Capt. of the situation, suggested that we light off the donkey and put it on main propulsion. Explained that maybe temporary patches could be applied to the mufflers. Received permission to give it a try. Approached Herb Hayward (MoMM1c). He was short in stature and slender, able to crawl into areas I couldn't. He agreed to go with me. We assembled available supplies (sheet asbestos, sheet metal and aluminum and an assortment of wire). For moral support we included a couple of inflatable life belts.

We crawled into the superstructure patched #1 (strip of asbestos covered with strip of sheet metal, wired in place.) Lit off #1 eng., patch held. Repeated on #2, it held. No material left for #3. Returned below and next day out to sea in broad daylight affected repair to #3, #4 was intact. Thusly we completed our patrol. For our baling wire mechanics, Herb and I were recommended for the Bronze Star and subsequently awarded same. Just another example of the improvisation and patchwork repairs performed on sub patrols [Topor].

Topor's Bronze Star Citation stated:

For distinguishing himself by meritorious and heroic conduct in action as a member of the crew of the *U.S.S. Puffer* during the Fourth War Patrol of that vessel in enemy waters. In spite of the fact that he knew enemy men-of-war were in the vicinity and that his ship might be forced to dive any instant, Topor volunteered with another man to go topside at night and accomplish repairs to piping beneath the superstructure deck, thereby quieting the excessive noise being made by two main engines and eliminating a grave military hazard to his ship. Part of this work had to be done with his body in such a position underneath the piping that it is extremely doubtful whether he would have been able to extricate himself in time to get below had the ship been forced to dive. Topor accepted this risk with complete disregard for his own personal safety. His conduct throughout was an inspiration to the officers and men of his ship and distinguished him among those performing duties of the same character. Signed, T.C. Kinkaid, Vice Admiral, Commander Seventh Fleet [*ibid.*].

Resistance in the Sibutu Passage

The *Puffer* was ordered on June 6 to proceed to Darwin for a possible reload of torpedoes. Only two torpedoes remained aft. First the boat would have to run the gauntlet of the Sibutu Passage, now under the watchful eyes of Japanese air and destroyer patrols. The *Harder*, under the command of Sam Dealey, was also in the vicinity of the Sibutu Passage and had sunk a destroyer on June 6 (Alden, *Successes*, p. D-150). To stir up the hornet's nest further, the *Harder* sunk another destroyer on June 7, prior to the day the *Puffer* attempted to pass through. On the June 7 at 0455 the *Puffer* submerged and approached the northern entrance to the Sibutu Passage. Unfortunately a strong current hampered the progress. At 1606 Selby spotted a plane through the periscope and delayed surfacing. At 1930 the *Puffer* surfaced and had still not yet reached the narrow passage. A bright moon hung overhead and the seas were like glass, making the sub's wake easily seen by aircraft. For the next two and one-half hours the *Puffer* went undetected and Selby recharged the batteries. At 2245 with batteries charged, on all four main engines the *Puffer* started the sprint through the Sibutu Passage at 18 knots. Thirty minutes later an aircraft forced the boat to submerge (WPR).

By 0126 on June 8 the *Puffer* had progressed only halfway through the Sibutu Passage, with weaker but persistent northerly currents retarding the forward movement. At 0145 fast screws were heard starting up, suggesting a destroyer was waiting. The *Puffer* went undetected. However, due to the rapidly approaching daylight, Selby was required to submerge for the next 17 hours. At 1902 the *Puffer* surfaced again, and picked up radar interference. Two ship contacts were made in the next 45 minutes. With information that became known later, Selby conjectured in the war patrol report that the radar interference and ship contact was the *Harder* making another approach. At 2145 another aircraft forced the boat down for 90 minutes. The

Puffer surfaced. Forty-five minutes later another aircraft contact was made, but it did not approach. Two more aircraft contacts early on June 9 forced the *Puffer* to crash dive again. By 2326 on June 9 the *Puffer* had finally cleared the hot area (*ibid.*).

Friendly Natives

The *Puffer* moved east through the Celebes Sea, and then south into the Molucca Sea with no more air contacts until 0721 on June 11. Forty minutes later the sky was all clear. Shortly after surfacing a small craft was detected. Selby decided to make contact with the natives. If unfriendly toward the Japanese, the local inhabitants might divulge valuable information about the location of Japanese vessels (*ibid.*).

> 0900 Sighted large sailboat bearing 116°T and changed course to close. The boat was a small two masted cabin schooner manned by natives. She carried a mainsail, a foresail and a jib, had the letters "PICKY" on her bow (some obliterated letters in front of the "P") and the numbers "R21 or P27" on her stern. She was a very clean, well rigged and shipshape looking boat though obviously fairly old. Took some pictures of her.
>
> After considerable gesturing and yelling got them to head into the wind and two of the natives to get in their dugout canoe and come over. This was all done with considerable reluctance on their part as they were apparently very much afraid of us—guess I would be, too, if I was in their shoes. They killed a lot of time unlashing their canoe and putting it over and then much more time in a very unseamanlike attempt to bail it out from the deck of the sailboat with a short length of line tied to a sail. I put up with all that nonsense and kept all hands away from the 20 MM guns on the bridge so that they would not become any more frightened than they were, for I wanted volunteers to come back with us.
>
> Two fairly old and very respectful natives came over for the parley. It was very difficult to get the idea across that we wanted one of them to come with us, even though I had a printed sheet of Malayan words taken from one of the BuPers Bulletins. Net result was that they didn't want to come with us unless they could take their boat and all passengers. They didn't like the Japanese but we were fine and they didn't have any fish aboard. We all parted the best of friends, they with my peace offering of two or three pounds of rice and five packages of cigarettes and we with nothing [*ibid.*].

After the friendly exchange with the natives, the next day Timor Island was sighted. Another plane forced the *Puffer* to submerge and stay down during the morning hours. The *Puffer* surfaced at 1207 and another aircraft at 1703 made for another crash dive. All clear 15 minutes later and surfaced again. During the night Selby received orders to remain at Darwin pending further orders and be prepared to take on torpedoes, fuel and stores on short notice. The *Puffer* had been out for 45 days, a typical length for a war patrol, but circumstances dictated redeployment if the gathering force at Tawi Tawi departed. On June 13 the *Puffer* arrived at Darwin, and awaited orders. Orders arrived the next day to proceed to Fremantle. Undoubtedly the crew was relieved. The *Puffer* headed south and arrived at Fremantle for repairs on June 21 and two weeks of rest and recuperation (*ibid.*).

Awards

Selby received a Navy Cross for the Fourth War Patrol. The citation credited the damage to the aircraft carrier.

> Aggressive and relentless in tracking the enemy, he expertly maneuvered and fought his ship throughout brilliantly executed attacks against hostile surface forces and by his outstanding

skill and daring contributed to the success of the PUFFER in sinking three enemy ships totaling 24,300 tons and in damaging a large aircraft carrier and another Japanese ship despite severe hostile countermeasures [Selby, *Biography*].

The boat was awarded the Navy Unit Commendation for the Fourth War Patrol. However this award was not presented until after hostilities had ceased. This award was established by the secretary of the Navy on December 18, 1944, and was awarded by the secretary, with the approval of the president. The Unit Commendation was conferred on any ship of the Navy, which after December 6, 1941, distinguished itself by outstanding heroism in action against the enemy, but not sufficient to justify the award of the Presidential Unit Citation.

11

The Fifth War Patrol

New Men and New Equipment

Twenty-two men left the *Puffer* for other duties. Six Fourth War Patrol transfers along with Creech, Julian Roberts, and Wilson from earlier patrols returned to the *Puffer*. Many of the veterans that helped save the *Puffer* during the First War Patrol left: Anderson, Brockhausen, Henger, Hetrick, Huddleston, Kellum, Lefferts, Love, Patsko, Sander, Solak, and Zelaznicki (RG24). Their combined expertise would be difficult to replace. Carl Dwyer also returned as executive officer after organizing and teaching a TDC school in Perth (WPR).

CREW TRANSFERRED AFTER THE FOURTH WAR PATROL

Name	*Service #*	*Rate Arr.*	*Fourth WP*	*Fifth WP*
Akeman, Robert Bruce	300 57 76	S2c	S1c	TRAN
Allen, John Chester	360 09 28	QM3c	QM2c	TRAN
Anderson, Robert Emil	250 45 32	EM2c	EM1c	TRAN
Brockhausen, Charles William, Jr.	223 47 23	QM1c	QM1c	TRAN
Coggins, Donald Grey	656 99 31	MoMM2cV6	MoMM2c	TRAN
Hannon, James Wesley	382 59 33	SC3c	25-Apr-44	TRAN
Henger, Vincent John	250 58 16	RM2c	RM1c	TRAN
Hetrick, William Herman	250 49 66	MoMM1c	19-Apr-44	TRAN
Hopkinson, Alfred Harry	222 98 51	CPhM(PA)	19-Apr-44	TRAN
Huddleston, Walter Carter	644 39 21	S2cV6	S1c	TRAN
Kellum, Raymond Herlong	268 17 81	GM2c	29-Apr-44	TRAN
Lefferts, Harry Edward	223 62 74	F1c	MoMM2c	TRAN
Lemar, John Edward	607 49 76	F1cV6	F1c	TRAN
Love, Oliver Willard	346 76 77	TM2c	TM1c	TRAN
Martinson, Kenneth Russell	665 12 72	RT2cV6	RT2c	TRAN
Orbovich, Michael MacAllen	258 50 07	S2c	TM3c	TRAN
Patsko, Demeter	250 38 55	Y1c	CY(AA)	TRAN
Prisby, Henry Bernard	622 24 82	EM3cV6	EM3c	TRAN
Sander, Harold Eugene	316 56 20	EM1c	EM1c	TRAN
Solak, John	243 82 28	F1c	MoMM3c	TRAN

Name	Service #	Rate Arr.	Fourth WP	Fifth WP
Switzer, Donald Raymond	411 18 66	MoMM2cV6	MoMM2c	TRAN
Zelaznicki, Joseph	410 31 59	EM1c	CEM(AA)	TRAN

New and Returning Crew Members

Name	Service #	Rate Arr.	Date Arr.
Bianco, Louis	807 36 30	F1c(EM)	4-Jul-44
Bollman, Eric Petter	555 58 73	RT2cV6	4-Jul-44
Bull, Maurice H.	403 72 62	CPhMV6	13-Jul-44
Corke, Robert Edward	647 16 61	S2cV6	4-Jul-44
Creech, Bishop Boggs	634 13 65	F3cV6	7-Jul-44
Dogan, Fred F.	283 51 66	MoMM2c(SS)	4-Jul-44
Gutensohn, John Peter	368 30 94	MoMM1c	4-Jul-44
Hagen, Arden J.	868 40 11	SC3cV6	12-Jul-44
James, Paul Daniel	652 44 71	S2cV6	4-Jul-44
Kemp, Thomas R.	375 99 09	CEM(AA)(T)	9-Jul-44
Kennedy, Robert Francis	622 45 19	S2cV6	5-Jul-44
Liggett, James David	636 49 86	F3cV6	4-Jul-44
Mays, Frank, Jr.	867 18 90	S1c(RM)V6	4-Jul-44
Musha, Donald Anthony	868 51 12	S1c(QM)V6	4-Jul-44
Nelson, John Joseph	243 56 66	MoMM1c(SS)	12-Jul-44
Nielsen, Howard Stello	368 56 98	SM1c	13-Jul-44
Parker, James Victor	268 75 37	MoMM2c	4-Jul-44
Roberts, Julian Alonzo	272 23 31	EM1c	5-Jul-44
Smith, Edward W.	337 60 69	S1c	4-Jul-44
Thoman, Andrew J. II	882 43 91	S1c(Y)V6	4-Jul-44
Weber, Lawrence R.	647 18 58	Y2cV6(SS)	4-Jul-44
Wilson, William Earl, Jr.	311 93 42	S2c	4-Jul-44

The crew received the usual two weeks rest and recreation while the boat was being repaired and refitted. Two improvements were installed: a JP-1 Listening Device, which gave the submarine superior sound information; and the long awaited SJ-1 radar unit with PPI display. The orders directed the *Puffer* to conduct unrestricted warfare against the Japanese in the Makassar Strait, the Celebes Sea, and the South China Sea (*ibid.*). The crew knew that after this patrol they would return stateside for a major overhaul at Mare Island, California. For many crew members it had been over a year since they had seen friends and family.

On July 14 at 1500 it was back to the grind for many of the crew who had been on board for three or four war patrols. For the next couple of days the *Puffer* moved north toward Exmouth Gulf for refueling. As usual something was not working properly. The pitometer log in spite of a second overhaul — the first had been done during training exercises — was not functioning correctly. During refueling a third attempt was made to repair the pitometer. The electrician mates worked all night and calibration runs were made the next morning with success. Operation was satisfactory on the surface, however a day later it was discovered, while conducting fire control training dives, the pitometer was still not working at slow submerged speeds. A two hour dive was again made to attempt repair of the irksome piece of hardware. The 3-inch and 20mm gun crews practiced on an old shipwreck. On July 20 the equipment was functioning properly under all conditions. Selby credited Thomas R. Kemp, EM1c, with a job well done for a week of untiring effort and professional ability (*ibid.*).

Return to the Makassar Strait

During the next week the *Puffer* proceeded through the Lombok Strait and northward into the Makassar Strait. In the southern entrance to the Makassar Strait many radar contacts were made on small craft. Undoubtedly some of these craft were Japanese patrol boats on the lookout for American submarines. Selby worked the area around Balikpapan before moving into the narrowest portion of the northern Makassar Strait, very close to where the boat operated during the First War Patrol. Selby described the most frustrating events (*ibid.*).

29 July

0401 Four miles off LABUAN BINI [a peninsula that juts out into the Makassar Strait toward Celebes Island] had to maneuver to avoid being sighted by a sail boat which I felt might possibly report our presence. As a result we did not reach the desired diving position and had to submerge at daylight off the above point. This was just about the poorest spot we could be in as it was the logical turning point. Thus began the most exasperating morning's submarine operations I have been through to date.

0505 Submerged 5 miles southeast of LABUAN BINI POINT. Could not safely head toward the beach in any direction until it was light enough to get cuts for there was a 2 knot southwesterly current running. Headed into current.

0516 JP sound operator picked up screws in the direction of LABUAN BINI POINT, bearing changing to northward. Went to battle stations and took estimated normal approach course at full speed. Visibility considerably hampered not only by the early morning darkness but also by numerous floating logs, also branches and the general debris characteristic of this area. During the last 15 minutes JP sound picked up one more bona fide contact and three false ones.

0535 (Ship Contact #8) Observed that screws belonged to trawler type coastal vessel hugging coast. Broke off approach and commenced looking for some of the other reported screws after going to 60 feet to get rid of 8 or 10 feet of seaweed trailing from periscope. Bumped large log with periscope on coming up. No damage.

0606 (Ship Contact #9) Sighted smoke bearing about 270°.

0618 Sighted two masts on bearing of smoke. Apparently a ship heading toward us to round LABUAN BINI POINT. Commenced approach. Could see beach well enough now to keep from being inadvertently set onto it.

0645 Recognized target as a small coastal steamer as he swung wide around the point and came to a northwesterly course, about 2 miles off the beach. We were in a good position to sink him with torpedoes set shallow, but I did not consider him worth torpedo fire and this was no time to let our presence be known for other reasons.

0700 (Ship Contact #10) Sighted smoke bearing 280°. Smoke developed into two medium freighters, zero angle on the bow, both hugging coast in column about 1 mile apart and headed for LABUAN BINI POINT on course 100°. Changed course to 100° to put them directly astern, while waiting to see whether they would hold their course or swing left up the coast. Considering the actions of the coastal steamer as it went around the point, this looked like a good spot to be in.

0705 Picked up the masts of an escort vessel.

0715 With the two ships still on a steady course, angle on the bow 5° starboard and range about 9,000 yards, it appeared that they were past their turning point. Being right on their track, I decided to pull out to starboard for a stern tube shot at the first one, and then swing for a bow tube shot at the second. Commenced pulling out for a 90° starboard track.

0721 No change in set up.

0731 Leading ship had swung left to course 040° hugging the coast. It was evident that I now could not close him. The second ship was still on course 100° but was undoubtedly due to follow the leader, so came left at full speed to close his track for a bow tube shot after his expected course change.

0736 Second target changed course to 040° as predicted.

0748 Second target now at range 5,000 yards with 110° starboard angle on the bow. I was

Opposite: The Fifth War Patrol — July 14, 1944 (Fremantle), to August 29, 1944 (Pearl Harbor) — 3,784 nautical miles in the patrol area. The *Puffer* patrolled the Makassar Strait, the Celebes Sea, the Sulu Sea, and the South China Sea. After stopping briefly at Pearl Harbor the boat returned to Mare Island, California, for an overhaul. The flags indicate where attacks were made. The rising sun flag shows an attack on the Imperial Japanese Navy; the lone sun flags show an attack on a merchant vessel (map artwork by Nancy Webber).

so disgusted at having wound up in this position, since, if I had played it differently, it should have been an easy shot on at least one straight target at close range, that I was determined not to let the second one go without firing. Also, he not only looked closer than 5,000 yards, but our estimated position was only 5,000 yards from the beach.

0749 ATTACK NO. 1
    Latitude 00-47 North.
    Longitude 118-50.7 East.
    Target course 040°, speed 12.5 knots, angle on bow 120° starboard, TDC range 5,150 yards, TDC torpedo run 6,000 yards, own course 000°, speed 3.7 knots, gyro angle 9 left. Commenced firing 6 torpedoes using a spread of 200% of the estimated target length.

The torpedoes put up such a heavy cloud of bluish white smoke that they partially obscured the beach to the north and made it very difficult to see the PC escort ahead of the target. In spite of the smoke, I watched the torpedoes run for a full two minutes before either the escort or target took any action. The PC headed in our direction with about a 30° starboard angle on the bow and a few seconds later the target came hard right. In the meantime we were swinging left to bring our stern tubes to bear.

The freighter came around until he presented 10° port angle on the bow, so we set up for a port track, the range having increased to about 3,500 yards. In the meantime, minelayer escort was spotted heading in our direction with a 30° port angle on the bow from abaft the target. He had apparently been riding on the port quarter of the target or I would have seen him before this—though how he could find any navigable water between the target and the shore is somewhat of a mystery.

0758 Three depth charges. Decided to evade at periscope depth as long as I could keep track of both escorts if they didn't get too close.

The target had now come back to his original course of 040° and was pulling away.

0800 Three depth charges. The minelayer must have dropped these for I was watching the PC when they went off and saw no sign of depth charges in his vicinity.

0803 Two depth charges. Minelayer headed back for convoy and PC stayed with us, echo ranging. Put stern to him, TDC set up, and stern tubes set on 2 feet.

0817 PC boat headed back toward convoy and we lost sight of him about 10 minutes later.

0838 Reload completed forward.

0842 (Aircraft Contact #1) Sighted dive bomber (RUFE) headed towards us from about 4 miles at low altitude. Went to 150 ft. and commenced pulling clear at 4 knots.

0930 Came up for look and navigational fix. All clear. Evasion of escorts and plane had taken us 7 miles out.

0939 Picked up echo ranging on approximate true bearing 290°T. Figured this was an A/S vessel sweeping for us but on the possibility that it was a target which hadn't gotten the news, headed for the beach at standard speed.

0956 Heard second pinger on same bearing and sighted smoke.

1007 (Ship Contact #11) Sighted two masts and top of bridge of large vessel and tops of two double masted escort vessels. Our only chance to get a shot at him was the possibility he might swing wider around LABUAN BINI POINT than the preceding two vessels had or that he was going slower.

1025 Couldn't close. Had been running standard and full speed for 45 minutes and his angle on the bow was 110° starboard, estimated range 5,500 yards.

This hurt for it was a valuable target. At this time I could not positively identify it because of the land background and a low haze on the water which distorted its appearance but its man-of-war bow, bridge, tripod mast forward, large size, and the fact that it had two large minelayer or destroyer escorts indicated it was valuable. Subsequent sighting of this ship on the 31st when it got past us again and on the 1st of August when it didn't, positively identified it as the submarine tender TSURUGISAKI of 12,000 tons displacement or her sister ship the TAKASAKI.

The first two freighters were MFM, well deck type, one similar to the OSAKA MARU type, 4,000 tons, page 132, ONI 208J, and the other similar to the KAHOKU MARU type, 3,300 tons, page 135.

1031 (Ship Contact #12) Sighted more smoke and masts on approximate bearing 280°T, so rang up full speed and held it. Was determined nothing else was going to pass between us and the beach at a greater range than 2,000 yards.

1042 False alarm. Of four vessels passing, one was a steam driven schooner with high masts which made it appear large from a distance (actually about three or four hundred tons) and the other three were sea trucks.

1048 (Aircraft Contact #2) Sighted observation plane (DAVE) apparently searching. Not close so kept an eye on him.

1052 (Ship Contact #13) While closing the beach one of the PC boats had been heard pinging as he came back toward us from the direction of the convoy. At this time he passed 1,000 yards astern using manual keying and alternating long pings and double pings. We were set up on him but he continued on his way without giving any indication of contacting us.

My purpose in keeping set up on shallow draft escorts when at periscope depth is not to shoot at them if they merely get within range but to be prepared to shoot if they get within range and start offensive action. I firmly believe that, regardless of how shallow the draft of an escort, a torpedo running under him or close to him convinces him that he is considered a legitimate target and thereby reduces his effectiveness as an A/S vessel considerably.

1103 Navigational fix one mile from shore so commenced pulling out to 4,000 yards to patrol parallel to the coast on a northeasterly heading to see if anything else might still be coming through.

1223 (Ship Contact #14) Sighted another PC on the port bow heading toward us from a range of about 7,000 yards. Believe he heard our air compressor running. He stopped and commenced lying to, listening, when we rigged for silent running. Put him astern and slowly worked away from him.

1327 Sighted another PC about 2 miles from first.

1414 All clear and quiet. Headed east to be about 15 miles clear of land on surfacing.

1916 Surfaced 20 miles east of LABUAN BINI POINT and headed out of MAKASSAR STRAIT. Since all today's targets were hugging the coast, decided to try and make contact off TARAKAN. Planned to get fix on SIPADAN ISLAND (Lat. 04-07N, Long. 118-38E) and then head for a spot 30 miles northeast of TARAKAN along the inshore traffic route from TARAKAN north [*ibid.*].

Shallow Water

After the frustrations of July 29, Selby decided to take a different strategy. He used July 30 to move north and east of Tarakan and submerged just outside the 100 fathom curve. There were shallows and reefs to the north. During the First War Patrol the *Puffer* ran aground in this area and was nearly lost. Very similar to the first patrol, the weather was not cooperating. July 31 was more frustration, but August 1 was a better day (*ibid.*).

31 July

0512 Submerged just outside 100 fathom curve with BUNYU ISLAND bearing 240°T, distance 20 miles and commenced closing 10 fathom curve.

It was necessary to make this approach to shallow water with the utmost caution as the 10 fathom curve is only 1½ miles from a three fathom bank which extends 11 miles from BUNYU on this bearing. The only navigational points for cuts are the right and left tangents of BUNYU and high peaks 45 miles to the north and northwest. These peaks had been identified the previous day but on this particular morning were unfortunately clouded over most of the time. This meant, in effect, that when we were about two miles from the 10 fathom curve our position would have to be fixed by two tangents on a 500 ft. island 13 miles away. Add to this the fact that 7 or 8 fresh water rivers emptying into the sea here make depth control difficult (we regularly dropped from 65 feet to 80 ft. or rose to 50 ft.) and the fact that we had intermittent rain squalls all morning, and it was a tricky proposition.

All the above merely goes to prove that Fate can be most unkind. For, if we had been able to fix our position an hour earlier than we did, or if the two valuable targets which came past had been an hour later, we would probably have gotten in on them.

0919 Position fairly well established by regular use of fathometer in conjunction with cuts. We were 7 miles out from the 10 fathom curve so headed in.

0939 (Ship Contact #15) Sighted masts of what at first appeared to be two patrol vessels dead ahead in column on a northerly course. When a light rain squall in that vicinity cleared, a bridge was visible abaft the first mast and a stack abaft the second mast. Although I never saw the hull itself this was apparently a large tanker, 6 or 7 miles away with an angle on the bow close to 90° starboard. Commenced closing at high speed but he was too far away. He made one zig about 30 degrees in our direction but then zigged away again.

1006 (Ship Contact #16) Sighted smoke on port bow from direction of TARAKAN. Took a westerly course at full speed to close his probable track close to the 10 fathom curve.

1023 Picked up pinging of two ships on bearing of target. This target turned out to be the submarine tender previously sighted off MANGKALIHAT with two minelayer escorts similar to the YAEYAMA class. The outboard escort was doing the smoking.

1106 Closed this group at high speed until at which time the target's angle on the bow was 90° starboard and his range about 6,000 yards. We were just too far out to start with. As nearly as could be estimated, he was running between the 10 fathom curve and the 3 fathom shoals and in spite of this was zigzagging. It's no wonder that they go aground in this vicinity. Needless to say it was not pleasant to see him get past us again — to say nothing of the tanker.

Since no chase was practical here, decided to pull out for a couple of hours, surface and head for SIBUTU PASSAGE (4.82°N, 119.65°E) to intercept them at the eastern entrance to DARVEL BAY.

During the approach I made careful written notes of his appearance for I was still not quite certain what type ship it was other than that it was a man-of-war and probably some kind of tender. After the approach I made a sketch and then attempted identification. His characteristics were so striking and definite that only a sister ship could be mistaken for this vessel. Man-of-war bow, bridge forward, small turret forward of bridge, large tripod mast immediately aft bridge, long stretch of heavily loaded deck, stack aft, heavy goal post mast abaft stack, another turret aft of after mast and a cruiser stern. I had the Executive Officer [Dwyer] take two looks to check on any points I might have missed. One point we both missed at this range were his cranes just abaft the foremast. Those were seen the following day in the lowered position from a range of 2,000 yards.

The submarine tender shown on page 89 of ONI 41 dated 1941, resembles this ship in practically every detail and no other ship in any of the recognition manuals even comes close to it. According to the manual there are two of this class submarine tender, the TSURUGISAKI and the TAKASAKI of 12,000 tons displacement each. The following were the only differences observed.

1. Cranes were in lowered position lying almost flat on deck.
2. Some sort of cargo was loaded along the whole length of the deck between the cranes and stack. This was all covered with tarpaulins.
3. The picture indicates a single tall mast aft of the stack and a smaller mast and boom right on the stern. The latter was not seen. The mast abaft the stack was a heavy goal post type mast of approximately the same height as shown. Either the manual is wrong on this mast or it has been changed.

1128 (SHIP CONTACT #17) Two PC boats on A/S sweep passed us at 5,000 yards coming from direction of convoy and headed toward TARAKAN.

1323 Surfaced and set course for SIBUTU PASSAGE.
2230 Commenced transit of SIBUTU PASSAGE at 10 knots in bright moonlight [*ibid*.].

No postwar data was found on the identity of the Japanese ships.

Sibutu Passage

After the frustrating approaches Selby returned to the area that had been good to him on the Fourth War Patrol. Even though he gave a detailed analysis of the attack and subsequent depth charges, he found it appropriate to insert two humorous anecdotes. Undoubtedly a good sense of humor was a good trait of a submarine commander. The attack took place north of Sibutu Island (*ibid*.). The *Puffer* communicated with another submarine in the area using SJ radar pulses in Morse code. This means of communication was more difficult to intercept than voice communications on normal radio frequencies (Deem).

1 August
0147 Commenced patrolling eastern entrance to DARVEL BAY.
0508 Submerged in Lat. 5-06N, Long. 119-22E and continued patrolling eastern entrance to DARVEL BAY.
0935 (Ship Contact #18) Sighted smoke to southwest with true bearing changing to the right. Came to 340°T, the approximate normal approach course.
0952 Picked up echo ranging on bearing 242°T.
1004 Sighted foremast and top of bridge of TSURUGISAKI and tops of escorts on either side. Target was steering a constant helm plan with present base course about 050°T so put him astern while maneuvering to get ahead of him on his base course.
1031 Previous observation while he was on his extreme left course with the range 7,900 yards indicated that he had either altered his base course to the right or that he was varying the amount of his constant helm swing. This put us to the left of his base course so started right at full speed to close and shoot with the bow tubes on his next extreme left course.
1037 Target swung left, angle on the bow 40° port, range 5,000 yards. Port escort had a 5° starboard angle on the bow, was about 2,500 yards out on the port quarter of the target, and on our starboard beam.
1042 Angle on the bow 90° port. He had just started swinging back right. Escort still on our starboard beam, zero angle on the bow and about 2,000 yards away. Felt that I had to fire this one with a periscope spread as his constant helming had prevented our obtaining more than a rough estimate of his speed — somewhere between 13 and 17 knots. I was using very little periscope and there was a light chop on the surface so the chances were good that the escort wouldn't see the periscope.

1043 ATTACK NO 2(a)
  Latitude 05-07.2N
  Longitude 119-34E
  Target course 060°T, swinging right, estimated speed 15 knots, angle on the bow 110° port, range 1,750 yards, torpedo run 2130 yards, track 127° port, gyro angle 10° right, own course 100°T.
    1043-00 Fired One — aimed ¼ length ahead.
    1043-11 Fired two — aimed just ahead.
    1043-18 Fired three — aimed ¼ length inside bow.
    1045-26 Fired four — aimed at M. O. T.
    1043-54 Fired five — aimed ¼ length inside stern.
    1043-40 Fired six — aimed ¼ length astern.
  Swung periscope immediately to starboard beam to look for port escort but found him

instead 10 degrees abaft our port beam, angle on the bow 180° and starting to swing left. He had apparently run right across our stern.

1044-21 First torpedo explosion, loud and heavy. Could not look immediately as we were getting set up on escort who had commenced to swing left.

1044-30 Dull explosion which was barely heard. May have been an internal explosion on the ship, a torpedo dud, or a torpedo exploding in such a way that it didn't make much noise.

Escort was still swinging left presenting a 90° port angle on the bow. Commenced swinging right for a stern tube shot. Range about 1,500 yards.

Looked at target to see what had happened to him. He was slightly down by the bow and still swinging right. While I was watching at...

1044-51 saw another torpedo hit him just under the bridge. This was one of the most terrific torpedo explosions I have ever seen. It shook us up considerably. His whole bow and bridge were engulfed in huge cloud of smoke and spray which rose above the top of his foremast. I think the torpedo must have hit either a fuel tank forward or a magazine.

On swinging back to the escort, found he had a 50° port angle on the bow range still about 1,500 yards. When he steadied with a 10° port angle on the bow, his range was 1,200 yards.

1046-48 *ATTACK No. 2 (b)*

Range 1,050 yards, torpedo run 760 yards, commenced firing three down the throat in spite of a large right gyro angle. Started deep at the same time for I knew things would be hot if we missed. We did miss and things *were* hot, but not as bad as expected. The third torpedo was not fired by the Control Party because we had started down. This probably saved a torpedo as the set up was pretty much "from the hip." However, he had us spotted and it was a question of going deep or shooting and then going deep. If we had hit him we would have had a period of grace in which to observe the target and perhaps fire more torpedoes at it for the other escort had remained way over on the starboard quarter of the tender.

1048 to 1057 Thirty depth charges in salvoes as follows: four, three, five, four, six, three, five. This ended the depth charging. All were fairly close in that they shook the ship considerably, turned lights off and on, and made the cork fly; no damage to the ship, however.

To add to the growing list of classic remarks that are born on such occasions as this, one of our old timers in the Control Room came down with the following.

"Boy, *them* was close. I was so scared I smoked half the package of *my own* cigarettes before I knew what I was doing."

During and after the depth charging the QB sound gear was kept on a continuous sweep all around in an endeavor to pick up the targets screws while the JP was kept on the two escorts. The target's screws which had been very heavy and distinct prior to firing (sound had been furnishing continuous bearings to TDC), were never heard again after the first torpedo explosion. No difficulty was encountered in keeping track of the screws of the two escort vessels which were light, fast and easily distinguished from the heavy, slower boat of the target's screws. The JP sound operator had much the same experience. He picked up the target's screws during the approach about 10 minutes before the supersonic gear did and the fact that he was listening to the target was checked by periscope observations. After the first torpedo hit the JP operator could not pick up the target's screws again.

In view of the fact that the various sound operators did not hear the target's screws after he was hit and that the depth charging, which did not prevent our keeping track of the escort's screws while it was in progress, ended 12 minutes after the last hit thus giving us a completely clear field for listening. I feel that it is perfectly reasonable to establish as a fact that the target stopped his screws and did not start them again.

1057-1107 Escorts alternated listening and echo ranging. Maneuvered to keep one on each quarter.

1107 Screws of one escort faded out or stopped on true bearing of 122°. Target had been hit on true bearing 100°.

1122 JP and JK operators commenced hearing groaning noises and the crackling breaking up noises of a ship sinking from 100°T to 118°T. The JK and QB operators were familiar with this sound from two previous experiences in which the targets were observed to sink. Commanding Officer also put phones on and listened.

1128 Commenced coming up slowly to periscope depth. One escort alternately listening and echo ranging so could not speed up above 3 knots even though ship was heavy and progress slow.

1155 (about) Heard last of crackling, breaking up noise from direction of target.

1213 (SHIP CONTACT #19) Periscope observation. Escort in sight astern, angle on bow 200° starboard, range 6,000 yards. No sign of target or other escort. Commenced swinging slowly to right to head in direction of target and eventually go south through SIBUTU PASSAGE. Tubes #1, #2, and #4 reloaded forward. Commenced reloading remaining torpedo forward and two aft.

1248 Sighted smoke on bearing 119°T. It was the second escort approaching at high speed. This escort rejoined the first and they both took a northerly course and drew away at high speed. It appeared very much as if the one escort had come over to the target to pick up survivors about the time we heard the breaking up noise while the other looked for us. It was puzzling as to why they would go off and leave us until at...

1305 Picked up echo ranging from the direction of the western entrance to TAWI TAWI BAY.

1311 Lost sight of original escorts.

1330 (SHIP CONTACT #20) Picked up masts of two ships which turned out to be a type 40-44 PC boat and a converted trawler. The PC was echo ranging and the trawler listening. A third A/S vessel could be heard echo ranging farther in toward TAWI TAWI, but only the top of his one mast was ever seen. Looked like another PC. They made a slow sweep past us heading north on an east-west line of bearing. These ships came out of TAWI TAWI BAY probably to relieve the original two escorts. The nearest ship, the trawler, passed about 4,000 yards astern of us while we were on an easterly course.

1425 Lost sight of A/S vessels and resumed southerly course. Distant echo ranging heard for about another hour. We were making 4 knots and aided by a 2 knot southerly current so we made good time through SIBUTU PASSAGE.

1442 (SHIP CONTACT #21) Another small A/S vessel came up from the south, headed for scene of attack. Passed us about 5,000 yards—trawler type.

Although we passed close to the estimated position of the original action nothing was ever seen of the target or any floating wreckage.

I believe the sub tender sank for the following reasons:
(1) Screws stopped and never started again.
(2) Breaking up noises were heard for half an hour.
(3) Not in sight an hour and a half after being hit. In order to get clear he either had to go under his own power or be towed. With his damage forward he would have had to make a high number of turns to get clear in an hour and a half, yet we did not hear his screws. The two escorts available to tow him were observed to leave. A towing vessel would not have had time to come out of TAWI TAWI BAY and tow him clear in an hour and a half.
(4) During the night, TAWI TAWI BAY, the logical place to seek refuge if he was still afloat, was carefully reconnoitered with the SJ radar from a position two miles off TIJITIJI REEFS. Nothing was found there. Range 26,000 yards across the bay. Neither was anything seen in the bay the next morning by periscope. This search however was not as accurate as the one made during the night for intermittent rain squalls and haze prevailed.

One feature of this attack remains somewhat a mystery—plot shows that there should have been at least 4 hits. There were two very definite torpedo hits. One very loud timed explosion which was easily recognizable as a torpedo hit though not observed due to the necessity for watching the escort which was close aboard, and, the second terrific hit which was observed and jarred our ship considerably. There were thirty seconds between these explosions. Torpedoes were spread from forward aft with the resultant comparatively small physical spread. Any way our recorded data is plotted, it shows a minimum of 4 hits. The only readily apparent answer is erratics or duds. We did, of course, have the one low order explosion nine seconds after the first hit which might have been a dud. Another possible answer is that the first hit slowed him down so much that some of the torpedoes passed ahead.

2030 Surfaced halfway through SIBUTU PASSAGE having had no more indications of A/S vessels. The moon was intermittently covered with low clouds and passing rain squalls.

2120 SJ radar interference in direction of SIBUTU ISLAND.

2130 (SHIP CONTACT #22) Exchanged recognition signals and calls with RASHER by SJ radar. Told him he might expect A/S vessels in SIBUTU due to our action there for which information he thanked me. The ease of this first communication by means of our SJ radar keying circuit was amazing. The RASHER's estimated range was 10 to 15 miles.

2205 Experienced several minutes of difficulty with a friendly or tired sea gull. After making a couple of low, hovering passes at the bridge which caused all heads to be quickly covered, he attempted twice to land on the high lookout's head. Stopped laughing long enough to yell a warning to the lookout who seemed either unaware of or unconcerned with his plight. Came his answer: "Yes, sir, Captain, I know it. He tried to bite me a minute ago." Wherewith we gave the high lookout a broom for protection.

He next tried a landing on the revolving SJ mast and finally made it after nearly spinning in once. Five or six revolutions were enough — he had to balance himself with his wings like a tight rope walker. He finally flew down on the deck after what was one of the silliest exhibitions I have ever seen one of our feathered friends of the sea engage in [*ibid.*].

Glenn Stoy described the attack from his perspective in the control room.

August 1 — Cruising between the Sibutu Passage and Alice Channel having passed through to the northern end of the Passage on the mid-watch, submerged at 0500, BATTLE STATIONS at 0945, target is large submarine tender with escorts, made approach and fired six "fish" getting two bull's-eyes, came about fired two "swabbos" aft, here comes the escorts with their "ashcans," 300 feet and rigged for depth charge, although we are taking one helluva shellacking we did feel a little better to know we blew that tender to hell, the depth charging let up after about an hour and a half, we managed to get up to periscope depth for a look, spotted two patrol craft still searching for us but they were soon hull down, we tried to surface at 1900 but sighted an escort headed our way, did surface at 2035, found all clear, cleared the Sibutu Passage and are now back in the Celebes Sea, nothing sighted [Stoy].

Selby was quite certain the ship sunk was the submarine tender *Tsurugisaki* (or its sister ship the *Takasaki*) of 12,000 tons. Unbeknownst to Selby, the *Tsurugisaki* had been converted to an aircraft carrier in late 1941, renamed the *Shoho*, which was lost at the Battle of Coral Sea (Tully, *Shoho*). The *Takasaki* had also been converted to the light carrier *Zuiho* in 1942. Both were built in 1934 with a flexible design that could be completed as an oil tanker, submarine tender, or aircraft carrier as needed. As the war progressed the greatest need by the Japanese was for aircraft carriers. The *Zuiho* was later sunk in October 1944 at the Battle of Leyete Gulf (Tully, *Zuiho*).

Postwar analysis of intercepted Ultra messages identified the ship attacked by the *Puffer* as the *Sunosaki*, a 4,465 ton aviation fuel tanker. The tanker was damaged and towed to the Manila drydock for repair. However, before it could be put back into service, on September 21, 1944, the *Sunosaki* was bombed; shells in a magazine exploded, and the ship burned beyond repair. The hull was towed out of the harbor and abandoned (Alden, *Successes,* p. D-175; Somerville, *Maru Special,* No. 34, p. 47).

The *Sunosaki* identification was consistent with Selby's description that the second torpedo caused the "most terrific explosion I have ever seen or felt." Aviation fuel was highly explosive. The *Sunosaki* was supposed to support an air squadron (two medium aircraft carriers) with gasoline and other supplies and with an aircraft repair and parts shop. These aircraft carriers were unsuccessfully attacked by the *Puffer* during the Fourth War Patrol near Tawi Tawi. However, without fuel and parts the effectiveness of the aircraft carriers was diminished.

Basilan Strait Attack

On August 2 with visibility deteriorating Selby took the *Puffer* east into the Celebes Sea while the activity cooled off in the Sibutu Passage. August 3 was quiet except for a lone aircraft contact and flushing out of #4 fuel ballast tank. On August 4 orders were received to again transit the Sibutu Passage and patrol in the Sulu Sea for a week, and then proceed north toward Manila. The Sulu Sea is a shallow body of water that lies between the two archipelagos that stretch between Borneo and the Philippine Islands. On the way to the assigned area in the Sulu Sea, the *Puffer* made contact with the *Bluefish*, which was also headed north. Recognition signals were exchanged using radar pulses, and the boats closed for a short verbal exchange between Lt. Commander C.M. Henderson and Selby. The two boats ran a patrol line on the surface for about 90 minutes and then separated. Around noon on August 7 masts were sighted approaching from the direction of the Basilan Strait (6.81°N, 122.0° E) just south of the city of Zamboanga on Mindanao Island of the Philippines (WPR).

7 August

0522 Submerged with SAMPOAK POINT bearing 082°T, distant 5.5 miles and commenced patrol 2 miles off coast.

1143 (Ship Contact #24) Sighted masts of ship bearing 194°T approaching us from the direction of BASILAN STRAIT. Battle stations.

1153 Sighted new masts farther back and closer to the beach. I had absolutely no intention of getting left outside again so immediately closed in to one mile off-shore. From this position all I had to do was sit and wait as both of them were closing me with almost zero angles.

1228 It now appeared that the first target sighted would pass in a good position for a stern tube shot but that the second target which was closer to the beach and about a mile behind was going to be tougher to hit. Decided that if I hit the first one that the second would reverse course and that [I] could swing right and hit him with the bow tubes when he was half way around, or, if he held his course, I could shoot a "down the throat" shot.

Also could see now that the targets were freighters and not as big as first estimated. The mast of an escort was just showing up in line with and on the port quarter of the first target.

Our set up was checking so well on #1 target that I decided to fire only one torpedo since the range would be close.

1244 Single ping range of 900 yards checked with TDC set up.

ATTACK NO. 3(A)
    Latitude 7-50N
    Longitude 122-07.3E
    With range 950 yards, torpedo run 900 yards, angle on bow, 88° starboard, torpedo track 101° starboard, target course 030°, speed 9.5 knots, own course 131° speed 4 and gyro angle 179°...

1245-20 Fired #7 tube at M.O.T.

1245-55 Torpedo hit M.O.T. The only way to describe this sinking is that the target disintegrated in a cloud of smoke. He must have been loaded with gasoline or ammunition for he literally blew to pieces.

In this connection and in an effort to compare relative force of torpedo explosions, I would like to say here that despite the close range and the intensity of the explosion, it was not felt nearly as much on the ship as was the explosion on the submarine tender at 2,000 yards.

As soon as he was hit we commenced swinging right for the second target. He was acting as predicted except that he was reversing course toward the beach instead of away from it.

ATTACK NO. 3 (B)
With the range 1,200 yards, angle on bow 105° port swinging right, torpedo track 114° port increasing, gyro angle 34° right, target course 135°, speed 9.5 knots, own course 167°, speed 4.

1247-25 commenced firing two torpedoes aimed ¼ length inside the bow and ¼ length inside the stern respectively.

1249-25 Torpedoes had not hit, target had steadied on a course giving us a 135° starboard angle on the bow, and only the top of the escorts' mast was in sight to seaward so decided to fire one more.

1249-30 Fired #3 tube after feeding a series of continuous bearings into the TDC.

1250-14 Saw first torpedo explode on beach to left of target.

1250-49 Saw second torpedo explode on beach to left of target. The third torpedo was headed very nicely toward the target for what looked like a sure hit but after the second torpedo exploded on the beach, he swung left and showed us his stern.

1251-06 Third torpedo exploded on the beach ahead and to the right of the target after passing down his starboard side.

1251-32 First depth charge.

1254 Second depth charge. Escort was now headed in our direction but I couldn't make out what type he was having only seen the top of his mast and a zero angle on the bow view. He was small whatever he was. Started deep.

1255 Two depth charges.

1255—1346 Escort dropped 16 more depth charges, some in groups of two but most of them singly. He was pretty good—listened only and apparently attempted to place each charge rather than drop in salvoes. As it turned out his accuracy was probably due to an air leak in the blow down valve on the QB head which we could hear on our sound gear but were having trouble locating. As soon as this leak was located and stopped we had no more depth charges and at…

1417 His screws were growing faint on bearing 170°T.

1611 Periscope observation. No sign of target or escort. We were too close to the beach to surface and would not be able to overtake him after dark as he only had a 5 hour run to ZAMBOANGA so headed out to seaward.

The target sunk was very similar to the KOHOJU MARU, page 104, ONI 208J (rev.), 3,200 tons. His tripod masts fore and aft were so outstanding that I feel this identification may be considered positive. The target missed was most nearly similar to the HIYOSI MARU type, page 108, 4046 tons [ibid.].

Postwar analysis determined the ship sunk was the *Kyo Maru #2*, a 340 ton freighter converted to a sub chaser (Alden, *Successes,* p. D-177). Since this ship had been converted from a freighter to an auxiliary submarine chaser, its silhouette was that of a freighter and Selby identified it as such.

Torpedo Transfer

After the attack Selby noted a potential attack liability and commenced a risky operation to correct the situation.

Our torpedo distribution was now very poor there being one left forward and five aft. Since this would practically limit us to one salvo from the stern tubes decided to pull clear of the coast tonight and shift two torpedoes forward.

1904 Surfaced with SAMPOAK POINT bearing 134°T, distance 12.5 miles.

2145 Commenced transfer of two torpedoes from the after torpedo room to the forward torpedo room.

8 August

0107 Completed the transfer of two torpedoes to the forward room. This ticklish job was carefully planned and efficiently accomplished by Lieut. F. G. GOLAY, USNR and Lieut. W. M. PUGH, USN with volunteers from the deck force and torpedo force respectively, all under the supervision of the Executive Officer, Lt. Comdr. C. R. DWYER, USN [WPR].

Such a transfer of torpedoes was quite unusual. The WPR does not give details of how the transfer was accomplished. Neither Dwyer, Stoy, nor McDonald could recall the exact details of the transfer. With no cranes the most likely method would have been to float the torpedoes across the deck with the submarine decks awash. Selby singled out the following volunteers in the *Personnel Report* who transferred the torpedoes "without light in enemy waters and at considerable risk to their personal safety. The shift resulted in our being able to make one more attack than would have been possible otherwise (*ibid.*)" The crew included: Merritt Dayton Fallon (CTM), Glenn Earl Stoy (GM1c), Allen Harold Gordon (MoMM1c), William Earl Wilson, Jr. (Cox), Lloyd Joseph Kronberg (GM3c), Bernard Folsom Cassidy (S1c), Thomas Albert Bowden (S1c), William Warner Kimbrell, Jr. (TM3c), Phillip Clayton Sears (TM2c), Robert Edward Corke (TM3c), Donald B. McDonald, Jr. (TM3c), Clayton Edger Williams (TM3c), Calvin Coolidge Hamilton (TM3c), and Charles Anthony Darrah (TM2c). Stoy commented about the situation, "it sure didn't sound too good right in the middle of Jap waters with patrol craft still in the area, we would sure be done for if one of them was to stumble on us." Upon completion of the task "all hands sighed a breath of relief" (Stoy). For his efforts Stoy received a Bronze Star. Stoy's citation did not mention the true nature of the torpedo transfer. The operation merely referred to "repairs on deck" (Stoy, *Cita-*

Glenn Stoy receives the Bronze Star (photograph courtesy of Glenn Stoy).

United States Pacific Fleet
Flagship of the Commander-in-Chief

In the name of the President of the United States, the Commander in Chief, United States Pacific Fleet, takes pleasure in presenting the BRONZE STAR MEDAL to

GLENN E. STOY
GUNNER'S MATE FIRST CLASS
UNITED STATES NAVY

for service as set forth in the following

CITATION:

"For distinguishing himself by meritorious service in action against the enemy in the performance of his duties as a member of the crew in a United States Submarine during a war patrol. Though he well knew the risk involved to his own personal safety if the ship was forced to dive, he willingly volunteered to spend several hours assisting in making important repairs on deck at night. This resulted in his ship being able to sink a larger volume of enemy shipping. In addition, his exceptional skill and proficiency at his battle station assisted his Commanding Officer considerably in conducting attacks which resulted in the sinking of enemy ships for a total of over 30,000 tons, and in damaging enemy shipping of 10,000 tons. His coolness and efficiency contributed materially to the success of his vessel in evading severe enemy countermeasures, and in returning to port safely. His conduct throughout was an inspiration to all with whom he served and in keeping with the highest traditions of the naval service."

C. W. NIMITZ,
Fleet Admiral, U.S. Navy.

Glenn Stoy's Bronze Star Citation (image courtesy of Glenn Stoy).

tion). Probably the award board wanted to keep the nature of the torpedo transfer a secret and not encourage repeat performances by other commanders.

Cape Calavite Attack

After the torpedo transfer Selby moved the *Puffer* north through the Sulu Sea toward Manila. On August 11 the *Puffer* exited the Sulu Sea through the Mindoro Strait and moved north toward a point a few miles west of Cape Calavite. Cape Calavite is south of Manila Bay and near the west end of the Verde Island passage. Selby suspected ships moving to and from Manila from various directions would pass near this focal point (WPR).

12 August
    0120 (Ship Contact #26) SJ radar contact on small ship bearing 217°T, range 10,950 yards and closing fast. Swung to put him astern and attempt to ease slowly off his track while getting ready on 4 engines. Couldn't get rid of him at two-thirds, standard or full speed. The sky had cleared about midnight (the only time it was clear for a week) and he was apparently seeing us in the light of a quite bright quarter moon. When we swung to put him on the port quarter, he started to draw forward on the port side; same thing when we put him on the starboard quarter — range decreasing all the time. This situation wouldn't have been bad except for the fact that we were boxed in with CAPE CALAVITE 5 miles on the starboard bow, LUBANG ISLAND 6 miles on the port bow and the CALAVITE PASS entrance to VERDE ISLAND PASSAGE dead ahead. This latter I consider a place to enter only after careful consideration and then with a large degree of stealth and not while being chased at 18 knots.
    Could see our pursuer fairly plainly — well enough to recognize him as a small man-of-war. Probably a sub-chaser judging from the radar ranges but he looked big enough to be a destroyer.
    0142 Submerged to 60 feet and swung off the track to shoot with stern tubes if he was big enough.
    0145 Echo ranging commenced.
    0150 Pinging was getting closer and I still couldn't see him through the periscope so went to 250 feet.
    0225 After maneuvering for 35 minutes he passed close aboard once but gradually drew off toward CAPE CALAVITE.
    0240 Nothing in sight by periscope — pinging faint.
    0245 Surfaced and headed westward.
    0310 (Ship Contact #27) Picked him up again bearing 210°T, range 11,000 yards and opening.
    0340 Reversed course to head back for CAPE CALAVITE. This whole series of events during the night looked very much as if an A/S sweep was being made in the area in an attempt to clear the way for an incoming or outbound convoy. My guess was incoming because of the signaling 15 miles out but I was wrong — it was outgoing. The flashing white light must have meant that the coast was clear. I figured that even if the second A/S vessel had seen and reported us it was probably too late for a convoy coming from either direction and aiming to pass CALAVITE at dawn, to turn back.
    0442 (Ship Contact #28) Picked up SJ radar contact on three ships in direction of CAPE CALAVITE at 19,000 yards. Manned radar tracking party and commenced tracking at 17 knots.
    The ships were passing CAPE CALAVITE about 5,000 yards off and were headed on approximate base course 220°T. This put us about 10 miles off the track and it was commencing to get light but fortunately heavy weather had descended upon us again. Although our horizon to the south was clear they were in a heavy rain squall.
    0513 Range still 19,000 yards, 6 miles off the track — submerged and commenced closing track at 6 knots.
    Just prior to diving we had picked up what appeared to be radar interference on bearing 200°T but did not have time to check on whether it was friendly or enemy.
    0531 First look since diving. Targets were still obscured by rain squall although I could see some smoke and the faint outline of the tops of one large ship with a small angle on the bow.
    This whole approach was peculiar because of the continuously changing state of visibility. At times I could only see the escort who was coming down on the starboard bow of our target and at other times I couldn't see any ships at all. The escort's continuous pinging prevented their making any radical change without our picking up the change in bearing.
    0602 Could see large bridge and masts of target with a 10 degree starboard angle on the

bow. Target on port beam, escort on our port quarter with a 10° port angle on the bow—looked like he would pass close aboard.

0606 Target and escort made radical course change to left presenting a 60° to 70° starboard angle on the bow. Identified target as a large tanker and at the same time saw a second one to the left of him with a zero angle on the bow. Took normal approach course at full speed.

0614 Zig back to right—angle on the bow 10° starboard. Three ships were now in sight, two tankers and a freighter or passenger ship in column. Escort was a destroyer, passing astern and looked as if he would be well clear by the time the targets arrived within firing range. Range now 6,000 yards.

0618 Visibility cleared on the target's port hand and 4 more ships were seen in column of twos, one tanker and one freighter in each column. There were probably more but I couldn't see them. It later turned out that there were at least three more escorts although the one destroyer was all I ever saw. From this time on our target held a steady course until the time of firing. I expected momentarily that he would zig but it didn't make much difference for he couldn't get past us no matter what he did.

0629 First tanker had a 25° starboard angle on the bow, range 1,500 yards and the second tanker had a zero angle on the bow, range about 3,000 yards. Decided to shoot the bow tubes at the first one, swing right, pull off the track and shoot the stern tubes at the second one.

ATTACK No 4(a)

Latitude 13-17N

Longitude 120-07. 8E

Range 900 yards checked by single ping range, torpedo run 710 yards, angle on the bow 20° starboard, torpedo track 20° starboard, course 200°T, speed 8.5 knots, own course 066°T, speed 2 knots.

0631-00 Fired one at M.O.T.

0631-14 Fired two spread ½° right.

0631-21 Fired three spread ½° left. Saw first torpedo running erratic to the right and passing ahead of target.

0631-41 Saw and heard second torpedo hit about half way between bridge and bow.

0631-45 Saw third torpedo hit just abaft bridge. The tanker immediately burst into heavy flames all around the bridge and the bow commenced to settle. Started swinging right and at the same time the target started swinging right in what looked like an attempt to ram us though it may have been just loss of steering control. Caught a glimpse of the second tanker changing course to the right. Started to get set up for sound shot but sound was hearing so many screws it was too much of a gamble to shoot on sound bearings.

0635 Came back up to periscope depth. I can't give a very comprehensive account of the movements of any ships but our targets for it was pretty much a mad scramble with ships going every direction and continuous pop-popping of their guns as they fired into the water. Took a sweep around first to look for an escort. No escort. Next looked at our target who was dead in the water, still burning fiercely, and further down by the bow. I was contemplating firing one more at him when I looked astern and found the previously mentioned freighter-passenger ship crossing our stern with an 80° port angle on the bow, range 1,500 yards. As we were getting set up on him I could see another ship out beyond him on his starboard bow and partially hidden by a rain squall. The target was an MKFKM type with his composite superstructure amidships taking up about ¼ of his length.

ATTACK No 4(b)

Range 1,500 yards checked by single ping, torpedo run 1,470 yards, angle on the bow 90° port, track 98° port, course 240°, speed 8.5, own course 157° (had swung left while below periscope depth), speed 3.

0636-48 Fired #7 at M.O.T.

0636-50 Heard two depth charges—not close.

0636-58 Fired #8.

0637-07 Fired #10.

A few seconds after firing saw a large splash between us and the target and thought for a moment it was a premature until I saw three other splashes in the vicinity and realized it was more gunfire.

0637-41 Saw and heard first torpedo hit directly under bridge and stack.

0637-49 Saw and heard second torpedo hit inside bow.

0638-30 Heard third torpedo explosion. Did not see this as I was sweeping around with the periscope. This later turned out to be a hit in the bow of the second tanker which was on the starboard bow of the freighter. The original escort was now headed back in our direction coming up on our starboard quarter but still distant and the first tanker was still burning. The freighter took a heavy port list immediately and commenced settling rapidly.

0640 Two depth charges.

0641 Single depth charge. Escort was now approaching rapidly so rigged for depth charge and started deep.

On my last look the freighter was in the worst condition and seemed to be sinking quite rapidly but the first tanker had stopped settling for the time being. The second tanker, still in the outside edge of a rain squall was reversing course and appeared to be burning forward.

0643 to 0722 Conducting evasive tactics. That three other escorts had shown up was indicated from the echo ranging of our A/S vessels. They must have been to the rear and far side of the formation for I only saw one prior to going deep. Thirty-seven more depth charges were dropped but none of them were close. Believe there was too much confusion topside for them to conduct an effective search. During this period heard the typical breaking up noises of a sinking ship on the bearing of the freighter.

0735 Started up slowly. All but one pinger had faded out on a southerly bearing.

0806 Sighted two tankers dead in the water with a destroyer alongside the near one probably taking off personnel. What I wouldn't have given for a couple of more torpedoes at this point! The first tanker was still low in the water and down by the bow but the fire was out. His topside was a mess—badly burned and charred. The second tanker was also down by the bow, though not quite as much, was burning and looked bent about half way between his bridge and forward bow. We got two pictures of him later though they may not come out well due to the poor visibility. The freighter was no where in sight. I feel sure it sank, first, because it very definitely looked like it was sinking when I last saw it, secondly because we heard the breaking up noises and thirdly because it was not now in sight whereas the two damaged tankers were.

0808 (Aircraft Contact #18) Sighted plane circling over damaged tankers.

Spent the rest of the day following the two tankers which were drifting at about 2 knots in a northeasterly direction toward CAPE CALAVITE. Keeping them in sight was a three way battle with the plane, destroyer and the visibility which was growing continuously worse. After leaving the side of the first tanker the destroyer commenced maintaining a patrol around both ships echo ranging intermittently. About 1100 the weather got too bad for the plane and we didn't see him anymore. Sometime during the morning the fire was put out on the second tanker. I feel that both of the ships must have been in very bad shape internally for they both appeared entirely abandoned and no effort was made to get up steam on either one. This in spite of the fact that neither had been hit in their engineering spaces and that they were obviously drifting onto the steep beach at CALAVITE where they would surely break up in the heavy seas.

One tanker appeared very similar to the HUZISAN MARU class of tanker page 285, ONI 208–J (rev.). Single mast forward, bridge, kingposts abaft bridge, single mast aft and stack. The picture of this one may positively identify it. The other was the same size and had a single mast forward, single mast aft and stack aft but the after mast was almost amidships making it look more like the TEIYO MARU on page 276. I was not able to get pictures of this one due to the interference from the escort and rain squalls. The freighter was most nearly similar to the HOKKAI MARU class, page 77. The tankers were apparently empty when hit for they were riding high in the water. The freighter appeared to be loaded.

At 1323 got my last look at the group as a downpour of rain enveloped all of us for the rest of the day. The wind had increased to at least 40 knots and the seas were mountainous requiring two-thirds and standard speed to stay at periscope depth and full speed occasionally to keep us from broaching.

```
           USS PUFFER (SS268)

              THEME SONG

(Sing to the tune of "Oh, My Darling Clementine")

           On the PUFFER
           One greay morning
           Aswe lay off Borneo
           We saw three tankers
           Coming toward us
           And they were bearing 180

           Man the bow tubes!
           Man the stern tubes!
           Set the ready lights to go
           We can't give them
           Too much angle
           Cause their not moving very slow.

           Came the escorts
           Came the escorts
           Ploughing wildly through the sea
           Two ships sinking and one damaged
           And their as made as they can be.

           Rig for depth charge!
           Rig for depth charge!
           Take her down 300 feet
           Watch your angle Mr. Decker
           Cause the waters' might deep.

           Roberts, listen
           Roberts, listen
           And the JP listen, too
           Those little noises may be fishes
           And again they might be screws.

           At night we surfaced
           At night we surfaced
           And went merrily on our way
           We have met him
           And harrassed him
           And we'll return another day.

           Oh! the PUFFER
           The mighty PUFFER!
           She's as mean as she can be
           Throwing pickles
           At Jap shipping
           As she goes from sea to sea.

                  * FINIS *
```

The USS *Puffer* Theme Song as originally typed (image courtesy of Jack Thoman).

We maintained contact with the destroyer by heading on the same true bearing as his pinging but visibility was not more than 500 yards. This was very discouraging as I felt sure the heavy seas would finish sinking the tankers and I wouldn't see it. If they didn't sink it looked like they would hit the beach for sure for a tow in this weather seemed out of the question.

At 1700, with our estimated position 8 miles off CAPE CALAVITE, I began to get a little worried that this heavy sea might pile us up on the beach. I wasn't sure at all that we weren't in a typhoon although we had not had any of the advance warning common to a typhoon. Headed out on course 330°T. Heard echo ranging until 1810.

1900 Surfaced making full speed with the sea (050°T). No contacts on the SJ radar except with land. The wind was 40 to 50 knots and the rain still pouring down so I decided to pull clear of the coast and get a contact report off concerning the rest of the convoy, and the fact that the two tankers were adrift off CAPE CALAVITE.

1920 Picked up strong radar interference on the SJ radar. It was an extremely powerful radar trained directly on us and, according to the radar technicians, was not another SJ radar as it had very peculiar wave form characteristics. A sketch is included under remarks on SJ radar.

In order that they wouldn't be able to train on our radar, we secured the transmitter, taking a sweep once a minute. The bearing indicated that the radar was located on or just off CAPE CALAVITE. After being trained on us continuously for about 5 minutes, he turned his radar off and from then on used it only intermittently.

1952 Lost radar interference.

2135 Completed transmitting message. Decided to stay clear of coast until weather abated somewhat and visibility improved. I didn't think they could do much about the tankers until the seas calmed down and it didn't seem advisable to take any risks with the ship in the weather since we were capable of no offensive action [*ibid.*].

Stoy colorfully summarized the events of the day in his diary.

BATTLE STATIONS at 0450, have contacted a convoy of about eleven ships coming through the Passage, steamed at full speed to head them off, submerged at 0510, started our approach, in position, fired three "fish" forward getting two hits on a large tanker, we were so close he turned to ram us as he sank, we started for the bottom but a last look through the scope showed we'd cleared him so we came back up to periscope depth and let them have it with our last three fish getting three hits, at this point the escort had us pretty well spotted and started to close in on us, we hit 300 feet and rigged for depth charges, wee lad really had a lot of "ash-cans" aboard, for he peppered the whole ocean for a solid hour and though he did us no damage, he sure shook us up and made a lot of noise, we were able to get up to periscope depth for a look in a couple of hours, found another tanker and a large freighter in a very sinking condition, if we had only had a few more "fish" for they were sitting ducks, [we] sat by helpless while they were taken in tow headed for Manila, we were stuck in the tail end of a typhoon at this time, went deep to ride it out, are in hopes the crippled Japs will be broken up in this weather [Stoy].

On August 13 Selby stayed in the area observing the two battered tankers. The first tanker sunk was the *Shinpo Maru* (sometimes listed as *Shimpo* or *Shinko*), owned by the Iino Kaiun Company, a 5,135 ton ship pressed into military service. Twenty Japanese crewmen were killed. The damaged ship was run ashore under tow by the *Shoei Maru* and the *Kyoei Maru*. Selby suspected the heavy seas would break up the *Shinpo Maru*, but the task was completed by the *Bluefish* on August 17. The *Bluefish* discovered the beached maru near Golo Island, an island just north of the Calavite Passage, where it had been towed. The *Bluefish* further demolished the ship with a salvo of torpedoes on August 17. Even though towed to the beach, Japanese sources considered the vessel a total loss after the *Puffer* attack. The *Puffer* should be given full credit for the destruction of the ship (Alden, *Successes*, p. D-178; Somerville, 1995).

The *Teikon Maru* attempted to ram the *Puffer* during its attack on the *Shinpo Maru*. It was a bad decision. Postwar analysis also credited the *Puffer* with sinking the *Teikon Maru*, a 5,113 ton tanker. Built in 1913, the tanker *Teikon Maru* was formerly the German ship named *Winnetou*, sold to the Japanese in 1942 to aid the transfer of much needed petroleum. It was also owned by the Iino Kaiun Company. There were no casualties. The submarine *Pogy* (SS 266) had previously attacked and damaged the *Teikon Maru* about 60 miles west of Okinawa in February 1944. Postwar analysis could not account for the third tanker claimed as damaged by the *Puffer* (*ibid.*). The crew members composed a song about the attack on the tankers.

Another Assignment?

The *Puffer* was supposed to head for Pearl Harbor, but later in the day at 1612 Selby received a message to maintain his position for a possible special operation (WPR). Special operations usually involved evacuating people from the Philippines or a surface gun action. Four hours later the special operation was rescinded and the *Puffer* was ordered to return to Pearl Harbor. The return route took the *Puffer* north between the Philippines and Taiwan and then east for the long 14 day ride home to Pearl Harbor, with a final destination of Mare Island Naval Yard in San Francisco Bay, Vallejo, California, for overhaul. After a stay at Pearl Harbor for two days to complete some minor repairs and test-fire electrically powered torpedoes, *Puffer* arrived in San Francisco on September 6, 1944 (*ibid.*).

Awards

Selby received a second Navy Cross for the Fifth War Patrol. The text praised him for his boldness.

> Skillfully maneuvering his ship to penetrate strong enemy escort screen, Commander Selby launched four bold, aggressive torpedo attacks in the face of severe countermeasures to sink four enemy ships totaling over 32,000 tons and damaged an additional vessel of 10,000 tons [Selby, *Biography*].

For his skill on the radar during the Fifth War Patrol Jay Deem received a Silver Star. The citation signed by C. W. Nimitz, fleet admiral, U.S. Navy, credited Deem for his coolness and expertise.

> For distinguishing himself conspicuously by gallantry and intrepidity in action against the enemy in performance of his duties as Radio Technician in a United States Submarine during a war patrol. His skill and ability in maintenance of his equipment and exceptional proficiency in furnishing accurate information to his Commanding Officer contributed directly to the sinking of enemy ships of over 30,000 tons and in damaging enemy shipping of 10,000 tons. His coolness and efficiency contributed greatly to the success of his vessel in evading severe enemy countermeasures, and in returning to port safely. His conduct throughout was an inspiration to all with whom he served and in keeping with the highest traditions of the naval service [Deem, *Citation*].

Jay Deem in 2004 with Silver Star (author's collection).

30 Days Leave

After a brief stop at Pearl Harbor, with a year of war patrols completed, the *Puffer* and crew returned to the States. Many of the plank holders were still on board. The sight of the Golden Gate Bridge, a symbol of American greatness, stirred the emotions of Stoy. He recorded the joyous event of returning to San Francisco.

Underway as before, contact with escort vessel has been made, you can almost smell the states, there it is ... have sighted and passed under the Golden Gate Bridge entering Frisco Bay, navigated the channel and moored alongside dock in Mare Island Navy Yard for overhaul. Boy is it ever good to be back here! [Stoy].

Crew picture taken at Pearl Harbor after the Fifth War Patrol — Commander Selby left the *Puffer* after the Fifth War Patrol. *Front row (left to right):* Larry Picone, Ken Dobson, Frank Golay, William Pugh, Frank Selby, Merritt Fallon, Thomas Kemp, Morrow Decker, Carl Dwyer. *Second row:* Allen Gordon, unknown, Herb Hayward, Charles Darrah, Robert Corke, Earl Schley, John Perro, Howard Allen, Tony Sasso, Calvin Hamilton, John Gutensohn. *Third row:* Charles Wiseman, Gerald Camp, Robert Polk, unknown, LaMar Jones, Ray Roberts, James Parker, Jefferson Rawls, Louis Bianco, Thomas Bowden. *Fourth row:* unknown, Harris Steinke, unknown, Glenn Stoy, unknown, Jay Deem, John Shiflett, Ralph Troop, unknown, unknown. *Fifth row:* Julian Roberts, unknown, Eric Bollman, William Kimbrell, unknown (half hidden), James Liggett, John Sanders, Sam Smith, Robert Kennedy. *Sixth row:* Bishop Creech, unknown, unknown, Paul James, unknown (half hidden), unknown, unknown (half hidden), unknown, Frank Mays, unknown (hat only). *Seventh row:* Jack Thoman, Ray Voss, Ladislaus Topor, John Hensley, Joe Kronberg, unknown, Don McDonald, Bernard Cassidy. *Eighth row:* Frank Corcoran, Carroll Allen, Lawrence Golden, unknown, unknown, Jack Lane, unknown, Fred Dogan, James Goin. *Back row:* unknown, Maurice Bull, James Patton (author's collection).

Some of the crew found jobs and stayed in the area for the entire refit. Many of the crew headed for home, even if it meant traveling across the country. For Stoy the return to the United States became a special event in his life.

[I] was granted thirty days leave — so began a very eventful period for me — getting to come home during the war was quite a deal — a service man was held in high esteem at this time — everything was done to make leave so very enjoyable — as great as it was, thirty days was as a weekend — so it was back to Vallejo, the *Puffer* and the war — with still time remaining in the states I called home and asked my lady love to come out to California and we would get married — which we did the 18th of November — then on the 21st it was sailing time back to the Pacific — did not return stateside until September, 1945 [Stoy].

Left to right: Jack Lane, William "Willie" Wilson, and Donald McDonald in Sacramento, California (author's collection).

Andrew Thoman traveled home to Arizona. As with Stoy the 30 days passed too quickly and it was time to return to the *Puffer*.

> I was given a 30 days leave, first time home in 16 months. What a great day to see some family and relatives again. Three of my brothers were overseas battling the Germans and Japanese. While home on leave, Mother and Dad made arrangements for a weeks stay at Todd's Lodge, Oak Creek Canyon, Arizona. This area has to be among the tops in beauty and serenity. It was a favorite vacation area since we were kids—good stream for trout fishing, hiking, home made biscuits, fresh fruit, etc. Leave time passed very quickly and after sad goodbyes it was time to report back to the *Puffer* to complete the overhaul [Thoman].

Upon arrival in San Francisco McDonald informed his parents by telegram he was returning home for 30 days leave. He left San Francisco on the evening train with Joe Kronberg, whose family lived in Portland, Oregon. Joe had been drinking too much and was almost tossed off the train. From Portland to Tacoma McDonald's seat mate was a Catholic priest. He confessed he had not regularly attended Mass, but had worn the St. Christopher's medal his grandfather had given him.

McDonald returned home to Tacoma for the first time since he had left for boot camp in January of 1943, 20 months ago. While he was away the family had moved a block down South "M" Street to a larger house his father had always admired. Upon arrival in Tacoma he took a taxi to his new home and quietly snuck in the front door, found and opened the door into the kitchen and tossed his cap onto the floor where his mother was preparing dinner. The sound of the cap startled her, she turned, and the sight of her son brought tears of joy. McDonald brought back $600 in pay, a sizeable amount of money in the wartime economy. He purchased a fur coat for his mother and left behind much of the other money.

His return to Tacoma warranted a small newspaper article recognizing his submarine service in the Pacific. He was treated to the home cooking of his mother. "Pete" Peterson, a high school friend, was also home on leave. They attended the football game between Tacoma's crosstown rivals, Lincoln High and Stadium High. McDonald's shop teacher was taking tickets, but didn't recognize the young men in their uniforms. It was almost as if the clock had been turned back three years when they were both in high school. After the game they decided to stop at a local bar for a beer. However at 20 years old they were still too young for a beer, and were promptly asked to leave. Even though the daily newspaper headlines brought the latest news from the war fronts, the lazy days were enough time to mentally relax, and at times to forget about the war. Returning to the uncertainty of the war was especially difficult after the 30 days leave (McDonald).

McDonald returned to Mare Island. The refit of the *Puffer* was ongoing, and departure for the next war patrol was a few weeks away. William "Willie" Wilson had heard that the good looking women were a few miles down the road in Sacramento. During the refit the duty schedule was three days on and two days off. With money to burn and two days leave the duo thumbed their way to Sacramento. While in Sacramento the pair visited one of the local watering holes, the Argentina Club. Wilson, the adventurous one, sat down at a table with three women. McDonald followed and sat down next to Bernice Meyne, who was working in Sacramento as a bookkeeper at a local auto dealership. She had accompanied a friend to California from Iowa with the intention of returning, but found employment and decided to stay — the California weather was much better than an Iowa winter (*ibid.*).

Three days later McDonald and Wilson returned to Sacramento and brought along their other shipmate, Jack Lane, for the third lady. The three women were roommates in an apartment not far from downtown. For the next two weeks the threesome dined and socialized with the women. In their conversations the shy McDonald learned that Meyne had grown up on a farm and liked to fish the rivers and lakes of Iowa, a pastime he loved to do in the streams of Washington. The ladies all seemed to enjoy eating at the local restaurants rather than cooking for the sailors. Even on submarine pay, McDonald exhausted his pay. On McDonald's final good-bye, Meyne gave him 10 dollars to tide him over until the next pay day. They corresponded for the next year while the *Puffer* patrolled the Pacific (*ibid.*).

12

The Sixth War Patrol

A New Commander and a Larger Crew

During the overhaul at Mare Island, command was passed from Selby to Dwyer. Typically officers ready for command were assigned to new construction or another submarine. Dwyer was one of a very few officers given command of the same boat on which he had been executive officer. Ken Dobson, a veteran of the first five war patrols, left the *Puffer*. Three new officers Lt. (jg) Russell C. Frank, Ensign Robert D. Weeks, and Ensign Richard A. Heehs joined the other eight officers (WPR).

Prior to the Sixth War Patrol twelve crew members left and seventeen were added (RG24). The additional 5 crew members, for a total of 75, were adequate for watch assignments, but Dwyer felt another 5 crew members would be ideal (WPR). Eleven officers were on board allowing for more flexibility on watches. The officers stood two three hour watches each day, and also rotated decoding duties. An alert O.O.D. was essential. Even with radar, vigilant lookouts were critical. The additional men gave the officers and the crew a little more time for sleep. However, when the number of men exceeded the number of beds, it was necessary to share bunks. "Hot bunking" meant one man coming off duty jumped into the same bunk as another man going on duty. Space was limited in the officers' quarters, and as a result the junior officers spilled over into the chief's area (*ibid.*).

Crew Transferred before the Sixth War Patrol

Name	Service #	Rate Arr.	Fifth WP	Sixth WP
Bartorelli, Ralph Antonio	202 94 88	S2c	S1c	TRAN
Bull, Maurice H.	403 72 62	CPhMV6	13-Jul-44	TRAN
Corke, Robert Edward	647 16 61	S2cV6	4-Jul-44	TRAN
Engborg, Frank Thomas	206 76 65	EM1cV6	EM1c	TRAN
Goin, James Warren	393 26 12	FC2c	FC1c	TRAN
Hamilton, Calvin Coolidge	356 69 63	TM3c	TM3c	TRAN
Nielsen, Howard Stello	368 56 98	SM1c	13-Jul-44	TRAN
Roberts, Julian Alonzo	272 23 31	EM1c	5-Jul-44	TRAN
Smith, Edward W	337 60 69	S1c	4-Jul-44	TRAN
Thatcher, Roy Orlando	329 27 16	S1c	S1c	TRAN

Name	Service #	Rate Arr.	Fifth WP	Sixth WP
Topor, Ladislaus	238 52 61	MoMM1c	CMoMM(AA)	TRAN
Weber, Lawrence R.	647 18 58	Y2cV6(SS)	4-Jul-44	TRAN

New Crew Members

Name	Service #	Rate Arr.	Date Arr.
Branchcomb, Ellis Denton	883 06 10	FCS3c	28-Dec-44
Burger, Edward Andrew	725 08 01	Y2c	7-Nov-44
Holland, Francis Anthony	300 47 89	GM2c	28-Oct-44
Johnson, Charles Streck, Jr.	730 91 25	PhM2c	13-Nov-44
Markle, John Emery	755 02 03	EM2c	20-Nov-44
McCarthy, Peter Edward	250 78 79	SC3c	28-Dec-44
McEntyre, Kenneth Edward	272 99 03	TM3c	28-Dec-44
Messenger, Ernest Henry	258 33 30	S1c(SS)	31-Aug-44
Metz, Thomas Addison	844 97 54	S1c	12-Oct-44
Okoniewski, Theodore Joseph	807 24 30	EM3c	14-Nov-44
Reynolds, Arthur Dale III	879 99 39	S1c	8-Nov-44
Rohrbach, Frank	703 39 77	S1c	8-Nov-44
Samuel, Harry	243 77 95	EM3c	14-Dec-44
Stevens, Albert Mahlon	411 11 43	SM1c	23-Sep-44
Venatori, Louis Edward	807 86 85	S1c	16-Dec-44
Wright, Kenneth D.	559 49 49	S1c(SM)V6	27-Sep-44
Youra, John Anthony	653 94 35	EM3c	14-Dec-44

It was a small world. Two years earlier in Kansas Frank Rohrbach (S1c) had been a high school student in Lt. Frank Golay's math class. Rohrbach wrote, "Golay was strict, but a very good math teacher" (Rohrback). Shortly after his assignment to the *Puffer* Rohrbach broke his elbow clearing the bridge.

Another new sailor, Thomas Metz, came to the *Puffer* by volunteering for submarine duty, although he had not been to submarine school. He was not unique; many men served on submarines without going through the prerequisite testing at New London. However, they still had to qualify before they could wear the silver dolphins. Metz previously had various non-combat duties. Metz, as many men at the time, desired action. The duties he received on the submarine probably were not what he envisioned. Metz described his introduction to life on a submarine and what motivated him to seek out submarine duty. In the process he gave a description of life aboard the *Puffer* during its time in San Francisco (Metz).

> I had put in for Submarine School at New London, Connecticut. While we were waiting for assignment (in San Diego), we did gate escort duty. In about two weeks, I was transferred to Submarine Administration Pacific, Mare Island, California. There I was assigned to the Ship Service Department and worked in a beer hall for two months. At the beer hall I could see lots of the men bringing their subs back from the Pacific for navy yard overhaul.
>
> The Navy yard launched several submarines and one submarine tender while I was at Mare Island. I rode the ferry across the bay to Vallejo many evenings and spent much time at the theatres along Georgia Street and at the Salvation Army Canteen. There I met Virgil C. Mays, a preacher-sailor from the First Baptist Church of Dallas, Texas. He preached at the Salvation Army Canteen two or three times a week. He later got on a fleet submarine and made war patrols in the Pacific. Virgil organized Sunday school classes for the crew in the forward torpedo room while their ship was out on patrols. I saw Virgil out in the war zone at the end of

one of their patrols and he told me that at the close of one of these lessons, they went directly to battle stations and sunk a Japanese tanker.

By September, 1944, it became apparent to me that if I was going to do the U.S. Government any good in the Navy, I was going to have to go where the Japs were. And the quickest and most efficient way to do that was on a fleet submarine headed for the Pacific.

While subs were at Mare Island for a Navy Yard overhaul, they were turned over to a relief crew and the regular crew was sent home on leave. Each sub maintained temporary offices in a building across the street from our barracks while the boat was undergoing overhaul.

When I went to the office of the USS *Puffer* to inquire about getting aboard, the relief crew officer said that Mr. Stiles M. Decker, the regular executive officer, would be back from leave

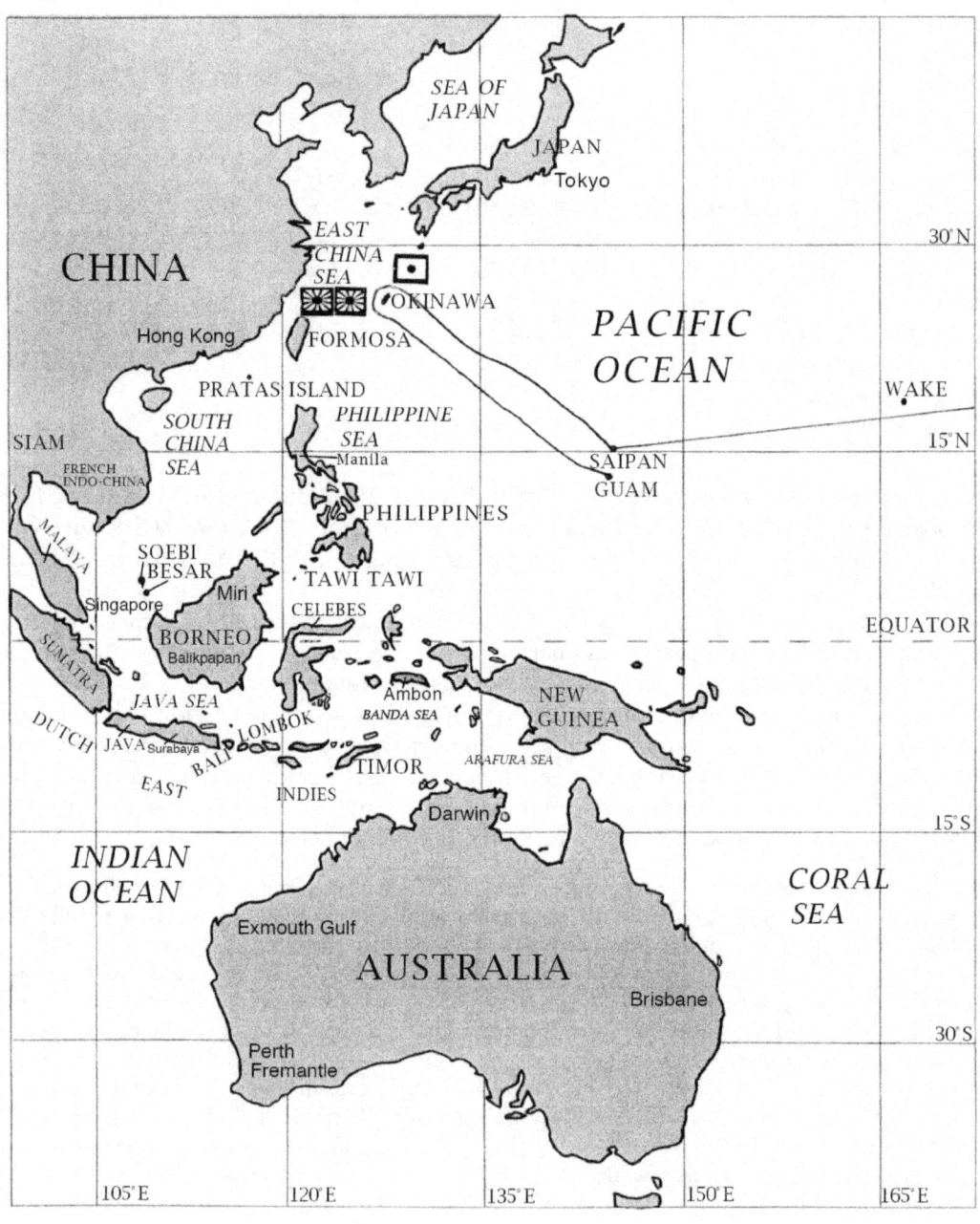

12. The Sixth War Patrol

The Dungarees crew picture taken at Pearl Harbor prior to the Sixth War Patrol. Note the censor's black ink covering the armament. *Front row (left to right):* Robert Biche, Larry Picone, Merritt Fallon, Richard Heehs, Morrow Decker, Carl Dwyer, John Gutensohn, Phillip McClure, Robert Weeks, Russ Frank, Frank Golay. *Second row (seated behind officers):* Robert Cochran, Howard Allen, Harris Steinke, unknown, Charles Darrah. *Third row (kneeling):* John Alexander, James Parker, Tony Sasso, Art Reynolds, unknown, Harold Sander, Louis Bianco, Bernard Cassidy, Paul James, John Shiflett, Sam Smith, James Liggett, Ted Okoniewski, unknown, Bob Polk, James Dickinson, Carroll Allen, unknown (half hidden), Ralph Troop, Jay Deem, Ladislaus Topor, (half hidden), unknown (CPO hat), Allen Gordon (on gang plank). *Fourth row (standing):* Bishop Creech, James Patton, unknown (arm in sling), Ray Voss, Robert Kennedy, unknown, unknown, Fred Dogan, Leo Evans, unknown, Merle Vogan, Frank Corcoran (half hidden), Roland Chamberlain, unknown, Larry Golden, unknown, Ken Wright, unknown (hat only visible), Bill Kimbrell, unknown, unknown (mostly hidden), Frank Mays, Thomas Metz, unknown, John Sanders, Eric Bollman, Ernest Messenger (tallest), William Wilson, Donald McDonald, unknown (author's collection).

Opposite: The Sixth War Patrol — December 28, 1944 (Saipan), to January 17, 1945 (Guam) — 3,784 nautical miles in the patrol area. After a short stay at Pearl Harbor to install a 5-inch deck gun and other modifications, the *Puffer* sailed to Saipan to top off fuel tanks. The *Puffer* and two other submarines were given the name the Clippers and patrolled the area around Okinawa. The crew returned to Guam for rest and recreation. The flags indicate where attacks were made. The rising sun flags show an attack on the Imperial Japanese Navy; the lone sun flag shows an attack on a merchant vessel (map artwork by Nancy Webber).

next week and that I would need to see him. I must have made a good impression on Mr. Decker when we met because he took me aboard although I had no sub schooling or sea experience.

A sub in overhaul at Mare Island has a barge tied along side to store parts and supplies on. It also has a small compartment used for a kitchen for the relief crew on duty. In this kitchen they can make coffee and fry eggs and bacon for snacks. Beside the door of this compartment was a slot machine, "a one-armed bandit," that operated on quarters. After watching the other men put money it, I thought it was time for me to try my luck. I put in a quarter and pulled the lever. The dials spun like wild but gave nothing back; so I tried one more time with the same results. Then I stepped back and looked that deal over. I had spent fifty cents and all I got was a good education. I've never tried gambling since. (The "profit" from the slot machine was used for a ship's party.)

While the *Puffer* was undergoing repairs, the crew attended classes to acquaint themselves with the technique and experience they would need when the ship went back on patrol. One of those special classes was on lookout schooling. This consisted of the proper way to report a sighting, training in aircraft and ship recognition, and techniques on how to see objects better at night.

When we moved back to the *Puffer*, my job was K.P. which was washing dishes, setting tables, peeling potatoes and keeping the kitchen and mess hall clean. On our first trip out from the pier at Mare Island, we took the boat out to a good shallow safe place and proceeded to trim the ship so it would barely sink. This is accomplished by rigging the ship for dive, opening the ballast tank vents and then flooding enough water into the trim tanks to cause the boat to submerge evenly. From down in the kitchen all this doesn't create much excitement, because there is no rough sea or steep dive angle. When we got back and tied up to the pier, I went home and reported to Orvie [his wife], "Woman, there isn't anything rough about sub duty at sea." A few days later we went out for an overnight cruise in the Pacific Ocean outside the Golden Gate. Man, the ocean was rough out there that night. The ship rolled and pitched and jerked and I think it must have been too rough to dive. The dishes slid off the tables right over the half-inch high edge around the table top. The ship rolled and pitched so hard I cut my fingers several times while peeling potatoes. You talk about sea sickness. I was the chief patient. The only relief I could get was to lie on a bottom bunk flat on my stomach and hang my arms off each side to keep me from falling off the bunk. When we finally got back to the pier the next day, I went home to tell Orvie a different story that night about sub duty. I was bleached out from being sea sick, about the color of paper, and I had bandaids on three or four cut fingers, but I wouldn't have quit if it would have killed me.

A few days before Thanksgiving, 1944, we loaded the ship with supplies, fuel, ammunition, food, water and torpedoes. Then we headed for Pearl Harbor along a [great] circle route up north near the Aleutian [Islands]. I was still on K.P. and the sea was extremely rough all the way. I stayed sea sick from the time we went under the Golden Gate Bridge until we walked ashore at Pearl Harbor. I had bleached out by this time till you could scarcely tell where the skin stopped and my white uniform started. I was so sick so long that they talked of putting me off the boat for shore duty; but they decided to try me on lookout duty so I could get some fresh air and sunshine. I have always given Mr. Decker credit for that decision. But I am glad they kept me on the *Puffer* for I got over the seasickness o.k. [*ibid.*].

New Weapons and Technology

Technical improvements were made to the radar systems, which allowed use of the radar through the periscope. Hydraulic leaks and vibration problems on the periscopes discovered during the voyage from Mare Island were corrected. The conning tower was enlarged and rearranged to accommodate the additional radar equipment. The external silhouette of the conning tower was lowered. The more depth charge resistant "T" shaped gaskets were installed on hatches, doors, and the induction outboard valve. Air conditioning was improved. Firepower was increased with the installation of a 5-inch deck gun at Pearl Harbor. Torpedo tubes were modified to accommodate the battery powered Mark XVIII torpedo. This model required charging equipment for the batteries and hydrogen burning circuits to burn off the hydrogen created by the charging (WPR). The Mark XVIII torpedo left no bubble wake, which made it virtually invisible to the enemy. However, if not properly maintained, the internal batteries exploded from a build up of hydrogen and quickly endangered a submerged submarine and its crew. The torpedo ran 12 to 15 knots slower than the Mark XIV, and the speed varied with water temperature, making for thorny firing solutions. Depth control and detonation were reliable (Gannon, p. 145).

Waikiki Bound

The *Puffer* departed Mare Island on November 22, 1944. The 7 day trip to Hawaii was filled with training dives, emergency drills, and drills of fire control problems (WPR). While at Mare Island the boat had acquired the new tunes of the day and the crew enjoyed playing the records while off duty, much to the chagrin of Metz.

> There was a "ten record" record player in the mess hall. All day long the boys would come by, put all ten of those records on the changer, turn it on, and listen to one or two of them. They would then go on somewhere else and leave me to listen to those records over and over as loud as it would play. The one song I remember most was about drinking rum and coca-cola in Trinidad [Metz].

With the new songs ringing in their ears and the thoughts of rum and coke, the *Puffer* crew arrived at Pearl Harbor on November 29, 1944. Metz described the Honolulu scene.

> We stayed in Pearl Harbor a few days. We got shore leave and went to Honolulu one afternoon. There we saw the block long lines at the "cat" houses. Had my picture made by a street photographer and he mailed the photo home for me when it was developed. We saw an aircraft carrier at Pearl Harbor that had just gotten back from battle and it sure was shot up [*ibid.*].

Golay described the Waikiki area as a permanent party.

> Waikiki, is a perpetual Mardi Gras, the streets lined with shooting galleries, skating rinks, bars, novelty shops and "Your Photo While You Wait" booths are filled with sailors, soldiers and marines.... Carl is going to let me have the station wagon one day and we're going over to the windward side for a swim and beer picnic [Golay].

Golay came on the *Puffer* starting with the Third War Patrol. In a series of letters Golay wrote to his family and future wife, he described many of the daily events of life and times on the *Puffer*. Golay wrote he "loved" the boat. That love was based upon earlier, aggressive, successful patrols with Selby. He had received a Silver Star as diving officer during Selby's tenure as commander.

It had been four months since the *Puffer* had been in combat. Unfortunately for the *Puffer* during that time the other American submarines had decimated a large portion of the remaining Japanese merchant fleet and numerous capitol ships (see graph). War patrols starting in September and October of 1944 were especially destructive to the Japanese.

Over the next eight months, with limited targets available as the war ground to an end, a toll was taken on Golay's morale. On the Sixth War Patrol he was given the engineering duties, which he did not like. According to one motor machinist mate he asked where the spark plugs were on the diesel engines (Topor). Of course, diesel engines have no spark plugs. He was probably overworked and had limited sleep. However, prior to the start of the patrol his morale was still high. The next event described by Golay demonstrated a pride in the *Puffer* by the crew as well as Golay.

> The Old Man [Commander Dwyer] got word last night that the Admiral was coming aboard this morning to look over our new conning tower arrangement — was left holding the bag as everyone else reported to an attack teacher session — just when I was beginning to be satisfied with the appearance of the boat a fuel oil line broke on a fuel truck on the dock and liberally sprayed us — the boat and everyone topside with fuel oil — everyone, and I mean everyone turned to and cleaned up the mess — just in time for the Admiral's visit — a damn nice guy and he accepted my invitation to the wardroom for coffee — [James] Patton and [Carroll] Allen very adequate hovering around in a haze of "Yes, suahs" [Golay].

Between December 4 and December 12, day and night group training exercises were conducted. Mark XXIII torpedoes were fired in low power (slow speed) to simulate the new electric torpedo, the Mark XVIII which was the primary torpedo for the remainder of the war. Tactics were practiced to fire torpedoes in the minimum time using both fore and aft torpedo tubes with large gyro angles (WPR). Exhausted by training exercises and anxious to return to sea, Golay wrote on December 9 and December 11 of his pride in the Submarine Service and the tiresome training. Golay longed for some recognition for the Submarine Service. For security reasons recognition of successes was always delayed two to three months to protect the location and identity of the submarines.

> Carl broke out the patrol reports today for us to read — and good reading they are — they make us restless and anxious to get out there — someday when the war is over and nobody gives a damn, they will publish a history of our submarines — the story is almost incredible, the announced sinkings lag far behind the actual sinkings.
>
> This flail must end some day — Edison [reference to Thomas A. Edison, the inventor, who slept very little] to the contrary, I can't get along without sleep — operations are the toughest part of this racket — the taxpayers took another beating as we lost another exercise fish — more of the same — battery, diving and the other thoroughly discussed headaches — a short day tomorrow — a traffic jam at the entrance delayed us past the closing hour of the beer hall — we missed the daily conference which is about the only chance to relax under the constant pressure — the boat is saturated with rumors — our area — refit and leave all coming up for complete analysis — am encouraging Allen to cut me in on the dope, the Forward Engine Room and Mess Hall seem to originate our operations plans — funny how often the rumors will turn out correct [Golay].

All the training exercises were finally over. Five days before leaving on the war patrol, in an act of defiance or bonding, all the officers except Commander Dwyer shaved their heads. Picone recalled he instigated the prank prior to Admiral Lockwood's inspection of the newly installed 5-inch gun (Picone). Much to Dwyer's surprise all the officers took off their hats below decks as Admiral Lockwood sat down at the officer's mess (*ibid.*). The wolfpack the *Puffer* joined was aptly named the Clippers (WPR). Golay described the "hair raising" sequence of events and other fun prior to leaving on patrol.

> Larry [Picone] appeared from the radio shack with his head shaved — and he shamed us into following suit — so we broke out the clippers and have been clipping and shaving like mad ever since — its amazing what is hidden by hair — a phrenologist would be in raptures with this display of bumps, dimples, misplaced divots — Bob [Biche] broke out his camera to record the event for posterity — Mac [McClure] evolved a pin head with a remarkable resemblance to "The Angel" — Bob has a gabled effect — won't repeat the unprintable and humiliating observations about my noggin — maybe I will let you see for yourself — will retain the pictures to see if

our kids look like their old man — Morrow [Decker] scalped me with his straight razor — had the Pharmacist's Mate standing by with plasma before he finished — must have been a blood thirsty reaction to his coiffure — a narrow ridge of hair fore and aft across his head — after the fashion of movie Indians — Bill [Pugh] is a wizened old man — Russ [Frank] a jolly gnome with a single short lock right in front — we painted Hitler's head on his dome — using the remaining hair for the moustache — everyone was a little sobered when Bill raised the question — "What if it doesn't grow back?" — don't know what

The station wagon road trip to the north coast of Oahu by some of the officers. The sign reads "OFF LIMITS / FOR TROOPS / *KEEP OUT*" (photograph courtesy of the Golay family).

Carl's [Dwyer] reaction will be — with his big-dealing tomorrow he'll be putting us under hack — that would be no hardship — who in hell would make a liberty looking like this.

Lost my eight bucks in the dice game — a pre-sailing ritual — instead of carrying a lot of dirty, useless money out to sea, we shoot dice until someone owns the bankroll — Russ almost has the game under control, and insists that his new daughter shall have a new war bond for Christmas.

Carl broke out his battle flag for his bunk cover and it should create the desired effect [*ibid.*].

Among the enlisted men there were minor tensions. "Joe The Horse" Kronberg was a good sailor but caused problems from time to time, especially when he had been drinking too much. His size and demeanor were intimidating. Kronberg had an athletic build and had played professional baseball prior to the war. Throughout the next eight months Golay continued to detail his problems with Joe. As a new shipmate, Metz described not feeling entirely welcome.

I had the back middle bunk on the port side of the forward torpedo room. The bed just pulled out from between the port reload torpedoes. One night I was laying on my bunk face down because that was the fastest way to rest. A lookout named Joe "The Horse," a man with several patrols, came off watch that night and he came in the forward room. He looked at me and commented to some of the other older hands, "Man, this bunch of new men we got this time are a crumby looking bunch. Look at that one laying there. He looks like a $(*&$#)." The other men didn't answer and neither did I [Metz].

On December 16, 1944, the *Puffer*, in the company of the *Blueback* and the *Sea Fox,* was ordered to conduct a patrol in the Luzon Strait. The wolfpack was under the command of M. K. Clementson on the *Blueback*. On route to Saipan, which was an advance refuel and re-supply stop, the *Puffer* and the *Blueback* made contact with the *Sea Fox* on December 22 (WPR).

On December 23 as the *Puffer* headed at full speed toward Saipan, Golay gave a report on the state of affairs on the boat. A field day was a cleaning day. Golay expressed his positive feelings about the crew, humorously detailed the "potato" problem, and talked of the social life discoveries of the crew while on leave. Christmas was coming and there were pictures on the boat to remind the men of their families (Golay).

Golay was concerned about the health of senior battle stations controllerman Polk (*ibid.*). Robert "No Smoke" Polk had brought a technique to the *Puffer* which allowed a rapid change of the load on the diesel engines from the electric motors. The electric motors ran the propellers both on the surface and submerged. When surfacing, large voltage changes would stress the diesels and create exhaust smoke, smoke that could betray the location of the sub. Polk's half voltage switchover technique created no smoke (Polk).

> Field day this afternoon, and to escape Simon Lagree Decker, I've found a sanctuary on the controllermen's bench in the maneuvering room — we are running ahead full on four and the motors and shafts are wailing like banshees — [Ray] Voss and [James] Bauersfeld just got an annunciator bell and looked very competent throwing levers and adjusting resistance to make the speed change. [Robert] Polk, one of the starboard controllermen and a damn good electrician, is on the sick list with an inflammation of the eyes — something like pink eye.
>
> A strange sea this morning — huge swells, the aftermath of some prolonged storm — fully a quarter of a mile between crests and sometimes our escort would be lost from sight for alarming periods as we wallowed in a trough.
>
> Tonight's problem — stowage for fresh potatoes — [Arden] Hagen's efforts with the dehydrated variety tonite was the last straw — Carl [Dwyer] gave up in disgust, and Russ [Frank] was stopped — of course the #1 stateroom was suggested, along with the engineering spaces — I'm a big hairy thing to the black gang if I let the mess cooks store food in the engine rooms — [Herbert] Hayward and [John] Perro haven't spoken to me since we left the islands — and if I argue with Russ and Morrow [Decker] they accuse me of being an uncooperative dog in the manger — the decision was to carry some potatoes in the superstructure — Bob [Weeks] produced a blue print with a topside locker titled "Potato stowage" — personally I'm looking forward to an effect from deep submergence that will match dehydration.
>
> Time out for rehearsal of Christmas carols.... "Omaha Trail" in the forward room in half an hour —

Frank Golay (right) receives the Silver Star (photograph courtesy of the Golay family).

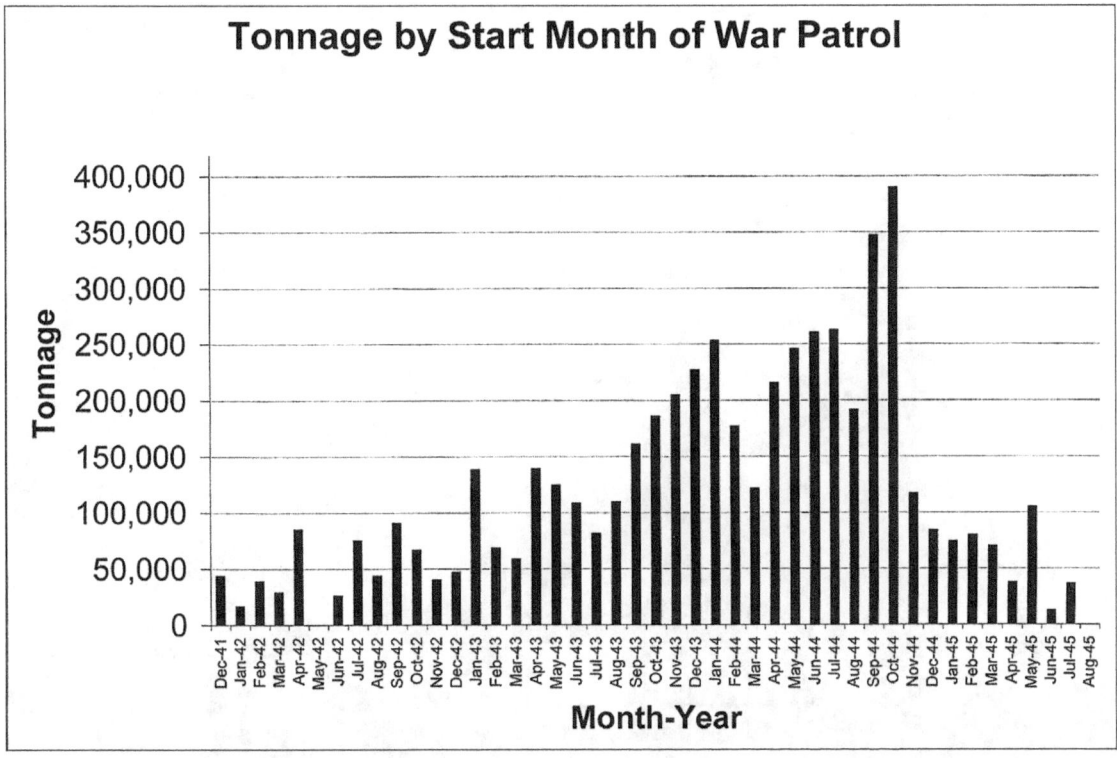

Joint Army-Navy Assessment Committee (JANAC) Evaluation of Japanese Tonnage Sunk (based upon data in *Silent Victory* by Clay Blair).

we're making water again — from the consumption — maybe the troops are trying to wear out the stills and force an issue of beer — the mail bag is stuffed again — the ship looks familiar again with a normal complement of pin-ups — and a surprising number of family group photographs — Dolphins, Combat Pins, proud wives and new babies — these are good shipmates and reassuring too — their letters home and the little shrines they make of their photographs.

[Allen] "Peach Basket" Gordon has removed Mabel's picture — a homely girl who haunted the control room for three runs — Gordon was very smug over his daily letter from Mabel, and would always make himself obnoxious when we returned from patrol by walking thru the boat nosily riffling a huge packet of letters like a pack of cards — he seemed a cinch to marry on leave and I sent him on leave with a quart of whiskey and my envious blessing — he had ambitious plans for a wedding at the Commodore and pestered everyone into a promise to try and make it — Mabel is a very touchy subject now — seems that her homeliness was not a sufficient guarantee of fidelity [*ibid.*].

On Christmas day the crew enjoyed the special programming from the Armed Forces Radio. The movie of the day was *In Which We Serve*, starring Noel Coward. Santa Claus visited each crew member with a present provided by the Honolulu Chapter of the American Red Cross, consisting of candy, cookies and other miscellaneous items (WPR). These small gestures brought back fond memories of home and were much appreciated. Turkey dinner with all of the trimmings was prepared by the excellent cooks — Carroll Allen, Arden Hagen, and the baker, Howie Allen. Christmas carols were sung, a small Christmas "tree" was decorated and there were Christmas cards for all from the Honolulu Junior Red Cross (Mays).

On December 27 the Clippers approached Saipan. Twenty miles from Saipan a low flying

Golay labeled the picture "More Disillusionment"— the clipped officers with Capt. Dwyer's battle flag (photograph courtesy of the Golay family).

"Joe The Horse" Kronberg relaxes at a club in San Francisco (author's collection).

B-24 settled into the rough sea waters. The *Puffer*, *Blueback*, *Sea Fox*, and an escort patrol craft (PC) from Saipan headed toward the crash site at maximum speed. The faster PC arrived at the location first, and picked up a rubber raft filled with survivors. The *Sea Fox* and the *Blueback* picked up two other survivors in the water. By the time the *Puffer* arrived at the fray all the visible survivors had been rescued. The PC and the Clippers searched for additional survivors without luck. By evening the Clippers were safely alongside of the submarine tender USS *Fulton* for fuel and minor repairs (WPR).

After a few days at Pearl, we headed out across the Pacific for Saipan. There we topped off our fuel tank and picked up a few supplies. The U. S. forces had just captured that place and it was in a mess. The two feet thick concrete bunkers that housed the coastal defense guns that the Japs used were just that much more shell riddled junk. After a few hours, we left Saipan for a patrol in the Empire Waters. I still had my job as lookout and

Christmas postcard sent by the crew to family members and friends back home. The inscription at the bottom reads, "The heroic deeds of Our Fighting Forces are an inspiration that will live forever."—F.D. Roosevelt (author's collection).

liked it very much. I could see very well, especially by day. I could spot a single engine fighter more than 35 miles away; that was before radar could find it [Metz].

Okinawa

The next afternoon the Clippers were headed for the Luzon Strait, in the Philippines, with the addition of the *Trigger*. The *Blueback* was delayed 24 hours for repairs. On December 30 the *Trigger* departed the Clippers for a separate patrol area, and the remaining boats were reassigned to an area north of Okinawa. The small island of Okinawa was Japanese territory and heavily defended, and would not be invaded until April 1, 1945. Submarines patrolled the area to prevent the re-supplying of the Japanese troops on the island stronghold. On January 2, 1945, the *Puffer* and the

Christmas card made by the Junior Red Cross of Honolulu and presented to each of the crew members of the *Puffer* (image courtesy of Frank Mays).

Blueback entered the patrol area. The *Sea Fox* departed for a patrol of the southern portion of the area. After some confusion and difficulties communicating with the *Blueback* concerning the assigned patrol areas, the *Puffer* remained in the original area (WPR).

On January 3, Commander Dwyer received a radio report from a patrol plane that Japanese freighters were seen heading toward the *Puffer*'s position as the convoy left the *Sea Fox*'s patrol area. The next day contact was made with two ships.

0540 (AP Radar Contact #5)
  0605 (AP Radar Contact #6)
  0616 DIVED. Paralleled Northern approaches to NAHA, OKINAWA, between YORON JIMA and OKINOYNRABU.
  0850 (Ship Contact #3) Sighted a sailboat. AVOIDED.
  1113 Heard pinging. Nothing in sight.
  1128 Heard pinging. Nothing in sight.
  1221 (Ship Contact #4) (See chart No. 2238). Sighted two masts bearing 215° T. Appeared to be two ships running N.W. corner of YORON JIMA from the Southwest. Began closing at high speed submerged. PUFFER is back in the war.
  1309 Obtained periscope radar range and a good cut. Targets were anchored N.W. of YORON JIMA. Closed target at slow speed.
  1637 Two targets are now well in sight. They are two masted stern driven luggers similar to lugger supply vessel type "J" shown on page 139 of ONI 222-J except they had two masts and were larger. The targets were anchored with bows headed towards the beach giving them a heading of 160° T thus putting the wind and sea on their starboard quarter. Figured they must be either beached or moored to two anchors to hold this heading. Plot shows targets anchored inside of the reef on an East-West line of bearing. This is unfortunate because the target length will not overlap on a good track. The North-South heading was a poor choice for them too as it required us firing across the seas to obtain a good track. Very inconsiderate of them. Due to shoal water to the North and East, PUFFER worked to the SOUTHWEST running as close as possible parallel to reef and looking the situation over. Could see several landing barges and several hundred men at the beach (Lat. 27-02.8 N; Long. 128-24.1 E). One boat with about 50 men in it came out from the beach and came alongside the near lugger for a while and then returned to the beach. The men on the beach seemed to be going in and out of caves there, about 200 yards inland. Could see what looked like concealed gun emplacements on the tip of HANEBU SAKI and to Eastward of the point. Decided that they were either unloading ammunition or holding landing exercises. Figured the targets had exceeded their life expectancy as they looked very old, so decided to attack. A gun action was the logical choice, but decided it was too early in the patrol to chance having the pressure hull holed by the shore batteries which were only about 1800 yards from us. In addition the visibility was very poor with intermittent rain squalls and heavy overcast. Torpedo attack did not look very promising due to heavy seas, shoal water, reef, shallow draft of targets, and lack of length in the targets. Decided to go in as close as possible, take a good look, and maybe fire a torpedo. Headed in toward targets and reefs, running at minimum speed, rigged in pit log, both sound heads, went to silent running, made preparations to destroy secret and confidential papers and material, taking fathometer soundings once a minute.
  1645 Plot shows one hundred and fifty yards from 10 fathom curve. This is minimum safe range so came right with full rudder for stern shot. Cannot see the reef. Believe these heavy seas are piling water over it.
  Looks like a torpedo set at zero depth could surf board over these waves and get over the reef. Decided to try experimental zero depth setting cross-sea shot.

1657 ATTACK No. 1 (a): Place: — Off N.W. tip of YORON SHIMA (27°N, 128.5°E).
  Anchored target holding 160° T, angle on bow 106°S, track 106°S, range 1200 yards, torpedo run 1200 yards, gyro angle 180°, depth set zero, own course 267° T. Set gyro on zero, did not use

TDC, set periscope on 180°, conned ship until cross wire was steady on point of aim (M.O.T.) for 5 seconds and then at...

1657-02 Fired my first war shots. It missed! Torpedo ran hot straight and normal. Naturally it broached repeatedly running across those heavy seas. The torpedo seemed to have a hard fight to maintain its course. A heavy wave would not only veer it off its course but also apparently move it bodily down sea. The torpedo apparently regained its heading very rapidly after each bounce. Its directivity surfboarding across those rough waves was amazing. Torpedo track was followed by watching the occasional broaching. The torpedo would disappear for a while and then apparently broach. From periscope angle the broaching looked like a whale blowing. What this would look like from a higher point is not known. Possibly the target can see the track and/or the torpedo broaching. It is believed that the spray of water thrown up about every 500 yards is due to the propellers coming out of the water. The torpedo is apparently going to hit the target in the bow. As it neared the target the waves are larger due to piling up effect in the shallow water. These waves bounced our MISS HOPE-FULLY just a little too far to the right and she passed the target's bow very close aboard, skipped along about 2000 yards beyond the target, hit a reef and blew up. The explosion sent a geyser of water into the air about 100 feet, the wind caught it, and the people on the beach were sprayed with a salt water shower. The explosion was hardly heard aboard ship. Sounded like the detonator click of a depth charge. Whether this lack of explosive noise received is due to the shallow depth explosion or the blocking effect of the shallow water between us and the torpedo explosion is not known.

1705 Came around and headed back towards reef for another experimental shot. Will close 10 fathom curve to about 500 yards, shoot and turn out. Visibility getting poorer.

1716 ATTACK No. 1-(b)

Same target as before, heading 160° angle on bow 100°S, track 100°S, range 1200 yards, torpedo run 1200 yards, depth set zero, gyro angle 000°, own course 080°T. With gyros set on zero, periscope on zero, steady on center of target,

1716-35 Fired one torpedo, ran hot, straight, and normal. Same characteristics as first one fired except that it seemed to be digging into the waves each time it was bounced, and thus moved to the left of the point of aim. Looked like it would hit the stern with only about 500 yards to go, its motion to the left is accelerated, this must be the reef's effect as this is the same spot where the first one moved off to the right. Torpedo passed astern of target about 10 yards, ran fairly straight for another thousand yards then hooked to the left for another thousand yards, hit a reef and blew up. Hardly heard the explosion aboard. After firing reversed course for another experimental shot. Rain is making targets hard to see. Seas are abating somewhat.

1724 ATTACK No. 1-(c)

Same target as before, heading 160°T, angle on the bow 90°S, track 90°S, range 1200 yards, torpedo run 1200 yards, depth set zero, gyro angle 180°, own course 260°T with gyros set on zero, periscope set on 180°, steady on center of targets.

1724-35 Fired one torpedo, ran hot, straight, and normal. Same running characteristics as the other two. Running straight as a die.

1726-47 Torpedo hit target about 10 yards aft of point of aim. Explosion sent a broad column of debris 400 yards into the air. Target disintegrated. Hardly heard the explosion aboard. I had hoped this explosion would hurt the far ship, but it was still there when last seen.

ATTACK RESULTS: SUNK — One lugger type supply vessel of about 500 tons. Cleared the area at high speed submerged in order to open out on land before surfacing.

1816 SURFACED.

1917 (AP Radar Contact #7).

2025 Sent PUFFER message No. 1 to COMSUBPAC giving weather and information on attack today.

2105 (Aircraft Contact #15), APR contact shows plane closing in, so DIVED.

2150 SURFACED [WPR].

Although postwar analysis could not account for the vessel sunk, there was little doubt the lugger was destroyed. The small lugger probably carried munitions and was under Japanese Army control, and therefore not recorded under the movements of naval ships. Dwyer had his first "kill" albeit a small vessel.

Dive! Dive!

January 5 was uneventful, except for the excitement of airplane contacts and two crash dives that followed. The following day the weather proved more problematic. The seas continued very rough. After an aircraft contact and subsequent dive, the *Puffer* was still only at 30 feet, which left the conning tower above water (WPR).

1404 Plane contact (Airplane Contact #17) on SJ at 10,000 yards. SUBMERGED, at the end of one minute we were still at 30 feet. Checked all vents open, negative flooded, maneuvering giving proper turns, pit speed 9 knots. Gave orders to fill auxiliaries, sanitary tanks, and bilges, and took a 20° dive angle. About this time we broke through the heavy seas that we were running into and went down like a rock. But not in time to prevent the C.O. from leaving a permanent set of left hand finger prints in the CRS hand rail in the conning tower. Decided to run down seas during daylight and into the seas at night in order to improve our diving time during daylight [WPR].

Andrew Thoman was on the bow planes during the sluggish submergence. With a 20° down angle and all tanks flooded he was sure the boat was headed to Davy Jones' locker.

After blowing every tank on board we slowly began to level off, another brown skivvies event. The captain was upset so we practiced diving. Later that day an alert lookout sighted a plane coming in fast, dived, rigged ship for depth charges. Ordered big down angle, made 300 feet in record time when one bomb exploded overhead. Mystery as to why the SJ radar didn't pick up the aircraft. Thank you alert lookout [Thoman].

1448 SURFACED.

1520 Alert lookout sighted plane (Aircraft Contact #18). No APR. DIVED. Rigged for depth charges. Ordered big down angle. Made 300 foot in record time when one bomb exploded overhead. No damage. This bomb sounded small and shallow [WPR].

If the same diving difficulties had developed during the second crash dive, the results could have been fatal. Alert lookouts with good eyesight, such as Thoman, were as good or better than the radar for detecting low flying aircraft.

Noisy propeller shafts had haunted the *Puffer* on and off since the First War Patrol. The depth charges during that patrol may have caused permanent damage. Even though the boat had been through a complete overhaul, the problem reoccurred. The defect now became Golay's problem as engineering officer.

On this dive our shafts started squealing at 40 R.P.M. up to about 70 R.P.M. All efforts to quiet them were fruitless. The squeal seemed to be in the strut bearings as you could hear it better in the After Torpedo Room than the Maneuvering Room. A stethoscope placed on the stern tubes indicated the same results. From this time on until the end of the patrol these shafts were noisy. This was naturally a constant source of worry to the C.O. as we had not been able to find any temperature gradient yet in this area. Do not believe we are justified in returning to the base for this as it may be impossible to hear it from deep depths. In addition it is not believed that it will help an A/S vessel if he is pinging, and if he is listening we can overcome this by heading up sea so he cannot listen as effectively. All of this wisdom is from the Executive Officer [Decker] who has had two years patrol work and commanded an SC and a PC. In addition our evasion doctrine calls for use of maximum speed up to cavitation point. At deep depth this will take us above the squeal speed. The only possibility to detect us would be for a listener to trail a mike deep in the water. This is a rare possibility. Based on these facts we decided to stay on station and continue the patrol. The noisy shafts will be remedied during next refit and thoroughly tested before we go out again. These noisy shafts are a distinct military handicap [WPR].

Heavy Seas and Heavy Action

The next two days were summed up as "one periscope, one mine, and many airplanes." The periscope was evaded at full speed. The airplanes were evaded by submerging. The mine was sunk with gun fire. Late in the day on January 9, the *Puffer* received word from the *Sea Fox* that a convoy was headed north. Although Dwyer headed for a midnight intercept point at full speed, he was slowed by the heavy seas, taking a steady stream of water down the conning tower and control room hatches. Normally the control room hatch would be closed, but due to the flooding of the main induction from the heavy seas, another supply of air was needed for the engines. The worst result was the water flooded the stash of sugar, a necessity for the gallons of coffee the crew drank (WPR). "Brown sugar in coffee is not a good combination" (Thoman). With the heavy seas Dwyer plotted a course to intercept the convoy around 0200 the next day. Contact came about an hour earlier than expected (WPR).

January 10, 1945:
   0055 SJ radar contact on the convoy at 252°T, 24,000 yards. (Ship Contact #5). Heard two pingers. That always helps! With the SEAFOX tracking astern this put us in good position for an attack on the starboard bow. However this would mean firing into the seas which will probably produce erratic runs. Decided to cross over to port bow and attack from down seas at the cost of darkness time. In addition the best background is to the northwest while crossing over the convoys fan, we get a very good idea of their disposition, and pick out the two large ships to attack. By now the seas had increased to make a successful attack problematical. Decided to go in and fire three experimental down sea zero depth settings using lower tubes, in accordance with COMSUBPAC patrol instructions. Went in for the attack with excellent background at about 8–10 knots pit speed, kept bows on, worked in astern of one of the side escorts and ahead of the port quarter escort.

ATTACK No. 2
   Range 1875 yards, track 100°P, gyros 350°, using TBT bearings, TDC offset. Two overlapping targets.
   0249-40 When TBT officer reported that he couldn't see all of the target any longer in his binoculars, fired one torpedo at port quarter of large target which had the second largest target in the convoy overlapping it and 300 yards beyond. Fired second torpedo spread. 1° L and third on 1° R. Came left and formed up with convoy about 1500 yards astern of port bow escort and about 1000 yards ahead of port quarter escort and waited to see results. Saw first torpedo hit the large target. Saw second torpedo hit the large target, followed by the ship blowing up and lighting up the horizon for miles around. Words fail to describe the scene. It looked like a Cecil B. Demille movie. Our position in the convoy looked a little stupid. Saw a third torpedo hit the target beyond the one just sunk. Saw this target sink. Two large pips disappeared on the radar. All the ships milled around now. Decided to pull out to about 4000 yards and watch their actions. The escorts milled around and dropped some depth charges. The two escorts on our side turned out to be small freighters. They looked as scared as the PUFFER felt when night turned into day for a while. Started pulling ahead for next attack. Convoy changed base course to the right to 110°T. This meant we would be firing in direction of SEAFOX who was astern of convoy. SEAFOX RATED NEXT ATTACK but she had a long end around ahead of her, and as PUFFER was in position to attack, decided to attack while SEAFOX was ending around the

starboard side. Sent message via WOPACO to SEAFOX info BLUEBACK THAT WE WERE ATTACKING AGAIN. No receipt from BLUEBACK.

0345 Exchanged calls over SJ with SEAFOX. Still not certain of exact bearing of SEAFOX so opened up on WOPACO with plain language voice, told her where PUFFER was and found out where she was. Her position was far enough south of the convoy so we could attack on good port track without fear of hitting her. About this time radar reported two intermittent pips astern and on the port quarter of convoy. Believed them to be airplanes. Next up comes word that these airplanes have ten centimeter radar. Something new has been added! Radar reports these pips are steady on the screen now and moving right along in our direction. Decided to go in and fire ten torpedoes while we could. Started in for the attack. On the way in we could see that our two "airplanes" had mounted 5 inch guns and were now large destroyers. Decided not to shoot at them as the seas were probably too rough for their shallow draft. With these two destroyers moving up along the port side of the convoy, it began to look like PUFFER and the two cans are going to arrive at the same place at the same time, so PUFFER speeded up. With the destroyer's 10CM radar, SEA FOX same, and PUFFER's SJ all filling the air at once, the screen was full of interference. Tried to use the ST but it was too rough. Decided to use SJ on intermittent sweeps excluding the DD sector. At this time one destroyer bore about 70° relative, and the near one about 60° relative. General plan was to cross ahead of the destroyers, shoot the bow tubes at the convoy, cross through the convoy and shoot the stern tubes at whatever was available. However, at this time the starboard lookout reported that the destroyer had seen us. Took a look and could see no change, but decided to take the lookout's advice as he had been designated to watch nothing but the destroyers. So forced to shoot at long range, started firing bow tubes at convoy using TBT bearings and radar ranges.

ATTACK No. 3 (a) (b)
    Lat. 27-01.3 N Long. 126-34 E.
    0528 Fired two torpedoes at a single ship aft of the main group, range 2600 yards, 56° port track, 12° gyro. Started firing four torpedoes at three overlapping targets, range 5100 yards, 81° port track, 55° gyro. During this time the far destroyer speeded up and started at us. By this time he was on the starboard beam. He pulled up alongside of the rear destroyer bearing about 70° relative now angle on bow zero. By this time there was no reason to doubt that the destroyers had seen us or had us in their radar. Had hoped to complete the bow shooting and move on over into the convoy so the destroyers couldn't shoot at us. Decided to feint to the left to get the destroyers off guard so came left with full rudder. Up to this time had tried to keep the destroyer information from the conning tower, but they sneaked an occasional sweep on the DD's just to be sure the bridge didn't go to sleep. A bridge PPI was needed in this type of attack.
    0528 When the full left rudder went on, the control party secured firing the bow tubes in accordance with PUFFER fire control doctrine and got set up on the two destroyers without being told. Forward TBT then shifted to the nearest destroyer. This target then cut right to head between us and the convoy. This was his mistake as it gave us a good track on him. The other destroyer turned out to port toward our stern. Started firing aft and steadying up.

ATTACK No. 3 (c)
    0530 Fired two torpedoes at near destroyer, range 1050 yards, 106° port track, 122° gyro.
    Fired two torpedoes down the throat at far destroyer, range 1200 yards, 0° track, 135° gyro.
    0530-53 Saw terrific hit under bridge of first destroyer.
    0530-59 Saw second hit in this destroyer in engine space. This destroyer sank immediately after the second hit without blowing up or taking any angle. One of the two pips disappeared on the radar.
    Situation looked a little tense so cleared the bridge of the three lookouts, QM, O.O.D., J.O.O.D. forward, and J.O.O.D. aft. The O.O.D. (Lt. F.H. Golay, USNR) volunteered to stay on the bridge. His assistance was an inspiration to the Commanding Officer. About this time the second destroyer seemed to have slowed down to a walk turned to port and then the sky

around was lit up with tracer fire. In addition nine random depth charges went off. The next few minutes saw a grand exhibition of radar controlled gunfire. Being in good position to observe the rake, it can be stated that there were straddles in range, deflection and morale. Ordered Lt. Golay below and returned to the cigarette deck, stood behind EIFFEL TOWER and watched the destroyer, Lt. Golay remained on the bridge. Heard one timed hit in second DD. His bow seemed to be smoking and only his after turrets were firing. He had now turned to starboard. This was very encouraging. At this time the conning tower reported his speed as 4 knots. This most welcome piece of news was accompanied by a cessation of firing these aforementioned tracers. Lt. GOLAY took the con and started end around.

0532 One timed hit in AK, followed by an explosion. Two less pips in SJ radar. Started end around on the convoy. Radar interference from SEAFOX indicated she had contact with convoy. Unable to raise BLUEBACK on WOPACO so sent convoy contact and new base course to BLUEBACK via COMSUBPAC (PUFFER #3). DD tracked us out on his radar and apparently lost us at 7000 yds. Too late for another night attack. Getting ahead of convoy's track for a submerged attack. Counted six ships as we passed convoy in addition to damaged DD astern. Believe we sunk five and damaged one.

At daylight sighted convoy on starboard beam and a smoking destroyer on starboard quarter. Will attack convoy and then go after damaged destroyer.

0655 As it began to get lighter now, the destroyer is getting closer on starboard quarter, still smoking heavily. SUBMERGED. Went deep and went ahead full speed parallel to convoy track.

0657 Several depth charges. Very large but distant.

0741 SUBMERGED. Smoke of convoy on starboard beam. DD far on starboard quarter. Started end around on convoy.

0746 AP Radar Contact #27. Plane radar getting closer.

0752 Dived. Went deep.

0755 Several bombs.

0807 SURFACED. Started end around again.

0825 AP Radar Contact #28.

0915 Closing convoy submerged. Convoy base course changed now to 160°T. This is a 50° change to right. Unable to close. Watched ships go by out of range, large track angle. Ships in convoy now are:

1— SHIGURE DD (SC #7).
1— AK — Similar to KOKI MARU (p222 — 208J)
1— AK — Similar to NISSYO MARU (p172 — 208J)
4— AK — Similar to KEIZAN MARU (p145 — 208J)

Very disappointing. Too much land in sight to end around now. They have headed down toward NAHA. Also one too many ships here if we sank 5 last night, unless the SHIGURE joined up after the attacks.

1140 Sound picked up pinging. Closed in direction of pinging.

1404 Sighted masts of two ships. (Ship Contact #8). Large angle on the bow. Identified leading ship as a small AK of the MFM type similar to SOYA MARU (p26 ONI 208J). The second ship in column was a destroyer with a PUFFERIZED bow. It looked as if he had run into the end of a dock making 30 knots. His forward turret was all messed up and elevated about 30°. There was no smoke coming out of the bow. Believe this DD was hit in attack No. 3(c). Closed at high speed, going deep between looks as DD is only making six knots and is pinging.

1446 Range 2640 yards, track 95°P, gyro 004°. Fired three torpedoes at DD aimed ½ ship length aft, M.O.T., ½ ship length ahead. This one ended up being aimed at M.O.T. of AK.

1448 Range 2800 yards, track 90°P, gyro 358° fired three at AK same type of spread. Used depth setting of zero due to shallow draft of targets and heavy seas. Could see torpedoes "blowing" every now and then. DD either saw them or heard them as he turned down the tracks and awkwardly tried to put a bone in that basket mouth of his. Came around for a down the throat shot but decided he was moving too much water in front of him. This would probably deflect a torpedo. Saw one torpedo headed on a collision course with AK and very close to him. He never changed course. With DD beginning to look like a cruiser in the periscope, went deep and rigged for depth charges [WPR].

"He dropped 22 depth charges. I never quit flinching as each exploded" (Thoman).

1451-14 One timed hit in AK. His screws stopped. No breaking up noises. Believe he blew up. Never heard screws again. Ran down starboard side of DD, crossed through his wake, and headed up sea to test depth plus, meanwhile he dropped 22 depth charges. Pulled clear of DD and came to periscope depth.

1615 DD about 5000 yards away still dropping DC's. No AK in sight. At his speed he couldn't have cleared the area. DD headed into NAHA.

1800 SURFACED. (AP Radar Contact #30)

1802 (Ship Contact #9)

Sighted two patrol boats. One challenged us with searchlight. Evaded on surface at high speed. We have to get flat battery up.

1921 (AP Radar Contact #31).

1932 SJ radar contact 270°T, range 14,000 yards. (Ship Contact #10). Radar pip size indicates a DE. Tracking until completion of battery charge.

1935 Received message from SEAFOX giving her position and requesting ours.

2000 PUFFER is being tracked by someone.

2048 Received congratulations from SEAFOX. Obviously this made us feel better about the whole deal.

2050 Exchanged calls with BLUEBACK. Received "WELL DONE" FROM PACK COMMANDER.

2149 Message from Pack Commander asking how many fish we fired.

2209 SEA FOX gave dope on her prospective movements.

January 11, 1945

Tracking target north of AGUNI SHIMA.

0039 AP Radar Contact #32.

This target is evidently patrolling. He is using a constant helm superimposed on zig plan with countermarches every hour and fifteen minutes. As PUFFER only had two torpedoes left forward decided not to attack until we knew his plan well enough. Did not believe he was zigging this radically so closed in to 4000 yards and ran the zig plan with him for an hour. Also determined at this time that the target was not the SEA FOX or BLUEBACK. Used TBT bearings. TDC calling zigs within the minute. Decided we knew the dope so at...

0121 Headed in for attack. Target let out a puff of black smoke. Cleared at high speed. Target evidently was blowing tubes. Started in again. Target countermarched. Another end around. Started in again.

ATTACK No. 5.

Lat. 26-45 N. Long. 127-09.5 E.

0250 Range 1400 yards, track 117°S, gyro 006°, fired last two bow torpedoes at depth zero. Came left slowly and passed about 500 yards astern of target, and headed out for a rain squall on his port quarter to watch him blow up. He didn't. Both torpedoes missed. No excuses are offered. PUFFER wanted this one badly after such a long attack. Analysis showed that the target did not hold his course on the far right leg when we fired for two or three minutes as he had been doing.

0315 Sent message to PACK giving dope on this patrol vessel.

0345 Exchanged recognition signals with SEA FOX.

0347 SJ contact on IHEYA JIMA.

0650 Sent PUFFER 4th [message] to COMSUBPAC.

1404 (Ship Contact #11)

Sighted masts of four (4) ships. Closed at high speed. JP heard sonic pinging. Ships are two trawlers and two PC's. The PC's seem to be circling the trawlers. Decided to go in slowly, go under the group at deep depth, come up on the other side and fire two remaining stern tubes at the two PC's. Then go deep, head into the sea and clear the area.

On way toward the group, heard muffled explosion. The batteries of the two remaining torpedoes had blown up (See Section K) in the tubes. Went deep, put target group astern and built up gradually to full speed.

1555 SURFACED. PC's and trawlers look closer from the bridge than from the periscope so, 1557 SUBMERGED.

1610 Situation in after torpedo room requires ventilation so SURFACED and evaded patrol craft on surface.

1654 Received COMSUBPAC Serial 9 ordering PUFFER to GUAM for refit. Reload at PERTH not available.

1724 AP Radar Contact #33.

1741 Torpedo in #7 tube now on fire despite all measures possible being taken. Cannot endanger the ship any longer. Surveyed one Mark 18 torpedo to the JAPAN STREAM [WPR].

The situation with the final two torpedoes was extremely dangerous. The batteries had exploded as a result of a faulty hydrogen detector. Use of salt water to put out the fire would cause a chemical reaction with the battery acid producing chlorine gas. The fire could cause the explosive in the torpedo to detonate, which would sink the boat. The only choice for Dwyer was to get rid of the torpedo.

In the *Comments Section* of the war patrol report Dwyer recorded the poetic description of the action.

> Captain, Oh Captain, come change sides with me.
> These are 40 mm tracers as you can see.
> Golay, old boy, your swap is a cinch.
> Here on my side, they're shooting five inch [*ibid.*].

In the *Personnel Section* of the WPR Dwyer lauded the fire control party for its good work.

The efficiency, calmness and accuracy of this group under severe attack conditions was inspirational to the Commanding Officer. During the attack on the two destroyers at 1000 yards, the only words spoken by the C.O. were "Angle of the bow — 90 port." The fire control party did the rest. Especially outstanding was the Executive Officer (Lt. S. M. Decker, USNR) TDC Operator (Lt. W. M. Pugh, II), and the Radar Operator (Deem, CRT) [*ibid.*].

Jay Deem in an interview elaborated on the events. Deem recalled that Captain Dwyer called him into his wardroom after the attack. Dwyer told him, "You are lucky we sunk that destroyer. If you had missed, I would have given you a court martial." Deem retorted, "That would not have been necessary, if we had missed, you and I wouldn't be here" (Deem).

The *Puffer* attacked six ships on January 10, and believed a tanker, a freighter, and an escort destroyer had been sunk. In addition it was thought two additional freighters had been damaged along with another escort destroyer. Postwar analysis gave credit for the escort destroyer claimed sunk, and also one damaged. The 740 ton corvette *Kaibokan No. 42* was sunk with all 170 hands lost. In the excitement and darkness, lookouts on *Kaibokan No. 30* initially misidentified the *Puffer* as another Japanese escort, but later made a proper identification and opened fire on the *Puffer* with their deck guns. Having seen the demise of *No. 42*, *No. 30* turned toward the *Puffer* and prepared to drop depth charges. Seconds later *No. 30* was also hit by a torpedo — the bow and bridge were wrecked and the forward gun mount was blasted off the ship. Having started a turn, *No. 30* had been lucky; a hit a few feet aft would have blown the forward magazine. Five crew members of *No. 30* were killed (Somerville, 1982).

Later in the war the Japanese had learned the value of anti-submarine escort vessels, but

Robert F. Kennedy drew the sequence of events that occurred during the multiple attacks on the Japanese vessels. The *Puffer*-ized bow of the escort is to the left of King Neptune's head. Note the shark's mouth on the bow of the *Puffer*, artwork that would become a reality after the end of the war (War Patrol Report from National Archives).

by that time it was too late. The *Kaibokan* class was equipped with radar, a technology only deployed on smaller escorts in the latter part of the war. However the effective range of the Japanese radar was far inferior to the American technology. The difference in radar capabilities left the escorts vulnerable to submarine attack.

Although not verified by postwar analysis, considering the observations made by Dwyer and observed by lookout Thoman, two small vessels probably were sunk and another damaged. Through the periscope the size of the vessels was overestimated during the excitement of the attack. Dwyer wrote in the WPR that the destroyer started to look like a cruiser. Dwyer mentioned the vessels originally identified as freighters turned out to be escorts, which were less than 1000 tons (WPR). The ships sunk were probably small army motorized luggers. There was no evidence of large freighters sunk by other submarines at this location and time (Alden).

The *Puffer* artist, Robert F. Kennedy, drew a cartoon that summarized the action of the last attack. Dwyer included the drawing as part of the war patrol report (WPR.). The microfilm image was quite thin, and it was necessary to enhance the image.

A Trap

The *Puffer* was ordered to return to Guam to repair the noisy prop shafts. On the way to Guam the *Puffer* received word of a downed B-29 pilot 100 miles southwest of Iwo Jima. Near midnight a white-blue rocket was sighted about 2 miles away. SJ radar was able to track something intermittently as it moved at 2 knots into the wind. Dwyer sensed a trap and ordered all ahead flank, and right full rudder. While the flank turn was being made sound reported high speed screws passing down the port side, believed to be a "Nip" 45-knot torpedo by the commander. An hour later the *Puffer* received a radio message containing "dope on the Jap trap" that confirmed Dwyer's suspicions. The *Puffer* had been lucky.

R & R at Guam

Without additional incident the *Puffer* arrived at Guam in the company of the *Drum* and an escort on January 17, 1945 (WPR). Only six months earlier on July 21, 1944, the United States liberated Guam from Japanese occupation. A poet on the *Puffer* proudly wrote of their accomplishments during the last war patrol and the crew's onshore activities—a possible reason for sending the crew to Guam. There were no women on Guam. The real reason was to keep the submarines closer to the front, but there may have been an ulterior motive as well.

> With a sudden thump and a hiss of air,
> The fish are on their way,
> And another ship of the rising sun
> Will come to us this day.
> For Carl and his boys are as good as can be,
> But don't let this be misleading to thee.
> While on our fair water this mood is maintained.
> When unleashed on the beach, their passions do flame,
> They'll woe a fair maiden without giving their name,
> And when she conceives they'll call her to blame.
> So! My dear daughter—them you must fear;
> They're a mad pack of demons when filled with beer.
> Tell the others my story and tell it well,
> Steer clear of the PUFFER or end up in HELL [*ibid.*].

Recreation at Guam—there were plenty of activities, but no women (photograph courtesy of the Golay family).

Camp Dealey had various activities to keep the crew entertained. There were still pockets of Japanese hidden on the island. A few months earlier submarine sailors who wanted to see more of the island had been ambushed by the Japanese. Metz described Guam.

There were lots of wrecked war machines strung along the beaches near Apra Harbor too; same as at Saipan. The U.S. used lots of concrete ocean barges to tow freight to the war zones, then they would sink them in shallow water around the harbor to make a better breakwater. After turning the *Puffer* over to a relief crew, we were transported from Apra Harbor to Camp Dealey by bus over a new highway, still under construction, for our two weeks rest.

Around the camp, coconut palms grew wild. The coconuts would eventually fall off to the ground and it was a good thing because I don't think any of us could have climbed those rough bark limbless trees. It didn't take us long to learn how to peel the outer hull

Thomas Metz receives the Combat Insignia (photograph courtesy of Thomas Metz).

off of those coconuts. Near the center of Camp Dealey, they had a Japanese two-man suicide submarine on display. It is mounted on two concrete pillars like a propane storage tank. There were Jap soldiers holed up in the mountains of Guam. They would come into camp and try to slip through the chow line.

We made a short walking tour of the country side which was thick jungle with only narrow paths through it. On this tour we came to one village where there were only very old people and a few small children. At the edge of the village was a long grave that the Japs forced the people to dig. Then they killed most all inhabitants, about 140 men and women, then the Japs pushed them into the ditch and covered them over with a dozer. One elderly man gave us a few small bananas. He explained they were so small because the stalks were cut too early. We saw several deformed people on this tour. This was probably caused by elephantiasis or some other jungle disorder. We saw one white girl that had lost one arm. She was French and had lived in Agana with her family before the Japs took over in 1941, so we were told. There was one civilian worker at the submarine refit complex at Guam, to correct some malfunction in the sound gear. He was the only civilian worker from the states I saw.

While we were at Camp Dealey, we had a pretty good place to rest. The camp was located on gently rolling terrain sloping to the beach on the east side, hemmed in by jungle on the other three sides. We lived in fifty man Quonset huts nestled among the trees. They offered swimming and softball games daily in their recreation program at the rest camp. The swimming hole had been blasted out of the coral along the beach. We got soft drinks, Coca-Cola and tropical candy bars for between meal snacks. The candy bars were made of light colored mealy textured chocolate that scarcely tasted like a state side candy bar.

Before we left Guam, we had an awards presentation ceremony aboard the *Puffer* for her crew. I, along with others, was awarded the submarine combat insignia with one star by a Captain from Admiral Nimitz's command. The Captain explained Admiral Nimitz usually made these presentations in person, but he was away from the island that day [Metz].

13

The Seventh War Patrol

A Full Boat and Refit

Robert Polk and John Sanders both left the *Puffer*. These two men would be reunited many years later. Starting in 1990 Polk, Sanders and John Gutensohn were instrumental in organizing the many *Puffer* reunions. The *Puffer* gained another 7 crew members; 10 crew members remained at Guam and 17 were added for a total of 83 enlisted men (RG24). There was only one change among the officers; Lt. Wilfrid Delafield replaced Lt. Lawrence Picone (WPR).

CREW TRANSFERRED BEFORE THE SEVENTH WAR PATROL

Name	Service #	Rate Arr.	Sixth WP	Seventh WP
Burger, Edward Andrew	725 08 01	Y2c	7-Nov-44	TRAN
Camp, Gerald Maurice	410 67 41	SM1c	SM1c	TRAN
Creech, Bishop Boggs	634 13 65	F3cV6	MoMM2c	TRAN
Dickinson, Master James	636 47 51	F3cV6	MoMM2c	TRAN
Fallon, Merritt Dayton	228 11 89	CTM(PA)	CTM(PA)	TRAN
Jones, LaMar	660 19 18	TM3cV6	TM1c	TRAN
Markle, John Emery	755 02 03	EM2c	20-Nov-44	TRAN
Polk, Robert Edgar, Jr.	656 56 30	EM2cV6	EM1c(T)	TRAN
Sanders, John Wiley	45 08 12	S1cV6	S1c	TRAN
Sears, Phillip Clayton	602 06 87	TM3cV6	TM2c	TRAN

NEW CREW MEMBERS

Name	Service #	Rate Arr.	Date Arr.
Baumgartner, Delmar D.	629 82 14	S1c(RM)	2-Feb-45
Berry, William R., Jr.	825 49 06	F1c(EM)	2-Feb-45
Bretz, James L.	313 43 86	S1c	2-Feb-45
Dauplaise, Louis B. E.	201 55 17	CQM(T)	4-Feb-45
Deiss, Harry C., Jr.	826 39 00	F1c(EM)	2-Feb-45
Frith, Otha L.	837 49 28	F1c	2-Feb-45
Giaimo, Anthony	201 49 92	CTM(PA)	2-Feb-45

Name	Service #	Rate Arr.	Date Arr.
Gibbs, Warren J.	802 43 92	S1c(TM)	2-Feb-45
Gooch, William C.	845 60 78	F1c	2-Feb-45
Hartman, Raymond W.	895 07 29	S1c(GM)	2-Feb-45
Henderson, Franklin	279 50 81	EM1c(T)	10-Feb-45
McCardle, Oliver P.	895 45 81	F1c(MoMM)	5-Feb-45
McPherson, George L.	637 96 81	RT3c	2-Feb-45
Pierson, Siegel H.	807 54 04	S1c(TM)	2-Feb-45
Thursby, Cecil H.	382 58 83	Y1c	21-Jan-45
Urbanski, James L.	895 83 88	S1c	5-Feb-45
Werner, Sondol	708 38 10	S1c(QM)	5-Feb-45

Although quarters were close among the enlisted men and officers, Dwyer felt there were advantages to the additional crew members.

> The eighty-three men carried on this patrol was an adequate number to stand all the watches and provide sufficient relief. This enabled us to man any and all of the equipment twenty-four hours a day without undue strain on anyone. Replacements have been trained for the expected loss of key men who have completed numerous patrols. The new men received from SubDiv-28 were of the highest caliber and were very well indoctrinated. School of the Boat was held daily for all the unqualified men. The Watch Officers supervised their respective section's training [*ibid.*].

Ensign Phillip McClure — commissary officer with a taste for beer and pilchards (photograph courtesy of the Golay family).

With the refit completed, which included work on the squeal in the prop shafts, noise in the QB sound shaft, and routine painting, the officers and men were back on board February 1, 1945. Realistic training exercises for the new crew members were limited by the few ships at Guam. On February 11, the *Puffer, Piranha,* and *Sea Owl* were to operate as a team, dubbed Bennett's Blazers for wolf pack commander C. L. Bennett on the *Sea Owl*. The patrol was the longest of the war for the *Puffer*, 71 days. Much of the time was spent on lifeguard duty (*ibid.*). With Japanese shipping nearly nonexistent, the role of most submarines changed to supporting the air bombardment of Japan.

> [The Seventh War Patrol was] the longest and most trying ordeal the crew was to endure. There were days, nights, and weeks, and months of looking for something to shoot at. By this time most of the Japanese ships had already been sunk. It was kind of like going deer hunting on the last day of the season. The monotony was sometimes broken when we operated in very shallow water near Hong Kong. The water was so shallow we painted the brass parts on the main deck black to make the ship harder to see when submerged [Metz].

In his letters Lt. Frank Golay described many of the daily events on the *Puffer* not detailed in the war patrol reports. As the *Puffer* was preparing to leave on the seventh patrol, as usual it was loaded with food stores in every nook and cranny. Ensign Phillip McClure, commissary officer on the *Puffer,* decided to load a new item.

> Our departure was more than a little embarrassing with Mac [Phillip McClure] and his working party sheepishly loading cases of beer up until we cast off the lines and the Commodore

Opposite: The Seventh War Patrol — February 11, 1945 (Guam), to April 21, 1945 (Midway). The patrol covered 15,653 nautical miles, 9,003 of which were in the patrol area. The extremely long patrol began with 11 days of lifeguard duty off Formosa in the company of other submarines. The *Puffer* then moved south in search of Japanese shipping near Hong Kong. The new deck gun was used to shell Pratas Island. After stopping at Saipan to refuel, the *Puffer* patrolled Wake Island for a week. Finally after more than 70 days at sea the boat went to Midway Island for R & R (map artwork by Nancy Webber).

frowning at the scene—we have a full load in the forward hold, a synthetic deck of beer, each [officer's] stateroom allotted a case of crackers and a case of tomato juice [Golay].

One of the irksome jobs of the officers was to censor crew letters. However, no one censored an officer's letters. As a result, Golay knew much about the crew and wrote freely about other officers and crew members. Golay had a keen sense of observation and at times was critical of some officers and crew. He was overly critical of Dwyer. Many crew members spoke very highly of Dwyer at the *Puffer* reunions (Polk; Sanders; Frith). McDonald found Dwyer friendly and a good officer (McDonald). Golay was also critical of himself. The monotony of the war was grating on him. His feeling of a lack of contribution to the war effort undoubtedly contributed to his negativity. At the end of the previous patrol he wrote, "You taxpayers have taken a beating this run, it begins to look like we aren't to earn our bread and butter and the only 'fish' we have fired was to jettison a defective" (Golay). Today he wrote about Reynolds, who was a topic of many future exploits.

> My other helmsman is [Arthur] Reynolds, the erstwhile lookout and mess cook, he seems to have found his niche and is much impressed with his job of steering—his report to the bridge when the watch is rotated has the ritual and formality of an Episcopal service—he is the principle problem we face as censors, his letters at first were not a brief synopsis of the patrol report and he felt that Mrs. Reynolds should be cut in on the dope—right now he is busy selling her the idea of migrating their brood to a tropical island after the war—and raise turkeys—he was hacking in Los Angeles when Uncle Sam sent his greetings [ibid.].

Lifeguard Duty

One day out of Guam, on February 12, Ensign James Goin developed symptoms of appendicitis, as diagnosed by Pharmacist Mate Charles Johnson. Two days later the *Sea Owl* was made aware of the situation on *Puffer*, and recommended transfer of Goin to an incoming submarine, the *Archerfish*. The contact was coordinated through Submarine Command Pacific, and the transfer was made on the morning of February 15 in the *Puffer*'s rubber boat (WPR).

> Jim Goin was hit hard by appendicitis early in the week, but instead of the customary imprudent, but dramatic amateur appendectomy aboard, we rendezvoused with a southbound boat and transferred him by rubber boat—I suspect that since he was able to survive the transfer, he will find the infection little trouble—the typical PUFFER unpremeditated flail complete with bringing the rubber boat along the weather side instead of taking advantage of the lee—Jim is a good shipmate and I hope he can rejoin us next run [Golay].

On February 16 Bennett's Blazers became the Blazer Lifeguard wolf pack. The new orders placed the *Puffer* southwest of Formosa on lifeguard duty. Golay noted, "It must be encouraging to aviators to learn that saving one of their lives has the same evaluation as sinking 10,000 tons of Jap shipping in our reward system" (*ibid.*).

As engineering officer, Golay had problems with noisy propeller shafts and unpredictable equipment essential to the offensive capabilities of the submarine. On February 16, less than a week into the patrol, the pitometer log was again out of use for additional repair. Without accurate pitometer data the TDC and navigational equipment were badly handicapped. Manual entry of data was possible, but this made attack approaches of Japanese ships much more difficult. The air conditioning was also problematic. Golay wrote of his frustrations. Keep in mind the submerged top speed of the *Puffer* was around 9 knots.

> My own particular cross, the Pit Log, is temperamental and yesterday [while] submerged, raced around the dial to indicate 26 knots, a new course record—and all the fire control and

navigational equipment raced merrily behind trying to catch up — have the electricians busy removing the "outboard" motors from the ventilation fans— the one at the foot of my sack sounds like a B-29 taking off— with or without my foot in it [*ibid.*].

On the route to Formosa Dwyer noted in the war patrol report a total absence of enemy shipping. With a shortage of escorts Japanese submarines were used for anti-submarine warfare, attempting to keep the American submarines at bay from the shipping near the home waters of Japan. Also there had been an increased number of air contacts in which airborne radar had been detected. Anti-submarine surface vessels, such as those sunk during the previous war patrol, were also missing. Friendly planes were not to be trusted, even though recognition signals could be exchanged. All airplanes were treated cautiously. Very heavy weather was expected during this time of year, and Dwyer's expectations were realized. Late in the day on February 17 the *Puffer* arrived at the first lifeguard station. The next couple of days were highlighted by aircraft contacts and frequent crash dives (WPR).

A Near Miss

On February 19 at 2104 the *Puffer* surfaced in the safety of the darkness, but immediately picked up Japanese scanning radar signals and aircraft, which were not broadcasting the IFF or "Identify Friend or Foe" signal. Dwyer took the *Puffer* back down for an hour and resurfaced. The batteries needed recharging. Contact with a ship was made about an hour later (*ibid.*).

2104 SURFACED. APR contacts 158 mcs, saturated. SD contacts 20, 21, 30 miles. No IFF.
2109 SUBMERGED.
2118 SURFACED.
2145 Exchanged dope with PIRANHA via SJ. He reports no targets. Do not believe a target of any size could have run between PUFFER and coast without being picked up.
2155 SD contact 23 miles. No IFF.
2225 Ship contact #1. Proceeding on base course north parallel to the southwest coast of FORMOSA at full speed on two main engines, fully surfaced condition, zig-zagging by Arma Course Clock, charging batteries on two main engines. Visibility conditions excellent with the moon high in the sky. Sea calm and wind light. PIRANHA radar (SJ) interference 065°T, estimated distance 15,000 to 20,000 yards. Closest land bearing 065°T, distance 30,000 yards. Very alert high lookout (BRANCHCOMB, E. D., FC3c) sighted a white object this side of the horizon and reported:
"Wake at 050° relative." (070°T).
The O.O.D. (Lieut. F. H. GOLAY, U.S.N.R.) could see a white wake at this bearing and came left with full rudder and went ahead flank speed on four main engines. Radar operator was coached on this bearing for investigation. By this time the regular operator had been augmented by the CRT (Jay Deem) and the Executive Officer (Decker). High lookout (BRANCHCOMB) amplified his original report to the O.O.D. by stating,
"It looks like a submarine."
At this time both the O.O.D. and J.O.O.D. (Ensign R. A. HEEHS, U.S.N.R.) could see a wake and the vague outline of ship with a low silhouette with angle on the bow large. The ship's phosphorescent wake was considerably more pronounced than the outline of the ship. The Commanding Officer arrived in the conning tower just as the radar (SJ) operator reported to the O.O.D.,
"Nothing on that bearing except PIRANHA'S interference with land behind it."
The Quartermaster [MUSHA, D.A., QM3c(T)] now sighted the phosphorescent wake at 170° relative and described it as looking like water pounding on a roof and could not make out

any ship outline. The Commanding Officer arrived on the bridge just as the port lookout (WILSON, W. E., Jr., Cox.) reported,

"Two wakes astern — looks like torpedo wakes — about 400 yards."

2226 CRASH DIVED. Destination — 326 feet. Sound picked light high speed screws which eventually disappeared to the southeast. The port lookout (Wilson) reported that in addition to the two wakes reported, he had sighted the other ship's wake beyond. The quartermaster reported that he had seen one wake this side of the other ship's wake [ibid.].

The situation was complicated by the timing of the events, because the enemy ship sighting coincided with the changing of the high lookout and deck officer. Shortly after 2225 Branchcomb was relieved from high lookout duties by Ray "Half-hitch" Hartman, and Branchcomb informed him of a possible ship's location. Branchcomb also informed Ensign Heehs, who was junior officer of the deck, but Heehs dismissed the object as clouds on the horizon (Branchcomb). At this time Heehs and Golay

Raymond "Half-hitch" Hartman, who helped evade two torpedoes fired at the *Puffer* (photograph courtesy of Raymond Hartman).

were rotating stations as dive officer below decks and officer of the deck. When Hartman looked at the object he told the port lookout Wilson that it looked like a submarine (Hartman).

As Golay arrived on deck he asked Wilson what "Half-hitch" had said to him. Wilson told Golay and seconds later Wilson reported the two torpedoes passing astern, also spotted by starboard lookout Francis Holland. In a 2005 interview "Sandy" Branchcomb recalled he had told Dwyer after the dive began, "You better get this boat out of here in a hurry. There is something out there, even if radar didn't pick it up" (Branchcomb). The near miss frayed the nerves of Dwyer. Jay Deem on radar at the time recalled Dwyer yelled at Wilson for not seeing the torpedo wakes earlier (Deem). Hartman was chastised by Golay for making a report to Wilson, and not directly to him as officer of the deck (Hartman).

2330 SURFACED. Sent message to SEA OWL and PIRANHA telling of the torpedoes fired at PUFFER [WPR].

As a result of Branchcomb's and Wilson's sharp eyes, and Lt. Golay's actions to evade, two torpedoes passed harmlessly astern of the *Puffer*. Once again the *Puffer* had been lucky. For their sharp eyes Branchcomb and Wilson each received a Bronze Star. Interestingly, Branchcomb's citation made no mention of an enemy sub or torpedoes, but refers to "a floating obstruction at a considerable distance from his ship." The citation continued, "By his keen vision and presence of mind in making an accurate report, he undoubtedly saved his ship from destruction" (Branchcomb, *Citation*).

In a 2005 letter Hartman recalled Branchcomb told him after the medal ceremony the medal also should have gone to him. Hartman wrote he was not jealous; he was not in the service for medals. The two remained friends. Hartman remembered Branchcomb loaned him money when he lost his wallet (Hartman). Golay also received a Bronze Star for his quick response to the torpedoes (Dwyer, *Ship's History — Awards Supplement*). In the darkness the phosphorescent algae wake of the Japanese submarine had assisted the lookouts in spotting it and the oncoming torpedoes. A day earlier Golay had romantically described the algae phenomenon, unaware the tiny organisms would help save the boat the next day.

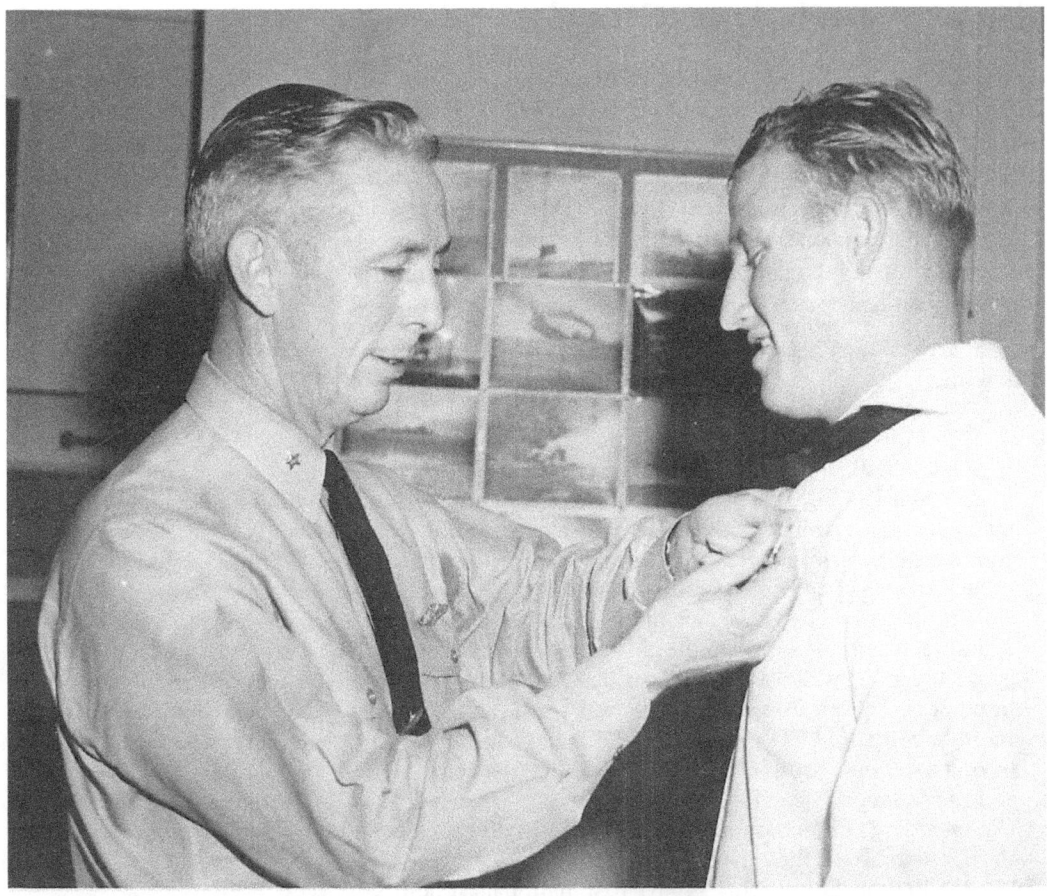

Ellis "Sandy" Branchcomb (right) receives the Bronze Star (photograph courtesy of Ellis Branchcomb).

Wish I might have shown you the sea last night — it was phosphorescent beyond belief — our bow wake made a huge neon "V" — one that would have warmed the cockles of Winnie's [reference to Winston Churchill] heart — it continued to glow halfway to the horizon — the light created by the violence of our screws was bright enough to read by — honor bright — each eddy, and small whirlpool in the turbulence of our wake was a writhing, glowing water slug and you had to convince yourself that they were not alive — and when we turned into the sea and water would ship over the bridge — our parkas would be brilliant with glowing sequins — and each wave breaking over the bow would look like the shower of sparks from an arc welder — strange how the minute sea life that are luminous travel or live in huge shoals — we ran out of this patch as if we'd snapped a switch [Golay].

The next day, February 20, the *Sea Owl* rotated into the position previously patrolled by the *Puffer*. The *Sea Owl* was also fired upon by two torpedoes which also missed. The *Puffer* moved from the Takao lifeguard station, off the southwest corner of Formosa, east toward the northern extreme of the Bashi Channel, which lay between Formosa and the Philippine Islands. On February 21 the *Puffer* was directed to the location of a ditched aircraft but along with numerous other vessels and planes was unable to find any survivors. The aircover overhead was welcome. The only object found was a ditched auxiliary aviation fuel tank. The wind was blowing at over 20 knots and the seas were increasing. The next day *Puffer* and *Piranha* continued searching for downed pilots, with no luck. The weather had now reached typhoon level (WPR).

Man Overboard!

On February 23 the weather continued extreme. For 27 hours it was impossible to get a fix on their location using the sun or stars. Radar was used to determine the range and bearing of a known location on Formosa. On February 24 the rough seas and a persistent Japanese aircraft complicated the conversion of a fuel ballast tank. This procedure was normally done during the night, but due to the heavy seas it was felt daytime would speed the process. The continual Japanese aircraft contacts delayed the completion of the job until after dark. One of the new crew members, Otha "Freddie" Frith, volunteered to perform the dangerous conversion in heavy seas (*ibid.*).

1700 Sent man on deck to convert #4 FBT to a MBT. Seas running heavy as usual. Put them astern.

1711 Sighted a Japanese aircraft at about 8 miles, SUBMERGED.

1735 SURFACED Resumed work converting #4 FBT.

1744 Sighted Japanese aircraft, range about 7 miles. SUBMERGED.

1831 SURFACED This persistent Japanese search plane has placed us in a difficult position. Darkness has descended with #4 FBT partially converted to a ballast tank. To leave it in this condition is dangerous because of several factors, least of which is the inevitable oil slick even though the tank is now supposedly full of salt water. To reconvert the tank to a fuel ballast tank will require as much or probably more time than continuing the conversion, as gasket holes will never stay centered when the chips are down. Although fuel ballast tanks are normally converted at night, it was decided earlier today that daylight conversion was best in view of the heavy seas. To wait for smoother seas was ruled out also earlier today on the basis of their improbability in LUZON STRAITS in February and in view of the military necessity for always having maximum speed available and keeping fuel consumption. Calculating the risks involved and the situation at hand, it was decided to continue the conversion to a main ballast tank. The Commanding Officer assumed full responsibility for the operation, took the con, and directed the operation from the cigarette deck.

1835 Resumed converting #4 FBT to a main ballast tank.

1839 An unusually large wave broke over the main deck coming from the starboard beam and normal to the direction of the seas. At first all appeared well with the workers on deck. However, in the dim light afforded by the moon through a heavy overcast, it was seen that FRITH, O. L Flc, had been swept loose and was being carried along by the water. He was carried slightly aft and hit the life line opposite the after five inch gun platform where there is a double wire only about 18 inches apart. Here he was caught momentarily by the life lines. Suddenly rising hope soon gave way to despair as the impact of the water tore loose his grip on the wire and swept him over the side.

Ordered "All stop, left full rudder," until the stern cleared the man overboard.

Calculated that a backing down recovery would give best chances of success under present conditions of poor visibility, heavy seas, and possibly limited time. Danger will be in having to dive while backing down. Decided to throw all caution to the wind.

Ordered "All back full — shift the rudder" in order to prevent the stern from working up wind and running down the man overboard.

After this time heavy clouds obscured the moon and total darkness descended. The man overboard had lost sight of the submarine by now and things looked even darker for him — Although shocked by the force of the seas which swept him over the side, FRITH had the presence of mind to take it easy in the water and conserve his strength. He checked his lifebelt, removed his shoes and other clothes, and started whistling.

Fortunately the searchlight was rigged and had not flooded out yet. Ordered it turned on and trained on port quarter. After backing down about two ships lengths, ordered "all stop," turned the con over to the Executive Officer, and then took station on the main deck aft to look and listen for the man overboard. Heard him off the port quarter and with some coaching got the searchlight on him. By now he was abeam of the conning tower up sea with the boat dead in the water. The situation looked good at first but it was soon apparent that the boat was drifting down sea faster than the man was swimming and that the man was tiring rapidly. Started twisting the boat to bring the stern up wind and at the same time dispatched a swimmer with a buoy and line to aid FRITH. Unfortunately the swimmer and the buoyed line parted company in the heavy seas. FRITH was found to be near exhaustion but still game in spite of the fact that he had now lost his life preserver due to the heavy seas. While the two swimmers were making their way back to the ship, the searchlight bulb burned out. Considerable trouble was experienced renewing the bulb as the one which burned out had blown up. The two persons in the water lost sight of the boat. After a space of time which seemed to them an eternity, the searchlight finally came back on, and they now found themselves on the starboard bow, downwind from the boat. As the searchlight was trained on the port bow, the two swimmers could not be seen. Luckily they were heard shouting on the starboard bow and then soon illuminated by the searchlight. The bow was swung down wind and a volunteer swimmer (DAUPLAISE, L. B. E., CQM) went over the side with a buoyed line to retrieve the two exhausted swimmers. The boat was flooded down to prevent anyone being bashed against the hull.

1855 All hands recovered safely.
1915 Continued converting #4 FBT.
1930 Completed conversion of #4 FBT to a main ballast tank.
2040 O.O.D. sighted a spherical type mine close aboard the starboard bow. Avoided.
2200 SUBMERGED Flushing out #4 FBT, 2237 SURFACED.
2245 Received Pack Commander's instructions to rotate areas. PIRANHA to "BLAZER LIFEGUARD," SEA OWL to North BASHI CHANNEL, and PUFFER to South BASHI CHANNEL [*ibid.*].

The war patrol report was not complete. The first swimmer mentioned in the WPR, but unnamed, was Captain Dwyer. Although Chief Dauplaise played a very important role in the rescue of Frith, in a 2004 personal correspondence, Frith insisted it was Dwyer that saved his life (Frith). Dwyer got to Frith first, but it was Dauplaise that reached them both with a line (WPR). If Dwyer had not gone in after Frith, the rescue attempt may not have been as vigorous. After the rescue Dwyer told Frith, "We left together and we're returning together" (Frith). By abandoning the boat in this manner, as the commanding officer Dwyer opened himself up to possible disciplinary action. Nothing occurred.

Thirsty Lookouts

For the next week the *Puffer* and the other two submarines stayed in the vicinity of Formosa. Submarine Command directed the *Puffer* to various downed pilots, but none were located. The crew was kept on edge by many enemy aircraft contacts, which required the boat to submerge and surface numerous times each day. On March 4 the *Sea Owl* and *Piranha* were ordered by Submarine Command to proceed west toward Hong Kong for patrol and lifeguard duty. The *Puffer* stayed off the southern coast of Formosa for continued lifeguard duty. The next two days aircraft contacts followed by crash dives became the dangerous routine (WPR). On March 3 Golay wrote to his sister about the crash dives, the need for a battery charge, the weather and the culinary delights cooked up by the inventive officers.

> The lookouts are awarded extra beer rations for planes sighted during this run, and we've dived so often I'm beginning to question how many are planes and how many are thirsty lookouts — can't quite force myself to stick around to see for myself — usually the words "Clear the Bridge" are involuntarily out before the lookout completes his report — we've been giving the Japs hell

sinking all the oil drums, belly tanks, etc that we find — Morrow [Decker] exploded a floating mine on his watch the other morning, without warning — the old hands were pouring to battle stations before the spray had settled.

Our can [battery] was flat and even before we could get a charge started they forced us down — nine times in my watch we surfaced, only to have the planes force us back down — everyone was more than a little worried, when we were finally able to slip into a rain squall, that destroys the effectiveness of their search equipment [radar] — it was a relief to get the charge in — a security in the knowledge that we have plenty of submerged capacity — to be caught with a flat can is one of the greatest hazards of this racket — imposes severe limitations on evasive tactics.

Mac [Phillip McClure] and Morrow just mixed up the afternoon's hors d'oeuvres — equal parts of garlic, anchovies and pilchards — you have to stop whatever you are doing and eat the stuff in self defense — pilchards are a variety of oversized sardines, and we seem to have a corner on the worldwide production of them for the past few years — experienced everything except pilchard ice cream in our valiant effort to eat our way thru them — Christ must have had pilchards to feed the multitude on the shores of Galilee, the miracle becomes plausible after eating them continually for two patrols [Golay].

Radio messages brought news of the loss of two more submarines, the *Escolar* and the *Shark*. The small submarine community usually knew someone on a lost boat. Golay commented, "The *Shark* was Bob McDonald's boat, he was a good guy" (*ibid.*). Practical jokes kept the officers and men entertained during the lulls in the action and helped boost morale. Golay wrote of a joke played upon one of his fellow officers which took their minds off the monotony of the patrol and allowed their nerves to relax.

One night last week we encoded a stork-o-gram for Mac [McClure] — a stork-o-gram is a message they slip into our other traffic to notify officers and men out here when they have become a father — "FOR PUFFER ONLY X STORK-O-GRAM FOR ENS PHILLIP ALBERT MCCLURE X RED CROSS REPORTS XRAYS SHOW LORRAINE TO HAVE TRIPLETS X EVERYTHING OK" — we encoded it and slipped it into the file of messages he was decoding — it was one of the funniest experiences I've had to watch him break the message — he was dumbfounded, slumped onto the settee and for once had nothing to say — when the shock wore off he proved adequate, getting magnificently drunk on torpedo alcohol while we strung along behind — our joke almost got out of hand, for we didn't cut Carl [Dwyer] in and when he came down off the bridge and learned the news, he broke out a bottle of scotch, passed the word over the PA and issued beer to all hands — Mac soon regained his voice and acquired stature commensurate with his accomplishment — until he passed out — he and the "Old Man" both survived the truth, Carl philosophical over his contribution and Mac visibly relieved — I shall never forget the moments as he broke down the message, it was almost like old times on the *Puffer* and we were civil to each other for a few hours [*ibid.*].

The crew was not above playing jokes on the officers as well. Golay was on the receiving end of such a gag.

[Ralph] Troop [S1c], one of the helmsmen — they man the sound gear submerged — delights in waiting until a comparative quiet moment of the watch or when we're busy with depth control and then tensely reports "Screws at 180" — this is the relative bearing from the bow in degrees and is dead astern — my reactions please him much, trying to simultaneously call the Old Man, raise the periscope, give John [Gutensohn] the word on depth, and cut in our position on the chart — until the chuckling in the conning tower brings me to a stop and I sheepishly realize that there are always screws at 180 — our own [*ibid.*].

March 6 proved different than the preceding ten days. The Japanese were up to new tricks. Slightly after midnight radar picked up an airplane on SJ radar at nearly 16 miles.

Within 20 minutes the plane had closed the distance to 6 miles and started a run directly toward the *Puffer*. Dwyer "pulled the plug" and the boat stayed submerged for 40 minutes, and then surfaced. Early in the morning at 0504 the plane was back, and *Puffer* submerged again. After three hours Dwyer surfaced again. Forty minutes later the plane was back again. This cat and mouse game continued three more times until around 1100 when the plane was gone. Later that evening at 2055 the *Puffer*'s radar picked up an airborne radar signal (WPR).

> 2055 — APR contact 150 mcs. Airborne, Very persistent searcher. Never closes the range to less than six miles. Cuts his radar off and on intermittently. Definitely has us but seems only to be a snooper plane.
>
> 2230 APR contact 176 mcs, 250 PRF, 2 uscc, PW. Shipborne. This is an entirely new type Japanese radar of which PUFFER has no knowledge. Cuts off after beaming on us for about 10 to 20 seconds.
>
> 2242 (Ship Contact #3) SJ radar contact bearing 050° relative, (345°T) range 2550 yards. Came left with full rudder, went ahead flank speed, and made ready the stern tubes. Visibility very poor, unable to make out target. Assumed target to be a small submarine or A/S vessel.
>
> 2246 Fired first "down the throat" torpedo from #10 stern tube using radar bearings, gyros 180, no spread.
>
> 2246-45 Fired second "down the throat" torpedo from #7 stern tube using radar bearings, gyros 180°, depth set 10 feet, spread about 2°R. by ship offset.
>
> 2247-30 Fired third "down the throat" torpedo from #8 stern tube using radar bearings, gyros 180, depth set at 0 feet, spread about 2°L. by ship offset.
>
> 2252 While standing on the port side of the bridge watching for that illuminating explosion that would mean that another ship of the Japanese Navy has been rocked in the "Cradle of the Deep," the Commanding Officer noticed a fluorescent streak in the water off the port quarter near and parallel to the PUFFER. By the time the fateful significance of this streak was registered, a Japanese torpedo of the 45 knot class was passing the PUFFER abeam to port, distance unmentionably close. In a voice slightly above high C, the Commanding Officer ordered "Sound the diving alarm."
>
> 2252 Another CRASH DIVE.
> 2255 Heard two end of run explosions,
> 2255-30 Heard one end of run explosion.
> 2320 Target screws disappeared.
> 2322 SURFACED [*ibid.*].

Once again the tiny algae had saved the *Puffer*. Dwyer "believed that the plane helped to vector the surface ship into attack position" (*ibid.*). The surface ship was equipped with a new type of radar, and had radar contact on the *Puffer* before the *Puffer* made radar contact. The *Puffer* had been in the area for 10 days; the other two subs for a week. It was only a matter of time before the Japanese retaliated. The lifeguard areas were relatively small, 15 miles in radius. Dwyer observed, as a "result of weather messages sent by various boats and aviators referring to lifeguard submarines in plain language on the VHF" radio frequencies, the Japanese must have been aware of their presence and location (*ibid.*).

On the evening of March 7 the Japanese continued to search for the *Puffer*. After submerging for the day, the boat surfaced at 1858. At 1948 SJ radar made contact with an aircraft at 7000 yards and closing fast. Dwyer submerged the boat and spotted an aircraft float light that marked their diving point. The *Puffer* surfaced an hour later and sighted a plane circling at about 5 miles with a searchlight on the water. The *Puffer* submerged again; the aircraft was leaving the area when the boat surfaced again at 2220 (*ibid.*).

Air Support

For the next five days the lifeguard duty continued. Submarine Command realized the vulnerability of the submarines on long term lifeguard duty. Command coordinated with Philippine based Army air forces to provide air cover for the *Puffer* while it was on the surface. Also the lifeguard submarines in the area were now only required on the surface during the actual air strikes. On the second of the five days at 1100 lookouts sighted the fighter cover in the distance and communication was established and recognition signals were exchanged. The P-38s gave Dwyer "a very nice feeling to see our own planes wheeling over us for a change." Dwyer was so appreciative that he performed a battle surface for the fighter cover and fired the 40 mm and 20 mm guns. He would have fired the 5-inch gun, but the seas were too rough. The fighters reciprocated when they departed with "an aerobatic exhibition that made our battle surface look like a cheapskate's alibi" (*ibid.*).

No air strikes were scheduled for March 10 and it should have been a good day. However, it was not a "sweet" day for the *Puffer*. While surfacing and opening the conning tower hatch the rough seas sent a cascade of water into the boat.

> The most serious damage was the salting of 700 pounds of sugar, teaching us the hard way not to put all of one thing in one place. Issued ration stamps for the small quantity of brown sugar remaining and learned to drink, but not like, a new brew: Navy issue coffee with brown sugar [*ibid.*].

Not only were the foodstuffs ruined, but the high seas also caused the water supply to be tainted. Golay as the mechanical officer lamented his role of attempting to keep all the systems operational. The rough weather took another toll on the *Puffer*; it damaged the batteries. Golay was very complimentary of John Gutensohn (CMoMM), Earl Schley (MoMM2c) and Ted Okoniewski (EM1c) for their skills in keeping the boat ship shape.

> This has been a lousy week of heavy weather — earlier in the week the violent rolling of the ship cracked some of the cell tops in the battery wells and threw acid over the adjoining cells grounding them out — and that ain't good — we've had a sixty hour flail hunting down the grounds and clearing the circuits with little rest for anyone — once when the end was in sight, we undid most of our work when we surfaced in a following sea and half flooded the conning tower and pump room — these weeks strengthen my resolve to leave the sea when the war is over and settle as far inland as possible — a submarine is just a prolonged mechanical headache — you eventually begin to anticipate the casualties in the sounds — the rolling has stirred up the sediment in our fresh water tanks and I'm being heckled badly at meals — but tonite I shall quiet my tormentors — have Schley making water from each of the stills and shall compare by taste and sight the water we made with the water that comes from the First Lieutenant's tanks.
>
> Another of my favorite characters is Okoniewski — "Ski" an electrician's mate we picked up in the states ... he's a very competent electrician and is indestructible — the department was in lousy shape when we came out of the yard and I'm indebted to him for his solid loyalty — and then too, I like to talk with him about his wife Mary — he was proprietor of a small "fixit" shop in Bridgeport, Conn. And they were married last fall — and the honeymoon of three days on Fisher's Island in the Sound — wish I could write you one of his letters to Mary — they're simple, full of love — with all the naturalness and sincerity in the world.
>
> Gutensohn and his men did a fine job this past week, replacing a fresh water cooler and the attached salt water pump on #2 main engine in 28 hours — they are competent, skilled technicians and are carrying the load for me — God knows I'm no engineer — talked Carl out of two cases of beer and celebrated the finish of the job when I came off watch one midnite [Golay].

The air strikes resumed on March 11, and the air cover located the *Puffer* in spite of the low, overcast ceiling. Another exchange of lend-lease shows was performed and the fighter

"The Luxury of Air Cover"— P-38s helped protect the *Puffer* while on lifeguard duty. The swimmer at the lower right was holding onto a finger of a mine; he was not holding a beer bottle. The image had to be redrawn from a very thin copy on the microfilm (War Patrol Report from National Archives).

cover departed amid profuse thanks for the *Puffer* exhibition. March 12 was the last day of lifeguard duty. Fighter cover and the *Puffer* were unable to find each other. The *Puffer* was ordered to leave the area and head southwest for Hong Kong, following the other two boats that had departed earlier. Dwyer received word from the pack commander that he would request an extension for the Blazers in an area with Japanese shipping. Unfortunately the *Puffer* was low on fuel (WPR).

During March 13 the *Puffer* relocated to the new area and made plans to rendezvous with the pack commander on the *Piranha* the next day. On March 14 the *Puffer* received word of a downed aviator, but was unable to locate the flyer. At 1000 the *Piranha* was sighted and closed. Information was exchanged and the *Puffer* took advantage of air cover to work on a fuel ballast tank with a split gasket. Twenty-two Chinese junks were sighted in midafternoon as they proceeded toward Hong Kong. The small craft continued to be a menace to navigation for the next 10 days (*ibid.*).

On March 15 air strikes were made along the China coast and lifeguard duty continued. No requests were made to rescue down pilots. The highlight of the day was a floating mine that was sunk with rifle fire. The cartoon included in the WPR showed the appreciation for the air cover and the contact with the mine (*ibid.*).

Junks

After one more day of lifeguard duty in extremely rough seas, the *Puffer* and the *Piranha* headed southwest toward the island of Hainan. The Blazers had been given a five day extension. The sea was filled with junks, and the *Puffer* and the *Piranha* were not sure of each other's exact location, causing some confusion. By early in the morning both boats' positions were properly known by the other. During March 17 and 18 the two boats moved into position near Hainan, joined by the *Thresher*. Seas continued very rough, which made submerging difficult. To get under the water in rough seas could take 2 minutes and 30 seconds, much too long if aircraft were closing (*ibid.*). Metz recalled the hazards of lookout duty at night in the typhoon.

> Sometimes the waves would get spaced out about 200 feet apart and about 40 feet high. You could look off high lookout position as the valley passed under the bridge and I bet it would be 50 to 75 feet to the water. Then as the valley moved aft, the screws would come all the way out of the water and you could hear them wind up like a racing car engine. At night during these storms, I sure dreaded high look-out duty for my hour, because you couldn't hear the other men on the bridge for the roar of the wind and sea. The starboard lookout was supposed to slap you on the leg if they dived the boat, but I was always afraid he might forget. But we never lost a man by diving out from under him [Metz].

The next five days were spent looking for Japanese shipping, but none was found. Dwyer even attempted to find out about Japanese shipping from the residents of one of the junks in the vicinity, but had no luck. Metz recalled the contact not detailed in the WPR.

> One day we entered a large group of junks at anchor and tried to learn about some Jap ships in the vicinity but to no avail. We did trade them cigarettes for fish and crabs which they kept in a home-made basket. In this area there were hundreds of these junks and one or more families lived their entire lives on them. A party of four men went aboard one of the junks and brought back a native man to the *Puffer*, but we didn't find out much about the Japanese shipping. One of the boarding party (Glenn Stoy) had a Browning Automatic Rifle. The native wanted to see it fire. The captain gave the gunner's mate permission and he rested it across the forward capstan. Then he expended one clip of ammunition in fully automatic. This sounded like a sewing machine running wide open and that pleased the native very much. The native brought his own small boat with him to the *Puffer* and tied it to the front starboard side near the bow plane by a long line. When he started back to his junk, he wanted the *Puffer* to give him a tow. So some of our crew held his mooring line while the *Puffer* pulled him through the water at 10 to 15 MPH for a short circle [*ibid.*].

Golay wrote, "We are still scrambling for a target everyday forced the probability of a dry run on our consciousness—and consequently this has seemed an endless patrol" (Golay). Golay recalled other details of the cross-cultural encounter, which in his mind did much to compensate for the endless patrol and lack of sinking Japanese ships. Later in life Golay became an economics professor at Cornell University, specializing in the Far East. The positive experience of coming in direct contact with the local people lifted his morale and may have been a seed for that interest.

The junks (photograph courtesy of Glenn Stoy).

We closed a fleet of three [junks] and they boarded us from dinghies—we broke out the Chinese-English dictionary for a conference — we bartered white flour and canned fruit for some fine croaker and two servings of crab and lobster — Mac and I went aboard with them — each junk seems to have a crew of two families—the well-deck amidships is paved with brick and here is the hearth for cooking—the tiller is a long bamboo pole and the rudder and rigging creaks, groans and squeals in almost intelligible Chinese—we became good friends with all the language obstacles and one of the boys of the family was persuaded to come along with us— until the time came for us to row back, when he had a change of heart—they were hospitable and liberal, forcing coolie hats on us while we were shamed by our comparatively mean gifts of flour and fruit—was reminded of the parable of the rich man and the widow with her mite— as they pulled away from the PUFFER, they turned and gave us a "V" for victory—Winnie's version with two fingers—which did much to compensate for our fruitless weeks on station [*ibid.*].

Artillery Action

Late on March 24, orders were received to bombard a Japanese radio tower at Pratas Island and then proceed independently to Saipan. On March 26 the Blazers arrived at Pratas Island. The *Puffer* surfaced at 0344 in preparation for the bombardment and to make contact with the *Piranha* and the *Sea Owl*. A Japanese bomber was sighted. It flew over the *Piranha* and the *Sea Owl* (WPR). Golay wrote, the Japanese pilot "decided they were small fry, and started a bombing run on the *Puffer*. When the pilot gave her the throttle, great balls of fire belched out of each engine, not a very good advertisement for Japanese AVGAS [aviation fuel]" (Golay). The *Puffer* made another crash dive. The sky was all clear 20 minutes later, but it appeared as if the plane was waiting to give the group of submarines a welcoming party. During the next 30 minutes the three subs pulled into a position 1,500 yards from the island and began firing their 5-inch guns at the radio installation. Dwyer suspected it was the "first submarine divisional bombardment on record." After expending all 5-inch shells at a radio tower and 40mm battery at a small boat the action was completed by 0708. The Japanese airplanes returned at 0846 and the *Puffer* submerged under the safety of the rough seas (WPR).

Return to Saipan

Dwyer was ordered to return to Saipan. On April 1, Easter Sunday, the day before the *Puffer* arrived at Saipan, Golay wrote of the events of the day. He was ready to complete the cold and stormy patrol. The patrol had been depressing; word of another lost submarine was received, and the *Puffer* had only burned fuel. Even the relatively good food was getting difficult to swallow. Some recognition had been given to the Submarine Service. Only mail from home could make the situation bearable.

> It's good to get out of the parkas and rain pants again — the seas falling off eases our fuel situation, more acute than we like to talk about — Ickes would revel in our conversation, we pump bilges to the fuel system to extract the last drop — Mail tomorrow — if we are not wallowing around out here trying to hitch a ride — navigation lately has been a process of stepping off the distance with dividers and then dividing in the fuel — and then in hushed whispers we debate the possibility of the weather picking up and slowing us down still more — I'm glad March is over, it is a lousy month to go to sea — one storm has followed another — but I'm glad that we didn't spend it up north — Please have mail waiting for me — your letters are the only reason for coming in.

The Southern Cross is in sight again — they asked one of the boats to open up tonite and report in by radio — this is only done if a boat is overdue and invariably precedes the announcement of her loss — this one happens to be Bob Hoopes boat — we had a beer together in Pearl only a short time ago — wonder what Mary will do — Bob said they were having a baby this spring. [Lt. Robert D. Hoopes, Jr., and 88 other men were lost on or about January 12, 1945, when the *Swordfish* (SS 193) was sunk in the vicinity of Okinawa.]

We have quit diving for planes, and stick around to exchange recognition signals and mentally shoot them down as they playfully make a couple dummy runs on us before resuming this lonely patrol — they seem as glad to see us as we are to see them.

Schley ("Trim King") just brought me the word the #6 just ran dry — leaving the Collecting Tank and after that there ain't no mo' — guess I'll overhaul my lifejacket and lung just in case — we are not going to be an orphan this refit, but will be alongside our own tender — home to mother.

This run has seemed longer than any other — probably because we had a dry run — I've lost the capacity to choke down canned vegetables — peas, string beans and asparagus are equally nauseating.

I will hit an all time low tomorrow if I don't score on the mail.

Dick [Heehs] is standing watches with me now — he's a damn good officer and by far the savviest of the J.O.'s. Wonder who will stay in this run — Carl told me that I was to go back out — this is O.K. — tiresome as these runs have become, it is still better than the relief crew or tender.

The latest box score on sub warfare — they now admit to 1070 sunk, and they finally announced one of the carriers that the boats have knocked off.

We've been holding "Battle Stations — Patrol Report" for the past week in order to finish the damn thing — Carl is busy elaborating our bombardment into a successful — we'll slink in tomorrow, don't think there's a miniature Jap flag in the lot [Golay].

On April 2 the *Puffer* limped into Saipan at 1230 on one engine. The boat was on the last gallons of fuel. Also for the last couple of weeks the food rations were limited (WPR). The crew may have complained about the food earlier in the patrol, but when the situation worsened, the men stopped grumbling and pulled together.

Near the end of first leg of this patrol we were making out on two meals each day and for one of them, we only got half a slice of bread and a bowl of soup. Servicemen are the world's worst to complain about the food but during this time when groceries were scarce, we didn't say one word bad about the chow [Metz].

Ensign James W. Goin reported back on board after his bout with appendicitis, which proved false, and John Gutensohn accepted an appointment as warrant machinist. As the *Puffer* pulled into Saipan late in the afternoon there was no fanfare and the boat was not properly attired.

The Quartermaster restricted to the ship for "Battle Stations — Sewing Machine." Carl wanted to fly our battle flags and miniature Nip flags only to find that they had been sent home for souvenirs, or traded for stills and belt buckles (on Guam) and we slunk alongside our own tender shamed by the colorful halyards of our friends — we were the last one in, even the band had been dismissed for late chow [Golay].

All the crew members were anxiously awaiting mail from home after seven weeks at sea. The mail for the *Puffer* was not found. Letters from home were the greatest morale booster for the crew. They would have gone without food before sacrificing word from wives, sweethearts, and family. In a week the *Puffer* was supposed to arrive at Midway and would have received mail there. Even another seven days would have been painful. Golay expressed his dismay and that of the entire crew.

NO MAIL!— some stupid S.O.B. dropped the ball and while everyone who boarded us was apologetic enough, the disappointment is still there — this didn't happen to any of the other boats— guess we didn't live right this run — they dangle the hope before us that possibly the mail will be on the plane tomorrow before we leave — for fifty long, tiresome days we have anticipated mail, and then to have some incompetent shore-based blankity-blank make a mistake like this— it turned the apples and oranges bitter— made arrangements to fuel and take on lube and water, but since we're the outboard boat in the nest they will get around to us early tomorrow morning — last one in and first out — gave myself the duty tonite, as I suspect the *Puffer* will be busy enhancing its reputation at the beer hall and in this mood, I wouldn't know when to quit [*ibid.*].

Ensign Richard A. Heehs, junior officer of the deck, stood watches with Golay (photograph courtesy of the Golay family).

The officers received copies of the latest war patrol reports from other boats. The secrecy of the Silent Service and the lack of recognition of its contribution during the war annoyed Golay. He wanted the accomplishments publicized.

Just finished reading the patrol report of the run for which Gene Flucky received the Congressional Medal — an unbelievable display of initiative and guts, he really took ninety men along for a ride and fought the most brilliant action of any submarine in the war — it's a damned shame that these boats are not publicized — when we know of the accomplishments of Sam Dealey, Red Ramage, Flucky, O'Kane and all the other skippers it makes us a little heartsick that their accomplishments can't be publicized [*ibid.*].

The *Puffer* stayed at Saipan for a couple of days, performing joint activities with the other boats in Bennett's Blazers. The submarine tender offered some of the comforts of home.

April 2 (Saipan arrival)
 The watches have become a deadly routine — am going over to the tender when Russ [Weeks] returns from the beer hall and treat myself to a long soaking shower and shampoo— shower with room to sing "Milkman, keep those bottles flying" — with appropriate gestures.
 The movie is no improvement on the *Puffer* fare — we included Charlie Chaplin's "Gold Rush" last run, and are trying to exchange "Bad Men of Texas" for "King of Kings"— but the other boat is holding out and wants us to throw in "Mexicali Rose."
 Supper today was a bowl of oranges and apples— but then if I go over on the tender, I'll get no mail off, the lure of recent magazines would be irresistible [*ibid.*].

April 3 (Saipan)
 We're lousy with fuel again and have been raving around on four engines trying to find the rest of the brood — we sortied with several boats, and the senior skipper must be a fugitive from Halsey's staff, all the elaborate formations and station keeping he expects of us — and just at dark the *Puffer* managed to trade places with the escort which happened to be station

guide—we were in the center of the formation and every time we tried to open out to our proper station, all the other boats would tag along, frantically keeping station on us and we would weave around in undeniable formation—we put on another engine on the line, there would be puffs of smoke from the other boats as they added turns—wonder what sarcastic message the Commodore will have for us in the morning—maybe we could dive and escape from the ring of hecklers—have a new respect for O.D.'s seems we're unique in always being out of station—can remember back before the war, when steaming in formation an O.D. who was caught 100 yds. out in distance or 5 degrees out in bearing could expect to spend his next liberties aboard working mooring board problems—and it was a particular "red-lettered" day when the J.O. was allowed to handle the stadimeter or give an order to the helm [*ibid.*].

April 4 (Saipan)
Seems the congenital confusion of the *Puffer* is contagious—spent most of my watch this morning chasing one of the boats trying to gain station—when we finally closed enough that I thought I could distinguish the type, decided she was not our boss and reversed course to find him—and when we closed the boat astern enough to exchange calls, found ourselves in the wrong gang and reversed course again to resume chasing the first boat.

John's [Gutensohn] commission came thru in our mail and he has been poisoning the boat with the vilest cigars he could obtain—they're suffocating even to bystanders.

We picked up John Goin, seems our Pharmacist's Mate is still batting zero in his diagnosis's—there was nothing wrong with Jim, and he is fat and sassy after two months on a tender.

Larry [Picone] is back out on another boat, which is a break for him—most of the men we left in after last patrol are back in the states for new construction [*ibid.*].

Puffer took on stores for a five day cruise to Midway. And much to the delight of everyone on the boat, mail arrived. Even the weather had improved.

MAIL TODAY!!!—four bags came aboard just before we shoved off—most of our first class mail I think—seven very wonderful letters from you—very reassuring letters—the sun is shining again—had the maneuvering watch and got underway, an unbearable two hours until I could go below and read your letters—and immediately reread them—and then leisurely reread them ... one hundred days without a single letter was quite a trial by fire [*ibid.*].

Midway via Wake

The original orders had directed the *Puffer* to return to Midway for refit. The Blazers, now consisting of the *Sea Owl*, *Piranha*, *Puffer*, *Pampanito* and *Thresher*, were directed to Wake Island (WPR). After the limited provisions of the last few weeks, the crew on the *Puffer* had been heartily eating from the new supplies, with the expectation of a short five day ride to Midway. Enough food for a week had been brought aboard. At Saipan the fuel tanks were filled with only slightly more than adequate diesel to get the boat to Midway. With mail and sunshine things were good on the *Puffer*.

April 5
Another lovely day to lazily sunbath up on watch—have practically turned it over to Dick [Heehs] and spend my stint heckling our fat quartermaster, [Harris] Steinke—keeping him from dogging it is my days work.

We're valiantly trying to keep station on another boat and since their zigzag plan consists of alternately running "all ahead frantic" for us and then reversing course and disappearing over the horizon leaves us to tag along with our tongue hanging out, like a younger brother—made a trim dive this morning, the first since fueling and taking on stores—only 6000 pounds out.

Movie today "Gold Rush"—can describe [Arthur] Reynolds to you perfectly—he's Charlie

Chaplin, the screen version, not the lover—complete to moustache and unbelievable turned up (and out) shoes.

Most of the men off watch are busy answering letters and the mail bag in the wardroom passageway seems to fill over nite [*ibid.*].

April 7

Just received a humiliating defeat (at acey-ducey) at the hands of the Marshall of Whitefish (Gutensohn) and decided it would be time better spent to write you—will forget to give him turns (power on the screws) the next time submerged when he is about to broach.

The most exciting game aboard is trying to anticipate the zigzag plan of our boss—he directed us to keep station on his beam at a prescribed distance and without any knowledge of his base course and speed—found myself scrambling to get on station late in my watch this morning and anticipating a zig, took what I thought would be a short-cut—missed his course about 90 degrees and ended up on the wrong side of him—and that ain't good—as is customary, the Old Man made a rare emergence from his nest and caught me with my pants down—feel kinda silly with only the alibi that I thought he was due to zig—had to keep the watch until we were back on station, which took most of Bill's watch.

Another fuel crisis—we didn't fuel to capacity when we hit the advanced base, only enough to take us in for refit and then last nite they give us a job to do on our way in—an indefinite amount of steaming—we're waiting for radio traffic tonite which will include our orders—the boat is beginning to cool off, we finished a test discharge of the battery last nite and after charging again, the battery is like a stove.

Our next rest camp will be much like the last one—with only gooney birds to talk to.

A hungry shark, the largest I've seen has been following us for days—he would have to carry a can opener to exist on our garbage for all the garbage is sacked and weighted—a throwback to the early days of the war, when our shortage of ships and men forced us to fight with zigzag plans, weighted refuse, confiscation of electric razors and radios.

The news from Europe is good almost beyond belief—have a bet with Carl that they won't reach Berlin before we reach port—and am beginning to worry—especially if this "little job" keeps us out for any time.

Morrow just looked in for about the fourth time, he usually gets a couple hours sleep before going on watch and I'm keeping him out of his rack [*ibid.*].

April 8

Just finished going through the boat with Dick [Heehs] and Bob [Weeks], they come up for qualification when we get in this time and will have no trouble, a submarine is a discouraging thing to a new man when he reports aboard, for the qualification requires that every man know how every piece of equipment operates and to be able to stand any watch aboard—this has paid a lot of dividends in emergencies and makes the men proud of their Dolphins.

That is they should qualify if and when we get in—our new job is most indefinite.

Movie tonite "Great Man's Lady" an improvement over the customary fare.

They've forgotten us—still no orders—if mariners return to port with tales of a new "Flying Dutchman"—one that resembles a submarine, take heart, the *Puffer* is still afloat—we are now eating two meals a day and Mac rigidly enforcing a "no seconds" rule.... Shades of the first cruise of the *Minneapolis* after the war started—we lived the last two weeks on rice and returned to port as slant eyed as the Japs.

Another submerged day, rough topside—leaving us low can and the broach officers tearing their hair—would have been better to send all my mail when we topped off, but at the time it looked like a short cruise in to the refit—Field day today which I spent in the sanctuary of the maneuvering room with housecleaning electricians underfoot.

[Donald] Musha, a quartermaster as you can tell from this story, gets the gold star after his name for this week—he sounded General Alarm by mistake on a trim dive at dawn this morning, and before they could "belay the word" over the 1MC, the ship was trembling at battle stations [*ibid.*].

Late on April 8 the orders to divert to Wake Island were received (WPR). Wake Island was still in the hands of the Japanese. An island prison, it had been bypassed by American liberating forces. Submarine Command suspected a Japanese submarine would try to re-supply the small Japanese garrison at Wake, which had held the island since December 1941. In 1941 captured American military had narrowly escaped execution as a result of the Emperor's intervention. Some men survived the internment in Japanese work camps. Ninety-eight captured American engineers and civilian workers that served as slave labor were executed by the Japanese in 1943.

It took one day to divert to Wake Island. For the next week the *Puffer* patrolled the north side of the island. Sinking the Japanese submarine would give a "successful" for the patrol. The routine was monotonous, submerged around 0500 and surfaced around 1830 (*ibid.*). There was good news from the European front. Stomachs were growling again as food stores dwindled and even clothes were in short supply. The weather was no longer sunny.

April 11
We surfaced too late for most of the news, but heard that the 9th Army is racing the Russians for Berlin.
Secured the washing machine to save water, but Sasso and Hensley had to open up for business as we ran out of clothes— my bout with battery acid had a detrimental effect on my shorts, seems that battery acid is harmful — spent half of last nite steaming thru a rain squall and just as we pulled clear, reversed course and steamed back thru — Bob just used half a box of matches trying to light a cigarette.
One of the boats slipped back in from patrol early and tried to laugh it off as a navigational error and the island was moving— this must be punishment for the communications flail we gave birth to back in our original area.
Mac trying to popularize fasting and gaining no recruits.
The bridge has been miserable and wet — equinoxial weather.
Have a new J.O., the Marshal of Whitefish, Montana — John Gutensohn, he is the Chief in charge of the Engine Room and has been recommended for Warrant — he's good company and is a raconteur of note — he wants to stay in next run and hopes to be able to make his way back to the states and his wife and son — he is a one man Chamber of Commerce and has just about convinced me that Whitefish is the place to make our home — he is going to provide economic opportunity by forcing thru local laws in his capacity of political boss and all his friends may then become bootleggers— he is busy saving box tops this week so that next week he can join the Dick Tracy secret message club [Golay].

On April 13, Dwyer recorded that a considerable number of the crew and officers were complaining of headaches about 1600 each day. Dwyer felt part of the problem was fatigue from 62 days on patrol (WPR). In addition the shortage of oxygen (hypoxia) and higher CO_2 level caused the headaches.

Late in the afternoon when there is no longer enough oxygen to support a flame, there are always men stopping by the wardroom coffeemaker which is turned on full, to light a cigarette from the glowing coils— and as he returns aft thru the boat each compartment gets a light off his cigarette [Golay].

As a result Dwyer changed the air in the boat by surfacing around noon each day or if that was impossible, circulating oxygen throughout the boat (WPR).
On April 15 word was received of the death of President Franklin D. Roosevelt. A memorial service was held in the forward torpedo room (WPR). To the younger men on the crew, Roosevelt was the only president they knew. A few days later Golay wrote about the new pinup girl for the *Puffer*. He also related details of a conversation with Carroll Allen, the officers' steward, about a building job he would perform for Golay after the war. Allen did become a

successful building contractor after the war. Personnel and mechanical problems were also on Golay's mind ... and finally the end of the patrol and mail.

April 18

The freon lines of the conning tower air conditioning plant leak so badly that we secured the plant — and each submerged watch is just a prolonged Turkish bath — wonder why we are surfacing.

In a little corner of the ocean we are sure giving the Japs hell, trying to starve out one of their by-passed garrisons and it begins to look like they will outlast the *Puffer* — there goes the surface alarm and the hammer of air into her tanks — Jay [Deem] stood her on her feet for this one, the greater the angle, the better the surface, for we bounce out far enough to avoid any trouble.

Much mail to censor, a letter from [James] Patton, [Carroll] Allen's boss to Lena Horne asking her to be the *Puffer* pin-up girl, that she has been unanimously selected by the crew — and I'm glad Carl let it go thru — we might as well have a pin-up girl and she'll do.

Allen and I have been reminiscing of Washington [D.C.] — and he deviates to tall tales of hunting in South Carolina — and the big snow of 1933 — Allen has promised to help us build a fireplace — he has "green hands" with fireplaces, they always draw [air] — and the craftsman, he becomes evasive when I try to question him of construction details — his mother took him out of school when he was thirteen and apprenticed him to a mason — he is quick to boast of his kids' marks in school, and just as quick to add that they were proud of his "dolphins."

[Thomas] Kemp anxious for a transfer busy with plans for a postwar chicken ranch — our searchlight was missing when we surfaced tonite — probably carried away when John

Carroll Allen became a successful building contractor after the war. The stewards were fully qualified submariners and wore the Silver Dolphins (photograph courtesy of the Allen family).

[Gutensohn] broached—"Ski" [Okoniewski] comes up to puzzle over the disappearance and to deny any accusation that he failed to secure the light properly just to have it carried away—it is a continual headache and we are relieved when we enter our area and can strike it below.

[I] am standing watch with Bob Weeks now, have had everyone of the J.O.'s this run, we neglect our job to talk sports and of San Francisco—our helmsmen are Kemp and "Peach Basket" two chiefs that we plan to leave in this time—and [Ernest] Messenger and [Donald] Musha enjoy their confusion when trying to execute the *Puffer* zigzag plan—if the sky hadn't been clear, think Kemp would have turned 360 degrees chasing the needle, which moves in just the opposite direction as the rudder—steering a good course is a talent that requires much experience.

Messenger is now a lookout and Bob [Weeks] and I look forward to seas that douse the lookouts—he always seemed to find the holes in the road when he was driving—Bill [Pugh] will be moving out of the #3 Stateroom, the "boar's nest" and maybe we can find the old cheese sandwich Bob lost in there back in P.H. and to which we attribute the unique and ripe odor of the place.

Allen just came in to set up for supper, a neat trick of arranging the silverware each place anchored by a knife and pouring water at each place to provide enough friction to anchor the chinaware.

One of the other boats accomplished our mission.

Mail soon [Golay].

On April 18 a Japanese submarine arrived on the south side of Wake Island and was sunk by the *Sea Owl* (WPR). As fuel dwindled, Golay joked, we "will probably have propulsion on the ice cream machine before we reach port" (Golay). Slowed by the diminished fuel supply, four days of slow travel put the *Puffer* at Midway on April 21 at 0900 for two weeks of well deserved rest and recreation, and additional training. The smell of steak and eggs drifted across the harbor. The submarine tender USS *Pelias* had breakfast waiting for the crew. Dwyer noted, "Very thoughtful to provide this for us" (WPR). Considering some of the men had lost 15 pounds, it was very thoughtful. Fresh fruit was delivered to the boat even before tying up at the dock, "the apples and oranges melted away before we rounded the entrance buoys and our old tender made us think of Perth" (Golay). About dinner that night Golay jokingly wrote, "tonite we had asparagus on the tender—but no pilchards" (*ibid.*).

14

R & R at Midway

Arrival

Frank Golay's letters and Tom Metz's recollections are the only written records of the four weeks at Midway. Golay detailed the arrival and the transition to living on solid ground.

April 20–21
    The tender band and sailors a calloused lot of cynical faces lining the rails as we came alongside, can remember the thrill of seeing my first boat come in flying battle flags.
    Some of the beards came off today and the boat was full of strangers.
    Laundry just left the ship, the ship's laundry made off with so many clothes when rags became short in the engine rooms that no one would patronize them.
    The last "fish" just left the [torpedo] rooms and they look like deserted gymnasiums.
    Other bad news that three more boats are down, and Chick Irish is on one of them — dammit if we knew what we're losing them to it would help a lot.
    Morrow [Decker] just ran me out of our love nest to pack his sea bag, amazing how complicated moving to the rest camp becomes weighing the chances of using all your worldly possessions and leaving nothing aboard ... he's a considerate roommate and a good officer, the best ship-handler aboard, the Old Man drives him hard and he drives us to produce results — and get no credit for the good job he does.
    Some major alterations that may keep us alongside additional time, which is O.K. with us.
    Rita Hayworth in "You Were Never Lovelier" which should start our hormones to racing again.
    If I go over on the tender to the movie, the wardroom hoard of new magazines will prove irresistible and this won't get mailed tonite.
    The daily ration of beer is three cans which should keep us out of trouble.
    "Cobber" [Wilfrid Delafield] hit the jackpot with three cans of cookies with chocolate lumps in them.
    It will be hard to get to sleep tonite, the birds are very noisy outside my window and then there is the subconscious rebellion to a firm steady bed after months in an active bunk [Golay].

Compared with Guam, Midway had very little to offer the sailors for activities. As at Guam there were no women. It was a flat, sandy island with very little vegetation. Midway was mostly relaxing, drinking, or playing sports — it had its own baseball diamond. There was a ping-pong table, but the ping-pong balls had long since disappeared. It was also much cooler.

"We had a ship's picnic this afternoon and fourteen cases of beer melted away like snow — the Black Gang (the Motor Machinists) won the softball game [Golay]" (photograph courtesy of the Golay family).

Gooney birds around the post exchange and barracks were the local entertainment (Knoblock, pp. 131–2). Metz described the buffoons of the bird world and his recollections of a tour around the tiny island.

> They can fly for hundreds of miles over the ocean without ever stopping on land, but they can't walk or land scarcely at all. They fall around like a drunken person. When they come in for a landing, their legs just seem to fold up and they come to a stop by rolling end over end and scooting along the ground.
> I took a sightseeing tour around the island one day. I started out from the P.X. and walked southwest by the airplane hangers and shops. I then went west along the south side of the island through the salvage yard where the remains of the SBD dive bombers were. These were shot up in the Battle of Midway and limped back to the island after their carriers were sunk or damaged. These planes weren't fit to be repaired and fly again, so they were put in this junk yard in rows and the good parts were taken off them and used to repair other SBD's. I proceeded from the junk yard along south shore to the northwest end. There the runway started at the water's edge and went near the north side of the island back toward the rest camp. The airplanes were kept in C-shaped sand bunkers beside the runway to protect them from shrapnel when the Japs bombed the runway. On the north side of the island near the east end of the runway was an old wooden army colored barracks. The barracks had a single wooden four-panel door. Above this door was a sign which read, "THROUGH THESE PORTALS PASS THE BEST SUBMARINERS ON EARTH." When I read this I thought it was bragging a little, but as the years passed and I gave the sign more consideration, I believe it was exactly correct. Through those portals did pass the best submariners of the best Navy of the best Country on Earth, although each and every one of them may not have been perfect [Metz].

Fun and Games

With two weeks to kill, limited activities, and two months' pay, some of the crew turned to their two favorite pastimes: gambling and drinking. Tony Sasso made his point at craps for a $600 payoff (Polk). Stills were constructed or purchased and anything with alcohol content was distilled. A hot plate powered still boiled over and set one of the huts afire (Deem). The alcohol was mixed with the abundant supply of pineapple juice. Many men suffered from huge headaches. Other men simply enjoyed the good food and peace and quiet of the island. Regular mail delivery was a luxury.

April 22
Poker and dice games running full blast and will continue until morning and on into the refit until only two or three of the experts are left and they know better than to buck each other.

Morrow [Decker] is living with the Old Man and will probably survive the two weeks in a fried condition.

Mail [arrives] three times weekly.

Huge steaks for supper, four or five to a cow with fresh vegetables, real celery — and poached eggs for breakfast this morning, unbelievable — you know how much a rest camp can mean and we are grateful to be here, wonder why the Navy doesn't use Red Cross personnel to staff these camps, but women in the tropics are a nuisance it becomes necessary to shave, wear clothes — unless it could be you.

Gooneyville Lodge — the Officers' Quarters. Enlisted men in front of the lodge. Note the warm clothing required on Midway. *Left to right:* Charles Wiseman, Frank Corcoran, Robert Kennedy, Ray Roberts and an unidentified crew member (photograph courtesy of Jack Thoman).

The steward just saved me the trouble by dropping by to ask if I wanted an extra blanket tonite, and also one for Bull, they will feel good.

"Cobber" [Delafield] talked me into a game of pool and I learn that he was a delinquent by Mother's definition, a pool room hanger-on — I had to live in a YMCA to learn to play pool.

This is going to be a good two weeks, we play another boat touch football tomorrow afternoon — boats in the lagoon for sailing, deep sea fishing trips can be arranged, can even practice golf shots out on the air strip — but I'm skeptical of swimming — no ping pong balls.

Bought a hat today for Jack Nelson who will be rated Chief the first of the month.

Someone is playing a favorite album of mine, Andre Kostelantez and much Cole Porter and other timeless tunes — and there goes the "Missouri Waltz" [Golay].

April 24

Two days gone already and we are sure there aren't as many hours in these days as those spent out on station, played tennis this morning and we won a touch football game this afternoon from one of the other boats 24 — 6, will be stiff tomorrow, but it feels good to be tired physically instead of mentally.

Bill [Pugh's] orders came through today, he is going to New Construction at New London and he and Doris will have six good months together — wish he could be with us, dammit — he is glad to be pulled off after eight runs and will be much happier on another boat, it was his bad luck that Morrow and I both joined the *Puffer* after she was commissioned, both senior to him.

We are not allowed to mail film from theatre, so I'll have Bill take along some film I was able to pick up to send along to you.

The movie tonite is "Arsenic and Old Lace."

The skipper's are setting up for the nite's poker game, funny how cautious they are, their games always have the least money involved.

Will try to shoot a roll of film tomorrow, if I can borrow Bob's camera [*ibid.*].

William Pugh (left) and Edward Dauplaise on the deck of the *Puffer*. Pugh left the *Puffer* after the Seventh War Patrol for new construction. Dauplaise would become chief of the boat on the next war patrol (photograph courtesy of the Golay family).

April 25

We had a ship's picnic this afternoon and fourteen cases of beer melted away like snow — the Black Gang won the softball game — have tickets for the USO show tonite, the plane flying their scenery, costumes and part of the cast was forced down and from all accounts last nite's show was pure corn.

The Germans in Italy and southern Austria have surrendered unconditionally.

[I] read Eisenhower's very candid report to the President of several weeks ago in a recent Time — he is a brilliant man and yet he has his feet on the ground — it would be a good bet right now that we elect a soldier for our next President.

Took some pictures this afternoon.

The beach was good this afternoon and my tan will be quite creditable when we leave here only to fade quickly away — the party moved south one room last nite and settled in room

The softball team at Midway (photograph courtesy of the Golay family).

The chief petty officers, from left: Carroll Allen, Edward Dauplaise, Herbert Hayward, John Nelson, and Roland Chamberlain (photograph courtesy of the Golay family).

#5—twelve empty dead soldiers (whiskey bottles) which means a new high mark—and getting a mess boy to do anything around here is a major operation.

We start the attack teacher sessions tomorrow afternoon, but that is alright for that is the most interesting and most practical phase of all our training.

We rated [Carroll] Allen the first of the month and he is resplendent in new khaki uniform and Chief's cap—he, [Herbert] Hayward, [John] Nelson, and [Roland] Chamberlain who all made Chief this last run were thrown into the fish pond to start the picnic off.

My poor tired feet are stone-bruised from too much tennis and I'm going to have to turn into sick bay in the morning, there is no rest once you leave on patrol and you're on your feet thru all the watches—hate to give up tennis though.

I have gained back another five pounds.

The Old Man is receiving a Navy Cross tomorrow.

[I] played tennis this morning; think the blisters and shin splints will slow me down to a walk about tomorrow—but I want to do a lot of sailing, for I'm still strictly an amateur.

Bill [Pugh] is sweating out a flight out of here [*ibid.*].

Navy Cross

April 26 AM

Lots of gooney birds.

This afternoon we have to attend the Command Performance, "Battle Stations, Navy Cross."

No mail today, a young gooney bedraggled and unable to move out of range of the sprinkler looks like I feel when there is no mail.

April 26 PM

We caught two thirty pound wahoo—truly a good namesake for a submarine, beautifully streamlined, sharp teeth for armament and lots of fight—by contrast the ridiculous puffer is deadly only to those that eat it.

Bob Hope in "The Princess and the Pirate" last nite ... and then there has been "Fighting Lady" a documentary film about one of our big carriers—the photography was supervised by Edward Steichen and has some fine Technicolor shots of the blue seas—he is now making a similar film of the submarine service and we are envious of the boats selected to carry his photographers [*ibid.*].

The *Puffer* was selected to carry a photographer on the Eighth War Patrol. Sondol Werner was chosen as the *Puffer* photographer (RG28). Unfortunately the comparable submarine movie to *Fighting Lady* was never completed. During the mid–1950s a television show documented some of the daring exploits in a program titled *The Silent Service*. However, the complete story of the submarine service was kept silent until the early 1970s when the war patrol reports were declassified. Intercepted coded messages sent by the Japanese were not declassified until the 1990s.

Werner also created a document given to each of the crew on the Sixth War Patrol. The document was Dwyer's way of sharing the credit for the Navy Cross, which he was awarded for the Sixth War Patrol. In a 2004 interview Dwyer said, "It was one of the best ideas I came up with" (Dwyer).

The Old Man finally got the Navy Cross and should be even safer to ride with from now on—the historic event recorded on thousands of feet of film and hundreds of flash light bulbs burned—he crashed thru with a case of whiskey for a ship's party and everyone had their morale bolstered by a picture of himself congratulating the Old Man—"Battle Stations, photography" until it became too dark for the camera.

Donald McDonald congratulates Captain Carl Dwyer for the successful Sixth War Patrol. Dwyer received the Navy Cross for the patrol and gave each crew member a document recognizing their contributions to the success of the patrol (author's collection).

A citation was presented to each crew member by Captain Dwyer. The citation read: "For distinguishing himself by meritorious conduct in action in the performance of his duties as a member of the crew in a United States Submarine during a WAR PATROL of that vessel. His proficiency at his battle station materially assisted his Commanding Officer in conducting attacks which resulted in sinking enemy vessels totaling over 18,000 tons, and damaging more than 9,000 tons, for which his Commanding Officer received a Navy Cross. His calm manner and devotion to duty contributed directly to the success of his vessel. His conduct throughout was an inspiration to all with whom he served and in keeping with the highest traditions of the United States Naval Service" (image courtesy of Glenn Stoy).

Carl finally passed out over at the Tavern and Mac [McClure] and Bob [Weeks] put him to bed and then put about a dozen young goonies in with him — and they aren't house broken yet.

There was a woman thru here about six months ago with an USO show — Betty Hutton was the latest fully a month ago and the Old Timers tell you with a far-away look in their eyes of her show.

They wouldn't give us our fish for the BOQ mess, seems they put them aboard the boats that are leaving on patrol [Golay].

April 30

The work that we have to do in dry dock is going to give us two extra days at the Lodge — another whole seven days, less tomorrow which is my duty day, but there is much to do aboard.

Steak (again) this evening.

John's [Gutensohn] orders came thru today to the relief crew and he is disappointed because he anticipated orders to the states and to his wife and baby.

Charlie [Dwyer] just came by to tell me that they were coming out of dock and that we were scheduled to go in tomorrow, a ticklish job that I'd rather let the Old Man do [ibid.].

Midway gooney and chick (author's collection).

May 1

News flash at noon of Hitler's death, but no details, I hope he was killed by his countrymen, as it will help to discredit him and keep him from being a martyr.

No strain getting her docked this morning, they sent along a tug to give us a hand — a ship in dock is disillusioning for invariably it must contradict the preconceived ideas of its submerged portion — and they become much larger, for four fifths of our displacement is below water.

The wardroom mess treasurer collected mess bills today and then pacified his victims with rice and curry and French fried onions for lunch and steak for supper.

They ran the engines last nite on a charge and everything is "Jake."

[I] found [Jack] Lane one of the radiomen floating around and talked him into making the walk to the lodge — two of my last week's beer chits for inducement.

Our battery grounds back down to five volts — and that is <u>good</u>!

We are getting a damn good refit and our poor tired engines no longer produce a smoke screen when the load is thrown on them ... the air hammers and power brushes are making hay — docking is a frenzied period the first Lt. trying to clean and scrape her bottom before the other gangs complete their work [ibid.].

May 5

We were up and out at seven for fishing, two wahoos and seven bonita and lots of sun and salt.

The Squadron Commander was out at the attack teacher session today to qualify Dick [Heehs] and Jim [Goin], and they did fine — blew my run, when they threw a high speed destroyer at me using a constant helm zigzag — the flail was almost out of hand when the chief running the problem zigged them around to a course for a good track angle and left them parading in front of me like ducks in a shooting gallery — presented the men topside with all my amassed beer chits, they saved the day [*ibid.*].

May 6 (Sunday)
Up early with Morrow [Decker] for mass and then we had to return to the boat after breakfast for the sound runs, one of our shafts is still noisy, which means we will have to go back into dry dock and perhaps delay our departure...

No mail now for three days [*ibid.*].

Victory in Europe Day

May 7
Today seems to be V-E Day, although not confirmed by allied headquarters, and little jubilation out here, for V-E Day has little immediate significance.

We move back aboard in the morning.

[I] am convinced that "Cobber" [Delafield] spent his childhood in a poolroom, he has been taking my money all afternoon by sinking all the balls in fifteen shots — a neat trick.

[I] have been working this afternoon on the Watch Bill with Morrow [Decker], many new names aboard the *Puffer*.

Everyone scored on mail today.

Shall have to leave my typewriter in hock to move out tomorrow — but talked the Squadron Engineer out of a job order to have it routined, am inclined to think that not all of the errors are mine, and I've actually caught it failing to backspace.

A newspaper arrived today containing an announcement of the loss of SWORDFISH, Bob Hoope's boat.

Will be busy fueling tomorrow and drawing spares and supplies — and we go back to a two man watch section — [Arthur] Reynolds is in sick bay with stomach ulcers and may not be able to go back out with us — I hope not tho, for he is a good shipmate — it makes you feel humble when you find yourself an officer, with men younger than you under your command, particularly when they are so specialized that you realize that you can never know their job as well as they do — a submarine officer is a jack of many trades and master of none, unless the smattering of knowledge about many things makes him an officer — the men respect you only when they recognize that if you specialized you would be their equals [*ibid.*].

Training

May 8
Stopped by in at the barracks on my way to the movies to see [Thomas] Kemp — learned that they have [Francis] Holland in the brig, the revenuers raided his still — the Old Settlers learn to drink "pink lady" torpedo alcohol straight and even less handy characters learn to handle the stuff after straining it thru a loaf of bread, but the new arrivals are sissies, they have to distill the damn stuff — a still will sell for as much as $500 when the owner is transferred, and Holland, flush from a crap game picked up a novel model — a two quart size for $300 and has spent his leave learning to operate the damn thing — there have been more casualties from exploding stills than from the bombing — to make possible a busy social career, he took his clock and covered most of the face of it with a disc of paper and then marked the disc off in segments of time, labeling each one 7–8 BREAKFAST, 8–10 REST, 10–12 AT STILL, 12–13

DINNER, 13–17 AT STILL, and so on — but today the Master of Arms raided the air raid shelter, suspicious no doubt of the fumes and smoke pouring from the entrance as they used diesel oil for fuel — and some joker scratched over the "AT STILL" on the clock face and penciled in "CHURCH."

Mac [McClure] is busy being a proud father, or about to be father, reading excerpts from Lorraine's letters and incidentally financing young McClure with a phenomenal run of luck with dice — has sent home about $1500 of winnings which will provide a knee action bassinet.

Canned food is drooling from every possible nook and corner — millions of blue points worth.

We are back in dry dock with all the brains gathered around our squealing shafts commiserating with each other and wondering if they can get us to sea on time.

The training has gone well, we've had hits with seven out of eight practice shots and the diving sections look good — this will mean more sound runs and so on ad nauseum.

Bob is loading the last of our exercise fish tonite, and his job is complicated into most of the nite by our being in dry dock.

After six years in the Navy the doctor discovered that [Thomas] Bowden "Alfred" is allergic to the dye in dungarees and will receive a medical survey —[Arthur] Reynolds and [Ray] Roberts just now came aboard with their sea bags and I'm glad.

I judged prematurely the new leaf that the *Puffer* hasn't turned over, and now Al [Shaw] and I are by ourselves and everyone else left for the beer hall — they made recordings of some of our approaches which came aboard tonite, and Al is playing them now —concentrated confusion [*ibid.*].

May 10

We were out before daylight and in after dark ... and we got much of our training out of the way ... our shaft squeal has shifted to the other shaft — and there was a nosy garbage lighter that supervised the whole proceedings forcing us to repeat all the runs several times— thought the Old Man would inflate and take off when they laboriously semaphored to us after flailing around for an hour, that our new signalman showing off the light was sending too fast for them.... Carl and Morrow were both at a lecture on some of the new equipment, and he said just after word came for us to get underway —"You take her out"— as nonchalantly as all that — which makes me feel good, and encourage me to think that I will relieve Morrow after this next run. Making Exec is a crisis in the life of a reserve officer in submarines— you either make it or they ease you out, and then too last nite Carl asked me how many runs did I want to do, and I told him I would like to ride her back to the states— I feel a little ashamed that I have so little feeling of loyalty to the Old Man, ... but he has done right by me [*ibid.*].

May 11

The Red Cross remembered the Navy today — exchanged our library (and did very well)— a carton of cigarettes per man and a bag with sewing kit, toilet articles, etc.

We're also very doggy now in Mae Wests— and will no doubt have to wear the damn things on the bridge — and the CO_2 cartridges will be robbed for the soda siphon and cokes.

I want to get back at sea and get this flail over with — life at sea is much more orderly.

My own particular cross, the pit log, is misbehaving and I'm harassed from all sides until it is back in commission.

We've certainly been on our good behavior for the division commander, even cutting the crusts off our lunch sandwiches, culture has entered our lives— BLUEFISH has a citation, the second boat of our squadron — and our record is much better than hers— this was the second boat — will be too tired to load the damn ship to go out on patrol — and there must be a remote control for the General Alarm in my bunk for it invariably sounds when I try to slip in for a little rest.

Clearing the bridge for one of our dives today, one of the inflating lanyards on my Mae West caught on the Conning Tower ladder and I inflated like a balloon — not only scared the hell out of me, but made it a tight squeeze thru the hatch ... have new lookout in my section, Doc

Johnson the Pharmacist's Mate, ex-helmsman — our passenger is OTC and we originate practically all the communications — but then the pit log is forgotten in the anguished screams for the Engineering Officer when the search light fails [*ibid.*].

May 12

News today the Krauts surrendered 300 U-boats, and now I shall have to worry for fear they will send me to one and we'll pass each other in mid-ocean.

One of our exercises today was indoctrinational depth-charging — king size — and the skipper of our escort with a perverted sense of humor suggested a repeat because one of the charges was a dud — and already the line was forming in the crew's mess waiting for the Pharmacist's Mate to "Splice the main brace" with medicinal brandy — can't say that I've grown any more used to loud-underwater explosions, or that I missed them last run — she has developed a new critical speed, or perhaps the rejuvenation of overhaul added a few turns — she flounces up the channel swishing her hips, the brazen hussy — today was depressing — alternate rain and mist — the rain made me think of the morning we said goodby in Washington — the fog closed in as we finished the last run and we were lucky to pick up the entrance buoys before it closed down completely — tho sounding kept shelving in and with no buoys in sight we were ready to haul out and spend the night running in circles — out too early and in too late for mail.

The wardroom is going to be congenial this run, we're a lucky ship with the officers we have, not only professionally competent, but they are all good shipmates — Al [Shaw] and Duke [Duguid] our new acquisitions are going to fit in, it's a deflating experience to move aboard the *Puffer* if you expect any get-acquainted period or formalities.

The picture of the Marines raising the flag on Iwo is a dramatic thing.

Let's hurry and have the end of this war, I want to be with you.

I'm writ out and its 0200 [*ibid.*].

May 13

A short month since the death of FDR, colors raised this morning, some of the boats remembering to hoist them all the way and others hesitate and then sheepishly fall into line ... I'm glad that FDR was given a Congressional Medal, he earned it and not because it was a posthumous award.

She has been well-behaved today — we traded our recordings today and have been trying them all — have the duty tonite and will be up till midnight to start the charge — the remainder of our op-order appeared tonite and they're breaking it off in us, an extra training schedule — I'd rather make a run than do the training [*ibid.*].

May 14

These training periods are diabolically planned to make you happy to go back on patrol — the men are beginning to call her the SS WINDOWSHADE — walked up to Gooneyville to see what the movie was showing and it didn't sound good so we walked on up to the Gyrene's club for a beer — we take out the Division Commander tomorrow, and no doubt he will be caught up on his sleep and we'll be up all night making runs ... taking on water and fish tonite and I'll have to trim before turning in.

[Fred] Thornberry our new Yeoman is from K. C.

The torpedomen in the after room usurped the top place quartermaster this morning when they blew down the tubes after I'd trimmed the boat and we dove 5000 lbs light — a little more angle and we would have been floating upright like a spar.

Rumor today [is] of another boat down.

Another supply of beer chits so it will be a wet nite out.

The Marshall [John Gutensohn] was just down for a cup of coffee and reports an empty bunk in his room, so I'll sleep on the tender tonite and avoid the session when the pub crawlers close the tavern.

"Cobs" [Wilfrid Delafield] and Al [Shaw] are aboard tonite with the duty and are getting in some good licks on their notebooks.

Think I will navigate this run, after Duke [Donald Duguid] gets his hand in as top watch stander — he's an old Perth hand and has had five runs — will be good to come off the watch bill, you can slip into a hampering lethargy from the monotony of two daily watches ... the endorsement of our patrol report should appear any day now, and we still have hopes that we may get a successful — should feed well tomorrow, the training officer always calls for good food and my nest in which to sleep it off, but then that is better than having him prowling around during approaches and our own ship's exercises consist of running all ahead frantic for the channel buoys [*ibid.*].

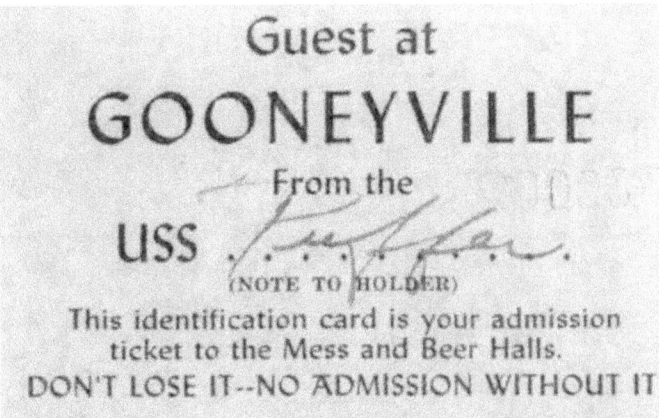

Admission ticket to the mess and beer halls at Gooneyville (image courtesy of Jack Thoman).

May 17

[I] went to the USO show with Carl — the show was pure corn.

Two approaches — altogether a good day — except for the cholera [shot].

The Doc couldn't turn me into sick bay, but built up the heel of my shoe with sponge rubber — the tendon was strained, which is logical for the heel on the tennis shoes is non-existent — hate to think of returning to the boat, but we have to soon [*ibid.*].

May 18

The movie "Tall in the Saddle" to make transition back to the *Puffer* easier.

A school convening soon for reserve officers who have been recommended for retention in the Navy and Carl told me he would give me a recommendation if I wanted to — a hard decision, wish they had not given us the chance and then it wouldn't be necessary to think the thing out — your letter weighing the advantages of Navy life make me consider it seriously ... would like to stick around for the end of this out here though.

One of our new officers reported in today, he was flown out from Pearl — looks like I will be working with Dick [Heehs] again, which is good.

The radio just played a medley of "Oklahoma" tunes.

More attack teacher and swimming this afternoon, and we arranged to go fishing tomorrow morning — fish tales tomorrow — fresh milk at lunch, overflow from the hospital's herd of five cows — another argument for not going to sea — one of the cows has only a stump of a tail, and they tied an extension of line so she can swish the flies off.

Am still battling cholera — have lost a razor and they're about impossible to replace, the company is probably busy making B-29's.

Many boats in now, the lodge too small and the overflow has to live at BOQ from all accounts we were lucky to get rooms for everyone at the lodge.

A news story today that the men shifted from Europe to this theatre are to be given furlough and tropical training in the states, God knows they've earned it — the Army is worried least they lose their will to fight in a psychological let-down — coming out of the [Mare Island] yard overhaul made a believer of me, only in the latter part of this run did the ship settle down and the men realize that they were back out to stay.

[I] was reading of the death of Sgt. John Basilone, the Marine who won the Congressional medal on Guadalcanal and was killed in the assault of Iwo — no doubt he wanted to return to combat, but you can only wonder how many of those men who come back are not motivated,

Midway Gang in front of one of the Quonset huts. *Front row (left to right):* Tony Sasso, Glenn Stoy. *Middle row:* John Hensley, Bernard Cassidy, Ted Okoniewski. *Back row:* William Wilson, Ken McEntyre (photograph courtesy of Jack Thoman).

at least in part by fear of censure on the part of his shipmates—and how much of it is the desire to surround themselves by friends they are sure of [*ibid.*].

Good-Bye

May 19

Two more hours before we can open her up, we are fumigating and I'm enjoying a beautiful sunset—the last few days have been warm and Morrow and I had a swim this afternoon after we "buttoned" her up for de-lousing—but then is that any way to talk of a lady—Morrow accidentally left the new issue of beer chits in the Wardroom and the crew are impatient home-bodies until we start ventilating and can go below again—our op-order appeared today and we've had all the charts out to look at the soundings—lube oil and battery water to come aboard tonite and then I'm thru.

This is a good-by letter and I have ships and shoes and sealing wax to discuss with you—and we are all going out on a pea green sea or is it a pea green boat—colors in five minutes, the SOP just hoisted prep—or as the limeys have taught us, Peter—one of our rest camp cronies pulled out today, after throwing all the new chiefs and qualified officers into the drink, and as the last line was taken aboard, everyone takes all the money and beer chits he has left and throws it over the dock—and the band settles for only one chorus of "Anchors Aweigh" and disintegrates to scramble for the loot—another reason for the mournful condition of tuba players—and taking their berth at our pier was a boat in from a long run and they are still draped around reading their mail—they are very hospitable at this base, and everyone drifts down to welcome a boat.

Everyone has picked up weight during this refit and looks much better for it.

The pub crawlers indulged in more head shaving last nite, but I'm going to pass this session up—Al [Shaw] and Duke [Duguid] made the sacrifice only after a struggle [*ibid.*].

May 19 PM and May 20

Dry drills this afternoon for a couple of hours, a chance for the new lookouts to learn how to clear the bridge from the high stations and the old hands break in the new JO's, its a game to see of you can ride the man just ahead of you down, and cauliflower ears and bruised fingers only make a good lesson — we are up and out early tomorrow, very early after the leisurely hours of the lodge — can't think of a thing forgotten — the control tower has word, the op-order is aboard, the tender is going to standby the fenders and lines, trash and garbage is in a cargo net ready to go off first thing, morning orders— it's quite a game played by skipper and O.D., the O.D. trying to remember everything, and the Old Man tries to catch him standing short, the Navy game — will have to stay up to start a charge at midnite a long day training tomorrow and we must leave with a full can.

[Ray] Roberts, our leading radioman was turned into sick bay this morning, a dietary deficiency, seems that all he eats underway are sandwiches—he's a good shipmate, always running, and is the best sound operator I've seen, especially at ranging — I hope we don't have to sail without him, he was married when we were last in the states and will talk a leg off about his wife — a reserve, he was a CPA when the war came along.

Free beer at the canteen tonite, to celebrate V-E day and this made my job easy, because there was no liberty until all the fish were aboard, the stores struck below and personal gear stowed in lockers.

The battery grounds are down to two volts— and that is good [*ibid.*].

15

The Eighth War Patrol

More Personnel Changes

John Gutensohn, a stalwart of the crew since the First War Patrol, left. Paul James was transferred during the Eighth War Patrol while topping off fuel tanks at Saipan. Ray Roberts, who Golay also feared would be disqualified for medical reasons, was still on the sailing list. However, numerous other men were transferred off the *Puffer*.

> The squadron was firm, so Carl had to transfer nineteen men — the personnel on the boat has been handled rather stupidly, and we find ourselves with about ⅓ of the commissioners aboard and they are tired — and you cannot give up too many of the key men until you can train reliefs — but this will be a good thing, we can get rid of some of the dead weight and can pick up some eager young men [Golay].

Dwyer held onto a few of the plank owners, and only 14 men were transferred while at Midway. Golay exaggerated slightly, at the end of the Seventh War Patrol approximately 25 percent of the First War Patrol crew, or 17 men, were still serving on the *Puffer*. By the start of the Eighth War Patrol the number of men from the First War Patrol was reduced to 12 (RG24).

> Morrow [Decker] and I had to go back to the boat this morning and work out our personnel problems — we are losing a lot of good men, and the squadron wants to replace them with rated men while we would rather pick up strikers and rate our own men — this makes for higher morale and keeps the men working — I am going to have a new assistant engineer [Al Shaw], we are picking up an ex-machinist who should be more help [Golay].

The squadron got its way — only McKee, Miller, Rafalko and Rama were seamen strikers. Many of the new men were rated chiefs or first class petty officers. Ken Martinson returned to the *Puffer* after a two patrol absence. With all the changes there were four enlisted men added to the crew (RG24).

On the Eighth War Patrol there were a total of 11 officers, four more than the first patrol, one more than the previous patrol. William Pugh left, and Donald Duguid and Al Shaw were added to the list of officers. Finding a place to sleep for all the officers and crew was difficult (WPR). Golay wrote about the new equipment, final disposition of the crew, officers and living conditions. The boat was getting overcrowded with the extra men and equipment.

15. The Eighth War Patrol

We picked up several new alterations this time, research in our weapons have almost crowded us out of the boats with new equipment and watch-standers to man the new gear — we picked up two new men and Carl moved two officers out of the wardroom into the Chief's quarters and there are seven men hot-bunking his run — someday they are going to realize we're running in excess of complement and take away our elaborate and effective watch bill [Golay].

CREW TRANSFERRED BEFORE THE EIGHTH WAR PATROL

Name	Service #	Rate Arr.	Seventh WP	Eighth WP
Bauersfeld, James Robert	608 86 03	EM3cV6	EM2c	TRAN
Bianco, Louis	807 36 30	F1c(EM)	F1c	TRAN
Bowden, Thomas Albert	376 20 12	S1c	Cox(T)	TRAN
Corcoran, Frank Howard, Jr.	647 33 81	MoMM2cV6	MoMM2c	TRAN
Gordon, Allen Harold	223 21 51	MoMM1c	CMoMM(AA)	TRAN
Gutensohn, John Peter	368 30 94	MoMM1c	CMoMM(T)	TRAN
Holland, Francis Anthony	300 47 89	GM2c	GM2c	TRAN
James, Paul Daniel	652 44 71	S2cV6	EM3c	TR @ Saipan
Kemp, Thomas R.	375 99 09	CEM(AA)(T)	CEM(AA)(T)	TRAN
Lane, John Nelson	225 10 12	RM3c	RM2c	TRAN
Liggett, James David	636 49 86	F3cV6	MoMM2c	TRAN
Messenger, Ernest Henry	258 33 30	S1c(SS)	S1c	TRAN
Shelton, Eugene Chester	291 64 17	S1c	MoMM1c	TRAN
Smith, Clark Sam	620 63 34	S2cV6	TM2c	TRAN
Vogan, Merle Francis	648 06 41	F1cV6	F1c(MoMM)	TRAN

NEW AND RETURNING CREW MEMBERS

Name	Service #	Rate Arr.	Date Arr.
Anderson, Edward C., Jr.	622 28 35	F1c	8-May-45
Brogan, Francis J.	892 34 99	MoMM3c	8-May-45
Gray, Earl A.	328 62 86	EM1c	30-May-45 (Saipan)
Hodges, Dale Lyman	316 04 49	CEM(PA)	8-May-45
Johnson, James T., Jr.	356 80 90	TM1c	8-May-45
Mappus, Karl W.	420 20 16	MoMM1c	8-May-45
Martinson, Kenneth Russell	665 12 72	RT2cV6	30-May-45 (Saipan)
McGraw, John M.	638 90 25	TM2c	8-May-45
McKee, Richard	574 14 98	F1c(MoMM)	8-May-45
Miller, Lawrence P.	356 08 99	F1c(EM)	8-May-45
Moore, Curtis	356 08 99	CSM	8-May-45
Owens, George D.	357 47 53	RT2c	8-May-45
Rafalko, Adam Peter	820 05 54	S1(TM)	8-May-45
Rama, Leonard Eugene	861 30 45	F1(EM)	8-May-45
Richenthal, Irwin	810 79 41	MoMM3c	8-May-45
Style, Norman	382 46 46	RM1c	30-May-45 (Saipan)
Thornberry, Fred K.	634 98 55	Y1c	8-May-45
Williamson, Jasper G.	360 48 82	Y1c	30-May-45 (Saipan)
Ziegler, Harold A.	821 09 75	EM3c	30-May-45 (Saipan)

Golay, from the state of Missouri, felt compelled to comment on the personality differences of crew based upon their home states.

The Eighth War Patrol — May 20, 1945 (Midway), to July 11, 1945 (Fremantle) — 5,918 nautical miles in the patrol area. The *Puffer* returned to Saipan from Midway and refueled. The primary purpose of the patrol was to sweep the South China Sea and Java Sea for any Japanese vessels. The sweep ended with a deck gun action on the north coast of Bali. The lone sun flag indicates an attack on a merchant vessel (map artwork by Nancy Webber).

One conclusion that is forced on you by the Navy is that there is a basic temperamental difference between men who come from the Northern United States and those from the South — the boys who come from the North are more adjustable, easily make small compromises necessary to live with fellow man and laugh easier, particularly at themselves, while men from the South suspect that everyone has designs on their personal rights and are the troublemakers aboard ship [*ibid.*].

Back to Saipan

On May 20, 1945, the *Puffer* left the submarine base at Midway Island in the company of the submarines *Tirante* and *Sea Owl*. During the nine day voyage to Saipan the boats trained, with one boat acting as a target, while the other two practiced coordinated approaches. Two days before arriving at Saipan Golay romantically commented about the scenery and sarcastically about the crowded condition of the boat. Markers left by fishing boats looked like periscopes. Training with multiple boats was trying. Mechanical problems haunted him and even the movie projector failed. The motor machinist mates had plenty of "rags."

Sunset [is] out of this world.

The northeast trades push us along and some days the sea is smooth like enamel and Jap glass fishing net floats are reported out to the horizon and the O.D. sends word down to ask the Old Man permission to pick it up — and he allows us one pass— and when we are lucky and take one aboard [Carroll] Allen comes grumbling to the bridge to scrub it up before taking it below to crowd further our pilchard like existence ... shower filled with soda crackers and the Wardroom looks like a nudist colony or a crowded rooming house the one day a week that we move the stores into the wardroom and choose up sides for a shower.

Joe "The Horse" [Kronberg] still is my helmsman and is breaking in on the sound gear and is still unable to distinguish fish noises from those more ominous and we courteously give all porpoises and other denizens of the deep a wide berth.

We're back among the fish net stakes, upright marker spars to mark fish nets, each one a periscope to perceptibly age the O.D.

We frantically race around trying to keep station and anticipate the zigzag plans— someday we're going to find someone junior to us and then will steam majestically around in circles blinking insulting message to junior "for Christ's sake get on station" — am busy wearing my engines but, just as the Pit Log settled down we blew a hole in a muffler and sound like a motorcycle and from the explanations that have been demanded of me I am beginning to believe I kicked the hole deliberately — and again the conflict with Russ over who's responsible for the ship's water — think the iodine taste must be from sea weed — nothing subtle about tastes on the *Puffer*— garlic and iodine.

We were busy showing our movies like mad expecting to exchange them when we topped off and the photoelectric cell that produces the sound gave up the ghost, so we revert to silent pictures, and I am of the opinion that our movies are improved without sound.

The engineering spaces with a new collection of pin-ups— Bob just volunteered to make zero floats, café and ice cream.

The bales of rags issued to the ship an unexpected morale booster and the engine rooms are festooned with pastel bra and panties— strangely

At a distance fish net stakes were easily mistaken for an enemy periscope by the lookouts and officers of the deck (The *Puffer* Film — National Archives).

Before departing Midway, in a show of unity the *Puffer* officers, except Dwyer, again received shaved heads on the tender USS *Griffin* (photograph courtesy of the Golay family).

inadequate to wipe down the floor plates, but now that the laundry is operating again we are not lacking for rags—["Freddie"] Frith and [Earl] Schley diminutive wipers look cool in scanties, but Larry Golden fierce in handle-bar mustache is still sorting rags to find unmentionables to contain his 225 lbs. [*ibid.*].

The day before arriving at Saipan the boat was spick and span. From a mechanical standpoint the boat was in good shape, until the unexpected occurred. The officers again decided to shave their heads.

They just called another Field Day and [Carroll] Allen and [James] Patton will be driving me out of the wardroom back to my haven among the electricians in maneuvering—since we have ceased to be a fighter, we keep clean as hell.

Carl up early to help us find the escort, eyes full of sleep and consequently in bad humor—he has so damn many St. Christopher and other medals that he has been issued another life jacket for additional flotation.

Just when Al and I finished congratulating ourselves last nite that the Engineering Department was in good shape with only some minor jobs to do, a motor in the air conditioning plant whined in anguish and expired just outside the wardroom and working all nite, [Henry] Smith and [Paul] James have failed to revive it and the temperature has crept up steadily to 90° and that isn't good—about the only solution to submarine air conditioning is to operate in an area with an injection of 50° air which will cool down the hecklers—and I'm ready to try a cold area.

[We] have a new quartermaster [Curtis Moore], a signalman from carriers, had both the *Lex[ington]* and *Hornet* sunk from under him by Jap aircraft so decided to try some safe comfortable submarine duty.

The shaved heads formal in caps … and without [*ibid.*].

On the way to Saipan numerous dives were made to train the new crew members. On May 29 the three boats pulled alongside the tender USS *Orion* at Saipan in Tanapag Harbor. The only defect found after the refit was a defective ventilation blower motor in the Control Room. No replacement parts were available at Saipan. Five more enlisted men were picked up in Saipan: Gray, Martinson, Style, Williamson, and Ziegler. Golay lamented the fact that Paul James was disqualified. James later rejoined the crew after the Eighth War Patrol (RG24).

> [I] have lost [Paul] James, one of my senior controllers who was disqualified by the Doctor,— and there seems to be no replacement available for him — and that ain't good — I will be glad when the time comes to drop the department [Engineering] in someone else's lap [Golay].

Back to War

On May 31, the *Puffer* and four other boats left the side of the tender USS *Orion* for the southwest Pacific. The orders sent the *Puffer* to shallow waters. Golay also belatedly discovered the reason for the happy sendoff from Midway.

> As usual our departure was dramatized by countless whistle signals — the Old Man I think reads the Rules of the Road just before we enter or depart and we use our whistle more than the rest of the Navy put together — the O.D. is no more than a glorified bell ringer on this sea going calliope — and if we hadn't given birth to enough confusion in the harbor, we met a large task force just at dusk and instead of courteously easing around to avoid breaking their formation we plowed right thru the middle, losing our escort guide and probably the little kindness yet entertained in the hearts of surface ship sailors.
>
> [Edward] Dauplaise busy breaking out a new chart portfolio — very interesting — the soundings disturbing — the new issue charts are frequently corrected for much of this Pacific war is being fought in areas where our existing charts are ancient and vague — each boat that discovers a new shoal by running aground or bouncing the bottom on a dive is dubiously honored by having the shoal named for her — *Stringray* Shoal, *Sculpin* Bank, etc. — would be nice if the *Puffer* could take a lead in this exploration and we might at that — from the soundings, we will be splashing water up on the shears with our hands to create the illusion that we are submerged.
>
> Started to unload the alcohol locker the other day to get some alcohol to clean a motor only to find the spigot nearly sawed in two and the tank dry — even the odor evaporated — which does much to explain the intoxicated flag-wavers, "get-one-for-me" [when we left Midway] [*ibid.*].

Paul James was temporarily disqualified for medical reasons. As senior controllerman he was difficult to replace (photograph courtesy of Avis Nelson-White).

Crew picture before departing Saipan. *Front row (officers—left to right):* Al Shaw, Anthony Giaimo (chief of the boat), Russell Frank, Wilfrid Delafield, Robert Weeks, Cmdr. Carl Dwyer, Morrow Decker, Phillip McClure, Richard Heehs, Frank Golay, Robert Biche, Donald Duguid. *Diagonal lines of the crew starting on the extreme left, front to back. First diagonal line:* unknown, unknown, Raymond Voss, William Kimbrell, Lawrence Golden, Joseph Kronberg, Bernard Cassidy, unknown, unknown, unknown, unknown. *Second diagonal line:* Herbert Hayward, Robert Kennedy, William Gooch, Raymond Hartman, unknown, unknown, unknown (half hidden), unknown, unknown, unknown, unknown, unknown, Kenneth Wright, George McPherson. *Center triangle of chief petty officers:* John Gutensohn, Edward Dauplaise, Jay Deem, Dale Hodges, Curtis Moore, John Nelson, Roland Chamberlain. *Center triangle of crew (behind CPOs):* Theodore Okoniewski, unknown, unknown. *Third diagonal line:* Charles Darrah, Earl Schley, John Alexander, unknown. *Fourth diagonal line:* John Perro, Arthur Reynolds, Anthony Sasso, unknown, Otha Frith, Ralph Troop, Harris Steinke, Delmar Baumgartner, Frank Mays, unknown, unknown, unknown, unknown, unknown. *Fifth diagonal line:* Glenn Stoy, unknown, unknown (half hidden), unknown, Henry Smith, Donald McDonald, unknown, unknown, unknown, unknown, Thomas Metz, Andrew Thoman. *Sixth diagonal line:* Howard Allen, Eric Bollman, unknown, James Patton, Frank Rohrbach, unknown, John Youra, unknown, Harold Ziegler (half hidden) (author's collection).

On June 1 the *Puffer* parted company with the other boats. On June 2 the *Puffer* met the submarine *Bream*. Commander Dwyer and Communications Officer Duguid along with paddlers boarded the *Bream* and returned after obtaining information on the Southwest Pacific area. The *Bream* was returning from lifeguard duty off the southern coast of Formosa, exactly where the *Puffer* was heading (WPR). The *Bream* had rescued five downed flyers, each of which was equivalent in the Navy's reward system to sinking 10,000 tons of Japanese shipping sunk. Such an effort made for a successful patrol and *Bream* was awarded the combat star.

Tragedy

About 30 minutes after recovering the rubber raft a tragic set of events was set in motion. At 1700 Frank Golay and Al Shaw went on deck to investigate an engineering problem that had appeared before the First War Patrol. "We flooded one of the engines yesterday when one of the exhaust valves salted up and failed to close completely" (Golay). The boat was moving "very slow, probably two to three knots on one engine so as not to flood the men working in the superstructure beneath the deck aft" (Metz). At 1717 "Al and I were down on deck working on the damn [exhaust valve] when we had a sound alert" (Golay). The sound men picked up noises that sounded like a Japanese submarine (Metz). "The Old Man gave maneuvering a 'flank' bell — they got all the engines on the line and Al's hand was badly crushed when the valve was closed on it hydraulically" (Golay). Shaw's scream of pain could be heard through the hull in the aft compartments (Mays).

The situation was extremely frantic for a few minutes. Shaw was trapped beneath the deck and the *Puffer* was about to submerge to evade the Japanese submarine. Dwyer became aware of Shaw's situation and ordered the exhaust valves reopened to free him, and this action also made it impossible to submerge. Golay and other crew members carried Shaw to the conning tower and brought him below deck to the mess table (Deem). The sound men lost contact with the noise.

Charles Johnson the pharmacist mate worked on Shaw's severe injury for the next two hours. The injury was probably beyond his level of training. He performed first aid to the best of his ability to stop the bleeding and save Shaw's life and arm (WPR).

> Our pharmacist's mate, very young and confronted with a complex problem, went to pieces as no doubt anyone would have done under the circumstances — Al was out from shock and it was necessary to get him to competent medical care [Golay].

"Several tendons have been severed and cannot be spliced without an operation due to recession of the tendons. Shaw stands the possible loss of the use of three fingers if he continues the patrol. Decided to send a message to ComSubPac and request advice" (WPR). Within the wound various blood vessels and tendons were clamped and the collection of clamps looked like bicycle spokes (Deem). Three hours after the injury had occurred at 2010 the *Puffer* exchanged recognition signals with an escort carrier and destroyer escort, the USS *Makin Island* (CVE 93) and the USS *Roberts* (DE 749). Dwyer established voice communications. He conversed with the doctor on the *Makin Island* who advised immediate transfer of Shaw to that vessel for further treatment. The *Puffer* maneuvered at flank speed to close the *Makin Island* (WPR).

Almost five hours after the injury occurred at 2155 the *Puffer* approached the *Makin Island*'s aft overhanging flight deck. The *Puffer* slowed to 10 knots and Dwyer chose Executive Officer Decker, Tony Giaimo (CTM), Roland Chamberlain (CTM), and Karl Mappus (MoMM1c) to perform the transfer of Shaw to the aircraft carrier. The plan was to bring Shaw to the deck through the forward torpedo room hatch (WPR). The transfer method suggested by the captain of the aircraft carrier would not be simple. "An aircraft carrier puts out waves off those screws at the back end about six feet higher than the main deck of a sub" (Metz). The transfer seemed unwise, "not realizing our low freeboard and poor sea qualities they suggested a direct transfer and we maneuvered to come alongside under the overhang" (Golay).

Chief Quartermaster Edward Dauplaise, an excellent swimmer, was also asked to assist with the transfer from the conning tower. He described what he observed in a 2001 letter.

> The Captain directed me [to] ask for help with our injured officer. It was decided that we should come close enough to the CVE's stern using their blue wake light as a guide; the carrier would lower a litter basket (they used this crane normally to retrieve their spotting plane). With everything agreed, the *Puffer* began to approach on the blue light; meanwhile below decks in the controlroom the Chief of the Boat, Tony Giaimo, was bewailing the fact that he was obligated to go on deck with 3 other sailors to receive this litter from the CVE. Tony was all shook up. I volunteered to take his place. I said, "I'm not doing anything. Ask the Exec if it's okay. Be happy to help you." "No, no," he said, "I've got to go up there, but I'd give anything not to have to do this." With this misgiving he went up on deck to stand by the bow to receive the litter. It was a dark night, light wind, and slight wave action. Being a spectator I was watching from the bridge as the *Puffer* drew nearer the CVE. With about 75 yards to go the *Puffer* rose up twice and dropped down into the sea, the third time it rose and paused before dropping down. I yelled "Lookout," as the *Puffer* dropped down a huge green wave swept over the bow and then one of the men on the bow yelled, "Man overboard!" And it was Tony Giaimo over the side wearing his life jacket as were the other men. I jumped up to man the 24" search light to try to keep the man in view. The Officer of the Deck immediately yelled for right full rudder, sped up to about 10 knots and began taking 2 minute legs at 90° turns, 4 turns and we were right back on our original course [Dauplaise].

Someone had the sense to throw over a marker light (WPR; Golay). Ellis Branchcomb started the TDC with a target speed of 0 and a range of 0 (Branchcomb). Dwyer maneuvered to pick up the man, using the searchlight for illumination. He shifted power to batteries and secured all engines so that a yell from Giaimo could be heard. Men were posted along the deck rails to hear the man in water (WPR). When the searchlight was turned on, the *Makin Island* captain irately informed Dwyer to turn off the searchlight over their PA. The carrier captain said, "If that damn light is not turned off, I'll shoot it out, because we cannot dive to avoid the enemy" (Dauplaise; Deem; Metz). The carrier rapidly departed the scene and sent the destroyer *Roberts* to assist. Within fifteen minutes Giaimo was located floating face down about 20 yards from the marker light (WPR; Golay). Karl Mappus went over the side to bring him aboard (WPR). Dauplaise also helped retrieve Giaimo.

> I shut the light off and found myself diving in to give a hand. We got him aboard. But while dragging him alongside I noticed that had he lifted his head but a few inches his mouth would have been out of the water. Several of us tried unsuccessfully using artificial respiration to bring him around to no avail [Dauplaise].

Metz observed, "Sure was a spooky feeling standing up on the lookout platform and looking down on those men trying to revive this man" (Metz). Golay described his emotions as he attempted to revive Giaimo.

> All of the miraculous resuscitations would become plausible if just one minor miracle would happen close to me — when we got him aboard his pulse was still strong and it was heartbreaking to work over him trying to rhythmically force "out goes the bad air — in goes the good" — only to have his pulse grow faint and his arms turn cold [Golay].

> Summoned back by the Captain I signaled the *Makin Island* again using the Blinker Tube giving a full report of the drowning and asked for the destroyer escort if they would send a boat with a Pulmotor. Didn't take them very long and they had the motor whaleboat alongside [Dauplaise].

About 20 minutes after recovering Giaimo the motor launch from the *Roberts* arrived to transfer Shaw. The chief pharmacist's mate on board the launch advised Dwyer to notify the

Makin Island if Giaimo did not recover consciousness. Artificial respiration efforts continued on Giaimo. An intravenous injection of coramine, a respiratory stimulant, was administered, all to no avail. The motor launch then left with Shaw. Artificial respiration efforts continued, and Dwyer requested medical advice from the *Makin Island* medical staff. Arrangements were made to transfer Giaimo. At midnight, an hour and 15 minutes after his recovery, he was transferred to the launch and then to the *Makin Island*. The chief pharmacist's mate from the *Makin Island* continued artificial respiration (WPR). A few days later the crew was informed of Giaimo's death and burial at sea (Metz).

Giaimo was probably not knocked unconscious by the wave that washed him overboard. There was no external evidence of an injury that would cause unconsciousness (WPR). "He was unable to swim, an inconsistency common among sailors but had the presence of mind to pull the lanyard to inflate the jacket, but the CO_2 cartridge was not properly secured and did not puncture. Last night was a depressing experience — someone should write Mrs. Giaimo" (Golay). Dauplaise wrote the letter and later visited Giaimo's widow.

> Next day following Tony's leaving via the destroyer's whaleboat, the Capt. asked me if I would be kind enough to drop his widow a line expressing sympathy and explaining how the accident came about. It wasn't but a few months later I and my family were on leave. I had decided to go via Chicago where Tony's family (wife and 3 year old daughter) lived. Upon meeting the wife I again expressed the Capt.'s and crew's and my sympathy. [Dauplaise delivered a collection given by the crew.] Trying to lighten her feelings I said that she would be receiving the $10,000 insurance money soon. She said no she wouldn't. They were not married [Dauplaise].

In a 2003 interview Charles Johnson, the young pharmacist's mate, recalled the guilt he carried for many years. Johnson felt he was partially responsible for the death of Giaimo. He could have disqualified Giaimo for not being able to swim, but Giaimo needed the pay-and-a-half from the Submarine Service for his wife and child. Johnson did not want to take bread out of their mouths (Johnson).

> It was foolishness, damn foolishness; he should have never been on the boat. I would doubt that for the better part of my life. I knew better, but I was going to be a buddy. It cost a man his life. It drove me crazy when I came back from the service. The first thing I wanted to do was go to Chicago and meet his family. I got talked out of that by my wife, my doctor, and my minister [*ibid.*].

Johnson's guilt seems misplaced; the entire transfer process of Shaw was misguided. The carrier should have sent a boat to the *Puffer* for Shaw (Golay). Giaimo's fear of going on deck was probably precipitated by his inability to swim. As a result of his emotional state of mind he forgot about normal safety procedures. The Mae West lifejackets were new equipment on the *Puffer*. Not familiar with the new device, Giaimo had not verified the condition of the Mae West before going on deck. Giaimo had also neglected to attach himself to the steel safety cable that ran the length of the boat (Johnson). The below deck agitation of Giaimo became a self-fulfilling prophesy; he was lost before he went on deck. "The whole damn procedure was a succession of stupid mistakes and incompetence — an expensive lesson even if we profit by it" (Golay). With the loss of Giaimo, Dauplaise became chief of the boat.

The South China Sea

On June 4 orders were received for the *Puffer* to take up station off Brunei, on the north central coast of Borneo. Along with the submarines *Bullhead* and *Kraken* the patrol line was to destroy any enemy vessels that might interfere with the capture of Brunei Bay. The British submarine *HMS Trenchant* was also operating in the area. On June 8 south of Singapore (01-59S, 104-57E) *Trenchant* had sunk the Japanese *Nachi* class heavy cruiser *Ashigara*. Golay wrote, "One of our English cohorts just finished a brilliant job in shallow water—a patrol that will make whatever medal they give him a mean award" (Golay).

Commander Arthur R. "Baldy" Hezlet, Royal Navy, was awarded the Distinguished Service Medal and the U.S. Legion of Merit, the highest honor the U.S. can bestow upon a foreign commander; the medal was presented by Rear Admiral James Fife at Subic Bay in the Philippines. *Trenchant*'s attack on the *Ashigara* was later described as one of the most brilliant attacks of the war, earning *Trenchant* the Battle Honor Malaya 1944–45. The *Puffer* had orders changed on June 9, which sent the boat off the east coast of the Malay Peninsula, near the track the *Ashigara* would have taken. The *Puffer* made contact with the British submarine on June 11 and sent congratulations to Hezlet.

Golay was prompted to write about the American and British navies after the contact. The jealousy he wrote about was not typical within the American Navy (Alden, email). He found Dwyer's congratulatory message lacking. Dwyer may have felt the British submarine stole a great opportunity from the *Puffer* and him.

> That the [U.S.] Navy [is] so permeated with a jealousy and hatred of the British Navy has been disillusioning—I think there is no American officer qualified to criticize the British tactics or bravery and yet I am forced to remain seated at the wardroom table while our leader explains these things to us—wonder how many more generations of Americans it will take to live down the memories of patronizing Englishmen and the "pressing" of American seamen—our futures have so much in common we can't afford to be so antagonistic—and I for one admire the English singleness-of-mind where the survival of England and the continuance of the Empire is involved—the greatest resource is their people and their inherent struggle for survival and the safety of their home is to be much admired—this was all prompted by the grudging, crude, boorish congratulations the Old Man signaled ... when we rendezvoused last nite [Golay].

Golay wrote of his evaluation of the American naval war effort and the lack of appreciation by the lay public. He also wrote of the mundane day-to-day events on the boat while in very shallow water. The many new men on board that needed to qualify were keeping Golay from his sleep.

> We have such superb Naval aviation and submarines that our attrition of the Jap fleet has been the monotonous performance of a deft surgeon removing a malignant growth before an audience of uninformed and listless laymen.
>
> The days are tiresome and monotonous.
>
> Every condenser on the ship should be full of mud by this time—we have scraped bottom several times today and only now has the Old Man changed course to head for deep water.
>
> The chore of taking men thru the boat to qualify them is upon us and interferes with my sleeping schedule.
>
> We converted the first of our fuel tanks [to ballast] last nite and surprisingly everything went smoothly and it is a relief to get the job done—but it does mean that we are down that much fuel and I have to go to the mat each morning with the Old Man trying to get him to slow down and save a little fuel for the long jaunt home—guess we could rig a sail to the periscopes, but she would sail within eight points of the southwest monsoon we have to hack on our way home.
>
> The ice cream machine has been converted again to reliable hand power, someday the mess cooks will learn that they can't leave the mix in until it solidifies.
>
> Another of these sage observations backfired on me, had "Cobber" [Delafield] open-mouthed with awe when I told him that as conclusion resulting from all my years at sea, that lightning at sea is a very rare thing—and since that night we have had daily visitations of this rare nautical phenomena—and I no longer try to laugh it off.

We're back in the bailiwick of long clearly defined slicks and paths of sea weed — think that the other day we crossed highway #66 which we patrolled up and down like a motorcycle cop back on our third run — we have finished our stint of training dives and from now on we're playing for keeps — the soundings on the chart which were merely numerals ten days ago now are the concern of the diving officer — Mac [McClure] has redecorated the wardroom with new editions of Varga [pinup girls from Esquire Magazine].

Can offer you the very best in sunrises — of course you'll have to endure a 0430 call by an inconsiderate quartermaster, a grouch O.D. who becomes civil only after having a cup of paint remover [ibid.].

On June 17 Golay wrote of a conversation with Steward Carroll Allen, which summarized the Malay patrol area, the highlight of which was an occasional contact with a native fishing boat.

> The latest Allen story — he is standing a half hour of volunteer lookout, and it is my good luck that he comes up just after sunrise from 0530 to 0600 ... thought I'd promote the conversation and suggested that we could use a target — Allen truthfully and succinctly observed — "You know, Mr. Golay — I kinda likes it peaceful like this" [ibid.].

Java Sea and Bali

After spending 12 days off the Malay coast, on June 21 the *Puffer* was ordered to patrol the East Java Sea between the Kangian Islands and Cape Seletan, northeast of Surabaya. The submarines *Icefish*, *Bullhead*, *Hardhead*, and *Baya* were similarly ordered. On June 23 the *Puffer* crossed the equator, and the new Shellbacks were initiated into the realm of Neptunus Rex. The purpose of the scout line was to report and destroy any Japanese naval forces retreating from the Dutch East Indies through the Makassar Strait that might threaten the operation to retake Balikpapan. On June 26 the *Puffer* and other boats arrived at the patrol line, already patrolled by the *Blueback* and the *Capitaine* (WPR). Shortly after arriving on station, the *Bullhead* made contact with two ships, identified as a minelayer and a *Chidori*, but missed with torpedoes set at 5 feet. Early on June 27 the *Blueback* sank a patrol vessel, *Cha 2*, probably the "minelayer" attacked by the *Bullhead* (Alden, *Successes*, p. D-306).

On June 30, the *Baya* and the *Capitaine* engaged a convoy of small Japanese freighters, sea trucks and a subchaser in a running deck gun battle. Ultra reports indicated no damage to any of the vessels. The *Baya* reported to the patrol line "targets were too small and made poor targets ... returning to patrol line" (WPR). At this time in the war there were no Japanese ships of any size remaining this far south, but the patrol line continued to scour the area with no additional contacts. In an effort to have a successful patrol the *Lizardfish* and the *Puffer* patrolled the north coast of Bali before heading home to Fremantle. Neither boat knew the intentions of the other boat. At 1152 on July 5 the *Puffer* surfaced near Bali (*ibid.*).

> *5 July 1945*: Patrolling across entrance of MADOERA STRAITS.
> 0235 APR contact 155/350/5. From later events it is believed that this radar is in BULULENG ROADS.
> 0302 SJ radar interference 130°T. Probably the LIZARDFISH headed for area E-5. They were due to transit LOMBOCK enroute to area tonight. Tried to exchange recognition signals off and on for an hour but could not raise them. Bearing holding steady. They must be making a sweep along BALI COAST.
> 0444 Submerged to close and investigate CHELUKAN BANANG BAY, BALI.
> 1152 Sighted a U.S. Submarine firing on CHELUKAN BANANG BAY with her deck guns. Very surprised by this scene.

1200 Position: Lat. 8°-09'S; Long. 114°-51'E.

1209 Battle surfaced. Exchanged calls with the LIZARDFISH. Began to close the coast along the West side of CHELUKAN BANANG BAY.

1220 LIZARDFISH completed firing. Secured all men topside and hauled out of Bay after starting two fires.

1222 Steamed close aboard Tg. TINGA TINGA and got a good look at the landing place. There were two boat houses, open native type with thatched roofs. Results of the LIZARDFISH gun attack are very evident by two fires. A wooden supply craft type lugger is on fire just East of the Western boat along the beach. The Eastern boat house was empty. There were five well camouflaged barges (type Super "A") (Ship Contact #4) in the Western boat house. Those barges were painted a mottled green and yellow. Selected those barges as the 5 inch gun target. Held the 40MM and two 20MM guns in ready condition in case a shore battery opened up. Did not mount or man the 30 and 50 caliber machine guns.

1224 With the barges bearing 310° relative (210° True), range 1,400 yards, commenced firing the 5-inch gun using controlled fire spotting between each shot. The third shell hit the far barge, followed by a terrific explosion of white flames about 300 feet in the air. Went to rapid fire. As each barge was hit, the explosion repeated. It was the most amazing sight I have seen in four years of submarine warfare. Took colored movies of the scene for Lieutenant Commander LONG's "SILENT SERVICE" picture. They should be something to see. It is believed that the barges were loaded with tins or drums of aviation gasoline to cause the explosions. The gun crew peppered the targets continuously with only 2 or 3 misses. Their shooting was magnificent. The targets were soon demolished and the boat house area a mass of flames. There seemed to be a gasoline storage just behind the boat house as 300 foot high flames leaped into the air from there continuously. It was noted that the fire on the lugger east of the boat house had died down and the hull was still intact so shifted fire to that target. First shell was a hit and it started burning again as before. Stepped up the rate of fire and demolished the lugger.

1234 APR contact of previous night is back again.

1248 With the barges and lugger destroyed, and the gasoline dump and boat house on fire and no more targets in sight, secured all guns and retired to seaward at high speed to join the LIZARDFISH who had been standing off the bay. Expended 33 rounds of 5-inch ammunition for about 28 hits. Decided to make a daylight coastal sweep of BALI Coast to westward looking for luggers, sea trucks, and barges. Closed to about 1,000 yards, stationed the crews at the 5-inch and 40MM guns. All gun crew members were put on sector lookout for planes. Started keying the SD radar. It is almost useless with so much land return.

1310 APR contact steady on us at saturation.

1330 Found TEMUKUS ROAD empty except for a sunken sea truck, and three native sail boats.

1340 Lost sight of LIZARDFISH.

1345 Sighted masts of several ships in BULELENG ROAD. This is stated by the Coast Pilot to be the largest trading station in BALI and also a Telegraph Cable Station. Jap radar is trained on us like a beacon but it cannot be seen.

1354 The BAY is filled with native fishing vessels of all descriptions in addition to one steel sea truck, one wooden sea truck, one powered Sampan, and one type "H" Landing Barge. (Ship Contact #5). The wooden Sea Truck is anchored farthest to the East and next is the beached Landing Barge, the motored Sampan and steel sea truck are farther west at the mouth of the river and to seaward of the anchored native sail boats. The greatest difficulty in this situation is to keep from hitting the native boats and homes. Fortunately there are no people along the waterfront. The steel sea truck and motor Sampan are well camouflaged with foliage. The barge appears to be very new, with a glistening coat of grayish-blue paint. With the APR contact steady on us at saturation pip, scanned the town and hills anxiously for a control station and possible shore batteries.

1358 Opened fire with the 5-inch gun on the nearest target, an anchored wooden sea truck with relative bearing 075°, true bearing 145°, range, 1100 yards. Three rapid hits amidships broke the target in two pieces. Got several more hits into the bow and stern sections before the remnants of the target disappeared from sight. At this close range it was a revelation to see the power and destruction of this 5-inch High Capacity ammunition. Fourteen rounds expended. Shifted to the next target in the line, the brand new, shiny landing craft beached at the waters edge. It looked as if it had just been put into the water so we proceeded to christen it with three rapid hits, relative bearing 060°, true bearing 130°, range 1200 yards. 5 rounds expended. This left the motor sampan and steel sea truck. Came left to unmask the 40MM gun and clear the PANARUKAN REEF. Shifted the 5-inch gun to the steel sea truck and the 40MM to the motor sampan. And then it happened! There was a wisp of smoke on the beach (at a spot we had previously passed at 800 yards) on our starboard quarter, the crack of a gun, and the splash of a shell about 15 feet off the starboard side near the bridge.

1404 Cleared the deck, sounded the diving alarm and pulled a blanket of water over our frightened skin. As the last man came down the hatch so did the water. Very close, but no damage there. Could hear the splashes of the shells around the conning tower as we went under. Headed out to sea. Hate to lose that chance at the sea truck. Pulled out from the beach to look the situation over. People are running around like mad on the beach. The well camouflaged bridge over the BULULENG River seems to be the traffic focal point. All those on the left bank are crossing to the right, all those on the right are crossing to the left. There are soldiers, sailors and civilians in the melee — what, no marines? [WPR].

Tom Metz wrote about his recollection of the events in 1976. With many men on deck it was a dangerous situation (Mays; Metz).

Along the north coast of Bali at the village of Chelukan Bawang, we found and destroyed two sea trucks and went on toward the Lombok Straits. At the village of Buleng Bali, we found six landing craft stored in a brush arbor built out over the water. We moved in and destroyed these crafts and shore installations with the 5-inch gun. After two rounds to zero the gun in, the 5-inch crew laid those 5-inch rounds right in that harbor. Fire, smoke and junk iron came boiling out of there. On the point of a mountain behind the harbor and ¼ mile away, a fuel storage tank exploded ... could have been flash fire up a supply line from the tank to the boats. Pretty soon the Japs got a gun crew together and commenced firing at us with probably a 3 or 4-inch gun. While this gunnery action was proceeding, I was on the 40 mm gun and we never got close enough to use it so I had some time to look around.

There must have been 40 men topside that day. When the first Jap shell hit near us, the Captain sounded the diving alarm. The boys that stood watches topside knew that we would be completely submerged in 50 seconds. The men started going below through the conning tower hatch, two at a time, one sliding down the hand rail. I knew that it was going to take some time for all of them to get below, so I dropped through the hatch with two other men, dropped on down to the control room and right on to the forward torpedo room.

There was an officer's steward by the name of James Patton on the 5-inch gun crew. There is an ammunition locker top side in front of the conning tower near the 5-inch gun mount that holds five 5-inch shells worth about $200 each. All of us white men had left the deck but the one black man topside did notice this ammunition locker open and stopped to close it and save that $1000 worth of shells. I've often thought of this in the past 30 years, especially when the people in the south were trying to tell everybody how no-account black people were. Anyway, we did get the *Puffer* submerged without losing any men [Metz].

Golay wrote about the events a week later as the boat neared Fremantle. He did not elaborate on the potential dangers of the situation.

We waited till the last day on station for a target and after another boat surfaced between us and the beach to show us it was safe ... we promptly surfaced and ran amok among the sampans and luggers until we ran into one that shot back ... two congratulatory messages tonite, the boats are so hard up for targets that even our small bag rates an ovation — and I'm sure everyone who was topside must be somewhat shamed for a bully [Golay].

Stoy gave another account of the events.

We open fire on a large shed containing five brand new landing barges — in short order all the barges were completely engulfed in flames — an aircraft radar contact was made at this time, forcing us to secure firing and to retire seaward — the contact was lost so we manned the gun and returned to finish the job — after destroying a considerable number of barges, sea trucks and luggers were forced to crash dive as we came under shelling by a Jap shore battery — it was touch and go for almost the entire crew was top side and we were almost dead in the water and as the Captain stated in his patrol report water came down the conning tower hatch with the last man to clear the bridge [Stoy].

After narrowly escaping Dwyer wanted to sink the sea truck he had seen in the small harbor. About 90 minutes later, with the *Puffer* submerged, he returned to the site of the shelling.

1549 Battle stations submerged, commenced approach. Worked down to the southwest and then cut back southeast to get the best track. The sea truck seems to be loaded with about fifty men aboard now. Getting a slight set to the northeast. Saw a truck load of Nip soldiers cross over the bridge.

1706 Fired tube #6 with depth set 0, range 1,250 yards, 60° port track, zero gyro, with torpedo aimed at center of target. Torpedo broached twice and drifted to the left at first due to the current and then moved to the right when the cross current hit it. Missed astern.

1706:35 Fired tube #5 with depth set 0, range 1,160 yards, 60° port track, zero gyro, point of aim ½ ship length ahead. Torpedo broached twice, moved over to the left at first then back to the right. Men are running around pointing at the torpedo.

1708:50 Saw and heard one hit. Target blew up.

1710:15 First torpedo ran up the river hit beach near bridge and exploded. Started a fire. Hope it hit a Jap installation there.

1711 Headed back out to sea. Getting too dark to see very well.

1807 Surfaced and headed for the LOMBOK STRAITS. Encountered several sailboats enroute.

2128 Commenced night surface transit of the LOMBOK STRAITS under a very clouded sky. Passage was uneventful, no contacts. However, just before we entered the strait between NOESA BESAR and the SW tip of LOMBOK, an enemy radar was detected on the APR — 162 mcs, 400 prf, 5 microseconds. He apparently tracked us through that part of our passage but no hostile moves developed.

2400 Completed transit of LOMBOK [WPR].

As a result of the destruction done to the Japanese sea trucks and the fuel dump, the *Puffer* was awarded the Submarine Combat Insignia for the patrol. What was supposed to be a morale booster to the crew after a long war patrol nearly became a disaster (*ibid.*). Lookout Ellis "Sandy" Branchcomb in a 2005 interview recalled the appearance of Dwyer immediately after they submerged. He remembered that the hair protruding out from under the brim of Dwyer's hat was singed. He speculated the burned ends of the hairs resulted from the heat of the Japanese shell passing over the conning tower within inches of Dwyer's head or it had turned gray from the experience (Branchcomb).

Fremantle

The boat stopped at Onslow, West Australia, for fuel and mail. The tides at Onslow were some of the largest in the world, hence the dock far above the deck of the submarine. "All I saw was a pier and lots of flat, sandy desert land and a country road leading to a village nearby, but I didn't go to the village myself though some of the other boys did" (Metz).

The remaining two days journey to Fremantle was no joy ride. It was monsoon season in the Indian Ocean and winter in the southern hemisphere. There was good news to celebrate, for real this time.

Russ [Frank], Dick [Heehs] and Bob [Biche] enjoyed themselves hugely when I went on nite decoding, but I'm having the last laugh as they struggle down from three hours of fighting the Indian Ocean monsoon — wet, cold and thoroughly mad because the Old Man drives her hard to get in a day early — the ship pitches violently and the watch in each compartment is alert to prevent a squeamish salt from flashing his cookies and then steal away without cleaning up ... and now I'm grinning and gloating over my moral victory [of being below decks].

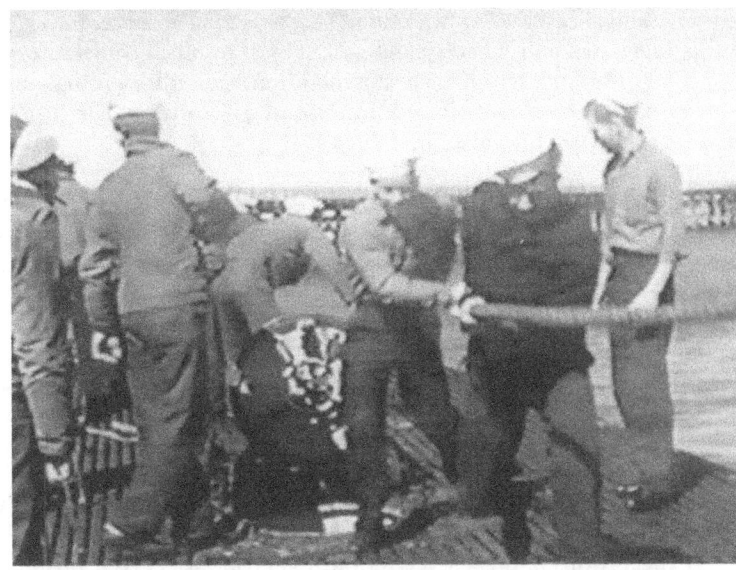

Preparing to dock at Onslow, Exmouth Gulf, West Australia. The *Puffer* took on fuel and much awaited mail (The *Puffer* Film — National Archives).

I had Mac's [McClure] stork-o-gram in my schedule the other nite — a 6½ lb boy — Carl was wary, but was finally convinced and contributed the medicinal brandy enough to knock the proud parent out — if Mac starts a bank account for his heir with all the money he has bet that it would be a boy the kid will not be in want [Golay].

R & R in Perth

As the *Puffer* approached Fremantle and Perth, thoughts turned to rest and relaxation. It was exactly one year since the *Puffer* had left Fremantle on the Fifth War Patrol. It was time for a comeuppance for two of the crew members. The crew was getting properly attired and stocked up with goodies to impress the Australian women.

We're still easing our way south and will just happen to find ourselves off Rottnest Light and Perth some morning — thought there would be no disapproval of this, but Hagen, one of our cooks expects to be met with a shotgun and minister — and Hayward unselfishly offered to stay close to the boat and watch over the refit — an irate Aussie must be home from the wars.

Blues are out all over the ship and the auxiliary load stays high with all the electric irons in use — and with all the swapping of blues leaves everyone scrambling for "crows" and Dolphins — a properly made suit of blues no longer fits if you gain five lbs of weight or lose weight on a boat. It's easy to understand the shortage of Dolphins, every girl out here has a collection.

Everyone busy bumming cigarettes, pleading for a drag — and even "shooting snipes" to smoke in a pipe — hoarding their own cigarettes for trading stock — the Nescafe has disappeared along with the chocolate and tea ... everyone scrambling like pack rats to assemble a sample case for "Down under"—after a long absence, the exchange rates for Nescafe, chocolate, nail polish and cigarettes is subject to much conjecture.

My God! Its cold! The air conditioning is still running—as well as the electric heaters which haven't been used since commissioning—Rottnest light just where she was supposed to be—and a magnificent sunrise [*ibid.*].

Metz wrote of the arrival at Fremantle and his introduction to Australian cooking.

We made our way down the coast to Fremantle, the port and submarine refit base for the rest camp at Perth. The sub crews stayed at the King Edward Hotel while at rest camp. The hotel was located down town Perth near the theatres, park, university and service men's clubs. We went to a café for dinner one day. A sign on the wall read "Pork Chop Dinner" for so much money, so I ordered one. The waiter had a good laugh. He said, "I haven't seen a pork chop in four years." Those Aussies served lamb or mutton everywhere everyday so I had a bowl of stew [Metz].

The American Red Cross was present in Perth, ready to serve the crew of the submarine and make their stay as comfortable as possible. From Golay's comments this was not the case 18 months ago. The behavior of submarine crews was probably not consistent with Red Cross expectations and caused friction. Everyone was given physicals.

The Navy must not be feuding with the Red Cross any more—there is a canteen on the dock and they were down soon after we arrived to offer to arrange our ship's party—which is welcome, otherwise it would fall to me.

The crew was not given liberty tonight and felt much abused.

The war is definitely on the wane—very detailed instructions regarding uniforms, salutes and conduct—the transition back to the peace time Navy is upon us—and we rebel—Russ [Frank], Duke [Duguid] and Bob [Weeks] managed to get themselves thrown out of the Officers' Club which is normal for the *Puffer*'s first nite in.

X-rays for everyone and I'm anxious to learn if [John] Alexander is tubercular—no news from Al Shaw, must get a dispatch off tomorrow to find if he will be available to go back out with us [Golay].

During the physical Tom Metz found out he needed glasses. Metz had to buy the glasses himself from a local optometrist. He also wrote of the servicemen's club and the Australian women he met there.

The American Red Cross operated a service men's club called "Swan Dive" which in peace time had been a private club, located on the Swan River near Kings Park. This club served soft drinks and knick knacks. They furnished music and had dances nightly. Young ladies from the University of Western Australia served as hostesses. One of these girls was named Priscilla Ladyman. She was a very nice young lady, one of the finest persons I've ever met. Her husband-to-be was in the Australian Air Force stationed in New Guinea. All the hostesses weren't as nice and considerate as Miss Ladyman. One of them asked me if I knew what was wrong with American men. I said, "No." She said, "They are over paid, over sexed and over here." I've often wondered what would have been her remarks to the same question three years earlier when the Japs were knocking on their northern coast [Metz].

Another popular night spot was the Pagoda Club as advertised with the flyer pictured on page 243.

Golay wrote of the current attitude in Australia toward Americans, which was much different than it was three years ago when the Japanese were knocking on the north coast of Australia. When Australian men were gone, the Americans were welcomed by Australian women. American servicemen romanced Australian women with promises of marriage and America. Australian women had no idea if their husbands were returning from POW camps

A Pagoda Club flyer attempted to entice the Yanks into friendliness and happiness and onto a marvelous dance floor (image courtesy of Frank Mays).

in Europe and Japan. Some Australian women had remarried American servicemen. The promises of wartime were easily made, and easily broken. Arden Hagen did keep his promise.

> The POWs are coming home — many men are returning home after as much as five years absence and their return must create complex human problems that cannot be really solved.
> The parties are turning into wakes, for everyone knows that the Yanks are not long for here — and will be missed — it will take some time for the surface hostility to be forgotten and then they will realize that we aren't so bad after all — the submarines out here have been effective good-will emissaries — but the men don't like us.
> Acting as a second in [Arden] Hagen's "shot-gun" wedding — much paperwork there.
> [Herbert] Hayward voluntarily staying aboard during refit to work in the engine rooms, with an irate "dinkey-di" (Australian slang for genuine; honest; the real thing) waiting on dock for him to appear [Golay].

Captain Selby was in Perth when the *Puffer* was refitted. "Capt. Selby is back here for a short tour of duty and had us out to his quarters for cocktails last nite — he is a beautiful man ... and has promised to come to the ship's party which will be a treat for the crew — they really loved that man" (*ibid.*).

After seven patrols Lieutenant S. Morrow Decker left the *Puffer* for additional training at the USNA. Golay became executive officer upon Decker's departure. As a result Golay was able to get rid of the engineering duties, for which he was obviously thankful. Even though he was giving up engineering, he wrote about the previous pressure of the responsibility. The progress of the refit and the relief crew's complaints reflected upon the prior upkeep of the *Puffer* and Golay resented it. He also found out that the Combat Star was awarded for the Eighth War Patrol, and lamented the fact that submarines had seen their heyday.

> We return to the boat Thursday, tho the tender and relief crew do not feel that they will be completed in time — the farther they get behind the more critical they become of our operation and maintenance of equipment — to justify their lagging — actually the *Puffer* has a fine machinery history and we are quite jealous of it — must admit tho that it has been a relief to turn over the Engineering to Bob [Biche], for you seem to live in dread that one of the engines will fall thru the bottom or an even more common dream that a salt water line will rupture in the battery compartment.
> We have our endorsement back on the patrol report and they gave us a successful for our last day's work — the old time patrols are all we have left to talk about — to set aside areas for our operations just hampers the air force which can now do our job more effectively so we look for the day when we will be pulled out of the war — what will they do with the boats, I

Left to right: **Delmar Baumgartner, Ray Hartman and Frank Mays relax at the Pagoda Club (photograph courtesy of Frank Mays).**

Captain Selby at the *Puffer*'s party surrounded by some of the crew members he earlier served with. *Front row (left to right):* Ken Martinson (shaking hands), Charles Wiseman, Eric Bollman, Captain Frank G. Selby, unknown, Harris Steinke, Frank Golay (foreground), unknown, Raymond Voss, Officer with drink—unknown, Howard Allen. *Back row:* Earl Schley, John Hensley, Joseph Kronberg, unknown, Herbert Hayward, Roland Chamberlain (in front of Hayward), Charles Darrah, unknown, Glenn Stoy, Paul James, William Kimbrell. *Standing in back:* John Perro, unknown (author's collection).

don't know, but can't convince myself that they will be laid up until months after the end of the war [*ibid.*].

Golay spent a week on an Australian sheep station north of Perth. He returned to Perth on July 24 "in time to do much work" (*ibid.*). On July 26 Golay wrote of the ship's party that all had gone well, even good news from Capt. Selby. Unfortunately the next day the news changed. Life became more complicated for new Executive Officer Golay. Golay was in charge while Dwyer visited friends in Albany, but Dwyer caught the flack. Golay was still upset with the refit crew and officers, who had taken over the quarters where the Airedale Cats scout plane pilots had lived. As Golay had written about earlier, the need for submarines was waning.

The ship's party last night a quiet affair—no fights, if that's any criterion and I've ignored the phone all day—believe we are going to avoid the usual session with the Ass't Chief of Staff explaining the behavior of the *Puffer* ... we return to the ship tomorrow and have a long day ahead, fueling and loading stores.

Selby has word that our recommendation for a Unit Commendation has been written.

We returned to the boat today ... and still it rains—think the *Puffer* leaves a permanent impression here—at least the stories will circulate for a long time to come—six of the crew, most of them torpedomen—leased one of the Roe Street bawdy houses including the chattels for a week for three hundred pounds and held open house for their friends—until the shore patrol and the *Sunday Mirror* simultaneously learned the story and drove the project underground—we are still bailing them out of jail—and then there is [Leonard] "Chickie-Bub"

The *Puffer*'s party July 24, 1945, at Rottnest Island (author's collection).

Evans, our fire controlman with the innocent face of a babe and the mind of a beachcomber — he took the first car with a key in it after the ship's party and it turned out to belong to the Chief of Police — Carl [Dwyer] has been taking a beating from the Division Commander for the short-comings—

[Arden] Hagen one of the principles in a shot-gun wedding since our arrival, asking for special liberty Sunday morning to christen his son. [Glenn] Stoy busy pre-dating letters to "Torchy" who has always had a daily letter.

The "Shack-masters" [refit crews] scrubbed and shaved, catching the 1610 liberty bus at the Wine Mess — and their little brown bags musical with clinking bottles — many of these jokers out here have made a good thing out of the war and there is little interest in returning the boats to sea in tip-top shape — it perturbs us no little — we are the only justification for the continuation of this base, and yet the submarines get the short end of everything — when they moved the "Cats" out of here, the quarters left by the Airedales would make a perfect rest camp for us, but instead, they are made available to the tender officers who already have quarters assigned aboard the ship — and everyone has transportation except the boats — things have changed much, but not for the better.

A liberty ship discharging Budweiser, which is like carrying coal to Newcastle — it can only suffer by comparison with Swan Lager and Emu Bitters [*ibid.*].

After two weeks of rest and recreation it was back to the boat for more training and approaches. At 0200 of August 2 Golay wrote of the events of the previous day and possible problems with the battery. At the moment the officers were trying to locate Rottnest Island and return to Perth. From Golay's remarks it was obvious he was ready for the war to be over.

We just secured for the nite after a full evening of approaches and tracking, Captain [Jesse L.] Hull let the escort and target group go — they lead a sad existence three days out of four, being pushed around by arrogant submarines who seem to want to stay out all nite and who cannot hear the sirens on Rottnest Island — however they do not complain and almost to a man are qualified "Shack-pappys" — should turn in, but will wait until we close land enough to cut in our position, [Carroll] Allen just brought me a cup of coffee which should do the trick — I'm tired of playing submarine — but it feels awful good to hear the word "This will be the last run tonite." — [John] Shiflett is baking cinnamon rolls tonite to appease Capt. Hull — and they're just as good as they smell — it's a cold wet nite to be running in circles out here — maybe the shower has been cleared, it would help to be clean once more — as I knew at the time, they were not pleased at our "quickie" battery discharge and we have an extra day to do it over — if the capacity is still down, it probably means that we will return to the states early for a new can — come on lets find that damn Island. I want to go to bed — and sleep and sleep and still more sleep — there must be simpler ways of making a living [*ibid.*].

The next day, August 2, training continued.

We fired exercise fish this morning and were in by noon.
War is Hell — no mail from you in a week [*ibid.*].

On August 4 Golay wrote about the battery problem and more parties for the officers thrown by grateful Australians. Dwyer and Golay were still feeling the heat from the staff as a result of unauthorized festivities on Roe Street. The *Puffer* would be heading back to sea on August 7. Golay made mental preparations for the departure and looked forward to the Ninth War Patrol. He was concerned about the increased losses of submarines. Unfortunately one more submarine was lost in the last days of the war.

It still rains — another battery test discharge and we are relieved to find that the can is normal and healthy just a faulty calibration of our ammeters.

Val Ambrose is giving a party for the *Puffer* tonite — she was housemother when we first opened the rest camp (eighteen months ago) and has a huge heart, each one of the boats of the old squadron that returns will find her ready with a party.... Selby will be there and is soon to leave so it will give me a chance to see him once more.

Carl and I have been before the Asst. Chief of Staff again who refuses to be pacified and who seems to have a blow-by-blow account of the festivities.

The major problem now is to get out of here without forgetting some important letter or report, am in the Yeoman's hair most of the day [*ibid.*].

On August 6 Golay wrote of the impending departure and continued personnel problems created by wayward crew members, Arthur Reynolds and "Howie" Allen.

We're ready — fuel, stores, water, everything — and now if only the crew will remember to return from liberty my troubles will be little ones from there on ... am still wearing the carpet thin over in the office of the Chief of Staff — and we aren't on a first name basis just yet.

Reynolds caught me napping the other day and asked me if I would give him permission to bring his girl aboard and show her the boat — tried to pass the buck along, by telling him that it was impossible to get a pass, but he scrounged one over on the British tender, how I can't imagine, and assuming he had my permission, he did it to me — a violation of some squadron order of long standing and I'm holding the bag — the man missed his calling, he should be a lawyer.

[Howard] Allen our baker, and a good one, talked when he should have listened the other nite and is in the hospital with a concussion when an Emu Lager bottle proved tougher than his head, and it doesn't look like he will be able to go out with us, and that isn't good, for he does much to make the run easier by turning out pies, bread and cake that makes you forget those mother used to bake [*ibid.*].

16

The Ninth War Patrol

The Last Departure

"Howie" Allen's head did not heal in time, and he was left behind. In his August 10 letter Golay hinted that he may not have completed all the personnel paperwork, which may be the reason the reports were missing from the National Archive files. "The mail transfer covered up a host of my sins as Exec, for much of the official correspondence was neglected thru my ignorance" (Golay). Golay also wrote about the personnel situation during the refit. The crew wanted to get back on board so that they would be headed toward home, and the relief crews wanted to stay put. The size of the crew was reduced.

> Everyone we transferred is scrambling to get back aboard, and those slated to go out are trying to find reliefs so they can stay in — they have cut our complement drastically — we always carried extra men for training and extra watches — we will go out with two fewer officers which will probably mean four hours on and eight off once more — but we will carry fewer stores and everyone [of the officers] will have a bunk [*ibid.*].

The crew lost 10 veterans and a limited number of replacements were unavailable. Seven new men made their first patrol on the *Puffer*. The crew now numbered 77, a net loss of three men. Golay wrote, "but everyone has locker space and only five men are hot-bunking so the boat is much more habitable" (*ibid.*). A veteran of the First War Patrol, Ray Roberts was temporarily transferred to the *Bullhead*, but returned to the *Puffer*.

Due to Golay's inexperience with his new personnel duties as executive officer, the crew roster was not available for the Ninth War Patrol. As a result it was impossible to determine who left the *Puffer*. However from an October 1945 crew muster list it was possible to determine seven crew members that were added prior to the Ninth War Patrol: Joseph L. Anglin (F1-MoMM striker), last crew member added during wartime; Thomas Russell Cali (PhM1c); Willie Coleman, Jr. (StM1c); Thomas W. Copeland (CMoMM); James Frank Edwards (TM1c); Wayne E. Johnson, Jr. (MoMM3c); and George W. Krans (MoMM1c) (RG24). Others may have come and gone in the interim. It was not possible to determine which 10 crew members left or when. In Golay's letter of August 9, he wrote, "One of our new torpedomen [Frank] Edwards has quite a gallery of tattoos — comely damsels with few clothes and a liberal text of names of ships, females and shore stations" (Golay).

On August 7 as the *Puffer* left the harbor at Fremantle, Golay wrote of the departure. He

The Ninth War Patrol — August 7, 1945 (Fremantle), to August 15, 1945 (Java Sea) — 806 nautical miles in the patrol area. The *Puffer* returned to the Java Sea to intercept any Japanese shipping. The war ended shortly after the transit of the Lombok Strait and the *Puffer* was directed to Subic Bay to await further orders (map artwork by Nancy Webber).

also talked of his career and the end of the war. Leaving Australia was not complete without another "Joe the Horse" Kronberg adventure. According to McDonald, who was on deck watch, it was Joe's intention to have "a last one for the road," return quickly, and have his absence go unnoticed; Joe neglected to sign out on the deck log, which could have gotten McDonald in trouble. He didn't force the issue with Kronberg (McDonald). Fortunately the brass had departed the scene early. Metz recalled the incident in his journal.

When we put out to sea on our ninth patrol from Fremantle, the harbor crew brought one of our men out in a speed boat. He had stayed in town too long. Joe was very belligerent and apparently did not want to go on the boat. In the process of dragging him aboard, he called one of the officers nothing more than a soap salesman [Metz].

Golay filled in the details of Joe's departure. Joe's antics gave way to Golay's complaining about getting the boat back out to sea. The weather looked bad, and it probably was his last visit to Australia. Golay and the rest of the crew were very ready and anxious for the war to end. Everybody wanted to get home.

Joe the Horse provided most of the entertainment at our departure, they carried him aboard sodden in liberty blues, AWOL and plastered — finally the Pharmacist's Mate [Cali] filled him with morphine so we could lower him thru a hatch — Joe has been one of the planesmen thru seven patrols — we came aboard together and have grown up together — he is probably the best lookout aboard — at sea a good man, but in port he is my most severe headache — he writes the kindest, most loving letters home to his mother — and all the time he is completely fouled up — the best story we carry away from Perth is of the Vice-squad pulling his amorous conquest of the evening out from under him in King's Park — he and I have regular man-to-man talks on the order of those indulged in by Andy Hardy and Judge Hardy and end up promising each other we are going to get along — but never do — yet you can't help liking Joe and he's a damn good lookout.

The rain cut short the parade of brass down to see us off — Captain Selby was down and gave me a pep talk about staying in the Navy — he talks a good story and it wouldn't be bad to ship over with him as skipper.

I'd rather be whipped than have to get a boat underway on a war patrol and this was no exception — they were publishing storm warnings this morning and by the time we were scheduled to get underway the harbor was frothy with white-caps and the wind was blowing so strong we could hardly twist her tail thru the wind — our comparatively large bow has a sail area which will take charge of the ship in a strong wind when we are backing down — the storm is picking up, but the latest message has the center moving to the south of us — the Navy has become storm conscious since those three cans [destroyers] capsized in the typhoon in the China Sea and weather messages make up much of our traffic as well as sternly worded billet-doux from Nimitz and Kincaid promising dire things to skippers who do not provide for the safety of their ships.

Probably my last view of Australia as we took departure and set the course.

The senior boat just released the escorts — a cheery exchange of "Good Lucks" and "Good Hunting!" which have become formal from much repetition — our days will be full of "Battle Stations" and dives as we will train on our way to the barrier.

Let's drop a few more atomic persuaders and get this war over — and get us home [Golay].

The *Puffer*'s orders sent the boat back to the coast of the Malay Peninsula via the Lombok Strait and Java Sea, retracing the course of the Eighth War Patrol. The bad weather continued, but appeared to be subsiding. The pit log that caused Golay so many headaches was operating normally. Bill "Cobber" Delafield had taken over commissary duties, and Robert Biche took on engineering. The boat concerns of the day were light, however Golay worried about the politics of Potsdam and when the war would end. On August 8 Golay wrote of the weather, the ice cream machine, and the war.

We are rolling deeply in the heavy, long swells that announce the end of a storm at sea — the bridge is wet and cold and I'm sissy and ask the O.D. to cease zigzagging and slow down for sights — the only compensation for the storm, we are mutually unanxious to begin training and practice dives.

The ice cream machine is back in commission and each batch of ice cream is completely supervised from the Exec, Engineering officer on down.

Movie today, but I'm sure that my nest is better than the violent pitching of the forward torpedo room — hot and humid with too many bodies— Dick [Heehs] just popped a huge pan of pop corn and I changed my mind — all the comforts of home.

The Potsdam Conference fizzled out into oblivion when they had to drag China into the declaration to replace Russia — Russia's absence means at least a year more of war [*ibid.*].

The next day August 9, Golay's outlook on the duration of the war changed. He felt Russia's entry into the war against Japan would hasten their surrender. There was also good news about the condition of Al Shaw, injured on a previous war patrol. The saga of "Joe the Horse" continued. Worst of all there was news of another boat lost, the *Bonefish*. The information was much delayed; the *Bonefish* was sunk June 18, 1945, with all hands lost. Similar to Golay, Frank Knight was executive officer on the *Bonefish*. The *Bonefish* was the next to the last boat lost.

Russia has declared war on Japan — pack your gear and catch the Queen Mary.

A letter from Al Shaw just before we sailed, he is in a hospital in New York and wrote the letter while home in Brooklyn — his hand is stiff and will be for many months, but the Doctors are encouraging and he says he hopes to return aboard — I hope he makes it.

Captain held mast on Joe the Horse Kronberg this morning and reduced him in rating — back to Seaman, he has been up and down in the Navy like a thermometer and this last punishment will be ineffective as his rate of Coxswain was being eliminated from Submarines and this will give him a chance to stick around.

A new announcement tonite that the BONEFISH is down, the fourth boat of our squadron, think Frank Knight is still aboard, he is too nice a guy to get a break like that this late in the war — used to play golf with he and Peggy, his wife, back in New London … now that the pickings are slim we aren't nearly so cocky, and is probably a good thing, but the scarcity of targets combined with the young skippers eager to make a record have accounted for much of the alarming increase in sinkings [*ibid.*].

Metz wrote of his reflections on his pending departure from Australia.

I got this far on my story and seemed to bog down. I've decided that inwardly I hated to leave Australia and the city leisure life and go back to sea and the war. At that time we had no idea the war was nearly over. The Americans had been losing several subs soon after they left Australia. We had been cautioned real thorough to tell nothing about our schedule to anyone [Metz].

Metz, Golay and even "Joe the Horse" were concerned about the next war patrol. Golay's apprehension was based upon the recent loss of an old acquaintance as well as his concern about the new skippers taking excessive risks to sink a ship, even a small ship, before the end of the war. Dwyer was experienced and made every attempt to avoid uncontrolled situations. However, seemingly harmless conditions, such as the deck gun action at the end of the last patrol, could turn deadly. One less degree of elevation on the Japanese howitzer would have holed the *Puffer*'s conning tower, or worse. With the live ammunition on and below decks a major explosion could have occurred. The *Puffer* would have sunk with many crew members lost. Metz, Golay and Kronberg all witnessed these events. No one wanted to be lost in the last days of the war.

The Numbers Game

Although very different people, Metz and Kronberg were apprehensive about another patrol. Both Kronberg and Metz didn't want to leave Australia. Kronberg showed his apprehension by trying to miss the boat. All men in the Submarine Service were aware of the arithmetic of lost submarines. Of the approximately 250 submarines in service during the war, 50 had been lost. The arithmetic was easy: one-fifth of all submarines were lost. To the submarine sailor that meant his number was up on his fifth war patrol. Beyond the fifth war patrol a sailor was living on borrowed time. Kronberg was on his eighth patrol; Metz was on his fourth.

The numbers were actually much better than computed by the sailors. Fifty-one boats had been lost at this time in the war: 46 subs were lost to hostile action while on war patrols, 2 ran aground while on war patrols, 1 was bombed in the Philippines while in overhaul at the start of the war, 2 were lost during training exercises, and 1 most likely was lost to friendly fire on route to Panama. By August 1945 approximately 1400 war patrols had been conducted. Therefore, the probability of being lost to hostile action on a war patrol was 46/1400 or about 3 percent, or 1 in 33. However, Golay's concern for the new skippers in the last months of the war was accurate. Of the seven boats lost in 1945, five were commanded by skippers on their first or second war patrols. The *Bonefish* and the *Swordfish* had more experienced commanders, respectively on their third and fourth patrols. The danger to submarines increased as the boats moved nearer to the Japanese homeland and into the Sea of Japan.

The *Puffer* and friend, the submarine *Capitaine,* proceeded up the coast of Australia toward their patrol zone. Golay was concerned about being bombed by friendly fire, the Airedales. Golay mentioned the first atomic bomb and underestimated its power, but he was sure the war would be over soon.

> The storm has played itself out and we lost the heavy swells along with the easterly set — this should really foul up our friend, they persist in hanging around the eastern edge of our lane and we are to the east of them which puts us over into the Airedales precinct — and they have little powers of discrimination when it comes to bombing — how can the Japs continue to fight on, altho they may choose race suicide to surrender — the news results are meager about the first atomic bomb and I suspect more publicity was given it than deserved.
>
> With the slackening of the wind we begin playing submarine with our friend and the day is full of exercises and drills — maybe we could lose him one of these dark nites and laze along by ourselves — we are arranging a rendezvous with one of the southbound boats and will be able to get off mail and also cover up many of my administrative, red-taped mistakes as an embryo Exec — the Old Man has been tolerant tho and we spend most of our time in mutual smoke blowing — we didn't look very good in our training period so going up in company with another boat will do much to smooth us out.
>
> The war will soon be over — have uncrossed my cramped fingers [Golay].

In the early afternoon on August 10, the *Puffer* met the *Cod*, which was returning from the *Puffer*'s assigned area, Pulo Tenggol, near the Malay Peninsula. Station KRCJ from San Francisco announced that Japan had asked for peace in accordance with the Potsdam Surrender Terms. But there was still no official end to the war. Golay was aware of the second atomic bomb and expected the war to end any day.

> We rendezvous with a southbound boat to transfer mail and get the dope on our area — which I don't expect we will reach — the war is accelerating and something is going to happen soon — the Old Man expects orders back to the Pacific, but mostly it's just sweating out the news [*ibid.*].

Later in the day Golay wrote about the events and the rapidly changing political picture on the world stage. He wanted nothing less than unconditional surrender.

> Hell, I'm forgetting the news — Japan will accept the surrender terms of Potsdam, providing the sovereignty of the Emperor is not jeopardized — and that means another atomic persuader — we hope that nothing but unconditional surrender terms are given them even if it means

prolonging the war — we have been out here too long and have given up too much of our time to settle for any less than total victory [*ibid.*].

In the late night hours of August 12 the *Puffer* was ready to run the barrier through the Lombok Strait, which remained a dangerous area patrolled by the Japanese. Prior to running the barrier, orders were changed; the *Puffer*, *Capitaine*, *Bullhead* and the HMS *Taciturn* and *Thorough* were assigned to a scout line east of Kangean Island. This assignment was similar to the patrol area at the end of the Eighth War Patrol. During the transit of the Lombok Strait the *Puffer* encountered a small patrol boat, "too small for torpedoes and the night is too dark for gun action," according to Dwyer in the war patrol. By 0230 on August 13 the gauntlet was traversed. By 1300 that day the *Puffer* had reached its position on the scouting line with the *Bullhead* and the *Capitaine* (WPR).

Golay described the transit of the Lombok Strait in the company of the *Capitaine*. The watch changed, allowing Golay to head for his bunk. He then contemplated awaking in the morning with the war over and how he would feel about leaving the *Puffer* behind.

> We ran the barrier tonight, and I shall write my daily page before turning in — we'll still be able to cut in on landmarks and I can sleep-in in the morning, although Charlie slept the nite thru, ignoring contact reports in his usual inimitable fashion.
>
> Our friend [the *Capitaine*] had some navigational difficulties last nite and seemed for a long time about to pioneer a new overland route, but finally got in close enough to ask a native where they were and followed us thru the slot after we had alerted the patrol boats — it is always a race to get started thru first, for the second boat is busy avoiding the Peter Charlies [phonetic alphabet for "PC" meaning patrol craft] and other of our little friends, who are wide awake and annoyed that one got by them — the dark of the moon was convenient and we were additionally protected by the blanket of overcast that has been providential for so many of our boats in here — the tide rips gave the O.O.D. many a bad time because a few hundred yards away it looks too much like a bow wake and our zigzag plan is benefited by many violent evasive course changes.
>
> We have been waiting all night for some super-duper message regarding our plans, but seems the Navy feels that all the boys may not have the word and it is business as usual tomorrow — hope they make it a submerged day, I'm bushed — they just called the 4–8 watch and Russ [Frank] and Dick [Heehs] staggered in eyes full of sleep — gulp down a cup of coffee and then up to the salt mines.
>
> It just doesn't seem to penetrate that the Nips have chosen peace instead of suicide — the atomic bomb must be quite a persuader ... tomorrow I shall suddenly wake to the idea that we are going home and that soon I shall be with you — five years now [in the Navy] and it won't be the same life — wonder how hard it will be to return to teaching — I shall miss much the Navy — it would be impossible to be so much a part of all this effort without carrying away some permanent scars — but the immediate reaction is a terrible tiredness and lethargy — not due in any part to tonite's work — you didn't feel it all along, but we have been pushing ourselves hard, and now there's nothing but tiredness ... the war is about to end [Golay].

On August 13 Golay wrote of the worldwide events and the daily events on the *Puffer*. The letter closes with his thoughts of the future. After three and one-half years of war he and many of the crew were ready to return to a more normal life and the simple pleasures of peace.

> Japan is willing to accept the Potsdam ultimatum — providing the sovereignty of the Emperor is not jeopardized — quite a loop hole — meantime it is business as usual out here — it will take twenty-four more hours to get another answer thru the Swiss, but we all are hoping that they have seen the light.
>
> Well worn charts, this is a familiar area for most of the SouthWestPac boats and we nose around trying to flush something out.

One of the men we picked up must suffer from claustrophobia—a wiper in the engine rooms [probably Anglin], he was up to talk it over with me this afternoon—the Pharmacist's Mate [Cali] reported that he was going to pieces for lack of sleep and he spends his time off watch in the Control Room at the foot of the ladder—have shifted him to lookout and hope that this new watch will ease his mind, for there may be forty long days ahead of him, each a little hell of its own, I suspect—wonder how he persuaded himself to try submarines, surely he had an inkling of this quirk—seems the psychologists back at sub school are not infallible.

Best food we have on patrol is the fresh frozen kernel corn—most vegetables lose much in freezing, but the corn is improved, if anything—and fresh frozen strawberries.

Stars come just now at 1900 and my enthusiasm for picking out a half dozen each evening makes the Chief [Dauplaise] grumble as he realizes we will be late cutting them in and even later for chow—he no doubt wonders why we don't settle for three—and that's a good idea, I'm hungry.

Men are busy studying to qualify and soon it will be time to take them thru the boat to see if they deserve dolphins.

The message just came thru and we are to continue on patrol and no change yet in our instructions—new mufflers all around and she purrs quietly around until a course with the wind astern and the faint exhaust sounds at times like a distant airplane.

Joe the Horse and I have made up again and are patting each other on the back promising to get along, when we get into port—that will be a neat trick—our interests conflict.

Russ sent down word that Jupiter is out and that leaves only a minute to finish this.

It's good to slip back into sea routine where there is time to write to you and to think of you ... they're going to pay us off with accumulated leave—let's take a honeymoon of three months—no, let's make it permanent—I feel it will never stop for me—and let's have a house with big rooms—leg room—a huge bed—Hollywood influence—a fireplace—and not hoard lights—and cheese in the refrigerator—and rye bread [*ibid.*].

Peace

August 14 was business as usual. Early in the evening, the *Puffer* received a message from HMS *Thorough* of a ten ship convoy, six escorts and four small ships with air cover. At 2230 the *Puffer* was directed to return to the original scout line. No attack on the convoy was made by any of the boats (WPR). The next day at 0718 a Subic Bay Radio broadcast was heard which announced the surrender of Japan.

Later in the day at 1300 the *Puffer* received "CTF 71 Serial LOVE directing cessation of offensive operations against Japan." Dwyer entered in the war patrol report, "The war is over!" (WPR). Golay wrote the exact same quote in his letter of August 15. Three hours later the *Puffer* was ordered to proceed to Subic Bay with the *Capitaine* (*ibid.*). Golay wrote about his immediate feelings and an overview of the war. He wanted to have the last submarine action of the war. Unfortunately the only recent loss was of another American submarine.

THE WAR IS OVER!! But it refuses to soak in—my reaction is to suddenly be tired, dead tired—and maybe the sensation of a heavy weight removed—this is an anti-climax after the news of two days ago and it will be the 16th back home, we already have been ordered to cease hostilities—the word came in as we were trying to establish contact with a target, wish we might have had the last submarine action of the war—rendezvoused with our limey friend and we nonchalantly—they are adept at it—came alongside to talk over the news.

The medicinal brandy has gone to celebrate the news and tonite we start taking atabrine for malaria prophylaxis—lets go home—the ship is tense tonite and yet tomorrow everyone will be fighting the let-down that must come in watch standing.

```
RADIO              U.S.S. PUFFER (SS 268)              14 AUGUST 1945.
                       U. S. NAVAL DISPATCH
NERK V NVB - FLASH - FLASH - FLASH - BT-

PRESIDENT TRUMAN HAS JUST ANNOUNCED THAT JAPAN HAS ACCEPTED OUR SURRENDER

TERMS! BT- END OF PRESS.




TOR: 2318 GCT /FM/ 9250 KCS. 14TH AUGUST 1945 - RECEIVED BY ALL HANDS.
     0718 LZT


FROM:              TO:                       INFO:
   RDO: SUBIC BAY     ANY OR ALL USN
                      SHIP OR STATION.
| Captain | Executive Off. | Engineer | Torpedo Off. | First Lieut. | Commun'ations | | |
```

The surrender notification message received by the *Puffer* on August 14, 1945 (image courtesy of Frank Mays).

Mac [McClure] just called in that he is breaking our orders now, cross your fingers and we'll head east — would like to pretend that my estimates of the end of the war were accurate, but I have been pessimistic — much too pessimistic — it's strange to look back to 1942 when we were scrambling for a draw and all the newspaper victories back in the States were bitter defeats to us and the ENTERPRISE was the only carrier we had operational — and we were busy fighting with multi-screened port holes, elaborate zigzag plans, weighted garbage and confining censorship instead of weapons — they didn't come until '43 and '44 and they gave us a superiority that hasn't been questioned since.

We're headed home and it's wonderful — a bone in her teeth and all four mains on line, carrying a zero float on Mrs. Dickenson.

The ship is warm with the water temperature at the maximum of 85°— the voltage regulators are not controlling the lighting motor generators tonite and each surge is translated to the wardroom as dimming lights and I wince sympathetically for Bob [Biche] — that was my baby last run.

The war is over — [Carroll] Allen consists mostly of a big white grin tonite and everyone is a little happy — gross understatement — "Charlie" [Dwyer] is the only one down cast, tormented with vision of returning to his permanent grade and having to give up his toy.

We were forbidden a couple of days ago to talk about going home — bad for morale, you know — our transcription of the hit parade has "Missed the Saturday Dance" as the top tune.

The impulse pressure is bled down in the tanks and the firing circuits are secured, the first time within my memory [Golay].

The Last Loss

Although the *Bullhead* was mentioned in the *Puffer*'s war patrol report as in the scout line on August 14, actually it had been sunk shortly after passing through the Lombok Strait on August 6. On August 12, the *Capitaine* ordered the *Bullhead* to take position the following day in a scouting line with the *Capitaine* and the *Puffer*. There was no reply and on August 15 the *Capitaine* reported, "Have been unable to contact *Bullhead* by any means since arriving in area" (WPR).

> We're missing one boat in our area and they keep asking him to report in, the most ominous silence you can experience — it's good to know that the odds have shifted heavily in our favor [Golay].

On August 26 the Navy announced the loss of the *Bullhead* and Golay described his feelings.

> They announced the BULLHEAD today, the 52nd and last boat lost in the war — we were together at the Majestic [Hotel] with her officers and they were a good lot — the last one must be the toughest one, at least to the relatives of the men it must seem particularly senseless [*ibid.*].

The most likely recorded attack of the *Bullhead* occurred on August 6, 1945, while the *Puffer* was still in Fremantle. On that day a Japanese army plane attacked a submarine with depth charges. The plane claimed two direct hits. For ten minutes there was a great amount of gushing oil and rising air bubbles. Because the position given was very near the Bali coast, it was assumed that the closeness of the mountain peaks shortened the *Bullhead*'s radar range and prevented it from detecting the plane's approach. Edward R. Holt, Jr., class of 1939, was commanding his first war patrol; it was the boat's third patrol (Commander Submarine Force U.S. Pacific Fleet).

Holt may have been looking for targets based upon conversations the officers held at the Majestic Hotel. The *Bullhead* was sunk very close to the same area where the *Puffer*

Frank Mays in 2004 holding the last American flag to fly on the *Puffer* during wartime (author's collection).

narrowly escaped a Japanese shore battery at the end of the previous war patrol. Earlier in the day while shelling the coastal fuel dumps, the *Puffer* radar had detected an airplane and they dove before it arrived. Luck had been with the *Puffer*.

In the *Remarks Section* of the last war patrol Dwyer wrote a fitting tribute to the Manitowoc Shipbuilding Company and the employees.

> I should like to thank and compliment the owners, managers, and workers of the Manitowoc Shipbuilding Company of Manitowoc, Wisconsin for the excellent submarines they built for us, and especially for the PUFFER. I have seen this vessel take the full measure of enemy punishment in one of the worst depth chargings of this War only to come back and even the score with the enemy during ensuing patrols. Although most of the credit for this comeback is due the former Commanding Officer, Commander F.G. Selby, no small part can be attributed to the inherent quality of the submarine itself. It is with great pleasure that the Commanding officer, officers, and men, present and past, of the U.S.S. PUFFER say to the Manitowoc Shipbuilding Company— "WELL DONE" [WPR].

17

Back to the States

54 or Bust

On August 17 the *Puffer* was near the equator and headed north on all engines—destination Subic Bay. The Navy had just announced a point system for discharging personnel. With the war over the spit and shine jobs were again in order. Upon arrival at Subic Bay the boat had to be ready for inspection. With the war over the War Patrol Reports were discontinued. However for the next month, the details of the events surrounding the *Puffer* and crew were contained in Golay's letters. Golay continued to refer to Capt. Dwyer as "Charlie" in his letters. "Stella" is Robert Weeks. Golay accounted the immediate concerns of the day.

> Everyone busy counting on their fingers—we picked up the news of the Navy point system in a broadcast this morning—we've had it broken off in us, the total probably includes all of the top one per cent—Darling (a wife) you're worth ten points, incidentally and that's enough—my total is about 45 and unless they lower the requirements it will be eight more months before I'm sprung—Mac has fifty-four points and is making a big, hairy thing out of himself rubbing it in—Stella [Weeks] and Russ [Frank] are sad with about thirty-five each, they have had [it with] the Navy...—the system seems to be unfair to the men with sea duty, as there is no discrimination made and no award for combat—the big problem is going to be to keep enough men in to man a respectable Navy—seems we picked the wrong service ... mostly today everyone is muttering to himself, counting on his fingers or laboring over columns of figures only to come up a little short of the coveted and elusive "54"—and those with the points go around smug and superior—Deem and Roberts are both happy as their Silver Stars are worth their weight in gold—Hayward is scrambling back to base after all of his enthusiastic tirades on becoming a civilian.
>
> The Japs still don't seem to have the word and fighting continues in most areas—I'm sure we won't stick around for pleasantries if they show up—have been piloting for twenty-four hours and we are steaming on four mains trying to make up a day—should cross the equator sometime tonite—the volunteers for extra lookout duty when the men are off watch exceeds the demand and the cigarette deck is cluttered with all shades and degrees of sun tan.
>
> The communicators don't realize the war is over and Bob [Biche] is snowed under with the decoding watch—our only concession to date has been to secure the watch on the high periscope—and we don't slow to convert the ballast tanks as they run dry of fuel.
>
> The days are perfect when the sun breaks thru, white clouds, the unbelievable blue sea and landfalls, a hazy blue turn into a lush green as we close.
>
> Tonite is shower nite for the wardroom and [Willie] Coleman [StM1c] is stowing the

passageway high with cases of crackers and bottles of coke syrup — the Pharmacist's Mate [Cali] secures early on the helm and goes down to the crew's mess to personally see that everyone swallows his atabrine tablet — the Quartermasters busy bringing the battle flag up-to-date and making miniature Jap flags.

[Harris] Steinke busy making the track chart for our report, he has become quite expert after seven runs — and to really portend the future, the brass on the bridge is losing the countless coats of paint and much elbow grease and brightwork polish are turning her into a shining hussy — and the peons are rebelling, it has been so long since the appearance of metal polish and the other weapons of peacetime that dormant memories are stirring [Golay].

Saturday, August 18

Much discussion of the point system on all sides — ten points for marriage certainly enhances a female's intrinsic value.

Steak with apple pie and ice cream, and we gorge on the best of our stores — someone will inherit most of our icebox of mutton — we hope.

Daily movies in an effort to show them all and be ready for a little horse trading when we get in — "Cabin in the Sky" today and [Carroll] Allen and [Willie] Coleman, our new messboy should be satiated with Lena Horne in three showings at least I suppose that explains their absence with Charlie ringing the pantry bell.

The limeys are firm in their intention of occupying Hong Kong and the Chinese just as determined to beat them there — will be interesting to follow and I'm pulling for the Chinese.

Laundry tonite and Charlie Wiseman is busy giving haircuts in the after torpedo room — I hope we will be able to store much of the spares and extra gear we have been carrying these past two years and we hope to reduce complement — and will have plenty of cooperation from the high scoring men — many sunbathers topside and no sun — much fresh air tho — flying fish stranded on deck, but they are too bony to eat with enjoyment or safety.

The Son of Heaven seems to have some subjects who haven't heard the word — we are still diving from planes although we don't hang around long enough to learn if they are friendly [*ibid.*].

Golay continued the letter on Sunday. He described the daily activities on the *Puffer*. He described his emotions about the end of the war and the future, which were probably similar to many other men on the boat. He reminisced about the ordinary events the war had taken away that he wanted to do and see in the fall months ahead.

Bob [Biche] was congratulating himself on catching the coding watch during this week, but he is swamped as the circuits are full of smoke-blowing and everyone is busy patting everyone else on the back.

Doubt if we will be moved off the ship when we get in which will not be good — the boats are badly crowded, even on patrol when one-third of the crew is on watch at a time, and we still have five men without bunks.

We have a new mess boy [Willie Coleman], a boogie fan who keeps the wardroom record player busy — it is piped into the 1MC and the crew can turn on their speaker any time — [Carroll] Allen revels in his new-found authority and is a slave driver — the most popular recordings are those of a program, all negro, called "Jubilee."

The last minute flail qualifying men for dolphins — it takes at least two hours to take a man thru the boat, so my days are full.

[We] have been fighting the inevitable let-down coming with the end of the war — a losing fight — the bridge watch has relaxed to little more than a daily sun bath and it seems to be my onerous task to drive them back — and this actively resented — but it can't be for long and I need jacking up myself as my only thoughts are of getting home and you and out of the Navy ... seems I'm drooling with self-sympathy this afternoon and will knock that off to tell you how much I love you and how much I long to be with you — you're irrevocably tied in with a tweed suit, soft white shirt, golf, cold fall weather, football, snow, pumpkin pie with whipped cream, females in sweaters, a filling station attendant animated by "fill her up," leaves turning on the trees, corn in shocks, magazines not sadly out of date, unlimited water in a shower — the lethargy and over-whelming tiredness that came with the end of the war have been replaced by a deep anticipation to leave all this and to steal your phrase to get down to the job of living — I love you much and would like to marry you [ibid.].

Monday, August 20, a day from Subic Bay, Golay's thoughts turned to the upcoming inspection by the admiral upon arrival. The crew and boat were expected to be spotless. Golay described the elaborate slight of hand which gave the boat the illusion of a normal naval vessel with a place for everything and everything in its place.

> Field Day today — the Admiral is reputed to make a tough and thorough inspection of arriving boats and we're going to have her spotless and shining — shower nite tonite and formal khaki pants, shirts with all the hardware installed are being laid out — preparing for an inspection in the Navy, particularly on a submarine is a battle of wits, trying to find hiding places off the beaten track for all the white elephants into the magazine, lock the hatch and then be the picture of chagrined surprise when the inspecting officer asks why the magazine is locked — and the key always conveniently leaves the ship with the Gunner's Mate who is promised mayhem if he botches the scheme up — and the pre-inspection party scrambling to keep out in front of the inspecting officer, loaded with cleaning gear, excess clothing and all the other accumulation that appears just when you think everything is in order — they circle around behind the inspecting officer, who is well aware of the subterfuge, and restore the compartment to the usual disorderly confusion.
>
> We will be tied up by noon tomorrow — it would be a break we can't expect if they pull us off and send us to rest camp after only two weeks underway — if we lose the "44-pointers" we'll no longer have to hot bunk — they are a happy lot, [Ray] Roberts with a wife waiting in Brooklyn, [Jay] Deem tired after too many runs, anxious to return to his old job — [Herbert] Hayward talking big, but after a rest of a few months, he'll ship over — and then there is [Phillip] McClure taunting us with his block "54" [ibid.].

Subic Bay Wait

Tuesday, August 21, Golay wrote about the arrival of the *Puffer* at Subic Bay. The boat was tied up to the tender next to other subs. The weather was rainy and the beer was equally as bad. It had not been a good day for Golay.

> We tied up shortly after noon, the Admiral down to welcome us and inspect the boat — physical and dental examinations, work and electronics conferences, cablegrams, all the usual flail designed to drive you muttering to the club and to drink.
>
> Charlie slowed to two engines yesterday afternoon and in spite of my repeated warnings that we would be late for the rendezvous, nothing happened — was up most of the nite trying to catch enough stars in the hazy moonlight horizon to learn where we were — and we were an hour an a half late, for which I caught hell and I've been sulking since.
>
> No mail — service from the states has been interrupted for no good reason, I'm sure, and much of our mail has been misdirected down south.
>
> The harbor is full of submarines and shipping — it has rained continuously since we tied up and she is pounding badly in the nest — not a good day — but the war is over and we're headed home ... even the beer was disappointing, export beer with labels of Budweiser, Ballantine, Schlitz and even Griesiedieck, to make us homesick — the bar opens at four and we were over promptly at three to admire the nudes, the sole décor and to officially open the bar — a rumor that the demand exceeded the supply and we greedily ordered a bale full and then felt ashamed not to make the effort to down the stuff— export beer, opaque and nauseating of formaldehyde

Crew members displaying the *Puffer* Battle Flag in Subic Bay. *Standing (left to right):* Ray Hartman and Harris Steinke. *Kneeling:* Frank Mays and Delmar Baumgartner (photograph courtesy of Frank Mays).

as a preservative — the rest camp a muddy puddle of Quonset huts and we are not disappointed in the least that we are not to go on leave — Russ [Frank] is aboard with the duty and is extremely indignant over the can of Pabst [a Minnesota beer] that I brought back to him — a righteous anger of a maligned Milwaukee-ite.

The troops are restless to go ashore, but have settled down to a round of visiting friends on the other boats of the nest — no doubt the sea stories are being elaborated — the boat was clean for the inspection and the Admiral was complimentary — our battle flag and miniature Jap flags, Charlie will fly with the slightest excuse.

We are not going to refit and will have to do our own work, but we will be able to give up some of our stores and "fish," which will help — looks like everyone with enough points will be pulled for transportation home — the navy will tie the ships up and throw up their hands if Truman declares the emergency ended [*ibid.*].

Wednesday, August 22, was not much better for the *Puffer* or Golay. The bad weather continued and the boats were pulled away from the tender. Each boat was anchored separately. The possibility of unloading unnecessary materials onboard was now minimal. There was plenty of food. Mail reached the *Puffer* with news of the celebration in San Francisco. The movies taken during the Eighth War Patrol were shown.

Boat troubles today to bore you with — the choppy water of the bay and constant showers plague us and keep us aboard — we were pounding badly with the nest pitching in the heavy ground swells — ...I felt that we should go out and anchor — the Divisions put a relief crew aboard this afternoon and we sloshed ashore for the wettest (literally) beer party of my experience — God it can rain here, and there seems to be no way to turn this shower off — the beer improved, perhaps we had a bad batch last nite ... Charlie just came aboard ... and broke up our poker game with a severe, glowering disapproval — the man just can't endure the sight of anyone enjoying themselves aboard ship — however I won't complain too much as I cashed in a winner for the first time in memory — enough to make a liberty next week.

The bay is full of shipping and the water is polluted for swimming, the seas show little inclination to be pacified and the monsoon season of eight months is due to start any time — we may not get alongside again to unload all the excess gear we are burdened with.

The supply ships are piling up in this area and our menus are full of fresh frozen strawberries, peaches, etc — stateside beef once more, and we give up the last of our sheep.

Bob [Weeks] had a letter today, our first mail — from his mother and father with clippings telling of the rioting in Market St. celebrating the surrender of Japan — not a nice story and a reflection on the Navy — but still if we had been in, I can name too many of the crew who would have been in the midst of the festivities [*ibid.*].

Subic Bay waters continued rough on August 23, and Golay continued to find the transition to the peacetime Navy equally rough. The laxness of submarine service was being replaced with the Navy he experienced prior to the war while on the cruiser *Minneapolis*. Dwyer, also a prewar surface ship veteran, more easily reverted to the old Navy ways. All members of the crew that were not regular Navy had enlisted for "Duration plus 6" or six months beyond the end of the war. The point system was still a hot issue.

Very rough in the bay this morning we are swinging at anchor waiting for the storm to play itself out — the war is over for sure, the Old Man squawked last nite because we were not showing anchor lights and this morning because there was no anchor ball — archaic impedimenta we lost back beyond memory — we are waiting the suggestion of white gloves and a telescope for the duty officer.

Carl is getting away on leave until next Tuesday which will be a welcome respite — a departure only tragic to him because climbing down the ladder into the boat, the boat lurched and he dropped his overnite bag full of whisky and broke most of his trading stock — the coolies are still sobering up after the beer picnic of yesterday and the constant rain prevents us from accomplishing much work ... three officers and two CPO's will be able to get away for a few days leave, (but not the crew).

Will pass up the movie tonite, it has been a long time since Abbott and Costello were funny — still no mail.

BuPPers letters are flying like mad, each of them entailing more work for the Yeoman and information about points, classifications and discharge information — haven't seen Mac [Phillip McClure] this evening, but he will be squelched by the latest directive which indicates June 1947 as the earliest he can get out — he has been flaunting his fifty-four points before all of us.

[Harris] Steinke fell down a hatch and may have fractured his leg, the Pharmacist's mate [Cali] just took him to the tender for an x-ray — if we are to leave here soon we will take about twenty-five extra men home for discharge and no one will complain of the discomfort once we head east.

Everyone is completely tired of the war and the unnatural femaleless existence [*ibid.*].

For Golay Friday, August 24, was a better day. The storm had quieted and the Old Man was gone for four days. The waiting was still making life difficult. When would the boats head east for Pearl Harbor and finally home? The hot weather was not making the boat hospitable. Finally, he remembered the good news of a long awaited promotion.

The storm outside has quieted much during the nite but the ground swells are still running too strongly to go back alongside [the tender] — the largest complication in this humid existence is finding enough to keep the men occupied — much field day and inventory of stores — anyway it is a respite from Charlie and that is good.

Dick [Heehs] has the duty today and is the most dependable of all the watch officers, I sometimes wonder what a kick in the face all the fresh caught reserve officers are going to find when they have to work for a living — the Navy has certainly not been able to accomplish this.

The bay is filled with rumors of all kinds, mostly about going home — and every other imaginable place.

Tokyo broadcast today of the casualties from the atomic bomb, 60,000 dead in Hiroshima more causalities than suffered by Britain in the blitz — quite a persuader.

It looks clear enough to show the movie topside tonite, the boat is hot from successive battery charges and the air conditioning plant is inefficient with the hatch open.

The engineers have found cracked lines and believe they will have number four back in commission by Sunday.

Joe the Horse and I are still feuding, he managed to attract one of the many native boats alongside and was trading ships stores for tuba, a nauseating but potent drink made of coconut milk — no trouble with liberty parties, a few hours ashore and they come back aboard to see the nightly movie.

I forgot the important news, Capt. Scott our division commander and a hell of a nice guy signaled over this morning that I was included in the last promotion and sent a boat out to take me over for a physical — and tonite the crew at quarters gave me new oak leaves and threw me into the bay — will buy a box of cigars tomorrow and the deed will have been consummated — it has been a long time, 33 months and we had given up hope — will mean some back pay.

A little mail came thru today postmarked the 13th and 14th in the states and a news item tonite explains the lack of transport, all transport planes are being assembled in Okinawa to fly the occupation forces into Japan, much of the combatant Navy and a few submarines are going up — I would almost be willing to trade our chances of going home to anchor in Tokyo Bay [*ibid.*].

August 25 Golay wrote about the latest rumors, of which there were many. In spite of being colorblind he passed his physical for advancement. Clara had returned to the United States and that idea filled most of the letter to her.

We are deluged with rumors and little action — no one seems to know for sure what's in store for us— they deny it right and left, but it looks to me like the end of the war caught the Navy with its collective pants down — had the physical for promotion today and am elegant in gold oak leaves— as usual they threw the color charts— those damn pages of multi-colored dots that are numbers to most people, but are indecipherable mysteries to me [*ibid.*].

Sunday, August 26, brought news about getting home and the *Puffer*'s endorsement of the last run. Everyone was required to take atabrine to ward off malaria. Atabrine had a nasty side effect of turning the skin yellowish. Some of its other side effects were headaches, nausea, and vomiting, and in a few cases it produced a temporary psychosis. No wonder no one wanted to take the medicine. Golay wrote positively about the Philippines, a country he became an authority on as an economist at Cornell University. In the 1960s he returned to the Philippine Islands with his family.

Mac's [Phillip McClure] orders came in last nite and he will not be pleased, for it looks like his chances of getting home are lessened, however as most yeomen he is a big dealer and will probably be waiting on the dock in charge of the WAVE line handlers as he has promised.

Finally received the endorsement of out last patrol report, the usual smoke-blowing, and they up us to the minimum tonnage for a successful run — suspect that the Admiral was impressed by our Technicolor movies.

Darling, you must be prepared for this, we have to take atabrine here for malaria prophylaxis and if you've never seen a jaundiced atabrine addict it will be a shock, we are yellower than our little friends and still do not compare with the old hands who have been on the course for months— maybe we will bleach out the color on the long jaunt home — still nothing more

A shark's mouth was painted on the bow of the *Puffer* by Robert Kennedy while the boat was anchored in Subic Bay (photograph courtesy of Ellis Branchcomb).

> definite than rumors ... we are provisioned and fueled and chomp at the bit waiting for the word.
>
> We gorge exclusively on apples, oranges and ice cream ... bottled cokes, the first in months.
>
> I maligned the weather in my earlier letters, the days are warm and the green hills look much like Hawaii, each deep valley filled with misty rain clouds.
>
> Attended mass this morning on the tender at 0530—an impressive service with the sun rising in the east and all the ships at anchor coming to life with bugle calls, bosun pipes, sloshing down hoses and flag hoists.
>
> Flailing around today trying to draw our beer ration to issue to the liberty party and finally gave up in disgust—liberty consists of four hours ashore, submerged alternately in mud and dust drinking beer which is unpalatable with preservatives—but still the *Puffer* manages to alienate the S.P.'s and it is my job each morning to go over and pacify the tender Exec.
>
> Captain Scott called me in this morning, a regular but pleasant summons, to show me a dispatch indicating that I have a second citation approved.
>
> We are trading our library of transcriptions—no more "Rum and Coca Cola"—[Carroll] Allen just insisted that this could wait until I made up my laundry ready to be taken over to the tender, he is no respecter of shiny collar marks [*ibid.*].

On August 27 mail arrived, which was good for the morale of Golay and the rest of the crew. The contents of Golay's letters were probably much the same as other crew members. Family and wives or girlfriends were anxious to hear from the stranded sailors and longed for their quick return. The waiting and rainy weather continued. Morale was dampened by a rumor that submarines were not to be included in the Tokyo Bay surrender ceremony. Daydreaming of the future was a way to pass the time.

> Two more wonderful letters from you in which you say the things that I long most to have you say to me, that you are waiting—anxious to have me there ... the long days are filled with much work—you should have a cable soon and a deluge of letters, when I think what an awful

beating a patrol can be without mail, it makes me anxious that you have not heard from me in two months.

The poker games are rather rugged with much money in evidence.

The roster of ships entering Tokyo Bay with the occupation forces does not include submarines, which seems a cruel slight, I know that is the universal opinion of the wardroom, everyone is more than a little perturbed and feels hurt — we're still sifting the rumors, if we could go to any port in the world — our officers should return from leave tomorrow and Dick and both Bobs should be able to get away and if we hang around long enough it will be my turn on Friday — the rain has resumed ... the war is over — the boat next to us had a fifteen minute session of calisthenics this morning — a reluctant crew took quite lightly.

Maybe we will be back in time for the football game we didn't see — and there will be snow for the first time in five years— and there'll be you beautiful and affectionate and desirable — and that's mostly what I think of, all the hours of the day [ibid.].

With nothing left to do, the crew decorated the boat. Robert Kennedy directed the operation, which included a large puffer fish on both sides of the conning tower. Battle flags were added for each ship sunk or damaged and palm trees for gun actions. In addition the bow of the boat was painted with a shark's mouth and the stern with a bee stinger. The decorations became a competition among the boats and the honor of the *Puffer* was defended.

She is elegant today with a huge *Puffer* insignia (as on the letterhead) in color on the conning tower fairwater and Kennedy will stencil the miniature flags tomorrow — the idea is contagious and all the boats are colorful with their devices— and probably tomorrow afternoon we can paint over them all when some brass hat takes a dim view ... the most important crisis of today was an invasion in force by one of the boats from the port nest, a flanking movement aimed at capture of our paint gun —frustrated when we paraded our power, Joe the Horse and three hundred pound Charlie Wiseman — we'll need it tomorrow to paint the conning tower [ibid.].

Pride ran high after a copy of the Unit Citation was made public for the Fourth War Patrol. The recreation facilities were improved with the application of some Yankee ingenuity. Golay's arch nemesis Reynolds was after him again.

Saw a copy today of our recommendation for a Unit Citation, very thrilling, but hardly recognizable.

[I] was ashore for a few hours this afternoon for a swim, they have thrown a dam across one of the crystal clear mountain streams above the rest camp and have made a fine swimming hole with rafts to lie on and soak up the sun — it was hard to quit and return to the ship.

Movies topside tonite, the boat is hot and the evenings are cool — will ask [Carroll] Allen to move a cot topside tonite, the most efficient rain producer yet discovered...

Mac [McClure] and the other officers did not return from leave today, probably they have a good thing there and can't give it up.

A letter today from Kansas City with news of the celebration on the 15th [VJ-Day]— by the time we return, celebrating will be frowned upon.

Bob [Biche] has all his engines in commission ... the tender will no longer approve work items, which is the best rumor of today.

[Arthur] Reynolds heckling me for permission to organize an expedition to hunt for his father, whose ship he believes is someplace out here — and so soon after the flail in Perth when he caught me in an absent moment and I gave him permission to bring his girl aboard [ibid.].

August 29 was no different than the previous days, more waiting. The day was spiced with WACs aboard. With the war behind him, Golay romantically recalled life on the boat and his fond memories of crew members, sights, sounds, and smells. However, no matter how pleasant those memories were in his postwar state of mind, Golay wanted to move on to a life of his making.

We swing easily and restlessly in the nest — why don't they send us along — we are ready to get underway for home on ten or even one minute's notice.

[I] am driving down in the morning with Mac [McClure] to catch his plane — a five hour trip which will be a treat after a monotonous week aboard — the hills are beautiful and make you restless to go ashore and tramp around — but they take a dim view of that as the guerrillas go out each nite to dig out the few remaining Japs holed up within sight of the bay — the native boats, little more than hollow logs with outriggers come alongside each day loaded with the small and delicious bananas that grow everywhere ashore — and their few souvenirs are eagerly bargained for by the sailors with money to burn and no place to spend it.

She has a new coat of paint and looks smart again — trust clean up below decks in the morning — WACs aboard today to stop all time and work — women are a nuisance out here — as long as there aren't enough to go around — half hour before their boat came alongside a messenger down from the O.D. to give us the word to have everyone in uniform, and from that moment on all work stops, the rails are lined by sailors — uninhibited sailors — and they all are — General Ben Lear would go mad to hear the whistling. [General Lear, a strict disciplinarian, disciplined soldiers who called to passing women while on maneuvers.]

Sailors have much more fun than people anyway — they devour comic books, spend hours talking about the last liberty — waste hours visiting on the other boats, an obvious evasion of work — an open ice box with the best food obtainable — there's an easy-going camaraderie and that they should be able get along so well together in such close confinement is amazing — this has turned into a recruiting officer's pep talk.

There will be many things that have become a part of life that will take adjustment to replace — the sea always beautiful and often friendly — the noises, engines, motors, hydraulic gear — the smells, hot electrical insulation, diesel fumes, the battery gassing at the end of a charge — living like a sandwich, unable to escape from people.

Some things won't be missed — the out-house with ten valves to open and close to operate — binoculars nudging your conscience to use them — the high periscope obstinate in a rough sea.

The vivid memories of Allen and Patton, Joe the Horse, Reynolds — all of them — packed like sardines in the forward room for a movie — the spontaneous grin that appeared when we fired our last fish of a run — with loud, underwater explosions holding no threat — we are going home — the sunrises and sunsets of the 4–8 watches — the Control Room and the satisfaction of knowing exactly what everything was for, what it can do, and how to use it — making a landfall — the reception when we return from a run — Golden Gate Bridge to welcome us home — the ship heeling with full rudder and, the powerful surge shuddering the ship as Maneuvering answers a "flank" bell.

But I want these things to be only memories — to be married to you promises me all things, more happiness than I thought possible — and a purpose that never existed before — and salvation from an oppressive mediocrity — you'll take much living up to — and I want to work at that all the rest of my life [*ibid.*].

On August 30, Golay took a trip to Manila to put Phillip McClure on a plane home. He saw for the first time a country that he would grow to love in the future. He criticized America for our colonial policy, a subject he wrote extensively about while teaching at Cornell University.

That was the most satisfying shower I've had and its wonderful to feel and smell clean once more — Bob [Biche], Stella [Weeks] and I drove down to Manila today with Mac to catch his plane — 140 km, which if I can recall any high school General Science is about 100 miles and felt like five hundred before we got in tonite — and after we reached Manila we had to go on to Cavite — a long, hot dusty day — Manila was a new experience to me, but would be an old story to you — the destruction even after six months of rubble clearing and rebuilding is complete and thorough — and we failed to meet Doug [MacArthur] who is on his way to Tokyo.

The livelihood of the people are the American troops — the villages and cities a succession of pathetic, friendly, taverns, cabarets and gin mills with each town supporting a "Duffy's Tavern," "Stork Club," "Trocadero," "Top of the Mark," etc — but none of them seemed to do any business, even after dark — and the bill boards are beginning to bloom again all extolling the harmless, nourishing merit of "Old 98," "Eagle," "Four Freedoms" and many other old established brands of Scotch Whiskey — and Colin Glencannon and all his Scotch compatriots must be whirling in their graves— and the Army keeps apace with frequent scoreboards recording the deaths to date from bootleg whiskey full of fusol oil and other poisons— more fatalities and blindness than would be experienced in a campaign — the inflation must leave the people helpless and desperate — and the soldiers and sailors ashore their pockets full of money accentuate the problem — but still there is no comparison to the Japanese occupation currency which is sold in bales as souvenirs and called "Mickey Mouse" money.

The plain north of Manila a beautiful panorama of rice fields that promise much to these people — their economy dependent on water buffalos, ungainly vicious looking beasts that look, a little apologetic for their ersatz fierceness— they have the outlook and disposition of Ferdinand and each is tended by a very small, very naked brown Philippine baby only large enough to cling to the neck of the beast.

Our colonial policy, paternalistic and much abused intensified itself here — the Filipinos are loyal and still worship the Americans— their troops are proud and smart in their cast-off American equipment and the heroic stories of the resistance here are not fiction — they drove the Japs mad with their indifference to cruelty and to the later Jap policy of kindness.

Travel is simplified, everyone hitchhikes with the Army convoys which eventually reach Manila packed, with a colorful noisy, uninhibited load. And the driver who runs out of gas turns into the nearest air field or Sea Bee camp and bums a tank full of gas— the acres of maturing rice paddies drained of water supporting the economy with acres of drying GI summer tans, pounded clean on the rocks lining the streams.

But the only impression we could carry back is of dust and more dust — it was good to return and soak in a shower with little muddy rivulets washing the day's accumulation of dust off— we have been placed on eight hours notice and I'm tired, and am going to bed — today |I've had Manila and particularly Cavite, which can only be reached by a succession of the biggest chuck holes in the road, mislabeled National Highway — a succession of Warrensburg street intersections of PWA vintage when Chris Johnson was city engineer — Darling I'd like to report that the Red Cross took good care of us today and we gave their doughnuts a beating [*ibid.*].

Off to Pearl Harbor

On August 31 word finally came of the impending departure from Subic Bay. The first of the month was an adequate event for the Navy to begin the departure.

Mail closed today without notice and we are getting under way soon for a long wonderful voyage in your direction — the Admiral is coming aboard each boat this afternoon to say good-bye — it will be a little sad only for him as his command is disintegrating and he will be left an Admiral with no ships to command.

Everyone is wearing a grin all over their face — we are going home — the tender with her brood of eighteen boats all in one nest is a beautiful sight each boat is flying their battle flags and the devices have been painted on all Conning Towers— and mama hen not to be outdone has dressed ship with their signal flags— this morning has been a succession of passing honors, a tribute to each of the British boats underway, each boat is rendered honors as they pass the nest — until you go below to accomplish any work — they are a good lot and fight their ships well.

We are hot bunking about twenty men and have two new officers— the tender has been loading men from landing craft all morning, men with point totals approaching the coveted

"45"—the ships and storerooms filled with cots and hammocks, they are rumored to be taking on 2800 men for transportation.

As in accordance with old Navy custom, they use the last morning, filled with the thousand things to do, to shift the boats around in the nest and we have had the maneuvering watch stationed all morning—I still feel grimy after the dust of yesterday—this is one boat no one will miss, the men have returned promptly from liberty since we were put on eight hours notice—expect we will be steaming in formation with the attendant flail of station keeping and needling the controllerman back in maneuvering until they give the exact turns asked for.

Later [that day]—submarines with running lights—and that is news—three columns of six boats with the tender shooing her brood along—suppose everyone was caught short and had to rig a stern light—we were underway from Subic Bay about 1500, destination Pearl Harbor and five thousand miles closer to you—we will be past the narrows of Verde Island Passage in another hour and I can turn it over to Dauplaise the Chief Quartermaster and turn in—lights to cut in for positions once more.

The Old Man could make this a pleasant trip with time to sun bathe topside, a relaxation of war-enforced life jackets, red glasses, high periscope, etc—but then knowing Charlie, the prospect is doubtful—the last time we were in these waters a ten ship convoy came out of the passage and before the morning was over our fish were gone and we were headed for the Golden Gate—a providential convoy, for it made it possible for me to be in the states while you were still in Washington—you may be aghast at all the details, but censorship has been lifted east of the 180th meridian and that will be my first chance to get off mail—it has been a full day, but a good one to experience.

Darling, when can we be married—Charlie is having the time of his life playing submarine and has the O.D.'s talking to themselves—the most essential quality of a *Puffer* officer is to be psychic, for reading the Old Man's would be the only way to pacify the man—but being a short timer I can do these last few weeks standing on my head—each day will be magnified knowing that you are home [*ibid.*].

On September 1 the long trip to Pearl Harbor started. The submarines could at best make 400 miles per day. That rate meant at least a 20 day voyage to Hawaii. Golay continued to poke fun at the transition of the submarines to a postwar Navy mentality. Censorship had finally been lifted. Golay told of one misled crew member, James Urbanski, who enlisted for four years, instead of duration plus six months. His sister was the talk of the boat; she attended the same finishing school as Grace Kelly.

We just took departure from San Bernardino Straits—a good day piloting and sight seeing—the islands are green and lovely from out here—Dauplaise and I can go off watch—taking departure is logging the last good position while piloting and setting the Dead Reckoning Keeper—Watch Officer's Guide, Knight's Seamanship and Rules of the Nautical Road much in demand—and the Wardroom full of argument and discussion of formation keeping and all the attendant visual signals—these are going to be long, dull days with little news of which to write—the tender making colors this evening and catching us flat-footed—and the *Sea Owl* promised us WAVE line handlers when we tied up in Pearl.

They've lifted censorship and there should be a million things to tell you.

We have just enough grass on her bottom that our two tired engines can't quite keep up with the youngsters fresh out of the builder's yards—orders for two boats of our squadron to the east coast and partial commission.

Dick [Heehs] received another shipment of popcorn while in Subic and he and Bob [Biche] just brought in a huge dishpan full—and I'm stuck with the job of making cokes—the penalty of mastering the fizz-bottle—a strain on my mechanical aptitude ... am envious of all the packages that come to the others—Russ [Frank] makes out best, with a huge box of food of all kinds every week or so—and Dick makes out well too—but what the hell am I beefing about with my locker still full of fruit cake—

The helmsmen are all folding up — three of them are off watch now — the Wardroom strangely quiet with Mac [McClure] gone — an inoffensive extrovert — and they are rare — he has been trying to talk himself out of the Navy after eight years and has Lorraine convinced — and what women wouldn't be enthusiastic over the prospect of her man leaving the Navy — he takes much knowing, but is a good guy and dependable, which is important.

The *Puffer* is changed, everyone grinning and turning-to with a smile — now would be the time to have us available for a V-J celebration — we could do it justice now.

[James] Urbanski is sad, of all those aboard, seems when he enlisted, he was told one thing and signed for something else and the Yeoman in checking his record finds that he will be around on a regular enlistment for some time — he is the best seaman aboard — completely lacking in ambition to get ahead in the Navy, he refuses to strike for a rate — he was a good high school athlete back in Pennsylvania and has two scholarships to the University of Pennsylvania — one an athletic and one for scholarship — and unless he finds a loop-hole he's stuck in the Navy for four more years — he's a little bitter — he writes good letters home, I would be wise to copy them — and his pin-up girl is a picture of his sister, a Powers Model, who has everyone aboard whistling — usually a man with a good looking sister is the go-between in originating correspondence between his shipmates and his sister — but we are all too awed with Ski's sister [*ibid.*].

Three days later on September 4 Golay wrote of the events en route to Pearl Harbor. Dwyer allowed the men on deck for relaxed sun bathing. At the same time the independent ways of the Submarine Service during the war were paradoxically replaced with regular Navy protocol. Work was found to keep the crew busy. It was obvious to Golay that some of the boats must remain in the Pacific. He hoped the *Puffer* would not be one of those subs. All the crew wanted to return to the states as soon as possible. He was amused by the contradictory policies which came from various branches of Naval Administration.

Another steaming day — and still another way to look at it — 14 times 24 or 336 miles and leaving only ten days to go — the monotony relieved by the unnecessarily complicated maneuvers to clear the outer columns of the formation so the center column can dive.

The bridge crowded with sun worshipers — in search of a sun, as it has been overcast since we left San Bernadino Strait — their Mae West's a 180 out of phase and drooping below the belt to give a non-cooperative sun a maximum chance — [Jay] Deem, [Ray] Roberts, [Herbert] Hayward, [Siegel] Pierson and the other short timers looking happy and very smug — one of our new officers and still another of the new men call Kansas City home and with eight of us who can qualify, we're planning the final word in homecoming celebration — we are drinking our way thru the accumulated beer and [Carroll] Allen will be glad to see it go from his cluttered wardroom passage way — which doubles as the cargo hold.

Lunch today a gastroatomic mixture of lobster salad, ice cream and beer — Doc [Thomas Cali] busy extolling the value of salt tablets and making few sales — Charlie busy accumulating bed sores which keeps him out of our hair.

The formation is acquiring polish and smoothness and the O.D.s are becoming acquainted with stadimeters and alidades — it used to be a good day when the J.O. was allowed to man either back in 1940 — the boat immaculate after Field Day — re-conversion on the *Puffer*, a painful process of starting all the "make work" records and inventories that permitted a naval officer to have a conscience in peace time.

The watchword "Things are tougher on the *Puffer*."

Too many boats are being ordered to the states and we all know that not all the boats can be accommodated in the yards at once — and that isn't good.

Up early with Duke [Donald Duguid] for stars — the tender navigator rather obviously setting the clocks ahead an hour — long before we reach the meridian — an old privilege to permit Navy to eat a leisurely lunch before LAN [Local Apparent Noon] occurring between 1300 and 1400 and evening stars after dinner.

The movie today "My Favorite Wife" and the snatches drifting back thru the wardroom sound vaguely familiar.

It would have been interesting to be with the squadron going to Tokyo, but still would not trade willingly with them.

Re-conversion is developing into something akin to multiple births—the Chief of Naval Operations, BuPers, and all the other Bureaus participating—and no one seems to coordinate policy—it would help if they would make up their minds, define a policy and method—each successive dispatch either changes some short-lived procedure or introduces another—one today permitting Naval Officers to wear civilian clothes outside of working hours—where in hell would we keep another wardrobe on a submarine—and no doubt we can look forward to white in Pearl and mine are cached away in some good hiding place which I have long forgotten.

No more censorship and tomorrow's episode will be full of radar and all the other dark secrets that have been thoroughly explained in recent magazines—the TIME of August 14 with enough information about the atomic bomb that each house holder should be running off a batch like home brew.

Bob Staff, one of our new officers, a trade school lieutenant with much carrier experience is the authority on station keeping, flag hoists, signals, etc—it has been so long since we had any of that it means learning it all over.

Waiting restlessly to reach you [*ibid.*].

A few days later on September 7 Golay gave the latest developments on the *Puffer*. It was still unclear where the boat would be stationed. As Golay suspected a couple of the boats were left behind at Guam. Injuries took a toll on the helmsmen and other key men. Thoughts were turning to the pending arrival at Pearl Harbor. The exploders were thrown over the side making the torpedoes harmless. Golay paid tribute to the excellent job done by the Pharmacist's Mates on board submarines.

We pick up another hour tonite and suddenly it's very late for me to be up, even to write to you—and now we can't wear civilian clothes, and someone back in the Bureau had their mind made up for them.

Still another helmsman on the binnacle list as Joe the Horse [Kronberg] injures his hand—and our last baker takes to his bed—and the poor navigator is cutting a tooth—maybe a wisdom tooth, but he sure is in one hell of a bad humor—and each day the tender pulls out of formation with one of the boats to transfer a patient—and then the Yeoman come off the wheel to catch up on all the records—wonder if [Carroll] Allen can steer.

Our turn to dive tomorrow—hope someone remembers to secure the air to the whistle—no chance to pick up fishing net floats—we might throw a man over the side and use that as an excuse—they seem to have written off our chances of making up a day and we settle down to a steady two engine speed—the tender showing movies topside tonite, but our station is too far astern, even using the high periscope—one result of peace, we can pick up short wave news broadcasts that formerly were jammed by the Nips.

We lose three boats that must be a little sad to see us steam on without them—they are stopping to visit with George and their chances of seeing the Golden Gate this year are practically nonexistent—we take the exploders out of the fish and give them the deep-six—and everyone breathes easier once they're over the side—today was a good day, much sun and the slight sea on the bow gives her a soothing rocking motion—Dick [Richard Heehs] and John moaning because the clocks go ahead and they have to give up their cribbage game to go on watch—you might send along a teething ring.

Each time we leave something behind—the equator, date line, Guam and all the other names—its impossible not to feel a little nostalgic, even if we are headed home—and wonder if it is for the last time.

An occasional plane out to check up on us—circling warily until they're sure we all have the word—a new laundry business in the after room to renovate whites for liberty in Pearl—and

Carl has [Leonard] Rama, one of the Electrician Mates strikers, an ex-tailor in to survey the possibility of stretching his whites.

The sound gear idle for weeks now — wonder if it still works.

The crew takes much satisfaction out of the lifting of censorship — if they could realize what an impersonal act censoring letters becomes, they wouldn't resent it.

I wish I knew what was going to happen to the *Puffer*, then we could make definite plans.

Doc [Thomas Cali] busy with all his patients running from one room to another — he takes a beating — preparing trays of food for each of his patients, dress their cuts and wounds— rub them with alcohol — give enemas— and mother them generally, seeing that they take the vitamins, iron pills, salt tablets, atabrine — he's a good man and has a hell of a responsibility on his shoulders— when you imagine all the situations that they have come face-to-face with on war patrols and they take care of their men with gentleness and compassion — was reading of one boat that sailed with an undiagnosed case of mumps and eventually had only one watch section on their feet — and the three appendectomies that had to be performed on early patrols off the empire — with no Coronados to come out and take off the sick men [*ibid.*].

On September 9, another key crew member was on the sick list — the baker. A new point system was created, but no orders for the *Puffer*. The new slogan on the boat hoped for a return by October 15.

[John] Shiflett is much improved, which we have been hoping for — the seas have picked up so much in the past twenty-four hours that it would be tricky business to transfer him — Doc suspected a ruptured appendix and peritonitis, but looks like he'll settle for something not nearly so serious— Duke and Stella a miniature edition of a watch section — one lifting the other around the middle so he can read the compass repeater for a bearing — [Peter] McCarthy trying his hand at baking, with Shiflett off watch, and taking a ribbing from the crew when his bread fails to rise and the mess cooks pile three loaves, one on the other to make a respectable sized loaf for slicing — but he redeemed himself with pound cake and cranberry sauce for shortcake.

A Honolulu broadcast station and Polaris high enough for a sight tonite, the first time in months.

Bill [Wilfrid Delafield] drops the atomic news that we are out of potatoes— and our record of standing short on every patrol remains intact.

One of the radiomen just came by and says the revised Navy point system is coming in — and probably means more work for the harassed yeomen.

Shower nite tonite — and issue of *Liberty* with styles in swim suits— the French influence of which you wrote, very much in evidence — and interesting too.

Not a beard left aboard which has the same significance as birds in predicting landfall — she's beginning to pound heavily and the O.D.'s blow up each hour with the turbo-blower as she rolls the air out of the tanks thru the flood openings— we're losing time and may be a day late — the principle reason for not transferring Shiflett to the tender yesterday — Carl was afraid of the wrath of the Squadron Commander if we held up unnecessarily — it seems that the safety and comfort of a man is not of sufficient importance now to out-weigh the military considerations.

Dick O'Kane and some of his crew were found in a prison camp and there should be survivors from some of the other boats including the persistent rumor that Mush Morton and some of the men of the Wahoo got ashore — and survivors of the *Houston* are appearing from prison camps.

The bridge is wet as they ship an occasional seas— and keeping station, can't quite persuade Duke [Duguid] to slow down for sights.

The Doctor's mate a psychologist as well as medical practitioner — humoring Charlie's hypochondria to get back in his good graces— he told the Squadron Medical Officer down in Perth that he was a lazy, blank, non-combatant — the Old Man got him aboard and cast off the lines just ahead of the SP's— right now they confer daily searching for an imagined allergy that keeps Charlie's throat sore, and will soon be a contributing cause to his annex — and the daily session with the atomizer — precedes the elaborate, voluntary treatise on allergies which have most of us passing up meals — we intercepted a visual message from one of the boats listing the symptoms of a man that they suspected had Dengue fever and before the message is in, Carl is nodding his head in agreement — and he is still taking atabrine — the course stopped when we got underway.

The slogan now — "Home for Navy Day" — it was a year ago yesterday that we returned to the states — can you steer, there's a vacancy on the *Puffer* right now for a helmsman — several of them — orders for boats every nite, but no mention of us [*ibid.*].

On September 11, the *Puffer* crossed the International Dateline. Golay reported on the health of the crew; the progress of the flotilla of submarines back to Pearl; and plans for the submarines, Navy Day, and his personal future, all of which were yet to be determined. Golay commented on Truman, a fellow Missourian. The contribution of the submarines to the war effort began to trickle out in the Navy Department reports, and Golay knew the price had been high. In spite of his complaints, Golay was proud to have served on the *Puffer*.

Yesterday was the 11th too — we should be in before they close the net next Friday, but we're eight hours behind and the head seas hold us back — no more trim dives to save time — and one boat with an O.D. with a broken leg hesitantly suggests that they would like to transfer the patient to the tender.

Our baker, [John] Shiflett, is sitting up now and taking nourishment — and [Peter] McCarthy will soon be delivered from his non-rising dough — only one man left on the sick list, which is a new high for the run.

The formality of interviewing each of the men to ask if they want to re-enlist in the Regular Navy, or, when they go out, if they wish to go into the Fleet Reserve — but few sales.

Bob comes off watch to get experience navigating which leaves me with even more time on my hands — and the task of filling all the time with a semblance of work —

My nite to make the cokes again — the water is inviting, and we could call away swimming with a cargo net over the side if we were alone.

We've been anticipating it all week, and it happened this morning — one of the boats lost steering and had the formation scrambling out of their way — and two hours later sheepishly crawled back into their station — but the commodore busted them back to the end of their column where they could do little harm.

Charlie busy with the Register, looking up signal numbers to see where we will be when they line up to enter port — and for once we have someone junior to us.

[Arthur] Reynolds advocating unionism before a heckling audience in the crew's mess, but he holds his own in any argument.

The new evaluation of overseas duty and still few additions to the list of men eligible for discharge — if repeated adding of columns could change their totals, we'd have no crew.

We only have dispatches referring to Submarines, but imagine that all the fleet is heading east, converging on Pearl and the west coast — there are a few indications that a review of the fleet is planned for Navy Day — Roosevelt was a good sailor, and looked the part bundled up in his boat cloak, but imagine Truman will cut about the same nautical figure that Coolidge was — his only concession was seasickness and a sailor straw hat — and if they do take the fleet to the west coast for Navy Day, I'll show you San Francisco even lovelier with the fleet swinging at anchor and the hundreds of searchlight beams stabbing into the darkness.

Do you think you would like a short tour of Navy life if we operate in the states — if I can stay in rank for another ten months, we'll have enough money to return to school for the graduate work that I need — but that's out if we're sent back out here — its hard to make plans with the future so indefinite.

At least you know that we are safe, the Navy Department has released word that all boats are back in port except for those previously listed as missing — forty-nine of them by our count — at least forty-six of those operational — one fifth of all the fleet boats that made war patrols — and our pay and a half does not seem such a racket — our casualties when compared with the number involved will be higher, far higher than any other service — wonder if it's wrong to feel a little proud of that [*ibid.*].

September 13 the *Puffer* prepared for arrival at Pearl Harbor. The same thought was on the minds of the crew and Golay — what will be the future of the *Puffer*?

> Shower nite tonite — whites out for renovation and modernizing with new "crows" [rating badges with spread-eagle insignia] — [Willie] Coleman muttering at the injustice of all the new boots to shine.
>
> Should have the dope on entry and berths tonite — we are halfway prepared for whatever may be in store for us — refit, overhaul, de-commissioning, de-mobilization — but if later directives have not undone most of our work, I shall be surprised — and also the yeomen.
>
> I have a lot of letters to mail to tide you over until I can talk to you.
>
> Channel fever and Bob [Biche] and I will get little sleep tonite with the suspense of a landfall — and the clocks go ahead another hour which make the nite even shorter.
>
> If they drop the point total to forty, we will release only thirteen men, which gives you an idea of how reluctant the Navy is.
>
> A blanket will feel good tonite — we're running into the northeast trades which will cool the boat.
>
> If they really intend to make the buoy on schedule, we better go to four engines soon.
>
> Two months of our mail is still missing — this should be the place for it to overtake us — rumor has much mail lost on the *Indianapolis* [Golay].

Friday, September 14, the *Puffer* was safely at Pearl Harbor and mail had arrived. This was the last Golay letter. The *Puffer* stayed a few days at Pearl Harbor and then was ordered to San Francisco. Golay was ready to go immediately, but the boat remained three days.

> Bob and I were up early for the flail of forming up for entry into the harbor and it lived up to expectations — the final order of entry having no resemblance to the steaming formation — we were tied up by noon tho — definite information about personnel and demobilization procedures is impossible to dig out and the Navy is thrashing around waiting for Congress to enact legislation.
>
> Oahu is just as lovely as we remembered — the approach from the south with Diamond Head, Koko Head, the Pali, Tantalus and all the other features emerging to recognition and then you can see the brilliant green fairways of Oahu Country Club hidden in the deep Nuuanu Valley — in Hawaiian, every letter is pronounced every time in exactly the same way — many of the cane fields were being burned in the plains around Pearl, and the pall of smoke laying over the harbor looked too much like December 7, 1941.
>
> The usual stereotyped welcome that Pearl has learned to mass produce — complete with band and bored receiving line of Commodores and Captains.
>
> Earlier tonite we took in the USO show at the ball diamond — much entertainment — returned to the ship to write to you and found it crowded and noisy with the dregs from the session at the beer hall — the old man is going into town tonite, so I'm writing at his desk.
>
> [Jay] Deem just came in clutching a .45 which he said he took away from the Marine sentry at the gate — a highly improbable story and no doubt I will be furnished all the missing details tomorrow morning by the Flag Secretary when he learns the *Puffer* is back in.
>
> We were scheduled to leave in the morning, but [Dwyer] "big-dealed" a few days here ... we are leaving here soon, very soon and will go directly home — and then I should be able to get away from the ship before too long.
>
> Jim is trying to locate enough gear for a golf session and we may be able to work it in tomorrow afternoon — after I get a cable off to you.
>
> The movie just started topside after the remaining stores were struck below.
>
> The critical item in the Navy now is Yeomen and I'm about to lose one of mine — after hoarding him thru three war patrols as a helmsman.

The shark *Puffer* moored at Pearl Harbor (photograph courtesy of the Heehs family).

U. S. Navy photograph of the battle flag taken while the *Puffer* stopped in Pearl Harbor (author's collection).

The *Puffer* returned to the United States on September 24, 1945, and anchored at Tiberon Bay. Many of the current crew members had not been on the *Puffer* during the war (photograph courtesy of Jack Thoman).

WAVE's should be at a premium with all this turmoil over demobilization ... no WAVE line handlers and we feel let-down, and little evidence of them around the base — BOQ had its share tho, each of them entrenched in a defense in depth of Ensigns — no infiltration — the O-club dance tomorrow nite.

[John] Shiflett did have appendicitis and we are going to lose him — bakers are almost as hard to get as yeomen.

Fuel, water, lube and stores and why in Hell can't we shove off this morning.

In Pearl we are besieged with requests of the crew for special liberty to look up brothers, cousins, friends — [Glenn] Stoy today found his brother's carrier in and they had a reunion two and a half years waiting [*ibid.*].

Arrived Pearl Harbor — found the carrier USS *Wasp* in port aboard which my brother was a crew member — after mooring to dock received permission to go over to the *Wasp* — met brother had happy reunion — took him back to the *Puffer* for steak dinner after which he wanted to transfer to sub duty immediately [Stoy].

San Francisco

According to Tom Metz, Dwyer was in no hurry to leave Pearl Harbor. Crew members were housed on the boat; no Royal Hawaiian Hotel treatment was given. Personnel were shifted around to accommodate west coast and east coast crews.

```
NAVY WEEK      October 21 - 28, 1945     MARTINEZ, CALIFORNIA
    USS PUFFER ---- Skipper ---- Lt. Commander C. R. Dwyer
               Submarine will arrive in Martinez Wednesday
               October 24th and leave Monday October 29th

                        PROGRAM OF EVENTS

WEDNESDAY
              Reception committee welcomes officers and crew of the
              USS PUFFER.
              Presentation of key to the City of Martinez to command-
              ing officer by Mayor Jack Fries.

THURSDAY
              Automobile sight-seeing trip to St. Mary's Pre-Flight
              School and luncheon at Moraga for the submarine crew.

FRIDAY
              Luncheon for submarine crew at Veterans Memorial Hall at
              12 noon.
              Football game at Alhambra Union High School Grounds
                       3:00 PM (Crockett vs Martinez)
              Dinner for Officers at Paul's Place 7:30 PM

SATURDAY
              Parade in the afternoon 2:00 o'clock
              Dance at the Martinez Sportsmen's Club for crew members
              9:00 PM

SUNDAY
              Special services and prayers at all Churches.
                 St. Catherine's Catholic Church    10:30 AM
                 Protestant Churches                11:00 AM

OPEN HOUSE AT MARTINEZ CANTEEN
              All personnel of the USS PUFFER are invited to make their
              headquarters while ashore at the Martinez Canteen - USO
              opposite the Southern Pacific Station - Open 7 AM to 11 PM
```

The *Program of Events* for Navy Week, October 21–28, 1945 — The *Puffer* crew was hosted by the city of Martinez, California (image courtesy of Frank Mays).

We transferred some of our east coast crew men and took on west coast men that were on their way to San Francisco. The Captain seemed pretty well acquainted at Pearl Harbor and didn't seem to be in any hurry to get back to the States. On the 17th of September we left Pearl Harbor with Admiral Halsey's Task Group headed for San Francisco, and passed under the Golden Gate Bridge in parade column on September 24th [Metz].

Stoy wrote, "Anchored in Tiberon Bay — no room in Mare Island for us."

The *Puffer* crew members are welcomed at the Martinez Canteen with a fruit bowl. Fruit was a scarce item on submarines during the war. *Sitting and standing (left to right):* Delmar Baumgartner, Ted Okoniewski, Willie Coleman, Dale Hodges, (Martinez ladies in center), Harry Deiss, Ray Hartman, John Youra, Ellis Branchcomb, unknown, unknown. *Kneeling:* unknown, Francis Brogan (photograph courtesy of Ellis Branchcomb).

Navy Day Celebration

The *Official History* of the *Puffer* described the arrival at Tiberon Bay.

Arrived 24 September 1945 and reported to Commander Submarine Squadron NINETEEN on U.S.S. AEGIR (23) in Tiberon Bay. There the *Puffer* began a brief refit getting into good shape for Navy Day. On 24 October 1945 *Puffer* went to Martinez, California, to represent the U.S. Navy on Navy Day, 27 October 1945. She was welcomed royally and presented with the key to the city of Martinez by the Mayor [Dwyer, *History*].

According to the Martinez newspaper, Mayor Fries encouraged the citizens of the city to "show their appreciation to Navy personnel and other military visitors for their splendid accomplishments during World War II" ("Navy Week," 1945).

On Wednesday the *Puffer*'s officers were treated to a luncheon, where Commander Dwyer told the story of the harrowing escape during the First War Patrol. The local newspaper quoted Dwyer's recollection of the events.

Then, for 38 hours, exactly on the hour, the Japs came over us. We could hear the thrum of her engines and the release of the ashcans. The men would start counting the seconds awaiting the whoomp of the depth charge explosions. The Japs not only tried to write us off but they tried to worry us to death. We took one hell of a shellacking ["Submarine Crew," 1945].

Chief Herbert Hayward greets the Martinez visitors (author's collection).

The newspaper inaccurately reported that "many of her personnel, their nerves shattered by the experience, went to hospitals and out of the service" (*ibid.*).

The enlisted men were luncheon guests of the American Legion on Friday, October 26. The crew were treated to female companionship.

> The luncheon at Memorial Hall yesterday proved a pleasant social affair. A pleasant feature was the distribution of members of the Commercial Girls Club among the *Puffer* crew members.... Frank Donley, Pat Taylor and Chief of Police Neilson protested against the Commercial Girls sitting alone and distributed them as company for the guests, to the delight of the boys from the submarine ["Navy Day Fete," 1945].

In this chance meeting of young women from Martinez, Ellis "Sandy" Branchcomb met a young woman he dated and later married (Branchcomb). Branchcomb still lives in Martinez. On Saturday the population of Martinez was invited to tour the *Puffer* from 9 to 11 A.M. and from 1 to 5 P.M. Metz had a surprise visitor.

> On this day many people saw the inside of a submarine. Lines of people passed through the *Puffer* from front to back most of the day. Late that afternoon some people that formerly lived near London [Arkansas], and I had attended high school with their children, came through the after torpedo room where I was on watch. Sure was glad to see someone from home. While we were at Martinez, we were taken on a tour of the country near there and went to a college where they train aviators. A trampoline instructor gave us a demonstration on how to perform on one of them and he was really good. The local citizens treated us to good food, hospitality and friendship [Metz].

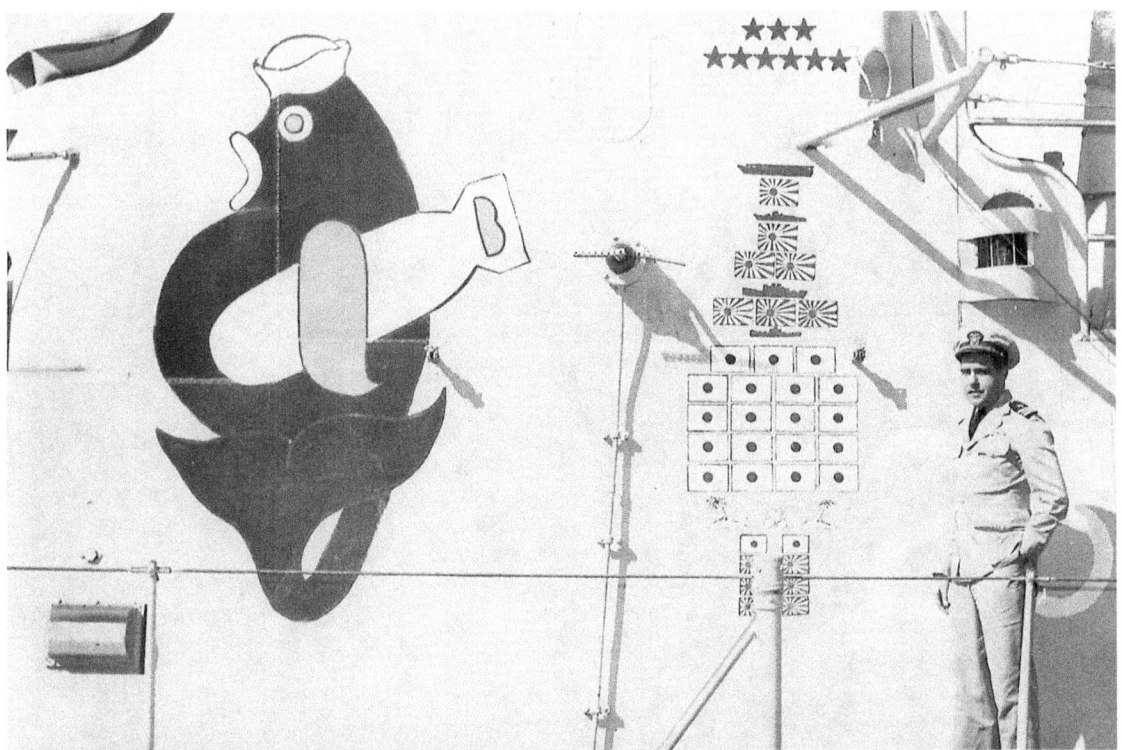

Commander Dwyer on Navy Day (photograph courtesy of the Dwyer family).

The *San Francisco Chronicle* also paid tribute to the Submarine Service and invited the public to visit the boats about which little was reported during the war. The officers and crew were now able to speak freely about their accomplishments.

> The end of hostilities has brought some relaxation in the security regulations that cloaked the activities of the "silent service" during the war.... Peace has brought another notable change to the submarine service. Gone is the reticence of the crews, once known as the most close-mouthed men in the navy ["Secrets," 1945].

Home Again

After five wonderful days at Martinez, California, the *Puffer* returned to Tiberon Bay to complete the refit and train the many new crew members. While part of the crew was celebrating in Martinez, other crew members with longer service records were allowed to go home on 30 days leave. McDonald was one of those men. After a year's absence he returned to Tacoma, Washington. He recalled riding the train with "Joe the Horse" to Portland. Other crew members were allowed to go on leave after Navy Day (McDonald).

Tom Metz described the typical refit activities done after the Martinez celebration. With the war over the emphasis was on shine. He was finally given 30 days' leave to return to his family in Arkansas. Upon his return he was given more tough jobs to do on the *Puffer*.

> Then we began to convert the *Puffer* to a peace time boat. We got rid of all of our extra equipment. When the tender could not take the extra, we would stack it on the top deck during the day and push it over the side at night, according to orders.... Soon as we got rid of all the extra

Some of the *Puffer* crew at a Christmas party at Club Casino — San Francisco (photograph courtesy of Bob Polk).

gear we carried while on war patrol, we commenced to shine the Old *Puffer* up for the peace time navy. The eight hours each day we used to stand watch and the four to eight hours each day we used to service torpedoes and keep the ship in shape, we now spend filing rough brass castings so they could be shined with Brasso — then there were hundreds of feet of copper tubing to have the paint removed so they could be shined each week. Then for days we crawled up under the forward tubes to scrape and paint the bilges. But thank goodness, for me this didn't last long till it came time for 30 days leave.

I bought myself a round trip ticket and caught the bus for Arkansas. Didn't even have the measles on my way home this time. Orvie [his wife] met me there at my folks and we really enjoyed ourselves for the next three weeks, just loafing, visiting and getting acquainted all over again. One of the Chief Petty Officers of the *Puffer* came by here and visited with us for a few days on his way home. We took him to the mountains in north Pope County on a deer hunt one cold December morning. We killed two or three squirrels, but saw no deer. That was my first and last deer hunt. The chief went on home and when my leave was nearly up, I headed back to the *Puffer* to wait on my time for discharge.

When I arrived back on the *Puffer*, to my surprise, they had saved the rough casting to be filed and the bilges to be scraped and painted for me. I worked at this by day and went to San Francisco on weekends to get away from the paint fumes.... In a barber shop one day we saw an army sergeant who had survived the death march from Batan — then was put on a Jap ship in the holds with 534 other fellow prisoners to be transported to work in the salt mines. When the American sub sank this ship and others with it, only ten of these American prisoners survived. We let him do the talking and we mostly listened. He didn't seem to be overly bitter about the whole matter despite his 44 months in prison and barely escaped death twice [Metz].

New Year's Eve 1945–1946—*left to right:* Curtis "Gabby" Moore and Vi Moore, Herbert and Ann Hayward, Glenn and Mildred Stoy celebrated the peace of the New Year at the Barrel Club in Vallejo, California (photograph courtesy of Glenn Stoy).

By the end of December most of the crew members with two years' service were transferred to one of the tenders to wait for discharge (RG24). During January and February these men were discharged, fulfilling the duration plus six months enlistment or adequate points. Metz wrote about his separation from the Navy.

In the process of time my number came up for discharge, so two other men and myself left the *Puffer* on our way home for good. They gave me our three sets of records and sent us by the tender to be forwarded on. Would you believe, I left our records on the yeoman's desk at the tender, so when we arrived at Treasure Island for processing they had to start us some supplementary records till the originals caught up with us.

We didn't get discharged at Treasure Island but did get certain processing done, and either sent home or threw away our unnecessary clothing. Those boys leaving the navy would actually throw away truck loads of blankets, sheets, pillow cases and clothing each day. I put mine in my sea bag and sent them home. They all came in useful for the next few years. I still have one dress uniform.

We were sent to Norman, Oklahoma by troop train for final processing. There we went before a group of American Legion men who wanted to know if we had obtained any injuries or defects while in the service. My answer was no. They said, "No fungus or anything?" Again I said no, because I didn't know athlete's foot was the same, so consequently, I got to doctor my own ailments.

An officer spoke to us about re-enlisting. He explained that this was his job, and he intended to do it, but if we had anything worthwhile to do at home, to go ahead and take our discharge.

So with my discharge in its envelope and my ditty bag in the other hand, they dropped us off at the bus station in Oklahoma City to catch a bus home. After one year and fifty-one weeks, I finished my navy career with a submarine battle insignia and four battle stars [*ibid.*].

Peter Keane was discharged in May 1946 and getting home was a problem. However, Americans were still grateful and helpful for the sacrifices made by the servicemen. Keane related his homecoming in a 2004 letter.

At the time of my discharge in May, 1946 there was a transportation strike and trains were not running. I was discharged in California so the Navy arranged for me to fly commercially. That trip from L.A. Airport to N.Y was supposed to take 9 hours leaving at 1 PM from the west coast and arriving at 10 PM in N.Y. (non-stop). Due to thunderstorms in St. Louis the pilot felt he needed additional fuel so we stopped in Albuquerque, New Mexico. This made the flight later and we still had to fly through the storm over St. Louis.

We arrived in N.Y. about 2 AM and with no further transportation I started to walk or get a lift to the city's outskirts to get a ride home. After only going about 3 blocks a police car stopped me and asked where I was going. I told them I was trying to get out of the city to get a ride home and they in turn told me I was headed into a rough section of town and could be robbed. The cops said to get in their car and they then started to pass me from patrol car to patrol car until we arrived at a place where another sailor was standing along side of an officer and his motorcycle.

This officer was stopping every semi heading north and west until he got both of us a ride up to where we lived. The semi driver was great; he bought us breakfast, indicated he had a son in the service, and got both of us as close as he could to our home towns so it would be easy to get a ride the short distance that remained. Pretty nice — the citizens during the war were very nice to the servicemen [Keane].

For the crew members left behind in San Francisco there was plenty of work to keep the *Puffer* shined and polished and time for Christmas and New Year's celebrations as well. The *Puffer* left for Hawaii on January 2, 1946. Shortly after arriving at Pearl Harbor, Stoy was transferred to Naval Recruiters School at San Diego, California.

Although I was pleased no end with my service on the *Puffer* I had looked forward to some time stateside after the war ended to be able to get home once in awhile. Being sent back out to the Pacific within thirty days was my only reason for requesting a transfer from the *Puffer* [Stoy].

What Next?

Other men not returning to Hawaii, such as McDonald, were transferred to the tender within a few weeks after their return from 30 days' leave. McDonald had gone home to Tacoma, but was required to return to Mare Island until the Navy was finished

Bernice Meyne and Donald McDonald were married on February 6, 1946 (author's collection).

with him. During those 10 weeks he relocated his girlfriend from a year ago, Bernice Meyne. They dated when leave was allowed from his naval duties. Probably because it was close to his home town, the Navy wanted him to travel to Bremerton, Washington, for his final discharge. He was discharged on January 30, 1946 (RG24).

McDonald returned to Sacramento with a wedding ring in his pocket. As with many men whose lives had been put on hold for three or four years he was ready to get on with living. Meyne was Lutheran and McDonald had been raised in the Catholic Church. Marriage in either church presented complications. They were ready to get on with their lives without added complications, so they decided to take the night train to Reno, Nevada, where marriage was simplified. On the morning of February 6, 1946, they caught a taxi at the Reno train station for the downtown of "The Biggest Little City in the World."

McDonald wanted to look around town, but Meyne wanted to get married as soon as possible. The taxi driver took them to a marriage chapel. The taxi driver and the wife of the minister served as witnesses to the ceremony. Upon return to Sacramento they moved into the apartment where Meyne had lived; her roommates had since departed. With the help of the Navy, McDonald found employment at a fledgling airline, Pacific Airlines, in Sacramento. By August of 1946, the newlyweds were expecting their first child, and their lives were on fast forward (McDonald).

After discharge some crew members joined the reserves upon return home. Although McDonald moved to Iowa, the Navy found him in late 1950 and recalled him to active duty for three months during the Korean War. That was the end of McDonald's naval service.

18

Postwar Service

Hawaii

On January 2, 1946, the *Puffer* left San Francisco and arrived in Honolulu on January 9. The boat reported to commander, Submarine Squadron Twenty-one, commanded by Captain R. W. Grenfell. The duties consisted of training submarine crews, and training surface craft and aircraft in anti-submarine warfare techniques. Some of the exercises included maneuvers with captured Japanese submarines. Plank holders Wilson, Hayward and Dwyer were still on the crew.

Left: Harris Steinke adorned with a newly acquired eagle tattoo. Steinke made a serious contribution to the Navy with the invention of the Steinke Hood, an escape device that replaced the Momsen Lung (photograph courtesy of Howard Baird). *Right:* Howard Baird relaxes during duty in the Hawaiian Islands (photograph courtesy of Howard Baird).

Some of the crew that went back to Hawaii, taking a break from drydock work. *Front row (left to right):* Charles Darrah, unknown, Chief Herb Hayward, unknown, Jim Bretz, unknown. *Back row:* Ted Okoniewski, unknown, unknown, Edward Dauplaise, unknown, Howard Nielson (photograph courtesy of Jack Thoman).

The *Puffer* Hawaiian Luau in February 1946. *Front row (left to right):* Kenneth McEntyre, John Alexander, James Landry, James Bretz, Harry Dehosse, unknown (half hidden), Garth Stocker, Herbert Hayward, Wayne Johnson, Peter Keane, Dana Washburn, Bernard Meister. *Second row:* William Wilson, James Urbanski, Ensign Lunchbaugh, Edwin Chaffee, Lester Owens, Capt. Carl Dwyer, Executive Officer Robert Reilly, unknown, David Hatt, unknown, John Poe. *Third row:* Gordon Williams, George Krans, unknown, Frank Freeman, Rene Veber, Carl Pitsch, unknown, unknown, Erwin White. *Back row:* unknown, Joseph Kupiec, Forrest Ramser, unknown, Ensign Rosenberg, unknown, unknown (photograph courtesy of Howard Baird).

The *Puffer* in drydock while James Urbanski and William Wilson (partially hidden) inspected the anchor (photographs courtesy of Howard Baird).

These duties were short lived. There was a rumor the *Puffer* would go to Bikini Island for destruction by a nuclear bomb test ("To Use *Puffer*," 1946), but that proved untrue. On February 15, 1946, orders were received to begin a pre-inactivation overhaul immediately. *Puffer* was put in drydock.

Baird recalled the ice cream machine continued to cause problems for the crew. Tim Dineen, the baker, lost part of his finger urging the ice cream machine to turn. When Baird visited Dineen in sickbay, Dineen joked that he didn't throw out the ice cream as no one would notice blood in chocolate ice cream (Baird). With Dineen's finger healed and the overhaul completed, on

Right: The *Puffer* ready for the return voyage to San Francisco — Bill Hahn (TM3c) on deck (photograph courtesy of Howard Baird).

Tim Dineen in the *Puffer* control room. Dineen, a cook, lost part of his finger in the ice cream machine (photograph courtesy of Howard Baird).

March 12 the *Puffer* began the return journey to San Francisco.

The *Puffer* arrived on March 19 and moored alongside USS *Aegir* in Tiberon Bay. The boat remained at that location for three weeks and then reported to the commandant, Navy Yard, Mare Island, for inactivation and decommissioning. On April 17 the long awaited Navy Unit Commendation for the Fourth War Patrol, commanded by F. G. Selby, was awarded by Captain C. W. Wilkins on behalf of James Forrestal, secretary of the Navy.

The *Grapevine* of July 12, 1946, announced the decommissioning of the *Puffer*. The *Puffer* was the 52nd and last submarine to be inactivated (image courtesy of the U.S. Navy).

Puffer Decommissioning Ceremony Marks Final Sub to Join 19th Fleet at Mare Island

The U. S. S. Puffer was decommissioned last week, 52nd and last submarine to join the Mare Island Group, Nineteen (Inactive) Fleet.

High-ranking submarine officials were on hand at the colorful decommissioning ceremony which marked the first Navy unit to complete its inactivation program.

Captain C. W. Wilkins, U. S. N., Commander, Submarines, Pacific Fleet, Administration Mare Island, and Captain Howell C. Fish, Commander Mare Island Group, Nineteen Fleet, Captain F. C. L. Dettman, Officer-in-Charge of the Submarine Decommissioning Detail, and many other submarine officers and men participated in the ceremony aboard the U. S. S. Puffer as the submarine's ensign and battle flag were hauled down for the last time.

Praising the work alike of the Shipyard, the Decommissioning Detail and the officers and men of the submarines who worked a twenty-four hour shift toward the end of the program to make their 1 July deadline, set last September, Captain Wilkins said:

"The success of the inactivation program marked a new high in cooperation between the Navy's forces afloat and the forces ashore. The Decommissioning Detail's foresight in organizing and laying out the work, the tenders' efforts in giving each ship a fine pre-inactivation overhaul, the conscientious craftsmanship of the Mare Island and San Francisco Shipyard workers and the cooperation and help of the 19th Fleet all played a part in completing the program successfully.

"I wish particularly to praise the magnificent spirit of the officers and men of the Submarine Service, who worked night and day to finish the task of laying up their own ships in the finest manner possible. Many Reserve Officers and men voluntarily extended their time in the service to help in this work, and I can honestly say that the submarines themselves are in the best possible condition to serve again in the defense of their country if the need should ever arise."

Nineteenth Fleet submarines now berthed at Mare Island are the Archerfish, Aspro, Barbero, Bashaw, Batfish, Baya, Bluegill, Bream, Devilfish, Dragonet, Guavina, Guitarro, Gurnard, Hackleback, Hammerhead, Hardhead, Hawkbill, Icefish, Jallao, Kraken, Lamprey, Lionfish, Lizardfish, Macabi, Manta, Mapiro, Menhaden, Mero, Mingo, Moray, Pampanita, Pargo, Perch, Pintado, Pipefish, Piranha, Puffer, Roncador, Sandlance, Sawfish, Seahorse, Sealion, Spadefish, Spot, Springer, Steelhead, Stickleback, Sunfish, Tilefish, Tinosa, Trepang and Tunny.

Blowin' the Breeze

Said the WAVE to the sailor "Before we go on this date, I want it clearly understood that may be a seaman second class but I'm a lady first."

A dashing young fellow named Joe
Had lost all his happy glow.
He used to be sunny,
He had lots of money—
But that was two blondes ago.

Briefing: "You men will hold this position, at all costs, and there's an explosion one of the platoon sergeants will blow whistle. Any questions . . ."

The *Smith Cove Naval News* announced the 1947 arrival of the *Puffer* in Seattle, Washington (photograph courtesy of the U.S. Navy).

Selby was present for the presentation and received the award. Immediately after the ceremony Lt. Commander R. F. Reilly relieved Commander Dwyer as commanding officer (Dwyer, *Ship's History*). The crew members presented Dwyer with a watch so that he would remember them. At the 1990 reunion Dwyer was still wearing the watch and emotionally recalled the presentation and recollection of the crew twice a day: every morning when he wound the watch; and every night when he took it off (Polk and Sanders, Reunion 1991)

Seattle

On June 27, 1946, Reilly turned the *Puffer* over to Commander Mare Island Group, Nineteenth Fleet. The *Puffer* was officially decommissioned. After sitting in mothballs for about a year, the Navy decided to send the *Puffer* to Seattle, Washington, as a Naval Reserve training boat. In this role the *Puffer* was not an oceangoing vessel. Naval Reserve members came to the *Puffer* to draw diagrams of the systems and compartments, similar to the

The decommissioning ceremony at Mare Island officially ended the *Puffer*'s active duty. Raymond Voss (extreme left) and Carl Dwyer (extreme right) were part of the commissioning crew in Manitowoc, Wisconsin (image courtesy of the U.S. Navy).

In 1951 the *Puffer* remained in exactly the same state as in 1947. However, the boat was no longer seaworthy because the propellers had been removed (photograph courtesy of the U.S. Navy).

UNITED STATES NAVY

SUBMARINE USS PUFFER (SS268)

Welcome on Board

The U.S.S. PUFFER is a Fleet-Type Submarine similar to the ones that accounted for a large number of enemy ship sinkings in the past world war. It is 312 feet long, and 27 feet wide at the widest point. On the surface it is powered by four diesel engines; while submerged, it uses electrical energy generated by two tremendous storage batteries. It takes less than one minute for a submarine to completely submerge.

There are men stationed in each compartment to assist you and explain the various mechanisms and functions performed in that compartment. Please feel free to ask questions. However, should the answer to your question be classified information, the men have been instructed to say "I don't know", even if they do know the answer - so please do not press your question any further. We also ask you not to touch any valves, turn any switches, or attempt to operate any equipment. Please be careful in going through the ship.

We desire that you enjoy your visit on board the PUFFER, and become acquainted with a vital component of your Navy.

The U.S.S. PUFFER was built in Manitowoc, Wisconsin by the Manitowoc Ship Building Company. The keel was laid February 16, 1942. In a dramatic side launching into the Manitowoc River, the PUFFER was first water borne on November 22, 1942.

After exhaustive trials conducted in Lake Michigan, the PUFFER was accepted by the Navy and was placed in commission on April 27, 1943, with LCDR H. J. JENSEN, USN, Commanding. She did not receive her baptism of salt water until she was transferred to New Orleans, Louisiana, via the Chicago Ship Canal, Illinois River, and the Mississippi River. After fitting out and training of her crew, the PUFFER proceeded to the southwest Pacific to commence her deadly damage to enemy shipping.

She departed Australia for her first war patrol on 7 September, 1943. On October 9, 1943, the USS PUFFER received one of the most severe depth charge attacks experienced in the war, when she was battered by heavy and close depth charges and was harrassed and kept down for thirty-eight hours.

One of the most successful war patrols was held in the Madoera Straits, Makassar Straits, and Sulu Sea areas. During this patrol, she acted as "Life Guard" for the first carrier strike on Soerabaja. She sank a 7500 ton freighter after evading enemy patrols, damaged an enemy aircraft carrier in Sibutu Passage, and sank two tankers which were enroute to refuel the enemy fleet prior to the battle of the Philippine Sea.

The USS PUFFER in her short career of twenty-six months, sank twenty (20) enemy ships, for a total of 103,324 tons, and heavily damaged eleven (11) other ships totaling 39,560 tons.

The historical information sheet given out to visitors of the *Puffer* (author's collection).

wartime qualification procedure. The *Smith Cove Naval News* reported the arrival of the *Puffer* in the May 16, 1947, issue. Ken Martinson, a wartime *Puffer* crew member, directed the movement of the boat from San Francisco to Seattle (Martinson).

The *Puffer* remained at this location for the next 13 years. By the late 1950s the crew had been reduced to a three-man ship-keeper crew. The propellers had been removed and the

Opposite, bottom: The 2000 *Puffer* reunion was held in Phoenix, Arizona. Clockwise from the top left, the participants were: Larry Picone, John Solak, Morrow Decker, Jack Thoman, John Sanders, Charlie Brockhausen, Charlie Brown, Frank Corcoran, Karl Mappus, Lorraine Kerls (widow of Charles Kerls), Fred Frith, Robert Polk, Edward Dauplaise, and Walter Mazzone (photograph courtesy of Robert Polk).

The first *Puffer* reunion was held in 1990 in Kissimmee, Florida. *Front row (left to right):* James Hargrove, James Dickinson, John Gutensohn, Tony Sasso, Carl Dwyer, Fred Frith, Peter Keane, Joseph (Zelaznicki) Zell, Norman Trudeau. *Back row:* Mike Kutscherousky, Russ Tidd, George McPherson, Charlie Brockhausen, Jack Lane, James Parker, Ken Martinson, John Sanders, Bob Krotzer, Robert Polk (photograph courtesy of Robert Polk).

The 2002 *Puffer* reunion in Buffalo, New York, was well attended. *Front row (left to right):* John Sanders, Ken Dobson, Edward Dauplaise, Robert Polk, Fred Frith, Russ Tidd. *Back row:* Don Switzer, Harold Ziegler, Glenn Stoy, Peter Keane, Charles Brown, Walter Mazzone (photograph courtesy of Robert Polk).

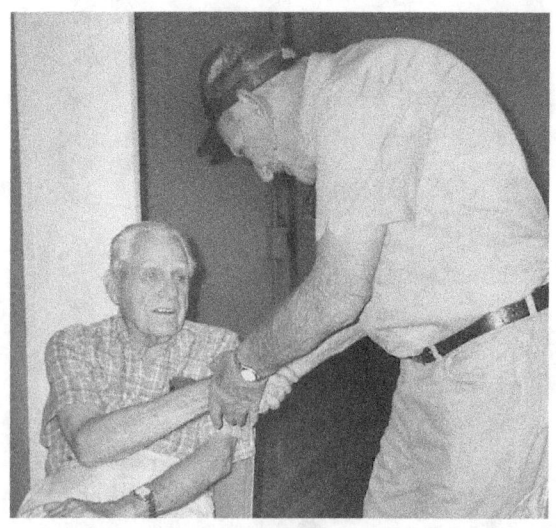

John Allen (standing) greets Capt. Carl Dwyer at the 2001 *Puffer* reunion in St. Louis, Missouri. Allen and Dwyer were both on the near fatal First War Patrol of the *Puffer* (author's collection).

vents were welded shut. The war record stenciled on the coning tower remained as painted in 1945. No modifications had been done, such as a snorkel. Deck armament remained as in 1945, a single 20mm and 40mm cannon, and a 5 inch/25 cal. deck gun. Boy Scout troops took tours of the boat and some slept overnight on the boat (Williamson).

The End of the *Puffer*

In an e-mail message of March 18, 2002, Elmer C. Williamson YNC(SS), USN (Retired) described the last days of the *Puffer*.

I was the last crew member on the *Puffer*. At one time I had the last flag that flew on the *Puffer* but gave it to the XO of the new (nuclear) *Puffer*. I note on the web site showing the *Puffer* being towed. That bridge is the Fremont Draw

Bridge in Seattle. *Puffer* was on her way for scrap. As I remember, I think some outfit in Portland, Oregon bought her. Probably made razor blades out of her. *Puffer* had a great record. *Puffer* was replaced in Seattle by the USS *Bowfin* as the reserve training submarine. *Bowfin* as you know is now a museum out in Pearl Harbor [Williamson].

The picture mentioned by Williamson and other photos can be viewed at www.navsource.org. Williamson used a World War II next of kin list that remained in the personnel records of the *Puffer* to locate veterans of the *Puffer*. A few *Puffer* veterans or their parents lived at the addresses on the report and were able to come and take small pieces of the boat as souvenirs. Jay Deem received a copy of the *Ship's History* mailed to his boyhood Illinois home address. Other crew members in the Seattle area salvaged the ship's clock, compartment name plates, and even the sink in the commander's quarters. The *Puffer* was officially placed out of service on June 10, 1960, when the *Bowfin* became the Naval Reserve training boat at Seattle. The *Puffer* was struck from the Naval Register on July 1, 1960. The hull was sold for scrap November 4, 1960, to Zidell Corporation of Portland, Oregon.

Reunions

Although the *Puffer* was gone, many of the submarine veterans that served on the boat attended regional submarine reunions from 1950 to 1990. Starting in 1990 the *Puffer* crew held yearly reunions in conjunction with the national meeting of the World War II Submarine Veterans Conventions. As the number of *Puffer* veterans dwindled, the last reunion of the *Puffer* shipmates was probably held in 2006.

Glossary of Terms and Abbreviations

Acey-deucy: a version of backgammon.

AK: a cargo ship.

Angle on the bow: the angle formed by the direction of the target vessel and the line of sight from the submarine, measured either to port or starboard; a parameter used by the Torpedo Data Computer (TDC). See http://www.fleetsubmarine.com/periscope.html for a complete explanation of submarine approach procedures. (All original content (c)2002 by FleetSubmarine.com. All rights reserved.)

Angle on the boat: the angle of the sub's keel measured from the horizontal; either up (surfacing) or down (diving); controlled by the bow and stern dive planes.

AO: an oil tanker.

AP: a troop transport ship.

APR: a radar detector; could detect radar being directed at a submarine from Japanese ground installations, airplanes or ships.

Ash cans: depth charges.

Ballast tanks: tanks filled with water or blown dry used to control the buoyancy of the submarine: positive buoyancy (caused the boat to rise when submerged or stay on the surface); neutral (maintain constant depth when submerged); negative (caused the boat to sink deeper when submerged).

Bathythermograph (BT): measured and recorded water temperature variations; used to find layers or boundaries between two water masses with temperature differences. A submarine could hide from enemy SONAR under a layer.

Bk: ship's Baker: followed by class: 3c, 2c, or 1c; or preceded by C for Chief; this crew member baked fresh bread daily, prepared pastries for breakfast and baked cakes and pies for the daily meals.

Black gang: the diesel engine room crew: firemen (F) and motor machinist mates (MoMM).

Boat: a term commonly used to describe a submarine; not used for any other type of naval vessel.

Bow: the front of the boat.

Bow planes: horizontal wing-like structures on the front of the submarine used to control the angle of the boat. (See also stern planes.)

Broach: to inadvertently surface.

Bulkhead: a watertight wall separating compartments within a submarine.

BuOrd: Bureau of Ordnance; Navy department charged with weapons development and production, such as torpedoes, deck guns, shells, etc.

BuShips: Bureau of Ships; Navy department charged with ship building and maintenance.

BuPers: Bureau of Personnel; Navy department charged with deployment and use of people.

CA: a heavy cruiser, a ship smaller than a battleship, with smaller deck guns.

Can: the storage battery. Also short for "tin can," an enemy destroyer.

Captain: the title used for the officer of any rank in command of a submarine. Typically captains were lieutenant commanders, or commanders; many were under 30 years old.

Chidori: a Japanese anti-submarine vessel class; a term used by sub commanders to describe most anti-submarine vessels regardless of size; armed with depth charges and deck guns capable of sinking a submarine; equipped with SONAR.

Chief of the Boat (COB): the senior enlisted man on a submarine.

Christmas tree: a panel of red and green lights used to monitor openings in the submarine hull. A green board indicated it was safe to submerge — all hatches were closed; monitored by the diving officer.

Ck: a cook; followed by class: 3c, 2c, or 1c; or preceded by C for chief. Subs had superior food, but it still required a skilled crew member to prepare it properly.

COMSUBPAC: Submarine Command Pacific.

Conning tower: the compartment above the control room; navigation and attacks were conducted here.

Controllerman: an electrician that controlled the distribution of the electricity to the shaft motors, recharging the batteries, and other needs of the submarine.

Cribbage: a card game widely played by officers and crew. Points are tallied on a board with holes and pegs.

CV or CVE: an aircraft carrier or escort aircraft carrier.

DAVE: a Japanese observation plane.

DD: a destroyer. A *Chidori* is a Japanese class of destroyer.

Displacement: the weight of water displaced by a vessel, measured in tons; the larger a vessel the greater its displacement of water.

Distance to the track: Range in yards from the submarine to the line defined by the target's course. A parameter estimated by the commander and required by the Torpedo Data Computer (TDC) to solve the torpedo firing problem. See http://www.fleetsubmarine.com/periscope.html for a complete explanation of submarine approach procedures. (All original content (c)2002 by FleetSubmarine.com. All rights reserved.)

EM: electrician's mate, followed by class: 3c, 2c, or 1c; or preceded by C for Chief. These men were responsible for the electric circuits, batteries and motors on board.

FBT: a fuel-ballast tank.

Fireman (F2c or F1c): part of the Black Gang. For example, F1c, Fireman first class. A similar rate as a seaman, but these men typically became motor machinist mates.

Fish: torpedoes.

Fleet-type submarine: attack submarines built between 1940 and 1945. "Fleet" is a misnomer as the submarine typically operated independently of the fleet.

Foo-Foo: anything with a pleasant odor; difficult to find after weeks on patrol. Foo-Foo dust is talcum powder. (I never knew where this term came from in my dad's vocabulary until I read about the Submarine Service.)

Fox schedule: radio communications sent at predetermined times. Submarines must be on the surface to receive radio messages.

"Fuel King": nickname given to the enlisted man in charge of fueling and monitoring fuel use.

GM: gunner's mate; followed by class: 3c, 2c, or 1c; or preceded by C for chief. These crew members were responsible for the various small arms, machine guns, 20mm and 40mm cannons, the deck gun and ammunition for each.

Gyro angle: after firing the angle through which the torpedo would turn in order to hit the target. The turn was controlled by a gyroscope within the torpedo. The TDC updated the gyro angle with an electrical-mechanical signal up to the instant of firing the torpedo. See http://www.fleetsubmarine.com/periscope.html for a complete explanation of submarine approach procedures. (All original content ©2002 by FleetSubmarine.com. All rights reserved.)

Head: the highly complicated toilet on a submarine; required 10 separate steps to flush.

Hot: torpedoes running properly as in "hot, straight and normal."

I-boat: a Japanese class submarine; similar in size to the American Fleet boats.

IFF: Identify Friend or Foe signal.

JAKE: a Japanese twin float observation plane.

Jam air: to compress air into the tanks. Compressed air and a full battery charge were essential to a submarine's survival.

JANAC: Joint Army-Navy Assessment Committee — after the war the official committee which evaluated and awarded credit to submarines for enemy ships sunk.

JK: sonar amplifier.

J.O.O.D: junior officer of the deck; lower ranking officer assisting the O.O.D.

JP sound: passive single fixed-head listening equipment used from mid–1944.

KATE: a Japanese torpedo bomber.

Kedge: to drop an anchor and then by taking in the chain pull the boat toward the anchor. When the *Puffer* ran aground during the First War Patrol this technique was considered to pull the *Puffer* off the coral reef.

Limber holes: drain holes along the length of the submarine's outer structure.

Maru: any Japanese merchant vessel; abbreviated as M or M. in the war patrol reports.

MoMM: motor machinist mate, followed by class, 3c, 2c, or 1c; or preceded by C for chief. These men were responsible for the maintenance and operation of the four diesel engines that powered the submarine.

M.O.T.: middle of target.

MTB: Motor torpedo boat.

Old man: the skipper of the sub; typically a lieutenant commander. None were old men; most were between 28 and 32 years old.

1MC: the on-ship communications systems.

ONI: Office of Naval Intelligence. Produced Japanese ship manuals used extensively by sub commanders in the identification of size (height and length) of the vessel and therefore allowed the range of enemy targets to be calculated through the periscope.

O.O.D. or O.D. or OD: officer of the deck; officer currently in command of the boat.

P.: port side

Periscope depth: with the keel at 67 feet the periscope can be exposed about three feet.

PhM: pharmacist's mate; followed by class: 3c, 2c, or 1c; or preceded by C for chief; single crew member responsible for the mental and physical health of the crew.

Pitometer log (pit log): a piece of equipment used to measure the submarine's speed through the water. This speed was automatically fed to the Torpedo Data Computer.

PPI (Position Plan Indicator): an improved radar display implemented in 1944 which displayed the sub's position at the center of a circular display screen and the enemy ships as glowing dots.

Pressure hull: the internal cylindrical hull built to withstand heavy pressure from water and depth charges; the thinner external hull contains the ballast tanks.

QB: sonar amplifier, listening phones.

QM: quartermaster, followed by class: 3c, 2c, or 1c; or preceded by C for chief. QMs stand watch as assistants to officers of the deck (OOD) and the navigator; serve as helmsman and perform ship control, navigation and bridge watch duties. QMs procure, correct, use and stow navigational and oceanographic publications and oceanographic charts. They maintain navigational instruments and keep correct navigational time. Usually the first man on deck after surfacing.

Range: Distance from the submarine to the target in yards. See http://www.fleetsubmarine.com/periscope.html for a complete explanation of submarine approach procedures. (All original content ©2002 by FleetSubmarine.com. All rights reserved.)

RT: radar technician; followed by class: 3c, 2c, or 1c; or preceded by C for chief; RTs maintained and operated the radio, radar and other electronic equipment.

RUFE: a Japanese dive bomber.

S.: starboard side.

Seaman (S2c or S1c): seaman second class, or seaman first class; men who were still striking for a specific rate, such as torpedoman, electrician, yeoman, radio tech or quartermaster.

SD radar: air search radar.

SJ radar: surface search radar.

SONAR (SOund Navigation And Ranging): equipment used for underwater sound detection; either passive (listening only) or active (listening for the reflection of a sent wave or ping). Ranges are measured from the time taken for the reflected sound to return to the source.

Spread: firing two or more torpedoes in a manner such that their paths diverge. If there were errors in observations input to the TDC, this technique increased the probability that at least one torpedo would hit the target.

Spitkit: very small vessel; fishing boat.

ST radar: miniaturized radar installed in the periscope; used in the last months of the war.

Station: a submarine's assigned patrol area; expressed as "on station" when within the assigned area.

Stern: the rear of the boat.

Stern planes: horizontal wing-like structures on the back sides of the submarine used to control the angle of the boat. (See also bow planes.)

StM: a steward's mate, followed by class: 3c, 2c, or 1c; or preceded by C for chief; typically an African American crew member responsible for the officer's quarters, uniforms, dining area, and service of their food. Each submarine usually had two such crew members. These men were fully qualified submarine crew members.

Striker: a seaman or fireman in training for a specific rate such as TM3c or MoMM3c, respectively. Advancement in rate was by exam.

TBT (Target Bearing Transmitter): binocular-like apparatus on the bridge, both fore and aft, used to transmit target headings directly to the TDC.

TDC (Torpedo Data Computer): analog computer using gears, not electronics, to find the torpedo firing solution; the TDC used the target's and submarine's relative positions, speeds and courses to automatically compute the gyro angle of the torpedo.

T. (True Bearing): direction of the boat, target or airplane as measured clockwise from a north-south line determined by star positions, not magnetic compass; north is a true bearing of 0°, due east is 90°, due south is 180°, and due west is 270°.

TM: torpedoman's mate, followed by class: 3c, 2c, or 1c; or preceded by C for chief; TMs are responsible for loading and unloading and maintaining torpedoes.

Torpex: the explosive used in torpedoes. Torpedoes contained 500 pounds of torpex.

Trim: ability to keep the submarine at a specified depth and angle on the boat or both. Any change in weight distribution (such as firing 6 torpedoes) altered the balance of the submarine; trim pumps were used to pump on or off ballast water to maintain the balance of the boat while submerged. Trim dives were a daily necessity as food and other equipment moved around on the boat.

U-boat: a German submarine; short for Unterseeboot. There were no U-boats in the Pacific.

Ultra: a decoded secret Japanese message which contained information about Japanese merchant ship locations and movements; also the name given to the project of breaking the Japanese codes. Ultra information was radioed to submarines on station allowing the commanders to intercept Japanese convoys.

V6: indicated an enlistment for Victory plus 6 months after a rate; for example MoMM2cV6.

Water slug: water taken into the torpedo tube after firing to compensate for the loss of weight of the torpedo.

WPR: the War Patrol Report — a summary of the action written by the commanding officer at the conclusion of each war patrol. The reports were distributed to other sub commanders and division commanders so they might learn from the successes and mistakes of other commanders.

Y: yeomen; followed by class: 3c, 2c, or 1c; or preceded by C for chief. These men keep the personnel records and type documents, and reports, including the War Patrol Reports. A good yeoman was hard to find.

ZEKE: a Zero, a Japanese fighter plane.

Appendix 1: List of Awards

Officers

Commander Marvin J. Jensen, USN — Silver Star.
Commander Frank G. Selby, USN — Navy Cross, Gold Star in lieu of second Navy Cross, Silver Star.
Commander Franklin G. Hess, USN — Bronze Star.
Commander Lawrence G. Bernard, USN — Bronze Star.
Lt. Commander Carl R. Dwyer, USN — Navy Cross, Silver Star, Bronze Star, Letter of Commendation.
Lt. Commander William M. Pugh II, USN — Silver Star, Gold Star in lieu of second Silver Star.
Lt. Commander Stiles M. Decker, USNR — Silver Star, Gold Star in lieu of second Silver Star.
Lt. Commander Frank H. Golay, USNR — Silver Star, Bronze Star.
Lt. (jg) Lawrence A. Picone, USNR — Bronze Star.
Lt. (jg) Robert C. Biche, USN — Letter of Commendation.
Lt. (jg) Kenneth L. Dobson, USN — Letter of Commendation.
Lt. (jg) Robert D. Weeks, USNR — Letter of Commendation.
Lt. (jg) Richard A. Heehs, USNR — Letter of Commendation.
Ensign Phillip A. McClure, USN — Letter of Commendation.

Enlisted Men

Jay A. Deem, CRT, USNR — Silver Star.
L. B. Edward Dauplaise, CQM, USN — Navy and Marine Corps Medal.
Roland J. Chamberlain, CTM, USN — Bronze Star.
Herbert D. Hayward, CMoMM, USN — Bronze Star.
Ladislaus Topor, CMoMM, USN — Bronze Star.
Merritt D. Fallon, CTM, USN — Bronze Star.
John P. Gutensohn, CMoMM, USN — Bronze Star.
Eric P. Boleman, CRT, USNR — Bronze Star.
Thomas P. Kemp, CEM, USN — Bronze Star.

Frank N. Stoltz, CRM, USN — Letter of Commendation.
Ray Roberts, RM1c, USNR — Silver Star.
James W. Goin, FCS1c, USN — Bronze Star.
Glenn E. Stoy, GM1c, USN — Bronze Star.
Allan H. Gordon, MoMM1c, USN — Bronze Star.
Raymond H. Voss, EM1c, USN — Bronze Star.
William H. Hetrick, MoMM1c, USN — Letter of Commendation.
Eugene D. Shelton, MoMM1c, USN — Letter of Commendation.
John L. Perro, MoMM1c, USN — Letter of Commendation.
Phillip C. Sears, TM2c, USN — Bronze Star.
John N. Lane, RM2c, USN — Bronze Star.
Charles A. Darrah, TM2c, USN — Letter of Commendation.
Earl S. Schley, MoMM2c, USNR — Letter of Commendation.
Charles E. Wiseman, RM2c, USNR — Letter of Commendation.
William E. Wilson, Cox, USN — Bronze Star.
Ellis D. Branchcomb, FCS3c, USNR — Bronze Star.
Clark S. Smith, TM3c, USN — Letter of Commendation.
Otha L. Frith, MoMM3c, USNR — Letter of Commendation.
Lloyd J. Kronberg, S1c, USNR — Letter of Commendation.

Appendix 2: Summary of Claimed Successful Attacks
Based Upon Data by Alden and Somerville

Cmndr	Ptrl	Mth/Yr	Day/Hr	Type	Name	Tons	Verified Claim
	Comments						
Jensen	1	Sep 43	17/03	AK	See Comment	None	
	WPR says hit heard, target stopped with port list then started again.						
	1	Sep 43	17/03	AP	See Comment	None	
	WPR says target disappeared, breaking up noise. Ultra report torpedo track at 04-20S 127-20E.						
	1	Oct 43	9/11	AO	Kumagawa M.	7508	Damaged
	WPR says hits heard, smoking aft. Ultra report 2 hits, towed to Surabaya, out until June 1944. [WIJN (see Alden) says AK converted to AO in 1943. Sunk on 12 January 1945 by aircraft.]						
Selby	2	Dec 43	13/05	AP-Army	Teiko M.		None
	WPR says hit heard, settled but continued. Ultra says 15,105 ton AP *Teiko Maru* report torpedo track at 14-29N 119-59E, no damage. [Later sunk 22 February 1944 by SS268 PUFFER; ex–French liner *D'Artagnan*.]						
	2	Dec 43	20/08	DD	Fuyo	820	Sunk
	WPR says stern blown off, sunk. Ultra position 14-45N 119-54E. [Fuyo rerated as patrol boat when sunk.]						
	2	Dec 43	20/09	AP	See Comment	None	
	WPR says 1 premature, possible hits heard. Ultra says 3212 ton AP *Gozan Maru* reported torpedo tracks at 14-40N 119-55E. [Sunk 30 March 1944 by aircraft.]						
	2	Jan 44	1/03	None			
	WPR says timed explosion heard on tender for the 8 or 10 smaller ships.						
	2	Jan 44	1/03	AK-Army	Ryuyo M.	6707	Sunk
	WPR says hit seen, orange flash, black smoke. Somerville says left Wasili, Halmahara,						

Cmndr	Ptrl	Mth/Yr	Day/Hr	Type	Name	Tons	Verified Claim
		Comments					

on 28 December for Manila with 88 passengers; about 0414 on 1 January at 08-36N 144-51E was torpedoed and sunk, 1 passenger and 6 crew killed.

| | 2 | Jan 44 | 7/15 | Trawler | Nansing M. #16 | 85 | Sunk |

WPR says sunk by 3-inch deck gun; ship identified by survivor.

| Selby | 3 | Feb 44 | 22/17 | AP-Army | Teiko M. | 15105 | Sunk |

WPR says stopped, boats in water, hit again and sunk. The *Teiko Maru* was carrying 906 passengers. Japanese records reported 201 casualties and 800 tons of cargo went to the bottom. Survivors were later rescued on February 24 and 25 and taken to Singapore. [Ex-French liner *D'Artagnan*.]

| Selby | 4 | May 44 | 18/05 | AK-Army | Shinryu M. | 3181 | Sunk |

WPR says hits seen, stern under, radar pip lost.

| | 4 | May 44 | 22/10 | CVE | Chitose | 11190 | None |

WPR says 2 carriers in company, hit heard. Torpedo exploded in prop wake of carrier, no damage.

| | 4 | Jun 44 | 5/10 | AO | Ashizuri M. | 7951 | Sunk |

WPR says seen sinking by bow. Somerville says left Yap 1 June 1944 for Balikpapan with *Takasaki* and CDs *Kanju* and *Miyake* (escorts); on 5 June was torpedoed, burned and sunk.

| | 4 | Jun 44 | 5/10 | AO-Gas | Takasaki M. | 4465 | Sunk |

WPR says burning, down by stern. Somerville says sunk.

| | 4 | Jun 44 | 5/10 | AO | See Comment | 856 | Damage |

WPR says took port list. Ultra report *Hishi Maru #2* damaged, arrived Surabaya 11 June. Somerville says escorts were *Kanju* and *Miyake*, not hit. [Probably misidentified; does not resemble target; left Surabaya in convoy 26 June; sunk 9 November 1944 by SS255 HADDO.]

| Selby | 5 | Aug 44 | 1/11 | AO-Gas | Sunosaki M. | 4465 | Damage |

WPR says big explosion on bow and bridge, screws lost, breaking up noise. Ultra reports position 05-08N 119-32E, reached Manila. Somerville says damaged by torpedo on 1 August, arrived at Manila 1 September and placed in Dewey drydock for repair, bombed there and burned 21 September, removed 4 October and left abandoned. [JANAC credits aircraft attack of 21 September 1944.]

| | 5 | Aug 44 | 7/13 | Sub Chaser | Kyo M. #2 | 340 | Sunk |

WPR says disintegrated.

| | 5 | Aug 44 | 12/07 | | None | | |

WPR says hits seen, target listed and settling.

| | 5 | Aug 44 | 12/07 | AO | Shinpo M. | 5135 | Sunk |

WPR says afire, down by bow. Ultra report aground off Golo Island. IJN says disabled. Somerville says continuation of convoy MI-13, left Manila 11 August, about 0730 on 12 August hit starboard side forward, 20 killed, towed by *Shoei Maru* and *Kyoei Maru* and run ashore, considered sunk. [JANAC credits jointly with SS222 BLUEFISH attack on 17 August 1944.]

| | 5 | Aug 44 | 12/07 | AO-Civilian | Teikon M. | 5113 | Sunk |

WPR says 2 AOs last seen abandoned and drifting. Ultra report sunk at about 1805.

Cmndr	Ptrl	Mth/Yr	Day/Hr	Type	Name	Tons	Verified Claim

Comments

Somerville says tried to ram sub when Shinpo M sunk, hit at about 0733 and sunk, no casualties.

| Dwyer | 6 | Jan 45 | 4/17 | Lugger | | 200? | Sunk? |

WPR says steam lugger, disintegrated.

| | 6 | Jan 45 | 10/02 | AO | See Comment | | None |

WPR says hits seen, target blew up and sunk. Somerville (4) says Coastal Defense (CD) 30 and Coastal Defense 42 left Keelung for Kagoshima 5 January with convoy, no record of damage to any maru. [See below.]

| | 6 | Jan 45 | 10/02 | AK | See Comment | | None |

WPR says hit seen, target sunk. [See comments above and below.]

| | 6 | Jan 45 | 10/04 | AK | See Comment | | None |

WPR says timed hit heard. [See comments above and below.]

| | 6 | Jan 45 | 10/04 | Frigate | CD 42 | 940 | Sunk |

WPR says hit under bridge, sunk immediately. Somerville says was on port side of convoy, hit by torpedo, blew up and sunk with all hands, 170 lost.

| | 6 | Jan 45 | 10/04 | Frigate | CD 30 | 940 | Damage |

WPR says timed hit heard, DD seen with bow down. Ultra report sub sighted, CD damaged at 26-45N 126-11E. Somerville says hit shortly after CD 42, bow and bridge wrecked, made 5 kts to Okinawa, 5 killed. [Sunk 28 July 1945 by aircraft.]

| | 6 | Jan 45 | 10/14 | AK | None | | |

WPR says timed hit heard. [See above comments.]

| Dwyer | 8 | Jul 45 | 5/13 | Barge | | 20 | Sunk |

Attacked as below.

| | 8 | Jul 45 | 5/13 | Barge | | 20 | Sunk |

Attacked as below.

| | 8 | Jul 45 | 5/13 | Barge | | 20 | Sunk |

Attacked as below.

| | 8 | Jul 45 | 5/13 | Lugger | | 200 | Sunk |

WPR says 5 landing barges burned and exploded from 5-inch deck gun hits. Ultra report says 2 subs shelled and torpedoed ships, Shuttle Boat #153 and 4 landing barges sunk, *Hihon Maru* a 112 ton vessel destroyed by fire. [See attacks by PUFFER below and above; also attacked by SS373 LIZARDFISH .]

| | 8 | Jul 45 | 5/15 | Lugger | Heiyo M. | 200 | Sunk |

WPR says sunk lugger previously hit by 373 LIZARDFISH.

| | 8 | Jul 45 | 5/15 | Sea Truck | Shuttle Bt #153 | 50 | Sunk |

WPR says broke in two from 5-inch deck gun hits. [See above comments.]

| | 8 | Jul 45 | 5/15 | Barge | | 20 | Sunk |

WPR says sunk.

| | 8 | Jul 45 | 5/18 | Sea Truck | Nihon M. | 112 | Sunk |

WPR says disintegrated. Ultra message reports torpedo attack, burning.

Total Sunk: 50,684 tons
Total Damage: 13,769 tons

Appendix 3: *Postwar* Puffer *Service Roster*

MEN WHO SERVED ON THE *PUFFER* AFTER HOSTILITIES HAD CEASED

Last Name	First Name	Service Number	Rate Received	Date Received
Asbury	Ralph H., Jr.	393 80 60	TM3c	11-Dec-45
Asman	Kenneth	378 61 55	ETM3c	21-Feb-46
Bailey	William H.	845 73 15	S1c	11-Mar-46
Baird	Howard D.	945 69 19	S2c	08-Nov-45
Banker	Robert Keith	381 85 01	MoMM3c	28-Nov-45
Bateman	Perry W.	375 66 87	CMoMMA	24-Aug-45
Battcher	George J.	713 83 66	S1c(RM)	21-Jan-46
Beaver	Donald D.	311 83 62	MoMM1c	26-Aug-45
Bechtold	Donald G.	246 37 04	MoMM3c	15-Feb-46
Bell	Theodore, Jr.	629 80 35	EM3c	11-Mar-46
Bergh	Gerald D.	412 86 73	QM3c	12-Mar-46
Borteski	John	819 41 69	Bkr3c	16-Sep-45
Brinkman	C. A., Jr.	381 96 23	F1(MoMM)	26-Nov-45
Browning	John F.	850 95 63	S1c	29-Mar-46
Bunkowske	Alvin W.	870 73 77	EM3c	12-Mar-46
Carr	Chester E.	606 36 07	MoMM1c	11-Mar-46
Carter	Fred	933 56 64	StM1c	21-Feb-46
Chaffee	Edwin W.	201 92 05	MoMM2c	06-Nov-45
Coghlan	Neil C.	378 65 70	ETM3c	01-Dec-45
Corbeal	Rodolphe N.	205 70 11	RM3c	06-Nov-45
Coughlin	Gale M.	316 67 12	RM1c	12-Dec-45
Crossman	Robert H.	857 55 57	QM3c	29-Mar-46
Dawes	Arthur P.	375 60 83	CTM	08-Feb-46
Dehosse	Harry V.	311 69 52	EM1c	30-Oct-45
Dickinson	L. R.	263 50 63	RM1c	11-Dec-45
Dineen	Timothy J.	201 84 65	Bkr1c	20-Dec-45

Last Name	First Name	Service Number	Rate Received	Date Received
Dullum	Henry	852 01 01	EM3c	29-Mar-46
Eaton	Karl Harris	609 75 40	RM3c	01-Dec-45
Fedor	Robert Carl	328 93 77	EM1c	06-Nov-45
Ferrie	Cornelius P.	225 53 37	S1(TM)	08-Nov-45
Fisher	Robert W.	274 63 72	CMoMM	26-Aug-45
Forbis	Eldon L.	842 65 52	RM3c	29-Mar-46
Freeman	Frank E., Jr.	396 04 76	MoMM2c	05-Dec-45
Gagneaux	Paul Reves	275 09 72	ETM3c	08-Nov-45
Galyean	Thomas	360 18 13	MoMM1c	21-Feb-46
Grumbrecht	R. F.	708 95 20	MoMM1c	22-Dec-45
Hahn	William, Jr.	278 51 16	TM3c	10-Nov-45
Hale	Francis G.	866 91 23	F1(EM)	08-Nov-45
Hall	Merle	876 97 66	MoMM3c	29-Mar-46
Hatt	David D.	322 26 61	S1c(RM)	22-Feb-46
Holden	Eugene F.	372 36 41	RM2c	28-Nov-45
Hull	Leon Sylvester	246 00 72	Y2c	01-Dec-45
Kadlic	Keith Mervin	865 70 55	F1(MoMM)	26-Aug-45
Keane	Peter Joseph	601 60 59	F1(MMS)	26-Aug-45
Koenig	Elmer H., Jr.	735 87 45	S1c	29-Mar-46
Krotzer	Robert K.	311 47 23	CPhMA	21-Feb-46
Kupiec	Joseph L.	212 85 23	EM3c	02-Nov-45
Landry	James Joseph	275 11 97	MoMM3c	11-Dec-45
Levander	Walter R.	283 24 32	CMoMM	07-Feb-46
Lindmark	Algot O.	727 91 08	S1c	21-Feb-46
Marshall	Robert F.	280 55 06	GM2c	29-Mar-46
McGehee	Claude	300 73 45	TM3c	10-Oct-45
McKay	Thomas R.	234 40 09	TM2c	27-Nov-45
Meister	Bernard L.	329 29 35	Y2c	30-Dec-45
Miller	Roy Marlyn	321 86 95	MoMM3c	12-Dec-45
Millspaugh	S. C.	760 05 43	MoMM3c	30-Mar-46
Motusovic	John L., Jr.	910 58 43	S2c	05-Dec-45
Otto	Stanley W.	342 75 93	SM2c	01-Jan-46
Owen	Lester Eugene	268 67 75	MoMM1c	06-Nov-45
Papalexis	James A.	565 50 23	TM3c	11-Mar-46
Parker	John A.	287 06 76	CTM	30-Oct-45
Parkhurst	Robert D.	510 49 78	S1c(MM)	20-Feb-46
Pfeifer	Robert H.	632 01 37	TM3c	08-Nov-45
Pfeiffer	C. P. C.	316 33 91	GM1c	14-Jan-46
Pitsch	Carl Francis	566 16 15	S2(RM)	05-Dec-45
Poe	John Darrell	849 56 05	S1(SC)	05-Dec-45
Poling	George F.	756 17 89	GM3c	29-Jan-46
Preston	Jack G.	357 51 18	Bkr3c	10-Oct-45
Ramser	Forrest L.	857 41 6?	EM2c	15-Feb-46
Raney	Bernard	865 58 07	RM3c	26-Aug-45
Rasmussen	Calvin	301 04 18	GM3c	20-Feb-46
Romaszewski	A. S.	238 78 11	MoMM2c	13-Dec-45
Sauvageau	Joseph G.	311 29 37	CMoMMA	19-Mar-46
Schraier	Carl	381 98 43	S1c	08-Nov-45

Last Name	First Name	Service Number	Rate Received	Date Received
Scott	Leroy W.	306 32 59	EM3c	11-Dec-45
Simmons	Ted G.	683 78 34	RM3c	11-Mar-46
Simonson	Jack E.	300 49 61	TM1c	10-Oct-45
Stocker	Garth	376 39 97	QM1c	27-Nov-45
Strauhal	Frank E.	890 32 38	TM3c	11-Mar-46
Svacina	Richard H.	871 73 30	TM3c	21-Feb-46
Taylor	John Harry	937 00 17	StM2c	08-Dec-45
Thompson	James M.	840 69 99	EM3c	29-Mar-46
Veber	Rene Yvon J.	566 29 43	S2c(QM)	05-Dec-45
Walker	Earl Leroy	980 78 72	StM1c	30-Oct-45
Washburn	Dana R.	825 44 00	F1(MoMM)	21-Feb-46
Westman	Dale H.	865 88 89	EM3c	29-Mar-46
White	Erwin Libby	926 95 31	S1(RM)	05-Dec-45
Williams	Gordon B.	256 53 07	F1(MoMM)	21-Feb-46

Bibliography

Published Works

Alden, John D. *The Fleet Submarine in the U.S. Navy — A Design and Construction History.* Annapolis: Naval Institute Press, 1979.

_____. *United States and Allied Submarine Successes in the Pacific and Far East during World War II — Chronological Listing.* Second Edition. Delmar, NY: Published by the author, October 1999. Updated 2006.

Barker, Anthony J., and Lisa Jackson. *Fleeting Attraction.* Nedlands, Western Australia: University of Western Australia Press, 1996.

Blair, Clay. *Silent Victory: The U.S. Submarine War against Japan.* Philadelphia: J. B. Lippincott, 1975.

Bosco, Gerardo, et al. "Effects of Hypoxia on Circadian Patterns in Men." *High Altitude Medicine and Biology* 4, no 3 (Fall 2003): 305–318.

Casey, Robert J. *Battle Below — The War of the Submarines.* Indianapolis: Bobbs-Merrill, 1945. (Written in the spring of 1943, publication delayed by the Navy based upon national security.)

Dossey, Larry. *Space, Time, and Medicine.* New York: Random House, 1982.

Ffield, A., et al. "Temperature Variability within Makassar Strait." *Geophysical Research Letters* 27, 2000: 237–240.

"Flag Raising Ceremony on Hull 268." Manitowoc Shipbuilding Company Employee Newspaper: *Keel Block,* October 1972, page 13.

"4th Sub Will Be Launched Here Sunday." *Manitowoc Herald-Times,* November 21, 1942, pages 1 and 2.

Frankenhaeuser, Marianne, et al. "Behavioural and Physiological Effects of Cigarette Smoking in a Monotonous Situation." *Psychopharmacology* 22, no. 1 (March 1971): 1–6.

Gannon, Robert. *Hellions of the Deep: The Development of American Torpedoes in World War II.* University Park: Pennsylvania State Press, 1996.

"'Gob' Gets 3 Years for Killing R.A.N. Youngster." *The Mirror* (Perth, Australia), August 12, 1944, page 11.

Gugliotta, Bobette. *Pigboat 39 — An American Sub Goes to War.* Lexington: University of Kentucky Press, 1984.

Jensen, Marvin John. "Biography." United States Naval Academy, Annapolis, MD. *Shipmate,* June 1993.

Knoblock, Glenn A. *Black Submariners in the United States Navy, 1940–1975.* Jefferson, NC: McFarland, 2006.

LaVo, Carl. *Back from the Deep — The Strange Story of the Sister Subs Squalus and Sculpin.* Annapolis: U.S. Naval Institute Press, 1994. Pages 15–17.

Michno, Gregory F. *USS Pampanito: Killer-Angel.* Norman: University of Oklahoma Press, 2000.

"Navy Day Fete Here Nears End." *Contra Costa Gazette,* October 27, 1945.

"Navy Week Is Observed in Martinez." *Contra Costa Gazette,* October 23, 1945.

Nelson, William T. *Fresh Water Submarines: The Manitowoc Story.* Manitowoc: Hoeffner Printing, 1986.

Noble, Bruce J. *Physiology of Exercise and Sport.* St. Louis: Times Mirror/Mosby College Publishing, 1986.

O'Kane, Richard H. *Clear the Bridge: The War Patrols of the USS Tang.* Chicago: Rand McNally, 1977.

"*Puffer* Decommissioning Ceremony Marks Final Sub to Join 19th Fleet at Mare Island." *The Grapevine* (Mare Island Shipyard Newspaper), July 12, 1945.

Roscoe, Theodore. *United States Submarine Oper-*

ations in World War II. Annapolis: United States Naval Institute, 1949.
Ruhe, William J. *War in the Boats: My World War II Submarine Battles*. Washington, DC: Brasseys, 1996.
Sasgen, Peter T. *Red Scorpion — The War Patrols of the USS Rasher*. Annapolis: United States Naval Institute, 1995.
"Secrets of the 'Silent Service.'" *The San Francisco Chronicle*, October 17, 1945, p.13.
Somerville, William. *Maru Special*. No. 34, 1979.
_____. Translation of *Kaibokan Senki* (*Coast Defense Ship Military History*, published by Coast Defense Ship Association, 1982).
_____. Translation of *Senji Sempaku Shi* (*Wartime Ships History*, by Shinshichiro Komamiya, privately printed, 1991).
_____. Translation of *Senji Yuso Senda Shi, Part I*. (*Wartime Transportation Convoys History*, by Shinshichiro Komamiya. Tokyo: Shuppan Kydosha, 1987).
_____. Translation of *Senji Yuso Senda Shi, Part II*. (*Wartime Transportation Convoys History*, by Shinshichiro Komamiya. Tokyo: Shuppan Kydosha, 1995).
Spiegel, Leproult, and Eve Van Cauter. "Impact of Sleep Debt on Metabolic and Endocrine Function." *The Lancet* 354, 1999: 1435–9.
Sturma, Michael. *Death at a Distance: The Loss of the Legendary USS Harder*. Annapolis: Naval Institute Press, 2006.
"Submarine Crew Welcomed in Martinez." *Contra Costa Gazette*, October 26, 1945.
"To Use *Puffer* in Atom Bomb Test." *Manitowoc Herald-Times*, January 1946.
Tuohy, William. *The Bravest Man — The Story of Richard O'Kane & U.S. Submariners in the Pacific War*. Phoenix Mill: Sutton 2001.
"'Unlawful Killing' Verdict Against Yank." *The Mirror* (Perth, Australia), June 24, 1944, page 9.

Unpublished Personal Manuscripts, Documents, Videos, and Letters

Baird, Howard D. Personal history. *Rite of Passage into Submarines*; personal correspondence 11/9/2001.
Liggett, James D. Personal history. *The Trials and Tribulations of the USS Puffer (SS 268)*.
Metz, Thomas A. Personal history. *Two Years Navy Duty of Thomas Addison Metz*, April 10, 1976. London, AK.
Polk, Robert, and Sanders, John. Video recordings of World War II Submarine Veterans Convention — *Puffer* Reunion Breakfast, Orlando, FL, September 7, 1990.
_____. Video recordings of World War II Submarine Veterans Convention — *Puffer* Reunion Breakfast, San Antonio, TX, October 4, 1991.
_____. Video recordings of World War II Submarine Veterans Convention — *Puffer* Reunion Breakfast, Anaheim, CA, September 9, 1993.
Stoy, Glenn E. Personal diary. *Day by Day Account of the Third, Fourth, and Fifth War Patrols of the United States Submarine Puffer (SS-268)*.
_____. Personal diary. *Account of the Sixth, Seventh, Eighth & Ninth War Patrols of the USS Puffer (SS-268)*.
Thoman, Andrew J. Personal history. *What I Remember about the Submarine Service*; personal correspondence 4/20/2001.

Unpublished Government Documents, Research Notes, Citations and Commendations, Naval Archives, National Archives, and Library of Congress Sources

Allied Claims and Enemy Confirmation of Damage to Japanese Ships — October, November, and December, 1943. (Short Title: PSIS 200-10). Document SHR 184 (Part II). Pages 317–8. Naval Historical Center, Washington Navy Yard, DC.
Bernard, Lawrence G. Service record: Navy Office of Information Internal Relations Division (OI-430), 18 October 1971. Operational Archives, Naval Historical Center, Washington Navy Yard, DC.
_____. Citations and Commendations. Operational Archives, Naval Historical Center, Washington Navy Yard, DC.
Biche, Robert C. Officer Biography Sheet: Naval Personnel form 979, 4 April 1958. Operational Archives, Naval Historical Center, Washington Navy Yard, DC.
Blair, Clay. Research notes for *Silent Victory*: American Heritage Center, University of Wyoming. Laramie, WY. Accession Number 8295, Box No. 77, Folder No. 42. U.S. Pacific Ocean Submarine Fleet — *Puffer*.
Branchcomb, Ellis D. "Bronze Star Citation" from John L. Sullivan, secretary of the Navy.
Christie, Ralph W. Correspondence to Capt. Allan R. McCann. 9 December 1943. Personal letters at the Library of Congress, MSS collection.
_____. Correspondence to Homer Graf, USN, chief of staff, 7th Fleet. 15 February 1944. Personal letters at the Library of Congress, MSS collection.
Deem, Jay. "Silver Star Citation" from James Forrestal, secretary of the Navy.
Dwyer, Carl R. *Puffer: Ship's History*. With addendums:
   Reference: Alpac 202–45. Serial 100. 26 October 1945.
   Reference: Alpac 278. Serial 114. 12 November 1945. Awards supplement.

Reference: Alpac 318. Ship's History Supplement #2. 8 January 1946.
Reference: Serial 157. Ship's History Supplement #3. 27 June 1946 (by R.F. Reilly).
———. "Silver Star Citation" from James Forrestal, secretary of the Navy, prepared 29 September 1946.
———. "Navy Cross Citation" from James Forrestal, secretary of the Navy, prepared 1 November 1946.
———. Officer Biography Sheet: Naval Personnel form 979, 22 July 1955. Operational Archives, Naval Historical Center, Washington Navy Yard, DC.
———. Officer Biography Sheet: Naval Personnel form 979, 30 June 1965.
Frith, Otha A. "Commendation Citation" from C. W. Nimitz, fleet admiral. Operational Archives, Naval Historical Center, Washington Navy Yard, DC.
Hess, Franklin G. Citations and Commendations. Operational Archives, Naval Historical Center, Washington Navy Yard, DC.
Japanese Underwater Sound Gear and Methods. Internal U.S. Navy Document, *Weekly Intelligence* 1, no. 4 (August 4, 1944).
Jensen, Marvin J. Citations and Commendations. Operational Archives, Naval Historical Center, Washington Navy Yard, DC.
McCallum, J. L. P. Memorandum for: Task Force Seventy-two. 30 October 1943.
National Archives II. Records Group 24 (RG24). College Park, MD. Microfilm of USS *Puffer* Enlisted Men Muster Rolls, reel 6363.
National Archives II. Microfiche Publication M1752, Records Group 38 (RG38). U.S. Submarine War Patrol Reports, 1941–1945, USS *Puffer*. War Patrol No. 1, Fiche 00670; War Patrol No. 2, Fiche 00671; War Patrol No. 3, Fiche 00672; War Patrol No. 4, Fiche 00673; War Patrol No. 5, Fiche 00674; War Patrol No. 6, Fiche 00676; War Patrol No. 7, Fiche 00677; War Patrols No. 8 and 9, Fiche 00678.
Penzenik, William. "Case of William Penzenik, Motor Machinist's Mate Second Class, U.S. Navy, July 25, 1944 — Record of the Proceedings of a General Court-Martial Convened on Board of the USS *Griffin* by order of the Commander U.S. Naval Forces Western Australia," Document #103998. Obtained via the Freedom of Information Act.
———. United States Consular Reports from Perth during World War 2, National Archives, Washington, D.C. Suitland Branch, General Records 1945, Volume 5. Letter from Mrs. Ashton to U.S. Consulate Officer Turner.
Pruitt, John Alden. "Case of John Alden Pruitt, Steward's Mate First Class, U. S. Navy, June 2, 1944 — Record of the Proceedings of a General Court-Martial Convened on Board of the USS *Orion* by order of the Commander U.S. Naval Forces Western Australia," Document #128932. Obtained via the Freedom of Information Act.
Pugh, William M. Citations and Commendations. Operational Archives, Naval Historical Center, Washington Navy Yard, DC.
———. Biography. United States Naval Academy — Alumni Bureau.
Selby, Frank G. Biography. Navy — Office of Information, Internal Relations Division (OI-430), 25 July, 1968.
Somerville, William. Translation of *Tabular Records of Submarine-chasers*, Microfilm JD-208. Operational Archives, Naval Historical Center, Washington Navy Yard, DC.
Stoy, Glenn. "Bronze Star Citation."
Voge, Richard G., et al. *Operational History*. Command Submarine Pacific (ComSubPac), 1946. Operational Archives, Naval Historical Center, Washington Navy Yard, DC.

Personal Communications

A Personal Data Sheet was sent by the author to crew members. They answered the following: nickname, highest rate, other naval service, why submarines, events during boot camp and submarine school, activities while on leave, best friends on the *Puffer*, best and worst days while on the *Puffer*, activities after the war, sacrifices during the war, what they wanted most, other stories and recollections.

Alden, John. Radar specifications, letter, comments on manuscript, 6/30/2006.
Allen, Carroll. From son Bishop Harold H. Allen, e-mail and photograph 12/26/2003; from son Herman L. Allen, service record and photographs 8/16/2005.
Allen, John. Personal interviews at the World War II Submarine Veterans Convention in St. Louis, MO, on 8/20/2001 and 8/21/2001.
Bernard, Jon. E-mail correspondence with personal information and photographs of his father Lawrence G. Bernard 1/24/2006.
Branchcomb, Ellis. Personal Data Sheet 2/15/2005; phone interview 1/26/2005.
Brockhausen, Charles. Phone interview 1/31/2002.
Brown, Charles E. phone interview 1/15/2002; letter to the author with personal account and comments on the First War Patrol text, 1/30/2002.
Coggins, Donald. Phone interview 11/24/2004.
Corcoran, Frank. Personal Data Sheet 4/24/2001; phone interview 11/24/2004.
Dauplaise, Louis B. E. Personal Data Sheet 5/16/2001; personal letter to the author 11/20/2000.
Deem, Jay. Telephone and personal interviews on 6/25/2003, 12/19/2003, 2/23/2004, 4/5/2004,

10/18/2004, 10/24/2004 (in person), 7/11/2005, and 8/15/2005.

Deiss, Harold. Telephone interview 3/26/2004.

Dobson, Kenneth. Letter to the author 1/12/2002 with "Some Recollections of October 9 and 10, 1943"; letter to the author 12/3/2005; phone interview 1/31/2006.

Dufault, Ernest J. E-mail correspondence from John Harto 1/2002 and 1/2004, who had personal conversations with Dufault.

Dwyer, Carl R. Personal Data Sheet 5/10/2001; comments on First War Patrol text 1/15/2002; phone interview 2/9/2004.

Frith, Otha L. Phone interview 1/27/2004; letter to the author 1/28/2004.

Funk, Leonard. E-mail 5/23/2001 from R. E. Bouska, notes on personal conversations with Funk.

Golay, Frank H. Personal letters to Clara Wood between 11/14/1944 and 9/14/1945 and photograph collection.

Hartman, Raymond. Personal Data Sheet 2/10/2004; phone interview 2/25/2004; E-mail message 1/5/2006.

Hess, Franklin G. Personal letter to John Sanders from his son, Dan Hess; phone interview with Dan Hess 8/15/2005.

Johnson, Charles. Phone interviews 3/10/2004, 3/22/2004 and 4/14/2004; voice recording of personal history of his wartime service and recollections of the *Puffer* patrols.

Keane, Peter J. Personal Data Sheet 10/21/2002; letter to the author 10/21/2002.

Kennedy, Robert F. Phone interview with Kapryan Kennedy, son, 2/25/2004.

Lane, John, Personal Data Sheet 6/14/2001.

Mays, Frank. Phone interviews 1/14/2004, 2/4/2004, 2/27/2004, and 8/19/2004; personal interviews 4/15/2004 and 4/20/2005.

Mazzone, Walter. Phone interviews 6/18/2002, 7/28/2002, 11/6/2003, and 7/10/2006; e-mail correspondence 7/28/2002, 7/29/2002, 7/31/2002, 8/1/2002, 8/9/2002, 8/11/2002, and 8/12/2002.

McDonald, Donald B. Personal Data Sheet 4/30/2001; ongoing telephone conversations and personal interview 9/30/2003.

McGinley, Rear Admiral (Retired) E. S. "Skip." E-mail correspondence 8/15/2006.

McKee, Richard. Personal Data Sheet 6/7/2001.

Metz, Thomas. Personal Data Sheet 11/14/2001; letter to the author 4/27/2006.

Parker, James V. Personal Data Sheet 4/30/2001.

Penzenik, William. E-mail and telephone conversations with Charles Penzenik (son) and Elaine Penzenik (wife) during June 2004.

Picone, Lawrence. Phone interview 7/11/2006; letter to the author 7/17/2006.

Polk, Robert. Phone interview 11/25/2003.

Reynolds, Arthur. Personal Data Sheet, 3/5/2004.

Rindskopf, RADM Maurice. E-mail with comments on the TDC and Fire Control (FC) approach procedures, 8/31/2006.

Roberts, Raymond. Phone interview 1/29/2004.

Rohrback, Frank. Personal Data Sheet 11/15/2001.

Sander, Harold. Phone interview 9/26/2003; letter to the author 9/20/2004.

Sanders, John. Letters to the author 9/17/02 and 1/17/04.

Solak, John. Phone interviews 12/15/2001, 11/13/2003, and 5/7/2004.

Spalding, Kelan. E-mail correspondence about his brother, Robert.

Stager, Joel. E-mail 1/14/2002.

Stoy, Glenn. Personal Data Sheet and letter to the author 4/10/2001; phone interview 7/23/2003; letter to the author 10/6/2005.

Thatcher, Roy. Personal Data Sheet 5/21/2001.

Thoman, Andrew J. Personal Data Sheet 4/10/2001; letters to the author 4/10/2001 and 5/21/2001.

Tidd, Russell. Personal Data Sheet 5/24/2001; phone interviews 7/23/2003, 9/19/2003, and 5/19/2006; e-mail correspondence 12/31/2001, 1/2/2002, 2/7/2002, 2/10/2002, 2/11/2002, 4/7/2002, 8/9/2002, 8/13/2003, 4/30/2004, 5/1/2004, 5/2/2004, 5/4/2004, 5/5/2004, 5/6/2004, 5/7/2004, 5/11/2004, and 11/22/2005.

_____. Comments on "Get-Away at Forty Fathoms" in *True Tales of Bold Escapes* by Theodore Roscoe. Englewood Cliffs, NJ: Prentice Hall, 1965, pages 57–81.

_____. Comments on "Depth Charging of the *Puffer*" in *United States Submarine Operations in World War II* by Theodore Roscoe. Annapolis: Naval Institute Press, 1949, chapter section, pages 274–278.

Topor, Ladislaus. Letters to the author 9/18/2003 and 2/13/2004; phone interview 7/24/2003.

Trudeau, Norman. Phone interviews 7/18/2003, 7/21/2003, and 5/24/2004.

Washburn, Edgar W. E-mail from Greg Washburn, his son, 10/29/2004 and 10/30/2004.

Williamson, Elmer C. E-mail March 18, 2002.

Wiseman, Charles E. Phone interview 8/13/2005.

Internet Sources (Date of last access)

BBC — British Broadcasting: h2g2. "Sleep Deprivation." http://www.bbc.co.uk/dna/h2g2/alabaster/A261046 (accessed July 2002).

CNN. "Sleep Deprivation as Bad as Alcohol Impairment, Study Suggests." http://archives.cnn.com/2000/HEALTH/09/20/sleep.deprivation/index.html (accessed July 2002).

Commander Submarine Force U.S. Pacific Fleet. USS *Bullhead* (SS 332) History. http://www.csp.navy.mil/ww2boats/bullhead.htm (accessed November 29, 2006).

Dewey, Dr. Russell A. "How to Recognize You Are Under Stress." Psych web. http://www.psywww.com/mtsite/smsymstr.html (accessed October 2006).

DrugEducation.net, "Caffeine." http://www.drugeducation.net/caffeine.htm (accessed October 2006)

Frank, Lee. "Do We Really Need to Sleep?" http://www.viewzone.com/sleep.html (accessed July 2002).

Hackett, Bob, Sander Kingsepp, and Peter Cundall. *KUSENTEI!* Stories and Battle Histories of the IJN's Sub-chasers. http://www.combinedfleet.com/kusentei.htm (accessed October 26, 2006).

———. *CH-4*: Tabular Record of Movement. http://www.combinedfleet.com/CH-4_t.htm (accessed October 26, 2006).

Hackett, Bob, et al. IJN NAGATO: Tabular Record of Movement. http://www.combinedfleet.com/nagatrom.htm (accessed October 19, 2006).

———. IJN YAMATO: Tabular Record of Movement. http://www.combinedfleet.com/yamato.htm (accessed October 19, 2006).

Harris, Steve, MD. Carbon Dioxide Poisoning. http://yarchive.net/med/co2_poisoning.html (accessed October 13, 2006)

International Labour Organization: "Copper Sulphate (II) Pentahydrate." http://www.ilo.org/public/english/protection/safework/cis/products/icsc/dtasht/_icsc14/icsc1416.htm (accessed August 2006).

Kueh, Lt. H. S. "Notes of interview of Marvin J. Jensen" transcribed by Patrick Clancey. http://www.ibiblio.org/hyperwar/USN/ships/logs/SS/ss200-WP_1-3.html (accessed July 2002).

Mountain High E&S Co. *Hypoxia*. http://www.mhoxygen.com/index.phtml?nav_id=26&article_id=10 (accessed October 13, 2006).

NMHA—National Mental Health Association. "Seasonal Affective Disorder." http://www.nmha.org/infoctr/factsheets/27.cfm (accessed July 2002).

OutDoorPlaces.com. "Heat Injuries." http://www.outdoorplaces.com/Features/Hiking/heat/index.html (accessed July 2002).

"Submarine Veterans Honored in San Francisco." The United States Navy on the World Wide Web, Navy Wire Service, April 10, 2000. http://www.chinfo.navy.mil/navpalib/news/navywire/nws00/nws000410.txt (accessed August 17, 2006).

Transport Canada. *Hypoxia and Hyperventilation.* http://www.tc.gc.ca/CivilAviation/Cam/tp13312-2/section2/hypoxia.htm (accessed October 13, 2006).

Tully, Anthony P. IJN Chitose: Tabular Record of Movement. http://www.combinedfleet.com/Chitose.htm (accessed October 19, 2006).

———. IJN Shoho: Tabular Record of Movement. http://www.combinedfleet.com/shoho.htm (accessed November 1, 2006).

———. IJN Zuiho: Tabular Record of Movement. http://www.combinedfleet.com/Zuiho.htm (accessed November 1, 2006).

Twilight Bridge. "Survival Stress." http://www.twilightbridge.com/stress/complete/3apossiblesources.htm#Survival%20Stress (accessed July 2002).

———. "Symptoms of Stress: How Stressed Are You???" http://www.twilightbridge.com/stress/complete/4symptomsofstress.htm (accessed July 2002).

University of Virginia Weather Site. Apparent Temperature Chart and Explanation. Courtesy of the *Climate Analysis Center*. http://climate.virginia.edu/Climate/apparent_temp.html (accessed July 2002).

Wikipedia contributors. "Japanese Battleship Nagato," *Wikipedia, The Free Encyclopedia*, http://en.wikipedia.org/w/index.php?title=Japanese_battleship_Nagato&oldid=78336325 (accessed October 19, 2006).

———. "Torpedo Data Computer," *Wikipedia, The Free Encyclopedia*, http://en.wikipedia.org/w/index.php?title=Torpedo_Data_Computer&oldid=73048363 (accessed August 31, 2006).

———. "USS *Puffer* (SS-268)," *Wikipedia, The Free Encyclopedia*, http://en.wikipedia.org/w/index.php?title=USS_Puffer_%28SS268%29&oldid=65478453 (accessed July 24, 2006).

———. "USS S-39 (SS-144)," *Wikipedia, The Free Encyclopedia*, http://en.wikipedia.org/w/index.php?title=USS_S39_%28SS144%29&oldid=7149 1453 (accessed October 11, 2006).

Williams, Jack. *USA Today*. "Understanding Hot Weather and Its Dangers." http://www.usatoday.com/weather/wheat1.htm (accessed July 2004).

Williams, Rudi. "Veteran, Joined Navy with 'Wooden Ships, Iron Men.'" Armed Forces Press Service. January 14, 2003. http://www.defenselink.mil/news/Oct1999/n10141999_9910142.html (accessed October 12, 2006).

Index

Numbers in ***bold italics*** indicate pages with illustrations.

Aborigines 117
Aegir (tender) 287
Air support 200–201
Akeman, Robert B. 85, 142
Alden, John ix, 1–2
Alexander, John 121, ***163***, ***232***, 242, 285
Allen, Carroll L. 121, ***163***, 169, 172, 175, 208–209, ***209***, 210, ***215***, 216, 229, 230, 237, 247, 255, 259, 264, 265, 269, 270
Allen, Howard A. 22, ***163***, ***163***, 175, ***232***, ***245***, 247–248
Allen, John C. 85, 142
Allen, John F. ix, 22, 25, 33, 73, 76, 81, ***292***
Ambon, Dutch East Indies 56, 58
Ambrose, Val 247
Anderson, Edward C., Jr. 227
Anderson, Robert E. 22, ***25***, 74, 142
Anderson, William L. 34
Angler (SS 240) 37
Anglin, Joseph L. 248, 254
Anti-submarine (A/S) 109, 132, 136–137, 150–151, 193–194; airplanes 193, 197–198, 203, 204, 240, 256; techniques 71, 186, 198–199; vessels 61–62, 91, 185–186, 193
Api Passage 112
Archerfish (SS 311) 192
Argonaut (SS 166) 37
Asbury, Ralph H., Jr. 306
Ashigara (Japanese cruiser) 236
Ashizuri Maru 137–138
Asman, Kenneth 306
Atabrine 254, 259, 263, 271
Atomic bomb 250, 252, 253, 263, 286
Auxiliary Sub-Chaser 37 68

Auxiliary Sub-Chaser 41 68
Australia: Japanese invasion 103; social environment 114–116, 118, 242–243

Bailey, William H. 306
Baird, Howard D. 13–15, ***284***, 286, 306
Bali 88, 113, 237–238, 256
Balikpapan, Dutch East Indies 58, 144
Banker, Robert K. 306
Bartorelli, Ralph A. 85, 166
Bashi Channel 195, 197
Basilan Strait 153
Bateman, Perry W. 306
Battcher, George J. 306
Batteries 200, 219
Bauersfeld, James R. 99, 174, 227
Baumgartner, Delmar D. 189, ***232***, ***244***, ***261***, ***277***
Baya (SS 318) 237
Beaver, Donald D. 306
Bechtold, Donald G. 306
Beer 54, 78, 114, 115, 187, 191, 197, 200, 211, 214, 224, 246, 260–261, 269
Bell, Theodore, Jr. 306
Bennett, C. L. 191
Bergh, Gerald D. 306
Bernard, Alan C. ***38***, 39
Bernard, Caroline ***38***
Bernard, Jon M. viii, 39
Bernard, Lawrence G. ***25***, ***26***, ***27***, ***38***, 56, 75, 77, 80, 81, 87; biography 38–40; Bronze Star citation 80
Bernard, Lawrence G., Jr. ***38***, 39
Bernhardt, Ethan ix
Berry, William R., Jr. 189
Bianco, Louis 143, ***163***, ***163***, 227

Biche, Robert ***163***, 172, ***232***, 241, 244, 255, 265, 268, 273
Bikini Island 286
Blair, Clay 5
Blueback (SS 581) 173, 176, 178, 237
Bluefish (SS 222) 110, 112, 153, 161, 221
Bollman, Eric P. 85, 120, 143, ***163***, ***163***, ***232***, ***245***
Bonefish (SS 223) 251, 252
Boot camps 7–8
Borteski, John 306
Bowden, Thomas A. "Alfred" 121, 155, ***163***, 221, 227
Bowfin (SS 287) 45, 293
Braley, Charles F. 22, ***25***
Branchcomb, Ellis D. 167, 193, ***195***, 234, 240, ***277***, 278
Bream (SS 243) 232–233
Bretz, James L. 189, ***285***
Brinkman, C. A., Jr. 306
Brisbane, Australia 1, 54–55
Brockhausen, Charles W., Jr. viii, ix, 22, 25, 32, 57, 77, 88, 142, ***290***, ***291***
Brogan, Francis J. 227, ***277***
Brown, Charles E. viii, 59, 64, 69, 84, ***290***, ***292***
Browning, John F. 306
Brunei 235
Buchanan, Robert ***12***
Bull, Maurice H. 143, ***163***, 166
Bullhead (SS 332) 235, 237, 248, 253, 256
Bunkowske, Alvin W. 306
Burger, Edward A. 167, 189
Burlingame, Creed 86
Burris, Marvin M. 22, ***25***

Cali, Thomas R. 248, 249, 254, 259, 262, 269, 271

315

INDEX

Camp, Gerald M. 99, *163*, 189
Cape Calavite 156–157, 160–161
Capitaine (SS 336) 237, 252, 253, 254, 256
Capones Island 88
Carbon dioxide absorbent 69, 76
Caroline, Jack J. *12*
Carr, Chester E. 306
Carter, Fred 306
Cassidy, Bernard F. 121, 155, *163*, *224*, *232*
Celebes Sea 143, 153
Censorship 192, 268, 269, 271
Chaffee, Edwin W. *285*, 306
Chamberlain, Roland J. 121, *163*, *215*, 216, *232*, 233, *245*
Chambers, Wayne M. 22, *25*, 98
Chicago 30
Chidori (Japanese destroyer) 61–62, 89, 92, 93
China 251, 259
Chitose (Japanese seaplane carrier) 130, 133
Chiyoda (Japanese carrier) 130
Christie, Ralph W. 44, 45, 63, 78–80, 88
Christmas 92, 175, 177, 282
Cielakie, Chief William *12*
Clementson, M.K. 173
Clouse, Fred W. 22, 83, 120
Cochran, Robert H. 85, *163*
Cod (SS 224) 252
Coggins, Donald G. 85, 142
Coghlan, Neil C. 306
Coleman, Willie, Jr. 248, 258, 259, 273, *277*
Cook, Donald vii
Copeland, Thomas W. 248
Corbeal, Rodolphe N. 306
Corcoran, Frank H., Jr. 99, *163*, *163*, *213*, 227, *290*
Corke, Robert E. 22, 120, 143, 155, *163*, 166
Creech, Bishop B. 22, 84, 143, *163*, *163*, 189
Crevalle (SS 291) 79, 89, 96
Crossman, Robert H. 306
Crouse, John ix
Czatynski, John 85, 98

Darrah, Charles A. 99, 155, *163*, *163*, *232*, *245*, *285*
Darwin, Australia 78, 140
Dauplaise, Louis B.E. viii, 8, 11, 189, 197, *214*, *215*, 231, *232*, 234, 235, 254, 268, *285*, *290*, *292*
Dawes, Arthur P. 306
Dealey, Sam 139, 205
Decker, Clayton 11, *12*
Decker, Stiles Morrow 81, 99, *163*, 168, *163*, 170, 172, 174, 180, 185, 193, 198, 207, 211, 213, 220, 224, 226, *232*, 233, 244, *290*
Deem, Jay A. viii, 22, 31, 32, 33, 54, 69, 70, 98, 110, 115, 116, 121, 130, *162*, 168, *163*, *163*, 185, 193, 194, 209, *232*, 258, 260, 269, 273, 293
Dehosse, Harry V. *285*, 306
Deiss, Harry C., Jr. 189, *277*

Delafield, Wilfrid "Cobber" 189, 211, 214, 220, 222, *232*, 236, 271
Depth charges 2, 4, 65, 66, 67, 68, 70, 71, 73, 89, 95, 132, 136, 146, 150, 154, 159, 183, 222
Dickinson, Master James 23, 25, 84, 98, 99, *163*, 189, *291*
Dickinson, L.R. 306
Dineen, Timothy J. 286, *287*, 306
Discharge 281–282
Discharge Point System 258, 259, 260, 262, 267–268, 272, 273
Dobson, Kenneth L. viii, *25*, 26, 31, 59, 64, 65, 66, 69, 78, 81, *163*, 166, *292*; biography 42
Dogan, Fred F. 143, *163*, *163*
Dotson, Rodney *10*, 11, *12*
Drum (SS 228) 3–4
Dufault, Ernest J 22, *25*, 31, 75, 80, 98
Duguid, Donald S. "Duke" 222, 223, 224, 226, *232*, 232, 242, 269, 271
Dullum, Henry 307
Dwyer, Carl R. ix, 3, 4, 25, 26, 57, 62, 65, 75, 78, 80, 81, 89, 99, 133, 143, 155, *163*, 166, *169*, 172, 173, 174, 192, 197, 198, *217*, 226, 230, *232*, 240, 241, 244, 254, 255, 261–262, 268, 271–272, 273, 275, 277, *279*, 284, *285*, 288–289, *291*, *292*; biography 40; Eighth War Patrol *228*, 231–241; Navy Cross 216–218; Ninth War Patrol *249*, 250–255; Seventh War Patrol *190*, 192–210; Sixth War Patrol *168*, 173–187

Eades, Gilbert L. 307
Eaton, Karl H. 307
Edwards, James F. 248
Eisenhower, Dwight D. 214
Electric Boat Company 16–17
Engborg, Frank T. 121, 166
Enterprise (carrier) 36
Escolar (SS 294) 198
Evans, Leonard D. 85, *169*, 245–246
Exmouth Gulf 88, 101, 241

Fallon, Merritt D. 99, 155, *163*, *169*, 189
Farner, Charles *12*
Fedor, Robert C. 307
Ferrie, Cornelius P. 307
Fife, James 44, 45
Fisher, Robert W. 307
Fleming, William P. 85, 98
Flores, Arthur 118–119
Flournoy, James A. 84
Forbis, Eldon L. 307
Forest, Raymond F. 84
Formosa (Taiwan) 192, 193, 195
Frank, Russell C. 166, *169*, 172, 174, *232*, 241, 242, 253, 258, 260, 268
Freeman, Frank E., Jr. *285*, 307
Fremantle, Western Australia 1, 140, 241, 248

Friendly fire 252
Frith, Otha L. 189, 196–197, 230, *232*, *290*, *291*, *292*
Fulton (tender) 54, 55, 176
Funk, Leonard G. 85, 97, 120
Fuso (Japanese battleship) *103*
Fuyo (Japanese destroyer) 92

Gagneaux, Paul R. 307
Galyean, Thomas 307
Gar (SS 206) 117
Gardner, Theodore N. 23, 84
Garner, William E. 85, 120
Geraghty, Barry 11, *12*
Giaimo, Anthony 189, *232*, 233, 234, 235
Gibbs, Warren J. 190
Goin, James W. 23, 98, 121, *163*, 166, 192, 204, 220
Golay, Clara viii
Golay, Frank viii, 50, 99, 155, *163*, 167, *169*, 171–172, 173–175, *174*, 180, 182, 191, 193, 194, 195, 200, 202, 220, *232*, 233, 234, 236, 244, 245, *245*, 247, 253, 254, 263, 265, 266
Golay, Jon viii
Golden, Lawrence J. 23, *25*, 98, 121, *163*, *169*, 230, *232*
Goode, Claude 117
Gooney birds 212, 219, *219*
Gooch, William C. 190, *232*
Gordelle, Eddie 117
Gordon, Allen H. 121, 155, *163*, *169*, 175, 227
Gosselin, Victor J. 23, *25*
Gozan Maru 92
Graf, Capt. Homer 80
Graves, William 23, *25*, 98, 120
Gray, Earl A. 227, 231
Great Natuna Islands 102, 110, 111
Grenfell, Captain R. W. 284
Grumbrecht, R. F. 307
Guam, Camp Dealey 187–188, 189, 191, 270
Gutensohn, John P. 23, *25*, 113, 120, 143, *163*, *169*, 189, 198, 204, 207, 208, 210, 219, 222, 226, *232*, *291*
Guthrie, John W. 84, 98, 99, 120

Hagen, Arden J. 143, 174, 175, 244, 246
Hahn, William, Jr. *286*, 307
Hale, Francis G. 307
Hall, Merle 307
Hamid, Abdul 97
Hamilton, Calvin C. *114*, 155, *163*, 166
Hannon, James Wesley 121, 142
Harden, Dick *12*
Harder (SS 257) 84, 139
Hardhead (SS 365) 237
Hargrove, James *291*
Hartman, Raymond W. 190, 194, *194*, *232*, *244*, *261*, *277*
Hatt, David D. *285*, 307
Haycraft, Geoffrey D. 23, *25*, 85
Hayward, Herbert D. 23, *25*, 138–139, *163*, 174, *215*, 216, *232*, 241,

Index

244, *245*, 260, 269, *278*, *281*, 284, *285*
Heehs, Richard A. 166, *169*, 193, 194, 204, *205*, 206, 207, 220, 223, *232*, 241, 251, 253, 262, 268, 270
Henderson, Cmdr. C.M. 153
Henderson, Franklin 190
Henger, Vincent J. 23, 142
Henry, Melvin "B" 99, 120
Hensley, John H. 98, *163*, 208, *224*, *245*
Hess, Dan viii, 113
Hess, Franklin G. *25*, 26, 32, 57, 62, 64, 75, 78, 80, 81, 113, 117; biography 36–37
Hetrick, William H. "Foxy" 23, *25*, 60, 80, 98, 119, 121, 142
Hezlet, Arthur D. 236
Hitler, Adolph 219
HMS *Taciturn* (British submarine) 253
HMS *Thorough* (British submarine) 253, 254
HMS *Trenchant* (British submarine) 236
Hodges, Dale L. 227, *232*, *277*
Holden, Eugene F. 307
Holland, Francis A. 167, 194, 220–221, 227
Holt, Edward R. 256
Honolulu 171
Hoopes, Lt. Robert D. 204, 220
Hopkinson, Alfred H. 121, 142
Horne, Lena 209, 259
Horne, Van J. *12*
Hornet (carrier) 36
Hot bunking 166, 227, 248, 259
Huddleston, Walter C. 23, 142
Hull, Leon S. 307
Humor 198, 229–230

Ice cream machine 236, 250, 286
Icefish (SS 367) 237
Indianapolis (cruiser) 273
Iwo Jima 222

James, Paul D. 23, 120, 143, *163*, *169*, 226, 227, 230, 231, *231*, *245*
Java Sea 112, 237, 250
Jensen, Marvin J. 4, *25*, 26, *27*, 30, 31, 57–60, 62, 79; biography 34–36; Bronze Star Citation 36; First War Patrol *55*, 56–79; Letter of Commendation 80; Silver Star Citation 80
Johnson, Charles S., Jr. 167, 192, 222, 233, 234
Johnson, James T., Jr. 227
Johnson, Wayne E., Jr. 248, *285*
Jones, Rear Admiral Claude 16–17
Jones, LaMar 23, *163*, 189
Junks 202–203
Justus, Leonard E. 85

Kadlic, Keith M. 307
Kaga (Japanese carrier) 37
Kaibokan No. 30 (Japanese escort) 185
Kaibokan No. 42 (Japanese escort) 185

Karimata Strait 112
Keane, Peter J. 8–9, 9, 15, 282, *285*, *291*, *292*, 307
Kellum, Raymond H. 23, *25*, 30, 31, 60, 77, 97, 98, 121, 142
Kemp, Thomas R. 143, *163*, 209, 210, 220, 227
Kennedy, Robert F. 23, 76, 120, 143, *163*, *169*, 186, *213*, *232*, 265
Kerls, Charles J. 23, *25*, 31, 69, 85
Kerls, Lorraine *290*
Kersbergen, Don *12*
Kikusui Maru 103
Kimbrell, William W. 24, 85, 98, 99, 155, *163*, *169*, *232*, *245*
Koenig, Elmer H., Jr. 307
Koske, Kenneth R. 307
Koti Passage 111
Kraken (SS 370) 235
Krans, George W. 248, *285*
Kronberg, Lloyd J. "Joe the Horse" 85, 155, *163*, 173, *176*, 229, *232*, *245*, 249–250, 251, 254, 263, 265, 270, 279
Krotzer, Robert K. *291*, 307
Kumagawa Maru 62, *63*, 66, 67
Kumano (Japanese cruiser) 103
Kupiec, Joseph L. *285*, 307
Kuretake (Japanese destroyer) 103, 109
Kutscherousky, Mike E. 24, *25*, 39, 60, 83, 97, 98, *291*
Kyo Maru #2 154

La Freniere, Joseph L. 24
Landry, James J. *285*, 307
Lane, John N. 8, 85, 110, 115, 116, *163*, *164*, 164–165, 219, 227, *291*
Lankerd, Charles E. 85, 98
Laughon, Willard R. 86
Layer, water 58
Lefferts, Harry E. 24, *25*, *26*, 142
Lemar, John E. 99, 142
Lennon, Francis "Butch" D. 24, 70, 85
Levander, Walter R. 307
Liggett, James D. 24, 29–30, 54, 65, 75, 77, 101, 120, 143, *163*, *169*, 227
Lindmark, Algot O. 307
Lizardfish (55 373) 237–238
Lockport, Illinois 31
Lockwood, Admiral Charles 40, 172
Lombok 88, 113
Lombok Strait 88, 95, 101, 112–113, 144, 240, 250, 253
Love, Oliver W. "Pappy" 24, *25*, 97, 142
Lunchbaugh, Ensign *285*
Luzon Strait 173, 177, 196
Lyons, Roy D. "Tiger" 24, *25*, 98

MacArthur, Gen. Douglas 54, 266
Mae West (life vest) 221, 235, 269
Mail 175, 203, 204–205, 206, 213, 216, 220, 247, 260, 261, 264, 267, 273
Makassar Strait 58–60, 61, 67, 75, 88, 95, 101, 129, 130, 143, 144
Makin Island (escort carrier) 233–234, 235

Malaya 137, 250
Maloney, Herbert E. 99, 120
Manila, Philippine Islands 88, 92–93, 266–267
Manila Bay 89, 156
Manitowoc, Wisconsin 1, 29–30
Manitowoc Shipbuilding Company *17*, 16–20, 70, 257
Mappus, Karl W. 227, 233, 234, *290*
Mare Island, California, Navy Yard 143, 166, 167–168, 170, 171
Markle, John E. 167, 189
Marshall, Robert F. 307
Martinez, California *277*, 277–279
Martinson, Kenneth R. viii, 99, 142, 226, 227, 231, *245*, *290*, *291*
Mathis, Charles H., Jr. 99, 120
Maupin, Corwin viii, *12*
Mays, Frank, Jr. 143, *163*, *169*, *232*, *244*, *256*, *261*
Mays, Virgil C. 167
Mazzone, Walter F. viii, *25*, 26, 31, 74, *74*, 79, 81, *290*, *292*; biography 41–42
McCann, Capt. Allan R. 45
McCardle, Oliver P. 190
McCarthy, Peter E. 167, 271, 272
McClure, Phillip "Mac" *169*, 172, *191*, 191–192, 198, 219, 221, *232*, 237, 241, 255, 260, 262, 263, 265, 266, 269
McDonald, Donald B., Jr. 1, 2, 3, 5, 6, 7–8, *10*, 11, *12*, 83, 85–86, 97, *114*, 115, *155*, *163*, *164*, 164–165, *169*, *217*, *232*, 279, 282–283
McDonald, Lt. Cmdr. Robert 198
McEntyre, Kenneth E. 167, *224*, *285*
McGehee, Claude 307
McGraw, John M. 227
McKay, Thomas R. 307
McKee, Richard 226, 227
McPherson, George L. 190, *232*, *291*
Meister, Bernard L. *285*, 307
Messenger, Ernest H. 167, *169*, 210, 227
Metz, Orvie 170, 280
Metz, Thomas A. viii, 9–10, 167–168, *169*, 170, 173, *188*, 202, 232, 234, 239, 242, 278, 279–280
Meyne, Bernice 165, *282*, 283
Midway Island 206, 211–216, 229
Miller, Lawrence P. 226, 227
Miller, Roy M. 307
Millspaugh, S. C. 307
Mindanao Island, Philippines 134
Mindoro Strait 93
Miri, Sarawak, Borneo 102, 103, 109
Minnesota (tugboat) 31
Momsen Lung 11
Moore, Curtis H. 227, 230, *232*, *281*
Motusovic, John L., Jr. 307
Moynahan, Cornelius *12*
Musashi (Japanese battleship) 130
Musha, Donald A. 143, 193, 207

Nagata (Japanese battleship) 102–103
Namy, Phil ix
Nanrei Maru 37
Nautilus (SS 168) 37

Navy Day/Week 272, *276*, 276–279
Nelson, John l. "Jack" 143, 214, *215*, 216, 232
New Orleans 32
Nichols, P. G. 79
Nielsen, Howard S. 143, 166, *285*
North Ubian Island 134

O'Kane, Richard 11, 205, 271
Okinawa 177–178
Okoniewski, Theodore J. 167, *169*, 200, 210, *232*, *277*, *285*
Orbovich, Michael M. 24, 142
Orion (tender) 231
Osborne, Ed *12*
Otto, Stanley W. 307
Owen, Lawrence J. 121
Owens, George D. 227
Owens, Lester *12*, *285*

Pagoda Club 242, *243*
Pampanito (SS 383) 83
Panama Canal 32–33
Papalexis, James A. 307
Parker, James Y. 143, *163*, *169*, *291*
Parker, John A. 307
Parkhurst, Robert D. 307
Patacsil, Felix 24
Patsko, Demeter 24, 29, 142
Patton, James W., Jr. 24, 30, 69, *163*, *169*, 172, 209, 230, *232*, 239
Pearl Harbor 268, 273, 275
Pelias (tender) 86, 210
Penzenik, William 24, 31, 118–119, 120
Periscopes 62–63
Perlas Islands 33
Permit (SS 178) 102
Perro, John L. 24, *25*, 98, 116, 121, *163*, 174, *232*
Perth, Australia 116, 241
Petitt, Timothy T. viii
Peto (SS 265) 17–18, *32*
Pfeifer, Robert H. 307
Pfeiffer, C.P. 307
Picone, Lawrence (Larry) 99, *163*, *169*, 172, 189, *290*
Pieper, Alfred L. 85, 98
Pierson, Siegel H. 190, 269
Piranha (SS 389) 191, 193, 194, 195, 197, 201, 203, 206
Pitsch, Carl F. *285*, 307
Poe, John D. *285*, 307
Pogy (SS 266) 161
Poling, George F. 307
Polk, Robert E., Jr. vii, viii, 116, 121, *163*, *169*, 174, 189, *290*, *291*, *292*
Potsdam Surrender Terms 252, 253
Preston, Jack G. 307
Prisby, Henry B. 85, 142
Pruitt, John A. 24, 30, 69, 117–118, 119, 120
Puffer (SS 268): arrival at Brisbane 54; attack procedures 57–58; commissioning 19, *24*, *25*; conversion to peacetime 279–280; deck gun action 96, 203, 238–239; decommissioning *287*, 287–288, *289*; defects 56, 75, 86, 91, 180–181, 192–193, 209, 220, 221, 229, 230, 233, 247, 263; flags 18, 21, 256, 260, *274*; food 200, 204, 206, 210, 213, 221, 254, 264, 266, 269; fuel 206–207, 210, 236; improvements 86, 143, 170–171, 227, 254; keel laid 18, *19*; launched 19, *21*, *22*, *23*; lifeguard duty 124–125, 191, 192, 195, 197, 200–201, 231–232; Navy unit commendation 1, 141; personnel changes 4, 82–83, 84–85, 98–99, 120–121, 142–143, 166–167, 189–191, 226–228, 248, 276; post war 252, 255, 258–287; repairs 54, 86, 100–101, 121, 123–124, 138–139, 143, 162, 170, 191, 219; reserve boat (Seattle) *288*–289, 289–293; reunions 290–293; runs aground 59–60; scrapping 292–293; testing 27, *29*, 55, 87; theme songs 160, 187; torpedo attacks 57–58, 62–64, 91–92, 94, 104–105, 126–129, 130–131, 134–135, 146, 149–150, 153–154, 158–159, 178–179, 181–182, 184, 240; training 55, 56, 88, 90, 99–100, 123, 143, 162, 170, 171, 172, 191, 202, 220, 221, 222, 223, 225, 229, 231, 246–247, 252
Pugh, William M. *25*, 26, *27*, 62, 72, 76, 81, 133, 155, *163*, 173, 185, *214*, 214, 226; biography 41

Q-ship 56–57

Radar 88, 90, 94, 121–123, 149, 256
Rafalko, Adam P. 226, 227
Rama, Leonard E. 226, 227, 271
Ramage, Lawson "Red" 205
Ramser, Forrest L. *285*, 307
Raney, Bernard 307
Rasher (SS 269) 86, 123, 152
Rasmussen, Calvin 307
Raton (SS 270) 112, 117
Rawls, Jefferson W. 24, *25*, 120, *163*
Ray (SS 271) 112
Red Cross 175, 213, 221, 242, 267
Reilly, Lt. Commander Robert F. *285*, 288, 289
Rest and recuperation: Fremantle/Perth 2, 114–117, 241–246; Guam 2, 187–188; Midway 2, 211–224; Stateside 162–165
Reynolds, Arthur D., III 167, *169*, 192, 206, 220, 221, *232*, 247, 265, 272
Reynolds, William G. 118
Rhymes, Ralph W. 24, *25*, 85
Richenthal, Irwin 227
Rindskopf, Maurice ix, 3–4
Roberts (destroyer) 233, 234
Roberts, Julian A. 85, 143, *163*, 166
Roberts, Raymond viii, 24, 57, 78, 85, 98, 99, *163*, *213*, 221, 225, 226, 248, 258, 260, 269
Robertson, Eugene C. 99, 120
Roe Street, Perth, Australia 245
Rohrbach, Frank 167, *232*
Romaszewski, A. S. 307

Roosevelt, Franklin D. 208, 222, 272
Rosenberg, Ensign *285*
Ross, Oliver B. 24
Royal Hawaiian Hotel 275
Russia 251
Ryuyo Maru 95

S-39 (SS 144) 38–39, 60
Sabotage 101
Sado Maru 36
Saipan 2, 173, 175–176, 203, 204, 231
Samuel, Harry 167
San Francisco 272
Sander, Harold E. 25, *25*, 32, 54, 68, 142, *169*
Sanders, John W. viii, 121, *163*, *169*, 189, *290*, *291*, *292*
Sasso, Anthony P. vii, ix, 99, *163*, *169*, 208, 213, *224*, *232*, *291*
Saury (SS 189) 40
Sauvageau, Joseph G. 307
Schley, Earl Stephen, Jr. 85, *163*, 200, 204, 230, *232*, *245*
Schmidling, Charles J. 99, 120
Schraier, Carl 307
Scott, Leroy W. 308
Sea Fox (SS 402) 173, 176, 181
Sea gull 152
Sea of Japan 252
Sea Owl (SS 405) 191, 192, 194, 195, 197, 203, 206, 210, 229
Sears, Philip C. 25, 98, 121, 155, 189
Secrecy 205
Selby, Frank Gordon 4, 81, 86, 133, *163*, 166, 244, *245*, 247, 250, 287–288; Fifth War Patrol **144**, 144–162; Fourth War Patrol **122**, 124–141; Letter of Commendation 113; Naval biography 86–87; Navy Cross Citation (5th War Patrol) 162; Navy Cross Citation (4th War Patrol) 140–141; Second War Patrol **82**, 87–97; Silver Star Citation 97; Third War Patrol 99–113, *100*
Selk, Debbie ix
Shanholtz, Stanley S. 25, *25*, 85
Shark (SS 314) 198
Shaw, Ensign Al 221, 222, 225, 226, 230, *232*, 233, 234, 235, 242, 251
Shaw, William F. 25, *25*, 121
Shelton, Eugene C. 25, 227
Shiflett, John L., Jr. 121, *163*, *169*, 247, 271, 272, 275
Shinpo Maru 161
Shinryu Maru 129
Sibutu Passage 88, 102, 134, 139, 148–149, 152–153
Sieracki, Eugene *12*
Silversides (SS 236) 86
Simmons, Ted G. 308
Simonson, Jack E. 308
Singapore 102, 103
Smith, Clark Sam 25, 30, *114*, 116, *163*, *169*, 227
Smith, Edward W. 143, 166

Index

Smith, Henry N. 85, 230, *232*
Snyder, Harry F. 25
Soebi Besar 102–103, 111
Solak, John viii, 78, 142, *290*
Somerville, William ix
Sorrells, Lowell 31
South China Sea 101, 103, 143
Spalding, Robert B. 25, 65–66, *66*, 120, 121
Spritz, Charles, "Spritz's Navy" 15
Staff, Robert 270
Stafford, Vertis A. 25
Steeley, Robert S. 26
Steinke, Harris E. 85, 116, *163*, *169*, 206, *232*, *245*, 259, *261*, 262, *284*
Stevens, Albert M. 167
Stocker, Garth *285*, 308
Stoltz, Frank N. *25*, 26, 57, 70, 98
Stoy, Glenn E. viii, 99, 103, 129, 130, 133, 137, 152, *155*, 155–156, 161, 162–*163*, 163, 202, *224*, *232*, *245*, 246, 275, *281*, *292*
Strauhal, Frank E. 308
Style, Norman 227, 231
Sub-chaser No. 4 (SC #4) 62, 64, 67, 68
Sub-chaser No. 6 (SC #6) 68, 77
Subic Bay 88, 258, 260–267
Submarine environment: adrenaline effects 51–52, 71; caffeine 52; carbon dioxide poisoning 50–51, 68, 72, 208; heat and humidity 48–50, 71; hypoxia 50–51, 69, 71, 72, 73, 75, 208; lack of light 47; nicotine 52; perception of time on 48; physical hardships 6, 45–46; psychological (morale) 1, 4, 223–224, 236, 247, 251, 253, 254, 255, 259, 264, 266, 267, 277; sleep problems 47–48, 72, 172, 254
Submarines: American warfare theory 43–44; German V-boats 43; graphic 175; lack of targets 171–172; losses 5, 247, 251–252, 272–273; post war 244–245; tonnage sunk 175
Sullivan, Warren *12*
Sulu Archipelago 94, 95, 130, 134
Sulu Sea 88, 134, 153
Sunosaki (Japanese tanker) 152–153
Surabaya (Soerabaja) 124, 127, 130, 237
Suzuya (Japanese cruiser) 103
Svacina, Richard H. 308
Swan Dive Club 242
Swanson, Harold *12*
Switzer, Donald R. 99, 142, *292*
Swordfish (SS 193) 204, 220, 252
Szysko, Michael 98

HMS *Taciturn* (British submarine) 253
Taiwan 90, 92
Takasaki Maru 137–138, 152
Tarakan, Dutch East Indies 59, 147–148
Tawi Tawi 130, 134, 153
Taylor, John H. 308
Teiko Maru 90, 103–110, *106–109*
Teikon Maru 161
Thatcher, Roy O. 99, 166
Thiell, John E. 18–19
Thoman, Andrew J., II viii, 9, 10, 143, *163*, 164, 180, 186, *232*, *290*
Thommen, Harvey 11, *12*
Thompson, James M. 308
Thornberry, Fred K. 222, 227
HMS *Thorough* (British submarine) 253, 254
Thresher (SS 200) 34–36, 206
Thursby, Cecil H. 190
Tiberon Bay 276, 279, 287
Tidd, Russell E. viii, *25*, 26, 30, 54, 60, 65, 77, 83, 120, 121, *291*, *292*
Tinosa (SS 283) 63
Tirante (SS 420) 229
Tjerk Hiddes (Dutch destroyer) 132
Tombleson, Wesley *12*
Tone (Japanese cruiser) 103
Toowoomba, Queensland, Australia 54
Topor, Ladislaus viii, *25*, 26, *26*, *29*, 98, 121, *138*, 138–139, *163*, 167, *169*
Torpedoes: deactivated 270; depth tests 40, 44; duds 4, 63; excessive use 62; firing pin 45; magnet exploder 44, 92; Mark XVIII 171; morale effect 6, 44; premature detonation 4, 63, 92
Torpedo Data Computer (TDC) 57–58
HMS *Trenchant* (British submarine) 236
Trigger (SS 564) 177
Troop, Ralph T. 121, *163*, *169*, 198, 232
Trudeau, Norman viii, *25*, 26, *26*, 30, 31, 32, 69, 98, *291*
Truk 102
Truman, Harry S. 272
Tsurugisaki (Japanese carrier) 152

Unangst, William K. 26
Urbanski, James L. 190, 268, 269, *285*, *286*
USO 214, 219, 223, 273

Vaughn, John A. 25, 26, 85
V-E Day 220, 225
Veber, Rene Yvon J. *285*, 308
Venatori, Louis Edward 167
Vincent, Leonard R. 26, 121
Vogan, Merle F. 99, *169*, 227
Von Sternberg, Donald V. 26, 85
Voss, Raymond H. *25*, 26, 85, 98, 99, *163*, *169*, 174, *232*, *245*

WACs 266
Waites, Roy D. *25*, 26, 98
Wake Island 206, 208
Walker, Earl L. 308
Wanek, Bob *12*
Warner, Wilbur D. *25*, 26, 33, 121
Washburn, Dana R. *285*, 308
Washburn, Edgar W *25*, 26, 75–76, 78, 85
Wasp (carrier) 275
Waterbury, Cristin ix
Webber, Nancy ix
Weber, Lawrence R. 143, 167
Weeks, Robert O. 166, *169*, 174, 205, 207, 210, 219, *232*, 242, 262
Wells, Richard 11, 12
Wentworth, Wilton *12*
Werner, Sondol 189, 216
West, Charles: building submarines 16–18; Manitowoc Ship Building Company 3, 16; quality of submarines 18
Westman, Dale H. 308
White, Erwin L. *285*, 308
Wilkins, Captain C.W. 287
William B. Preston (destroyer) 101
Williams, Clayton E. 155
Williams, Gordon B. *285*, 308
Williamson, Elmer C. 292–293
Williamson, Jasper G. 227, 231
Wilson, William E., Jr. *25*, 26, 65, 77, 83, 98, 143, 155, *164*, 164–165, *169*, 194, *224*, 284, *285*
Wiseman, Charles E. 85, *163*, *213*, *245*, 259, 265
Wolfpack 173, 191, 207
Wright, Kenneth D. 167, *169*, *232*

Yamato (Japanese battleship) 130
Youra, John A. 167, *232*, *277*
Yukikaze (Japanese destroyer) 133

Zelaznicki (Zell), Joseph 25, 26, 29, 142, *291*
Ziegler, Emmert 118
Ziegler, Harold A. 227, 231, *232*, *292*

www.ingramcontent.com/pod-product-compliance
Lightning Source LLC
Chambersburg PA
CBHW080758300426
44114CB00020B/2750